PATRIOTIC PLURALISM

PATRIOTIC PLURALISM

Americanization Education and
European Immigrants

JEFFREY E. MIREL

HARVARD UNIVERSITY PRESS
Cambridge, Massachusetts, and London, England
2010

Library of Congress Cataloging-in-Publication Data

Mirel, Jeffrey, 1948–
Patriotic pluralism : Americanization education and European immigrants / Jeffrey E. Mirel.
p. cm.
Includes bibliographical references and index.
ISBN 978-0-674-04638-2
1. Immigrants—Education—United States—History—20th century.   2. Children of
immigrants—Education—United States—History—20th century.   3. Americanization.
I. Title.
LC3731.M58 2010
371.826'912097309041—dc22   2009051855

For Barbara

CONTENTS

PATRIOTIC PLURALISM

INTRODUCTION: THE IMMIGRANT INVASION

Throughout the developed world, few issues provoke more passionate debate than immigration, assimilation, political allegiance, and national identity. Whether one considers North African immigrants in France, Turks in Germany, Pakistanis in Great Britain, Koreans in Japan, or Latinos in the United States, the impact immigrants have on the politics, cultures, economies, and demographics of their adopted countries sparks emotionally charged disagreements about a series of questions. How can newcomers be effectively assimilated into the larger society? Is cultural pluralism a more worthy and democratic goal than assimilation? To what extent should the values and laws of the dominant culture take precedence over the values and traditions of the immigrants' cultures? Can a system of cultural pluralism ensure the political allegiance of immigrants in times of national crisis? Should immigration be restricted to only those people whose racial or cultural backgrounds align with the majority in the country of destination?

Of all developed countries, the United States has had perhaps the longest and most self-conscious struggle with questions about immigration and national culture. This struggle has ebbed and flowed throughout American history but was particularly intense in the latter part of the nineteenth century and the first half of the twentieth. Between 1890 and 1930, over 22 million immigrants, mostly from eastern and southern Europe, landed on American shores. Huge numbers of them settled in the great industrial cities of the Northeast and Midwest. Questions about how to deal with this massive influx of ethnically and religiously diverse foreigners were central to political and cultural discussions of this era. Such influential Americans as Jane Addams, Franz Boas, Louis Brandeis, Calvin Coolidge, John Dewey, Horace Kallen, Frances Kellor, Theodore Roosevelt, Edward A. Ross, and Woodrow Wilson, along with scores of less prominent political and educational leaders, struggled to define how the nation should respond to what one writer at the time called "the immigrant invasion."[1]

To a considerable extent, these debates and the policies they produced have had a lasting influence on American thinking about these issues. Indeed, some of the key terms that we use to discuss immigration today, such as "Americanization," "melting pot," and "cultural pluralism," became firmly embedded in the national vocabulary during debates about immigration and assimilation in the first half of the twentieth century. For better or worse, Americans today routinely see the experiences of immigrants from this period as the standard against which all later immigrants are judged.

This book examines the role that education played in the Americanization of adult immigrants and their children who arrived in the United States between the 1890s and the early 1950s. It deals primarily with two institutions: public schools and foreign language newspapers. During these years, public schools led the effort to Americanize adult immigrants and their children, and the foreign language press was the most important mass commentator on and interpreter of Americanization issues in immigrant communities. To be sure, a vast array of other institutions including movie theaters, radio stations, professional sports leagues, amusement parks, and even department and grocery stores contributed to the Americanization process.[2] But in these emerging institutions of mass culture Americanization was largely an implicit and often haphazard enterprise. This was not the case with public schools and the foreign language press. These institutions were *explicitly* involved in Americanization education and, consequently, devoted a great deal of attention to issues of civic and citizenship education, which were central to the Americanization project.

The first half of the twentieth century was a period in which Americans placed great hopes in the power of education broadly conceived to solve social problems. As a New York City high school principal exclaimed in 1902, "education will solve every problem of our national life, even that of assimilating our foreign element."[3] This was also the era in which mass-circulation newspapers, including a robust foreign language press, played a crucial educational role by reporting on and explaining the great cultural, economic, social, and political changes that were occurring in the United States. Like the public schools, the foreign language press also was enormously important in Americanizing the flood of European immigrants in this era.[4] For most of the twentieth century these Americanization efforts, especially those of the public schools, were viewed as a welcome and positive contribution to the making of American society.[5]

However, since the 1970s, that perspective has fallen on hard times. Numerous scholars have criticized early-twentieth-century Americanization programs both in and out of school as a form of "cultural imperialism" determined to unify the nation by forcing European immigrants to abandon their cultural backgrounds.[6] One scholar went so far as to state that Americanization campaigns were "no more and no less than attempts at cultural genocide."[7] More recently, a growing number of labor historians have argued that one of the main aspects of Americanization was encouraging European immigrants to embrace American attitudes about race, power, and privilege, a process that ultimately led them to become "white." As one scholar put it, "white supremacy made possible the Americanization of the immigrant."[8]

Given these interpretations, it is not surprising that today the terms *assimilation* and *Americanization* are often referred to with scorn. The sociologist Nathan Glazer has pointed out that "in recent years it has been taken for granted that assimilation, as an expectation of how different ethnic and racial groups would respond to their common presence in one society or as the expected result of sober social scientific analysis of the ultimate consequence of the meeting of people and races, is to be rejected."[9] This view of assimilation and Americanization has become particularly prominent among educational theorists and scholars who see the treatment of European immigrants in the early twentieth century as the template for current, culturally insensitive efforts to assimilate new immigrants. Drawing on these conventional ideas about Americanization education, one educational theorist concludes, "The challenge facing educators with regard to culturally diverse students is *not* to 'Americanize' them" (emphasis added).[10]

But was the Americanization movement in the early twentieth century as monolithic and as culturally imperialistic as many historians and educational theorists assume? This book challenges and complicates the dominant interpretations of Americanization education. It argues that in large part these negative views of assimilation and Americanization are based on historical accounts that are incomplete, that often generalize from the most extreme examples of aggressive Americanization and, at times, mistake the bombastic rhetoric of Americanizers for the reality of these educational efforts. While there is no doubt that many leaders of the Americanization movement in the 1910s and 1920s wanted immigrants to abandon their cultural backgrounds and merge imperceptibly into white America, whether Americanization programs realized these hopes remains an open question.

This book presents an alternative view of Americanization education on both the K–12 and adult education levels by examining the dynamic interaction between Americanizers and immigrants. Contrary to currently popular views of Americanization education, I argue that from this interaction emerged a broader, more cosmopolitan, and ultimately more democratic vision of American culture and national identity.

This book differs from other works on Americanization education in five ways. First, it focuses mainly on civic and citizenship education rather than on broader forms of Americanization. Second, it views the great debates and intellectual battles over Americanization education as part of a larger, historically rooted conflict between ethnic and civic nationalism in the United States. Third, it examines Americanization education on both the K–12 and adult education levels in depth and over time in three major U.S. cities—Chicago, Cleveland, and Detroit—each of which was an important site of Americanization initiatives. Fourth, it makes extensive use of three remarkable and underanalyzed collections of articles and editorials from foreign language newspapers in Chicago and Cleveland. Fifth, the book broadens the time frame for examining Americanization education to include developments in the 1930s and 1940s. What follows is a brief discussion of each of these features.

The first distinctive approach involves defining the key elements of Americanization education as those connected to political allegiance and identity, rather than the role education played in, for example, the economic and social mobility of immigrants. During the first half of the twentieth century, *Americanization* was a catch-all term that included a wide variety of goals ranging from learning English and becoming a citizen to, as one wag put it, celebrating Mother's Day, eating corn flakes, and "living beyond one's income."[11] In 1924, the author of a U.S. Bureau of Education report argued that over the preceding decades the term had been tossed about with such reckless abandon that "[p]robably no word in the English language to-day is quite as meaningless as *Americanization*" (emphasis in the original).[12] Yet educators working daily with immigrants and their children had a fairly clear conception of what they hoped to achieve in Americanization programs. They focused primarily on preparing adult immigrants and their children to be citizens of the United States committed to the democratic ideals of this country.

Writing in 1920, Frank V. Thompson, superintendent of the Boston Public Schools, argued that Americanization education, at its best, should teach a set of ideals that all Americans, immigrant and native, would share in common. These included devotion and allegiance to the United States, particularly to our democratic form of government; a willingness to defend the country in time of danger; respect for the law; a commitment to civility in political discourse; tolerance of diverse points of view; a belief in the principle of equality; and participation in political life. These ideals were expansive enough and resilient enough to define "what it means to be an American" to this day.[13] In practice, educators sought to teach these ideals by instructing adult immigrants and K–12 students in three core areas: mastering English, learning American history and civics, and understanding and embracing the democratic ideals of this country. These three aspects of Americanization education are the foci of this book.

The second approach involves placing the debates and controversies about Americanization in the context of the struggle between ethnic and civic nationalism in American history. Since at least the mid-1990s, scholars from various fields have used the concepts of ethnic and civic nationalism to analyze the development of different forms of nation-states.[14] As Michael Ignatieff explains, ethnic nationalists contend that the nation defines and creates the state: "What gave unity to the nation, what made it a home, a place of attachment, was not the cold contrivance of shared rights but the people's preexisting ethnic characteristics: their language, religion, customs, and traditions." For ethnic nationalists, states rest on a foundation of ethnic or racial homogeneity, not on ideals, values, or behaviors that one can acquire through education or any other form of "conversion" experience. By contrast, civic nationalists believe "that the nation should be composed of all those—regardless of race, color, creed, gender, language, or ethnicity—who subscribe to the nation's political creed. This nationalism is called civic because it envisages the nation as a community of equal, rights-bearing citizens, united in patriotic attachment to a shared set of political practices and values."[15] Put another way, the state creates the nation.

These concepts are particularly useful for analyzing Americanization education because they highlight the two broad responses that native-born Americans had to the huge influx of immigrants who arrived between 1890 and 1925. In terms of ethnic nationalism, as early as 1890, many native-born Americans regarded the newcomers with fear and dismay, largely because they saw most of them as members of inferior races. Arguing that education could never change these people into good Americans, racial restrictionists sought to ban the immigration of all people from non-Anglo-Saxon or non-Nordic races.

Opposing the racial restrictionists were a diverse group of educators, intellectuals, journalists, and social activists who maintained that with proper education the new immigrants *could* become good Americans, regardless of their racial backgrounds. While there were significant differences between members of this group—some called for complete assimilation, others advocated cultural pluralism, and still others envisioned America as a great racial melting pot—they all fit within a civic nationalist framework because they all believed to varying degrees in the power of Americanization education to achieve *e pluribus unum*. Given this dramatic difference between the ethnic and civic nationalists on this issue, Americanization initiatives in the first half of the twentieth century look quite different from the currently popular story of unremitting intolerance, insensitivity, coercion, or cultural genocide, although there certainly were ugly aspects and trends associated with these efforts. Rather, the history of Americanization education in this era is more the chronicle of a long-running, at times impassioned, negotiation between diverse groups of civic nationalists who held different ideas about how to balance the *unum* and the *pluribus*.

The third distinctive feature of this book is that it focuses more on local than on national developments. With few exceptions, the historians and sociologists of education who have examined Americanization education have concentrated on the *national* debates and actions, particularly on the great "Americanization crusade" that began in late 1914 and ended, for the most part, after the passage of the National Origins Act in 1924.[16] While this approach has produced a number of influential and insightful studies, it avoids some important aspects of Americanization education, aspects that demand a more longitudinal, case-study approach. Case studies are necessary because Americanization campaigns and Americanization education programs were overwhelmingly *local* enterprises. Without a closer look at these programs, a number of important issues fail to get the attention they deserve. For example, nationally oriented studies rarely attend to the huge number of adult immigrants who sought Americanization education in public schools and other venues well before the advent of World War I. Moreover, national overviews miss the nuances of the intellectual backlash of the 1920s that rejected the often heavy-handed efforts of Americanizers during and immediately after the war. Most important, local studies capture the continuation of Americanization efforts in public schools and other institutions during the 1930s and 1940s, efforts that contributed to an enormous surge in naturalizations during World War II.[17]

In order to more fully address these developments, this book takes a detailed look at Americanization education from the 1890s to the early 1950s in the Chicago, Cleveland, and Detroit public school systems. During the first half of the twentieth century, Chicago, Detroit, and Cleveland were booming industrial giants. In 1920, these cities were the second-, fourth-, and fifth-largest in the nation, with about 2.7 million, 990,000, and 800,000 residents respectively. In that year, of the ten largest American cities only New York and Philadelphia had larger percentages of foreign-born residents than Cleveland (30.1 percent), Chicago (29.9 percent), and Detroit (29.3 percent).[18] As early as 1909, over two-thirds of the students in the Chicago Public Schools had foreign-born fathers, as did almost 60 percent of the pupils in the Cleveland Public Schools, and over 53 percent of those in the Detroit system.[19] During the Progressive Era, public schools in these cities focused extensively on Americanizing their immigrant pupils and their parents. In addition, adult Americanization education programs in these cities brought together business, civic, and educational leaders in coordinated efforts to provide classes and services to the cities' immigrant populations.

The fourth different approach that this book brings to the study of Americanization concerns the difficult question of identifying how immigrants responded to Americanization education. Specifically, what aspects of these efforts did immigrants support? Which did they oppose? Did they grudgingly assimilate, staunchly support cultural pluralism, or try to balance the demands of these contending points of view? Did they take different stances for children and adults? These are challenging questions in large part because sources that can shed light on them are either hard to come by or quite difficult to use. Most historians who have tried to answer them have relied on immigrant authors who mastered English well enough to get published, on oral histories of aging immigrants, or, if one has the requisite language skills, on reading a variety works published by the immigrant communities in their own language.[20] Useful as these approaches have been, all of them have problems, for example, the unrepresentative nature of immigrants who could write publishable English, the worrisome nature of generalizing from the small number of immigrants who could be interviewed by oral historians, and the sheer number of languages one would need to master to read the available materials of just the major immigrant groups.

This book tries to overcome these problems by using three extraordinary collections of foreign language newspaper articles and editorials that spoke for and to the large immigrant communities in Chicago and Cleveland. These articles and editorials were translated into English in the late 1930s and early 1940s by researchers working for the Works Progress Administration (WPA). The two main collections, the Chicago Foreign Language Press Survey (CFLPS) and the Cleveland Foreign Language Newspaper Digest (CFLND), contain an enormous number of articles and editorials from the foreign language newspapers in these two cities. These articles and editorials were either fully translated in the CFLPS or abstracted in the CFLND. In both cases, the collections draw on the major newspapers serving the most prominent immigrant communities in their respective cities and provide superb material for examining how immigrant communities dealt with the challenges of life in the New World generally and with Americanization particularly. The third collection, known as Comments on Current Events (COCE), examines selected articles and editorials mainly from the Cleveland foreign language newspapers and deals with specific events and themes related to World War II. It covers the period from May 1941 to July 1942.[21]

The number of immigrant groups included in these projects is substantial—twenty-two in the Chicago survey (running alphabetically from Albanians to Ukrainians, with Czechs, Germans, Jews, and Poles predominating) and eleven in the Cleveland digest (with Germans, Hungarians, and Poles predominating). Most of the Chicago articles and editorials are from roughly 1895 to 1935 and contain a wealth of material on education and assimilation. The Cleveland digest provides almost daily coverage for all of 1937 and 1938.[22] Essentially beginning where the Chicago survey ends, the CFLND offers a rare view into how immigrants from various groups dealt with issues of Americanization while at the same time addressing the rise of fascism, Nazism, and communism in or around their homelands. The COCE broadens and deepens the picture of how various immigrant groups dealt with America's entry into World War II. In all, given the considerable amount of attention the Chicago and Cleveland foreign language newspapers paid to Americanization education and to such related issues as loyalty, cultural maintenance, and national identity, these three collections are invaluable for understanding how immigrants responded to the challenges of life in the New World.

Rich as these collections are, it is impossible to know the degree to which the papers included in them actually reflected the ideas and attitudes of their readers. One could argue, for example, that the papers were merely platforms from which editors could hold forth on local, national, or international issues, unconcerned about their readers' points of view. While this may have been true in some papers, even the most self-absorbed editor had to recognize that these papers were supposed to be profit-making enterprises and that they could not stray too far from their readers' interests and opinions if they wanted to stay in business. Another problem with the collections is the dearth of information about who chose the editorials and articles that were included in the collections and who did the actual translations. Despite these problems, the collections are still enormously useful, because they highlight writings from the most prominent and long-running newspapers in various immigrant communities. They offer a rare opportunity for bringing a wide array of immigrant voices into a conversation that heretofore has been dominated overwhelmingly by white Anglo-Saxon Protestants.

These newspapers have one additional attribute that makes them an excellent source for examining Americanization education. The foreign language press was itself an enormously powerful educational institution in immigrant communities. As one commentator on Americanization explained, the foreign language press was "an educational agency without equal among our immigrant communities."[23] In terms of Americanization education, these papers may have had as much, if not more, influence on what adult immigrants thought and learned about becoming Americans than did public school or other naturalization programs.

The dynamic relationship between the initiatives of Americanizers and the Americanization efforts of the foreign language press was a potent educational force. The interaction between the Chicago and Cleveland foreign language newspapers and the Americanization campaigns in the World War I and World War II eras demonstrates how this process was negotiated and revised in the first half of the twentieth century. Editors and writers of the papers in the CFLPS and CFLND strongly supported key aspects of Americanization (e.g., learning English, knowing American history, becoming citizens). Indeed, Americanizers often viewed the local foreign-language newspapers as allies in their Americanization efforts. But at the same time, the editors and writers in Chicago and Cleveland rejected the Americanizers' demand that immigrants give up key elements of their Old World culture to be accepted in the New World. Instead, they sought ways to maintain and pass on their native languages and traditions, fought for greater respect for their people in the public school programs and curricula, and repeatedly encouraged their readers to use the freedoms guaranteed by the Constitution to defend their cultural differences from mainstream American. The historian Lawrence H. Fuchs describes this stance as "a kind of *voluntary* pluralism in which immigrant settlers from Europe and their progeny were free to maintain affection for and loyalty to their ancestral religions and cultures while at the same time claiming an American identity by embracing the founding myths and participating in the political life of the republic" (emphasis in the original).[24]

As evidence from these sources reveals, Americanization efforts in this era were neither a monolithic enterprise nor a cultural juggernaut. Rather, they were part of a long-running and contested process of cultural change. In that process, immigrants had a considerable degree of agency, and they were able to shape Americanization in ways that made sense to them. As labor historian James Barrett explains, "Americanism was, in fact, a contested ideal. There were numerous understandings of what it meant to be an American, divergent values associated with the concept, and so many ways that an immigrant might 'discover' America." Barrett calls this process "Americanization from the bottom up."[25]

While Americanization education was a negotiated exchange between Americanizers and immigrants, many historians have rightly noted that the power relationships in these negotiations were clearly unequal. Americanizers determined most of what was on the table. Nevertheless, the immigrants, as represented in the foreign language press in Chicago and Cleveland, were active, creative, and tenacious in their efforts to use Americanization education to further their individual and group interests and to use what they learned in this process to promote a new vision of American society. In other words, they Americanized on their own terms, balancing a deep commitment to the United States with an equally strong desire to maintain crucial aspects of their cultural backgrounds and their composite American identity. I refer to this stance as "patriotic pluralism."[26]

The foreign language press in Chicago regularly propounded these ideas in the early decades of the twentieth century, but the great flowering of patriotic pluralism came in the 1930s and early 1940s, when many of its core concepts entered the cultural and educational mainstream. This development of the stance coincided with and contributed to renewed efforts to Americanize European immigrants during the Depression and war years, a move that was in large part a response to rising anti-immigrant sentiment in the United States and the triumph of militant ethnic nationalist dictatorships in many of the immigrants' homelands. On the adult level, these Americanization efforts were led by two federal agencies, the WPA and the Immigration and Naturalization Service; on the K–12 level, they were advanced by the growing popularity of what was known at the time as intercultural education. Unfortunately, there is a large gap in the literature about these efforts, because almost every previous study of Americanization education concludes in or before 1930.

Thus, the last new approach this book takes is expanding the time frame for examining Americanization education into the 1930s, 1940s, and early 1950s. Historians of education who end their examination of Americanization in or before 1930 have missed some of the most interesting and important trends associated with this project, particularly the gradual shift toward a more culturally inclusive approach to teaching American history, culture, and citizenship to adults and to K–12 students. Crucial to this change was the work of such prominent immigrant intellectuals and educators as Louis Adamic, Franz Boas, Leonard Covello, Norman Drachler, and Hilda Taba. In the late 1930s and the World War II years, these individuals took ideas about the diverse history and character of this country similar to those popularized by the foreign language press and introduced them to the country as a whole. In this process, these immigrant educators fiercely denounced ethnic nationalism both at home and abroad and affirmed a decidedly civic nationalist vision of United States.[27]

The 1930s and 1940s marked the closing of an important chapter in the nation's struggle between ethnic and civic nationalism. In the immediate postwar years, nativists were in retreat, at least temporarily, and the efforts by European immigrants and their native-born allies to reenvision American history and culture along more cosmopolitan lines were gaining traction. These developments signaled the success of Americanization education, not just in terms of integrating eastern and southern European immigrants and their children into the broader national culture. They also signaled the reciprocal influence that these immigrants had on this country. In the process of becoming Americans, the immigrants changed how America came to understand itself. They began an effort that ultimately replaced the narrow Anglo-Saxon conception of the country with a vision of the United States as a nation enriched by its diversity and united by its common democratic ideals. In this way, these immigrants both honored and advanced the civic nationalist creed that was at the core of Americanization education.

1

THE SINGLE GREATEST FACTOR IN THE AMERICANIZATION OF IMMIGRANTS

From the early 1890s to the mid-1920s, over 22 million immigrants, most of them European, entered the United States. Unencumbered by quotas and facing few restrictions, this was one of the largest migrations in human history. In their culture, language, religion, and experience with democratic institutions, the majority of these newcomers could not have been more unlike most native-born Americans. In 1890, most Americans had northwestern European ancestry, worshipped in Protestant churches, and had been exposed to at least the trappings of democracy. The immigrants, by contrast, primarily hailed from eastern and southern Europe. Huge numbers of them were Roman Catholic, Eastern Orthodox Christian, or Jewish, and the majority had been subjects of the great autocratic empires of Europe and Eurasia.[1]

Many native-born Americans viewed this influx of foreigners with great trepidation. As early as 1891, for example, a report to the National Council of Education, an elite group within the National Education Association (NEA), warned, "Foreign influence has begun a system of colonization with a purpose of preserving foreign languages and traditions and proportionately of destroying distinctive Americanism." Seeking some way to contain and control this dangerous flood of aliens, the report declared, "The only answer thus far given is 'education,'—education in its broad American sense for body, mind, and morals; for every position of manual industry, social or civil service." The educators called for stronger compulsory education laws to get children of immigrants into public schools and "educated as American citizens in the language, history, traditions, and governmental principles of their adopted country."[2]

In 1913, William Maxwell, superintendent of the New York City public schools, reiterated these concerns, declaring that "the majority of the people who now come to us have little akin to our language; they have little akin to our mode of thought; they have little akin to our customs; and they have little akin to our traditions." But, he argued, "it is a great business of the department of education in this city" to train "the immigrant child to become a good American citizen." Like the members of the NEA committee, he was confident that the schools were up to this task.[3] An editorial in the journal *Immigrants in America Review* summed up this position, declaring, "Education is the single greatest factor in the Americanization of immigrants."[4]

Yet not all Americans were convinced that education could work such magic. The same year that the NEA leaders were urging schools to redouble their efforts to Americanize the immigrants, Senator Henry Cabot Lodge (R-MA) disparaged most of the newcomers as the "lowest and most illiterate" members of "alien" races, whose assimilation was almost impossible. What should Americans do, he asked rhetorically, "to guard our citizenship against an infusion that seems to threaten deterioration?" His answer was to severely restrict the number of eastern and southern European immigrants allowed into the United States.[5]

Over the next few decades, proponents of race-based immigration restriction rejected the idea that education or any other aspect of the vaunted "melting pot" could transform most new immigrants into true Americans. By the 1920s, the ideas of "scientific" racism that viewed the vast majority of new immigrants as racially inferior increasingly became a key part of the argument against both Americanization education and continued immigration of people from eastern and southern Europe. George Creel, a nationally renowned journalist, summed up this perspective in a 1921 article that flatly declared, "The so-called Melting Pot . . . is not working now nor has it worked for several decades."[6] For these racial restrictionists the single greatest factor determining whether the immigrants could be Americanized was whether they descended from the Anglo-Saxon or Nordic race. "Close the gates to eastern and southern European immigrants"— not "Provide more education"—was their rallying cry.

Between 1890 and 1924, these hopes and fears coalesced into two broad, opposing camps to establish whether education or innate racial character was the greatest determinant of assimilation.[7] In many ways, these two camps reflected a fundamental struggle, not merely about whether civic or ethnic nationalism would drive American immigration policy, but, more important, about what kind of country people wanted the United States to be. Until the early 1920s, supporters of civic nationalism generally prevailed in this contest, assuring the nation that the transformative power of education could turn even the most backward eastern European peasant into a true American. But in the aftermath of World War I, as the nation experienced a violent Red scare and the rise to prominence of such racist, anti-immigrant groups as the Ku Klux Klan, ethnic nationalists gained a considerable following across the country.[8] Growing numbers of Americans accepted the idea that most of the new immigrants were *racially* incompatible with a country created by Nordic settlers and shaped by Nordic ideals and values. This racist argument played a major role in the passage of the 1924 National Origins Act, which established racial quotas for entry into the United States and virtually ended large-scale immigration from eastern and southern Europe.[9]

This chapter examines the conflict between ethnic and civic nationalists as it relates to education. I argue that the most important debate about Americanization was *not*, as many scholars have maintained, between restrictionists, assimilationists, and amalgamationists, who advocated Anglo-Saxon racial and cultural supremacy, on the one hand, and cultural pluralists, who espoused cultural and racial equality, on the other.[10] Rather, I see the great debate of this era as being between people who believed that education could play a major role in Americanizing the immigrants (i.e., assimilationists, cultural pluralists, and amalgamationists) and those who believed that race alone was the crucial factor in determining who could become an American (i.e., racial restrictionists). For this latter group, the belief that education could transform inferior races into Americans was absurd.[11] Grouping together assimilationists, cultural pluralists, and amalgamationists under the broad heading of civic nationalism does not deny the substantial and consequential differences between these positions. But in comparison to the views espoused by racial restrictionists, I see the similarities among these three groups of civic nationalists as more salient than their differences.

All such categorization schemes are to some extent arbitrary, and all fail to capture the messy, at times contradictory, nature of people's ideas and actions.[12] For example, some assimilationists, such as Ellwood Cubberley, were strongly wedded to ideas of Anglo-Saxon cultural superiority, ideas that at times sounded a lot like those of racial restrictionists. Henry Ford, an avid supporter of Americanization education, was also a relentless anti-Semite and racist. Horace Kallen, the "father" of cultural pluralism, described ethnic differences in ways that could be construed as biological,

a stance that put him uncomfortably close to the position of the racial restrictionists, albeit with a positive take on these ethnic groups. In addition,
many people use the great amalgamationist metaphor of "the melting
pot" as a synonym for assimilation (see the George Creel comment cited
above), which was not what Israel Zangwill, the metaphor's creator, meant
by it.[13] Despite such examples of the imperfect nature of this categorization scheme, it works admirably in highlighting the role that education
played in the Americanization of European immigrants. Specifically, assimilationists, cultural pluralists, and amalgamationists were all civic nationalists who believed in the transformative power of education, a stand
that clearly distinguishes them from the ethnic nationalism of the racial
restrictionists.

In exploring these positions, the chapter begins by sketching the urban
and educational contexts in which these controversies about immigration and education took place. It then briefly examines the importance of
World War I in shaping the nature and direction of Americanization education in this era. Next it turns to the different ideas that inspired the
three main groups of civic nationalists—the assimilationists, cultural pluralists, and amalgamationists—and discusses their different approaches to
Americanization education. The chapter concludes with an analysis of
the rise of ethnic nationalism in the early 1920s, highlighting the arguments of the racial restrictionists about the importance of race in determining immigration policy and the claims they made about the futility of
Americanization education with regard to the new immigrants.

The Changing Urban Context, 1890–1925

Beginning in the latter part of the nineteenth century and extending well
into the 1920s, the United States experienced a series of profound, inter-
connected transformations, changing from a rural to an urban country,
from an agrarian to an industrial economy, and from a largely northern
European, Protestant nation to one that was increasingly multiethnic and
religiously diverse. Nowhere were these changes felt more dramatically
than in the nation's great cities, particularly, but not exclusively, those of
the Northeast and Midwest. While cities in the Northeast had experienced dramatic growth since the 1840s, in the latter part of the nineteenth
century these trends greatly intensified. For example, between 1890 and
1920, the population of New York City exploded from 1.5 million to over
5.6 million. Similarly, during these years Chicago climbed from 1.1 mil-

lion to 2.7 million, Cleveland from about 261,000 to nearly 797,000, Detroit from nearly 206,000 to about 994,000, St. Louis from 452,000 to almost 773,000, and Pittsburgh from 238,000 to over 585,000. Los Angeles, which was not even one of the nation's fifty largest cities in the 1890s, leapt from a population of about 102,000 in 1900 to over 588,000 in 1920, making it the tenth-largest city in the country.[14]

These demographic changes were directly tied to America's rise to international economic preeminence, a process that began in the post–Civil War era and continued almost unimpeded until the Great Depression. In the first half of the twentieth century, cities were a driving force behind the nation's unprecedented economic growth. By 1920, New York was a global financial center, and it dominated the nation's garment and publishing industries. Chicago, a national transportation hub, was also the great midwestern *entrepôt*, the meatpacking center for the country, and a major producer of farm equipment, automobiles, and steel.[15] The great "single-industry towns" of Detroit and Pittsburgh produced more automobiles and rolled out more steel, respectively, than any other cities in the world.[16]

Cleveland provides a typical example of the robust nature of the urban American economy in these years. In the late nineteenth century, the city was already "one of the world's great steel-making centers." By the 1920s, it "had become one of the world's leading producers of transportation equipment, rails, construction materials, barrels, automobile engines and transmissions, valves, pumps, light bulbs, sewing machines, refrigerators, washing machines, vacuum cleaners, and office equipment."[17]

Immigration was a major factor in these dramatic demographic and economic changes. Lured by the promise of jobs and better lives, between 1911 and 1920 alone nearly 8.8 million immigrants entered the United States, almost two-thirds of them from Austria-Hungary (about 2.15 million), Italy (about 2.05 million), and the Russian Empire (almost 1.6 million).[18] As historians Leonard Dinnerstein and David Reimers note, 80 percent of these new immigrants settled in the "northeast quadrant of the United States," mainly in the great cities of this region. By 1910, "about three quarters of the population of New York City, Chicago, Detroit, Cleveland, and Boston consisted of immigrants and their children. Foreign enclaves also predominated in such cities as Philadelphia, St. Louis, Milwaukee, Buffalo, Baltimore, Pittsburgh, and Providence."[19] Regionally, by 1920 "40 percent of the white residents in the North were either foreign-born or had both parents born overseas."[20] In 1913, one commentator tried to put the size of "the immigrant invasion" into perspective by pointing out that the total foreign-born population in the U.S. equaled the combined native population of 22 states.[21]

These massive numbers of immigrants profoundly altered the character of every city they inhabited. Many immigrants settled in close proximity to their Old World compatriots, creating neighborhoods that quickly became known as "Little Italy," "Greektown," "Poletown," or "Ukrainian Village." While these ethnic neighborhoods were not as monocultural as those nicknames imply,[22] native-born Americans saw these immigrant settlements as "foreign colonies" in which Old World languages, foods, customs, newspapers, clubs, churches, and synagogues flourished. Compounding the problem and heightening fears about this foreign invasion was the sheer size of these colonies. By 1930, New York had more Jews than any city in the world, and more Italians than Rome (in addition to having more Irish than Dublin and more people of African heritage than any city in Africa). Chicago boasted more Poles than any city other than Warsaw, more Czechs than any city outside of Prague, and more Lithuanians than any city in the world. Only Budapest had a larger Hungarian population than Cleveland's.[23]

These tremendous demographic changes had serious social and political consequences. As newcomers flooded America's industrial cities, urban leaders and local politicians found themselves quickly overwhelmed by a series of seemingly intractable, interlocking problems. Throughout this era, every major American city suffered from a growing gulf between rich and poor, overcrowding and disease in vast and expanding slums, widespread political corruption, inadequate or incompetent public services, and rampant crime. Immigrants were implicated in all these developments.

Promising to clean out corruption and provide efficient city services, groups of "progressive" civic leaders launched political campaigns across the country that by 1920 had reformed city politics and restructured city government in almost all of America's great urban centers. A central feature of these reform efforts was changing the governance, nature, and function of the public schools, in large part to address the problems posed by the vast number of new immigrants.

The Changing Educational Context, 1890–1925
Americans often have expressed great faith in the power of education to solve social problems. The last part of the nineteenth century and the first

quarter of the twentieth witnessed a particularly exuberant expression of that faith, which came to be known as progressive educational reform. In 1897, John Dewey proclaimed, "I believe that education is the fundamental method of social progress and reform."[24] Over the next two decades educators across the country rallied to that call, but the challenges facing them in reforming America's great city schools were daunting.

The number of new students alone was overwhelming. For example, between 1890 and 1920, public school enrollments in New York City more than tripled, from approximately 308,000 to 942,000 and enrollments in the Chicago Public Schools jumped from 136,00 to 394,000. In just ten years, 1920 to 1930, the number of students in the Detroit Public Schools more than doubled, from 111,000 to 232,000.[25] In large cities and small, the children of immigrants accounted for a huge share of the rising enrollments. As early as 1909, the U.S. Immigration Commission found that almost 58 percent of the pupils in the nation's thirty-seven largest public school systems had fathers who were born outside the United States.[26] Moreover, the diversity of these students was staggering. In 1913, a district superintendent in New York City reported that in the previous year immigrants from ninety-eight different countries, who spoke sixty-six different languages, had arrived in the city, and their children were pouring into the public schools.[27]

Finding ways to accommodate this flood of immigrant students was one of the chief reasons that progressives sought to reform the public school systems in major American cities. Indeed, key aspects of the progressive educational agenda directly addressed problems that the immigrants and their children either caused or greatly exacerbated. For example, progressive educational leaders—for the most part well-to-do, old-stock Protestants—launched broad political and organizational reform efforts designed to introduce greater efficiency, bureaucracy, and professional control to major urban school districts. These reformers argued that if urban public school systems were organized like great manufacturing corporations, they then could build enough schools, hire sufficient numbers of teachers, and provide high-quality education to all the new students.[28] These changes had profound consequences for immigrant communities.

Central to the success of these reforms was the progressive effort to shift the locus of educational power in cities from ward-based school boards to boards either elected from the city at large or appointed by the mayor. Because of the considerable size of many "foreign colonies" in cities, ward-based school boards often provided important sources of power and patronage for politicians representing the largest and most politically active immigrant groups. Progressive reformers sought to break that power through citywide elections that gave a decided advantage to well-funded, old-stock reform candidates who could attract votes from the native-born pluralities that still existed in major cities. While these political battles over the structure of school governance usually centered on issues of corruption, efficiency, and educational vision, issues of ethnicity and religion often lay just below the surface.[29]

By 1916, progressive reformers had succeeded in changing the educational governance structure of every major American city. In some places, such as New York and Chicago, the mayor appointed the school board members, a practice that enabled large, politically powerful immigrant groups to still have some say in the selection of board members. In other places, such as Cleveland, Detroit, Los Angeles, and St. Louis, board members were chosen in at-large elections, which made it considerably harder for candidates from immigrant communities to gain seats. Regardless of which form of school governance a city adopted, the results were much the same. During this period, native-born, Protestant businessmen or professionals dominated urban school boards. These boards in turn generally appointed professional educators with similar backgrounds as key administrators in these growing school districts.[30]

Once in power, these reformers centralized school governance and administration, professionalized teaching staffs, increased funding, initiated massive school-building programs, introduced or expanded a multitude of new educational programs and services (e.g., kindergartens, playgrounds), and modified curricula and pedagogy to address the problems of accommodating and Americanizing the immigrants.[31] But amid all this change, educators continued such time-honored Americanization activities as teaching English, introducing Anglo-American culture, and imparting ideas about American democracy. As the associate superintendent of the New York public schools put it in 1913, "The school must of necessity assume the duty of instructing the immigrant in the language, customs, and political ideals of our country."[32]

By 1920, virtually every school system serving large numbers of immigrant children had woven aspects of Americanization through all areas of the curriculum. In addition to these efforts on the K–12 level, urban educators strongly promoted Americanization programs for adults. In chapter 2,

I return to the Americanization initiatives on both the K–12 and adult levels and look closely at how they evolved in several major industrial cities.

Americanization and the First World War Era

Nothing focused the nation's attention on Americanization education more intensely than did the outbreak of World War I, in August 1914. Prior to the war, Americanization activities, though extensive, were more reactive than strategic. World War I changed that pattern of behavior, making Americanization one of the most prominent educational issues of the day. As a New York school administrator stated in 1919, Americans were "thinking as never before of how they are to deal with the greatest problem of their time . . . the problem of Americanization."[33]

Throughout 1915 and 1916, American political leaders watched the escalating carnage in Europe, fearing at once that the country would be drawn into the conflict and that large numbers of immigrants might side with their homelands against the United States if the country went to war.[34] These latter fears were not trivial. From the beginning of the war in August 1914 until America's entry in April 1917, ethnic and foreign-born supporters of the Allied and the Central Powers respectively *had* sought to influence U.S. foreign policy. People of British or German ancestry loudly proclaimed the righteousness of their motherlands in the conflict. In addition, groups such as the Czechs, Irish, Lithuanians, Slovaks, and Poles supported one side or the other, hoping that the outcome of the war would result in freedom for their subjugated homelands. All these actions stoked fears among many native-born Americans about the true loyalty of the immigrants.[35]

These concerns intensified as the prospects for American involvement on the Allied side loomed larger. As historian David Kennedy observes, "Of those 32 million persons from families with close foreign ties, more than ten million derived from the Central Powers."[36] Once the United States entered the conflict, these fears stimulated two distinct but related reactions: first, a vicious but ultimately short-lived campaign against German-Americans; and second, a zealous nationwide movement to Americanize adult immigrants from all backgrounds.

Had it not been for the war, German Americans would probably have been the least likely group of newcomers to arouse anti-immigrant sentiments. Arriving in large numbers during the nineteenth century, the

Germans were viewed by most Americans as hardworking, honest, and law-abiding. They were also among the most assimilated of all peoples coming to the United States.[37] They were the model minority of the era.

Despite their reputation for ready assimilation, the Germans maintained strong links to their homeland and to German culture. Probably nothing better demonstrates that commitment than their largely successful efforts to have German used as a language of instruction in public elementary and secondary schools across the nation, but particularly in the Midwest.[38] While these bilingual programs provoked some political controversy and concerns about assimilation, by the early twentieth century they were well established in almost all major cities that had substantial ethnic German populations.[39]

In the early years of World War I, German American language newspapers (as well as Hungarian and some Scandinavian papers) staunchly supported the German and Austro-Hungarian war effort. Similarly, major German American organizations sought to use their considerable political clout to influence U.S. policy in ways that benefited the Central Powers. For example, in 1914–1915, German American leaders campaigned vigorously for an embargo on the sale of war materials to all the nations engaged in the war, claiming that such trade violated American neutrality by disproportionately aiding the British and French. Some American political and opinion leaders quickly denounced these activists as agents of a foreign power.[40] As rumors spread about sabotage schemes orchestrated by agents from the German embassy, and as growing numbers of Americans lost their lives in attacks by German submarines, American leaders increasingly denounced German Americans whose "dual loyalty" seemed to threaten the nation.[41]

Representative of such criticism was Woodrow Wilson's State of the Union address in December 1915. Just six months earlier, Wilson had stood before a group of newly naturalized citizens, praising them and welcoming them into the body politic. While he warned them about the dangers of dual loyalties, his call for American unity was neither shrill nor intemperate. But in his State of the Union address, Wilson unleashed a furious barrage against dual loyalty, clearly directed at German Americans. "There are citizens of the United States," he exclaimed, "I blush to admit, born under other flags but welcomed under our generous naturalization laws to the full freedom and opportunity of America, who have poured the poison of disloyalty into the very arteries of our national life. . . ." He then added ominously, "They are not many, but they are infinitely malignant, and the hands of our power should close over them at once."[42]

When the United States joined the war in April 1917, these sentiments swept the nation in a wave of anti-German hysteria. Fueled by patriotic zeal, many Americans attacked all things German. These assaults ranged from the ludicrous—calling hamburgers "liberty sandwiches"—to the horrifying—the lynching of a young German immigrant in Collinsville, Illinois. During the war, about 480,000 German men and women registered with the U.S. government; some 6,300 were arrested, and, of these, about 2,300 "were turned over to military authorities for internment." German language newspapers were investigated for seditious articles and editorials, and some of their editors were jailed. Supposedly pro-German university professors and schoolteachers lost their jobs, and ordinary German Americans came under intense scrutiny for possible signs of disloyalty, whether in the form of comments about the war, speaking German in public, not flying the American flag, or reluctance to purchase war bonds.[43]

One of the most enduring developments of the anti-German hysteria was the abolition of German language instruction in public elementary schools and in some high schools. Across the nation, but particularly in the Midwest, where bilingual German and English instruction had thrived for over half a century, school boards voted to end virtually all these programs by the end of 1918.[44]

In terms of Americanization education, these developments raised concerns and suspicions about the loyalties of *all* immigrant groups and helped launch an extensive national campaign to Americanize the large number of non-naturalized adult immigrants. Beginning soon after the war in Europe erupted, this campaign included a broad range of conservative and liberal Americanizers, but, as America's entry into the war became increasingly likely, many of the most outspoken Americanizers demanded aggressive, even forced, assimilation, touting "100 per cent Americanism."[45]

In many ways, the Americanization campaign that began in 1915 and extended into the 1920s was one of the most important and extensive adult education movements in American history. Educational and political leaders believed that this campaign was essential to national survival in the face of enemies both at home and abroad. Writing in 1916, Robert Livingston Schuyler, a distinguished historian at Columbia University, summed up these sentiments, stating, "The European war has not created the problem of Americanization, but it has revealed it to us as a vital, perhaps the paramount issue in our public life."[46]

In early 1915, a wide range of organizations came together to promote Americanization education throughout the land. Specifically, these groups united to bolster the patriotism of the already-naturalized new citizens, teach English to the approximately five million aliens in the United States who could not speak the language, and strongly encourage the naturalization of the estimated six million adult immigrants who had not yet applied for citizenship.[47] Spearheaded by the National Americanization Day Committee, which was composed of business, civic, and philanthropic leaders, mainly from the Northeast and Mid-Atlantic regions, the campaign officially began with the designation of July 4, 1915, as "Americanization Day." Frances Kellor, a member of the committee, described the rationale for using the July Fourth holiday for this purpose: "Nothing seemed more necessary and fitting than that American-born citizens and foreign-born citizens and future citizens alike should be brought together in common observance of the day and in a common understanding of America."[48]

These celebrations took place in some 150 cities across the country.[49] The success of this endeavor convinced the Americanization Day committee members to reconstitute the group as the National Americanization Committee (NAC) in order to promote educational activities related to naturalization, national unity, and patriotism.[50] While urban public school systems had been providing immigrants with evening school classes in English and civics for many years, the NAC spurred new efforts that went well beyond these school-based programs. The NAC encouraged community organizations to dramatically increase their involvement in Americanization education. By the time the United States entered World War I, the organizational network advancing the Americanization of adult immigrants included the small, but very active, U.S. Bureau of Education, the U.S. Bureau of Naturalization, newly created Americanization offices in state governments, public school systems, leading Catholic, Protestant, and Jewish organizations, the Red Cross, numerous women's organizations, such patriotic groups as the Daughters of the American

Revolution, the U.S. Chamber of Commerce and its local affiliates, major industrial corporations, some trade unions, public libraries, and newspapers from both the English and foreign language press.[51] Chapter 2 explores these developments in detail.

Civic Nationalism and Americanization Education

Americanization activities in public schools and national efforts to assimilate adult immigrants rested on the shared belief that education could transform the children of immigrants and their parents into good Americans. As historian David Tyack observes, most educators at this time were "confident that schooling could change the many into one people, *e pluribus unum*."[52] In other words, even educators who largely disdained the new immigrants were still civic nationalists, due to their belief that the new immigrants could learn and truly embrace Americanism regardless of their ancestry or birthplace.

But this broad belief in education as an effective instrument for Americanization did not lead to consensus about the goals, content, and methods of that process. In the early decades of the twentieth century, numerous educators, journalists, politicians, public intellectuals, and some prominent members of the growing immigrant communities all participated in a long-running debate about the content and methods for effective Americanization education. Scholars have generally placed these people and organizations involved in these debates into three broad categories: assimilationists, cultural pluralists, and amalgamationists (supporters of the "melting pot").[53]

THE ASSIMILATIONISTS

The assimilationist position, which maintains that immigrants need to divest themselves of almost every cultural trait they brought from the Old World and firmly embrace the culture of the New, has been part of the educational landscape almost since the inception of public schools.[54] In 1836, for example, Calvin Stowe, an active promoter of common schools in Ohio, warned that "unless we educate the immigrants, they will be our ruin." He added, "It is altogether essential to our national strength and peace, if not even to our national existence, that the foreigners who settle on our soil, should cease to be Europeans and become Americans; and as our national language is English, and as our literature, our manners, and our institutions are of English origin, and the whole foundation of our society English, it is necessary that they become substantially Anglo-Americans."[55]

As the flood of new immigrants surged in the 1890s and the early twentieth century, civic leaders and educators repeated these views with increasing urgency. Probably no one in this era articulated them more vigorously than Theodore Roosevelt.[56] Writing about the new immigrants in a 1903 essay, Roosevelt stated, "We must Americanize them in every way, in speech, in political ideas and principles, and in their way of looking at the relations between church and state."[57] More specifically, he declared, "where immigrants, or sons of immigrants, do not heartily and in good faith throw in their lot with us, but cling to the speech, the customs, the ways of life, and the habits of thought of the Old World which they have left, they thereby harm both themselves and us."[58]

Years later, as the First World War raged in Europe, Roosevelt published an article in support of Americanization Day, in which he succinctly reasserted these earlier views, stating, "There should be no hyphenated Americans; neither native-American nor foreign-American." He explained, "Each American of foreign birth or origin who sincerely desires to become a good citizen should show his good citizenship by being wholly and without reserve, and without divided allegiance, and with emphatic repudiation of the entire principle of 'dual nationality,' an American citizen and nothing else."[59] If immigrants followed that prescription, Roosevelt also argued, then native-born Americans should welcome them as full and complete Americans, regardless of their background. He stated in his 1915 article, "Americanization is a matter of spirit and soul, not a matter of a man's physical birthplace or his national origin or his creed."[60]

In his May 1915 speech to newly naturalized immigrants, Woodrow Wilson conveyed a similar message. Early in the century, he disparaged many of the newcomers as "multitudes of men of the lowest class from the south of Italy, and men of the meaner sort out of Hungary and Poland, men out of the ranks where there was neither skill nor energy nor any initiative of quick intelligence";[61] but in 1915, either experience or political expediency had led him to a more tolerant view of the immigrants. Yet even as he warmly welcomed the new citizens, he warned them, as Roosevelt had, that they must seek complete assimilation. "You cannot become thorough Americans if you think of yourselves in groups," he declared. "A man who thinks of himself as belonging to a particular national group in America, has not yet become an American, and the man who goes among you to trade upon your nationality is no worthy son to live under the Stars and Stripes."[62]

Many leading educators echoed these views. Perhaps the best, and certainly the most widely cited, example of the assimilationist position in education came from Stanford University education professor Ellwood Cubberley, one of the most influential educators in the nation. Writing in 1909, Cubberley declared that the "southern and eastern Europeans" who were pouring into the country were "of a very different type from the north Europeans who preceded them." He continued,

> Illiterate, docile, lacking in self-reliance and initiative, and not possessing the Anglo-Teutonic conceptions of law, order, and government, their coming has served to dilute tremendously our national stock, and to corrupt our civic life. . . . Everywhere these people tend to settle in groups or settlements, and to set up here their national manners, customs, and observances. Our task is to break up these groups or settlements, to assimilate and amalgamate these people as a part of our American race, and to implant in their children, so far as can be done, the Anglo-Saxon conception of righteousness, law and order, and popular government, and to awaken in them a reverence for our democratic institutions and for those things in our national life which we as a people hold to be of abiding worth.[63]

Despite his disparaging remarks about the immigrants, and even taking into account his patronizing phrase ("so far as can be done") about the prospects for educating their children, Cubberley's belief that education could make them worthy citizens willing to embrace the things that Americans "hold to be of abiding worth" is a clear statement of civic nationalism. Equally important, many educational leaders agreed with Cubberley and sought to use public schools to Americanize the immigrants along lines set out by the assimilationists.[64]

School leaders were not alone in extolling these efforts to Americanize the children of immigrants along assimilationist lines. One of the most widely cited discussions of Americanization education (both at the time and by historians) is the 1912 autobiography by Mary Antin, a Jewish immigrant from Russia, who warmly embraced the assimilationist project of public schools.[65] Antin describes her years in the Boston schools as the beginning of a wondrous metamorphosis that changed a frightened immigrant into a proud American. This transformation occurred despite a school regime that gave little respect to or even recognition of her religious heritage. Indeed she was compelled each day to bow her head and recite the Lord's Prayer in class.[66]

Nevertheless, when she learned about the American Revolution, she accepted the story as her own. "As I read how the patriots planned the Revolution," she wrote, "and the women gave their sons to die in battle, and the heroes led to victory, and the rejoicing people set up the Republic, it dawned on me gradually what was meant by *my country*." Her overall views on Americanization education were simple and direct. She stated, "The public school has done its best for us foreigners, and for the country, when it has made us into good Americans."[67]

But if Antin represents an upbeat view of Americanization education, Leonard Covello, a child of Italian immigrants who attended the New York City public schools, described Americanization as a bitter process of cultural oppression and loss. Reflecting on the history he was taught as a child, Covello declared, "In fact, throughout my whole elementary career, I do not recall one mention of Italy or the Italian language or what famous Italians had done in the world, with the possible exception of Columbus, who was pretty popular in America." This experience sent a none-too-subtle message that being Italian "meant something inferior."[68] He summed up the process by declaring that Americanization programs "were designed, therefore, to suppress or eliminate all that was conceived of as 'foreign' and to impose upon the immigrant a cultural uniformity with an American pattern."[69] The educators who denounced such efforts to erase the cultural backgrounds of the immigrants and argued instead that these cultures actually enriched the United States were the cultural pluralists.

THE CULTURAL PLURALISTS

The assimilationist project did not go unchallenged. Advocates of cultural pluralism rejected what they saw as its narrow, ethnocentric vision of American culture and identity. At the same time that Roosevelt and Wilson were decrying hyphenated Americans, such national leaders as U.S. Supreme Court Justice Louis Brandeis and such public intellectuals as Horace Kallen and Randolph Bourne were questioning the legitimacy and effectiveness of the assimilationist form of Americanization and articulating a different vision of civic nationalism.[70] These and other cultural pluralists sought substantial preservation of the immigrants' native culture "within the context of American citizenship and political and economic integration into American society."[71]

On July 5, 1915, in a speech at Faneuil Hall in Boston, Louis Brandeis reflected on the Americanization Day celebration that had taken place the previous day. While most of his speech echoed themes about embracing the American political ideals and values articulated by Roosevelt and Wilson, he parted company with them in one notable way. Rather than castigating hyphenated Americans, Brandeis paid tribute to the diversity of the American people, particularly the immigrants. Denouncing the "Russianizing of Finland, the Prussianizing of Poland and Alsace, the Magyarizing of Croatia, and the persecution of the Jews in Russia and Rumania" as efforts to compel cultural homogeneity, Brandeis proclaimed the superiority of the Unites States, because "America has believed that in differentiation, not uniformity, lies the path to progress." He continued, "The new nationalism adopted by America proclaims that each race or people, like each individual, has the right and duty to develop, and that only through differentiated development will high civilization be attained."[72]

Perhaps no one in this era captured this idea better than Horace Kallen, a Jewish immigrant who became a distinguished professor of philosophy. He maintained that proponents of assimilation ignored the fact that immigrants were deeply wedded to their home cultures. For him, Americanization was largely an "external" development that included "the adoption of the American variety of English speech, American clothes and manners, and the American attitude in politics." Kallen believed, however, that these external characteristics were far less important than the "internal" aspects of a person's character, most notably their ethnic background.[73] He argued that because these ethnic roots were so strong, the United States had to reject aggressive assimilation and become instead a "democracy of nationalities, cooperating voluntarily and autonomously through common institutions in the enterprise of self-realization through the perfection of men according to their kind." Kallen coined the phrase "cultural pluralism" to describe this arrangement. More poetically, he imagined a culturally pluralistic nation as an orchestra, with each ethnic group contributing a unique instrument, and all of them together performing a "symphony of civilization."[74]

Randolph Bourne, an essayist who was one of the leading social commentators of this era, shared Kallen's views about the wrongheaded nature of assimilationist Americanization efforts, particularly efforts aimed at forcing immigrants to reject their home culture in order to gain admission to American society. He described that process as simply the nation's "Anglo-Saxon element" imposing "its own culture upon the minority peoples." Moreover, like Kallen, Bourne believed that efforts to eradicate immigrant cultures would fail and that the nation was better for that failure, since survival of these cultures enriched the nation. "The foreign cultures have not been melted down or run together, made into some homogeneous Americanism," he explained, "but have remained distinct but cooperating to the greater glory and benefit, not only of themselves but of all the native 'Americanism' around them." But, unlike Kallen, who seemed to believe that the relationship between immigrant cultures and the dominant Anglo-American culture was one of immutable entities arriving at some mutually agreeable accommodation, Bourne saw this relationship as dynamic. Bourne's metaphor for the United States was a continuously changing transnational tapestry woven with "many threads of all sizes and colors." He argued, "Any movement that attempts to thwart this weaving, or to dye the fabric any one color, or disentangle the strands, is false to this cosmopolitan vision."[75]

How such a "democracy of nationalities" would operate was never clear. Neither Kallen nor Bourne described the political structures that would be necessary to ensure that this pluralist vision would not, as historian Philip Gleason has noted, "produce Balkanization and a clash of ethnic nationalities in the United States."[76] Later in his life, Kallen partially addressed this concern ironically by taking a page from the assimilationists' agenda. In an essay written in the mid-1950s, Kallen argued that all citizens in a culturally pluralistic America had to know, understand, and embrace the core democratic ideals and values contained in such canonical works as the Declaration of the Independence and the Gettysburg Address.[77] From this perspective, knowledge of and support for American democratic institutions and principles were necessary structures for cultural pluralism to thrive.

Around the same time that Kallen and Bourne were presenting their ideas, a number of prominent social reformers and educators were arguing for schools to adopt some form of cultural pluralism. In 1908, for example, when Jane Addams addressed this issue at the annual National Education Association conference, she balanced her praise of public schools as "the great savior of the immigrant district" with a stern "indictment" of the unhealthy view of Americanism they often conveyed. She argued that by relentlessly immersing immigrant children in Anglo-American culture and by ignoring the backgrounds of immigrant families, the schools were driving a wedge between parents and children, weakening parental authority, and creating serious problems of youthful alienation and delinquency.[78]

Addams's solution to these problems was for teachers to be more attentive and respectful of immigrant cultures and to bring these cultures into their classrooms. "Can we not say," she urged, "that the schools ought to do more to connect these children with the best things of the past, to make them realize something of the beauty and charm of the language, the history, and the traditions which their parents represent." She encouraged her listeners to take a modest step toward cultural pluralism, concluding, "In short it is the business of the school to give each child the beginnings of a culture so wide and deep and universal that he can interpret his own parents and countrymen by a standard which is world-wide and not provincial."[79]

In 1916, as some Americans responded to the war in Europe by espousing a xenophobic form of nationalism, John Dewey made an even more forceful plea for appreciating the cultural backgrounds of immigrants. Speaking at the annual NEA conference, Dewey called upon teachers to recognize the great cultural diversity of the nation and be sensitive to that diversity in their classrooms. Fearing that the war had emboldened some assimilationists to demand that immigrants adopt the dominant culture as a proof of their political loyalty, Dewey declared, "No matter how loudly any one proclaims his Americanism, if he assumes that one racial strain, any one component culture, no matter how early it was settled in our territory, or how effective it has proved in its own land, is to furnish a pattern which all other strains and cultures are to conform, he is a traitor to an American nationalism." As if responding directly to Theodore Roosevelt and Woodrow Wilson, Dewey added, "The way to deal with hyphenism, in other words, is to welcome it, but to welcome it in the sense of extracting from each people its special good, so that it shall surrender into a common fund of wisdom and experience what it especially has to contribute." For Dewey, the great genius of the United States was its ability to combine numerous cultural traditions "to create the national spirit of America." He argued that at the very least, "our public schools shall teach each factor to respect every other, and shall take pains to enlighten all as to the great past contributions of every strain in our composite make-up."[80]

In making these arguments, Dewey was not simply calling for greater cultural or curricular equity. Rather, his ideas flowed from the very different vision of curriculum that he and other progressive educators were advocating. Often regarded as the father of progressive education, Dewey challenged the notion of curriculum as "something fixed and ready-made in itself." He argued instead that curricula, like cultures, should change in response to interactions with the environment.[81] In this case, he rebelled against the notion that that there was a fundamental dichotomy between American culture and the culture of the immigrants. Rather, the situation he encountered daily, first on the streets of Chicago and later in New York City, was one of pervasive and complex cultural interaction and change.

This is not to say that Dewey believed educators should stop teaching the common culture. Indeed, in his 1916 book *Democracy and Education*, he clearly states that people in democracies must hold key things in "common in order to form a community or society"; these things include "aims, beliefs, aspirations, knowledge—a common understanding—like-mindedness as the sociologists say."[82] But in response to people like Roosevelt and Cubberley, Dewey argued for a broader conception of the common culture, one that more readily represented the diverse groups of people who, in addition to Anglo-Americans, made vital contributions to the nation. Beyond this, Dewey's plea for more culturally pluralistic curricula rested on his vision of subject matter as "the cumulative outcome of the efforts, the strivings, and successes of the human race generation after generation."[83] From that perspective, educators who taught only a narrow portion of that cumulative knowledge were shortchanging their students.

Finally, cultural pluralists employed another core progressive educational idea in their critique of assimilationist Americanization, namely, that "compulsion" was a less effective educational tool than "interest."[84] Cultural pluralists argued that forcing immigrants into Americanization programs and then compelling them to learn lessons that stressed Anglo-American cultural superiority were ultimately counterproductive. Many young people, they maintained, would resist or reject these lessons, and adults would quickly drop out of or stay away from such programs altogether.[85]

In short, the cultural pluralists argued that Americanization education must be a process of cultural exchange rather than blunt cultural imposition. Writing in 1920, Floyd Clayton Butler, the director of Americanization at the U.S. Bureau of Education, nicely captured this perspective, saying, "America is the child of many races, but is herself stronger and nobler than any of her progenitors. This is so because each people has brought with it a wealth of art, of song, of custom, of ideals, all of which form a wondrous heritage."[86]

THE AMALGAMATIONISTS

The amalgamationists introduced a third vision of civic nationalism. They believed that the mixing and remixing of these groups in the United States would produce an entirely new and more robust nation.[87] The enduring concept they added to the vocabulary of Americanization was the "melting pot," largely due to the popularity of Israel Zangwill's 1909 play that used that phrase as its title. Over the years, however, the phrase mistakenly has come to metaphorically describe the complete assimilation of immigrants into Anglo-American culture. In 1920, Julius Drachsler, a professor at Smith College, summed up that misuse, writing, "Put baldly, the devotee of the crude, current notion of the 'melting pot,' bid America take the immigrant whoever he was and wherever he came from, strip him of his cultural heritage, throw him into the great cauldron, stir the pot vigorously, speak the magic word 'Americanization' and through the mystic vapors would rise the newly created 'American.' "[88] This was the assimilationist model, which saw the melting pot as an instrument for melting down immigrant culture, and as historian David Hollinger explains, "the resulting liquid [would be poured] into pre-existing molds created in the self-image of the Anglo-Protestants." Throughout the early decades of the twentieth century and indeed into the present day, many people view the role of the schools as America's great assimilationist melting pot. But this was not what early proponents of this idea had in mind.[89]

Zangwill and other amalgamationists came from a very different tradition, one that envisioned the melting pot as mixing all the races in the United States into a new, composite people. This tradition traces back to J. Hector St. John de Crèvecoeur, whose *Letters from an American Farmer* celebrated the emergence of "the American, this new man" whose "strange mixture of blood . . . you will find in no other country."[90] While Crèvecoeur was speaking of the mixing of European peoples in the New World, Hollinger argues that such nineteenth-century thinkers as Ralph Waldo Emerson and Herman Melville expanded on that original vision considerably. In 1845, for example, Emerson used the term "smelting pot" to describe the creation of a new American race composed of "Irish, Germans, Swedes, Poles, and Cossacks, and all the European tribes—of the Africans, and the Polynesians."[91] Six decades later, University of Pennsylvania professor Marion Dexter Learned echoed Emerson, declaring:

> No nation on earth has the blood of so many nations in the veins, as the Americans. The English puritan, Seigneur and felon, the Welsh, Irish, Scotch, African Negro, Swedes and Scandinavians, the Spaniard, Frenchmen Hugnenot [sic], Portuguese, German, Hungarian, Slav, Russian, Russian Jews and other Jews, Italian, Greek, Armenian, Chinese, Japanese, and whatever else they might be called have all contributed to the remarkable mixture of races . . . as we call the American people.[92]

Nothing better captured this sentiment than Zangwill's *The Melting Pot*. Early in the drama, David Quixano, the Russian Jewish refugee who is the protagonist of the story, proclaims, "the real American has not yet arrived. He is only in the Crucible, I tell you—he will be the fusion of all the races, perhaps the coming superman."[93] Clearly, Zangwill did not imagine the melting pot as an instrument of Anglo-American conformity, but rather as an all-inclusive instrument of biological and cultural fusion in which immigrants and native-born Americans alike meld together to form a totally new people and nation.[94]

In the final, triumphant scene of the play, David and his Russian Christian fiancée, Vera, gaze into a brilliant sunset, which David imagines as the glow around "the great Melting Pot." He exclaims, "There gapes her mouth—the harbour where a thousand mammoth feeders come from the ends of the world to pour in their human freight . . . Celt and Latin, Slav and Teuton, Greek and Syrian,—black and yellow— . . ." Vera adds, "Jew and Gentile . . . ," and David continues, "Yes, East and West, and North and South, the palm and the pine, the pole and the equator, the crescent and the cross—how the Great Alchemist melts and fuses them with his purging flame! Here shall they all unite to build the Republic of Man and the Kingdom of God."[95]

For some social reformers, Zangwill's ideas resonated strongly. Writing in the post–World War I era, Graham Taylor, a leading proponent of the social gospel and a staunch advocate for the immigrants in Chicago, described his city in terms Zangwill would have endorsed: "If Chicago is a melting pot, we are all in it. Native and foreign born are being melted together. . . . If we Americans are a new-world race our life blood is that of a cosmopolitan people, our nation consists of international constituents, our new race is inter-racial."[96]

Reporting on a 1920 study he had conducted on patterns of intermarriage in New York City, Julius Drachsler offered evidence that the amalgamationists were onto something. He found a considerable amount of intermarriage, both among various immigrant groups and between immigrants and native-born Americans. Based on this finding, he argued that this process could create a society in which there would be "intellectual and emotional harmony among the differing cultural heritages and peoples" of the United States. Echoing Addams and Dewey, Drachsler argued that this would happen only if the children of "mixed marriages" were taught to appreciate all the various cultures that were blending within the United States.[97] This call for the appreciation of the diverse cultures that were joining together was educationally similar to cultural pluralism.

From this perspective, the idea of the melting pot was used in two quite different ways when referring to education. The first, and most widely used, is the assimilationist approach, in which the schools sought to melt away the immigrants' cultural backgrounds and reforge them in an Anglo-Saxon mold. The second, which was much closer to Zangwill's ideal, demanded that public schools teach about the diverse backgrounds of the people who were merging into the new American nationality, a stance that was akin in some ways to cultural pluralism.

Regardless of which educational aspect of the melting pot people used, these ideas provoked strong reactions from two quite different groups: supporters of racial restriction and leaders of immigrant communities. As described in the next section, one of the main arguments that racial restrictionists used in demanding an end to immigration was that members of "inferior races" were marrying native-born Americans and, thereby, diluting the strength and racial purity of the nation. For them, Zangwill's glorious vision of the melting pot was a nightmare and a call to arms.

On the other side of the debate, despite Drachsler's plea for greater sensitivity to and education about immigrant cultures, some leaders of immigrant communities feared the melting pot as much as the racial restrictionists did. These leaders also saw intermarriage as a demographic and cultural threat, but in this case to their continued existence as distinct peoples in a pluralistic nation. This has been a persistent theme for immigrants ever since. Writing almost a century after Zangwill's play appeared, Zadie Smith captures this concern in her recent novel *White Teeth:* "[I]t makes an immigrant laugh to hear the fears of the nationalist, scared of infection, penetration, miscegenation, when this is small fry, *peanuts,* compared to what the immigrant fears—dissolution, *disappearance.*"[98]

Despite these concerns, amalgamationists still joined assimilationists and cultural pluralists under the banner of civic nationalism. All three groups shared the belief that in one way or another immigrants could become true Americans; they simply differed on how that should happen. But this idea that immigrants genuinely could become Americans was precisely what ethnic nationalists rejected.

The Rise of Ethnic Nationalism

As the Americanization campaign swept the country and as assimilationists, cultural pluralists, and amalgamationists debated the nature of American civic nationalism, supporters of racial restriction regarded the new immigrants as a dangerous demographic and cultural threat to the country. Writing in 1922, one defender of the immigrants commented wryly, "In the last few years the immigrant has been graduated perforce from his position as a problem to assume the doubtful dignity of a menace."[99] For many individuals and groups, the only way that menace could be dealt with was ending immigration from eastern and southern Europe altogether.

Widespread, organized opposition to immigrants began in the United States in the second quarter of the nineteenth century. Mainly targeting Irish and German newcomers, early nativists established some of the basic themes that shaped anti-immigrant sentiment well into the twentieth century. Whether one looks at the Know-Nothings of the 1850s or the American Protective Association of the 1880s and 1890s, these opponents of immigration generally stoked fears about four great dangers that they associated with the immigrants: their religions, which imperiled the unity and security of the nation (initially targeting Catholics, but eventually including Jews); their political radicalism, which threatened to undermine American democracy; their low standard of living, which jeopardized the livelihoods of native-born workers; and their racial inferiority and fecundity, which threatened to debase and overwhelm the Anglo-Saxon character and culture of the nation.[100] Beginning in the 1890s, perhaps the most significant change in this collection of anti-immigrant sentiments was the increasing centrality and sophistication of the racial-inferiority argument in efforts to restrict immigration.[101]

Throughout the nineteenth century, many Americans had argued about immigration issues in racial terms, with people on the East Coast largely focusing on the "Irish race" and those on the West centering on the influx of "Asiatic races." Concerns about assimilation of these races generated fierce battles about education on the local level and such federal actions as the 1882 Chinese Exclusion Act. However, these developments were not supported by "scientific" data, but rather were simply outgrowths of prejudices related to color, culture, and religion.[102]

Things began to change in the 1890s, when ideas drawn from Darwin's theory of evolution and Mendel's work in genetics became increasingly prominent in discussions of race and immigration. As historian Audrey Smedley argues, this new "scientific racism" rested on a series of propositions maintaining that: human beings were members of distinct racial groups; these groups could be ranked hierarchically; physical differences were related to intellectual and moral capabilities; such racial differences were passed on genetically; and environmental factors such as education could not alter inherent racial dispositions.[103] Moreover, these propositions explained distinctions not only *between* broad racial groups, but also *within* these groups. Thus, scientific racists subdivided and ranked Europeans into such different races as Nordics (from northern Europe), Alpines (from central and eastern Europe), and Mediterraneans (from southern Europe), each of which had its own racial makeup and character. Some European nationalists took this idea even further, proclaiming the existence of English, French, German, and Italian races.[104]

In the late nineteenth and early twentieth century these ideas combined with more traditional fears about religion, radicalism, and cheap labor to provide a platform upon which a diverse coalition of individuals and organizations campaigned to end or at least severely restrict the immigration of people from eastern and southern Europe. The coalition included the Immigration Restriction League (IRL), founded by a group of elite Bostonians, the American Federation of Labor, and a number of prominent Progressive era academics, as well as the resurgent and fiercely anti-Catholic, anti-Semitic Ku Klux Klan. Drawing strength from almost every section of the country, this coalition eventually had more success in stemming the tide of immigration than any previous or subsequent effort in American history.[105]

Not all of these individuals and groups were ethnic nationalists. Indeed, many people who sought to limit immigration in this period did so without injecting race into their arguments. Labor leaders, for example, tended to focus far more on what they perceived as the threat immigrants posed to U.S. wage scales and the American standard of living than they did on race. Similarly, most black leaders and newspapers at the time also supported limiting immigration out of fear that immigrants would take jobs from African Americans and drive down wages.[106]

But beginning in the late nineteenth century and continuing into the 1920s, many supporters of immigration restriction increasingly used racial arguments in their calls for "closing the gates." They defined the United States as a primarily Anglo-Saxon, Nordic, or Teutonic nation (although after America's entry into World War I the term *Teutonic* was dropped), which was in great peril due to the invasion of Alpine (i.e., Slavic), Mediterranean (i.e., Italian and Greek), and Semitic immigrants.[107] Francis A. Walker, who taught at Yale and later became president of the Massachusetts Institute of Technology, described the new immigrants in 1899 as "beaten men from beaten races; representing the worst failures in the struggle for existence. . . . They have none of the ideas and aptitudes which fit men to take up readily and easily the problem of self-care and self-government, such as belong to those who are descended from the tribes that met under the oak trees of old Germany to make laws and choose chieftains."[108] Viewing this problem as racial rather than cultural, the restrictionists argued that no amount of Americanization education could instill these "ideas and aptitudes" for "self-care and self-government" in the new immigrants.

One of the earliest restrictionists to make this claim based on supposed scientific data was Alfred P. Schultz. His 1906 book *Race or Mongrel* drew on Darwin to argue that racial purity was essential to the survival of great civilizations and that intermarriage with inferior races led to their collapse. Schultz viewed the United States as the last refuge of the Germanic Anglo-Saxon race and was convinced that excessive immigration of inferior races was "destroying the Teutonic character of America."[109] As for education enabling members of these inferior races to assimilate, Schultz scoffed, "The opinion is advanced that the public schools change the children of all races into Americans. Put a Scandinavian, a German, and a Magyar boy at one end, and they will come out Americans at the other end. Which is like saying, let a pointer, a setter, and a pug enter one end of a tunnel and they will come out three greyhounds at the other." He bluntly concluded that "the school cannot instill the peculiarities of one race into the children of another race."[110] Over the next two decades, other ethnic nationalists would reiterate that argument.

In 1916, Madison Grant, a leader of the IRL, published *The Passing of the Great Race,* which further developed the idea that maintaining or losing racial purity was the driving force in human history. In this highly influential book, Grant likened the history of the United States to that of ancient Rome, rising to power as a racially pure nation, but courting disaster with lax immigration, citizenship, and miscegenation policies.[111] He described the new immigrants as members of inferior races, particularly the Alpine Slavs and the Jews, who would either interbreed with Nordic Americans and corrupt the race or simply overwhelm the Nordics with their fecundity. In either case, their entry into the United States was contributing to its seemingly inevitable decline and fall.[112]

Like Schultz, Grant utterly rejected the idea that education could solve the problems precipitated by the onslaught of the immigrants. He argued that neither public education nor any avowedly Americanizing institution could make these immigrants into good Americans, since it was impossible to transform inferior races into superior ones. At best, the inferior races could imitate true Americans, but in Grant's eyes that made them even more dangerous. He wrote, "These immigrants adopt the language of the native American, they wear his clothes, they steal his name and they are beginning to take his women, but they seldom adopt his religion or understand his ideals and while he is being elbowed out of his own home the American looks calmly abroad and urges on others the suicidal ethics which are exterminating his own race."[113]

Two prominent sociologists, Edward A. Ross from the University of Wisconsin and a member of the IRL, and Henry Pratt Fairchild from New York University, supported and complemented the racial rationale for ending immigration that restrictionists like Schultz and Grant were making.[114] For example, in November 1913, Ross joined the debate with the first of a year-long series of anti-immigrant essays in the *Century Magazine,* later compiled into the book *The Old World in the New.*[115] His ideas on immigration were wrapped in the cloak of academic authority and written in a lively style that appealed to a mass audience. But the substance of these essays was little more than a litany of racial stereotypes that Ross used to justify his call for immigration restriction. Depicting clever but avaricious Hebrews, sociable but violent Italians, hardworking but slow-witted Slavs, Ross warned that unless the entry of these groups into the United States was barred, the Anglo-Saxon character of the nation would be overwhelmed by unassimilable races. Like other ethnic nationalists, Ross had little faith that education could be effective in Americanizing the immigrants, due in part to inherent racial characteristics. He argued, for example, that these newcomers were innately less ethical and less moral than northern Europeans.[116]

Fairchild offered a similarly biting critique of immigrants and Americanization. Writing in 1916, he sarcastically dismissed Americanizers who touted the success of their programs by pointing to "the readiness with which the immigrants adopt American clothes, the eagerness with which they attend the night schools, the enthusiasm with which they sing 'The Star Spangled Banner,' and the fluency with which their children use American swear words." He believed education could not break the fundamental racial and national ties that linked immigrants to their homelands, a fact that would imperil the nation in time of war. Restricting their entry was the only way to protect the American way of life.[117]

He expanded on these ideas in his 1926 book *The Melting Pot Mistake,* arguing that America's experience in the Great War provided convincing evidence of the failure of Americanization education. Claiming that during the war, German Americans' "ultimate allegiance nevertheless was with the 'Vaterland' and not with the land of their residence," he reiterated his belief that it was absurd to rely on education to assimilate immigrants. "Education, information, and knowledge had been powerless to sever them from their natural loyalty to the country of their origin."[118]

If Americanization failed with the Germans, how could it possibly transform Alpine or Mediterranean peoples into real Americans? He dismissed Americanization education as deeply flawed, since it ignored the importance of race and nationality in determining character and loyalty. As he put it, "[u]nderlying all the detailed errors and shortcomings of the Americanization movement was one fundamental fallacy—the fallacy of assuming that assimilation can be produced by any deliberate, purposeful, artificial measures whatsoever."[119] In essence, Fairchild argued that the influences of race and nationality were far more powerful than those of education.[120]

By the early 1920s, these arguments became ever present in the calls for restriction, not merely among academics, but also among politicians, civic leaders, and journalists. In February 1921, for example, Vice President–elect Calvin Coolidge called for immigration restriction based on racial quotas because "[b]iological laws tell us that certain divergent people will not mix or blend." He added that if Nordics do mix with other races, "the outcome shows deterioration on both sides." Coolidge also questioned the effectiveness of Americanization education, noting that even at its best it prepared immigrants to "become Americanized in everything but heart." Even with better education, Coolidge argued, restrictive measures would still be necessary to protect the nation from immigrants who were racially unassimilable.[121]

These views gained added traction in the post–World War I years, due to several new developments. Perhaps the most urgent of these was fallout from the Bolshevik Revolution in October 1917, which led to a brief but violent postwar Red scare in the United States. Following the Bolshevik takeover in Russia, fears about anarchist or communist insurrections in the United States quickly replaced worries about Germany and Austria-Hungary. These fears heightened following a series of strikes, bombings, and May Day riots, in late 1918 and early 1919; many Americans were convinced that revolution was imminent. In response, U.S. Attorney General A. Mitchell Palmer ordered a flurry of raids in 1919 and 1920 in which thousands of suspected communist agitators were arrested. A large majority of them were foreign-born, and many were deported. This furor over foreign-born radicals unquestionably soured the national mood about further immigration.[122] In addition, xenophobic sentiments were fueled by the profound disillusionment that swept the nation following the war, the 1920–1921 depression, and the rumored millions of Europeans seeking to flee their war-torn countries for a better life in the United States.[123] By 1921, such prominent racial restrictionists as Lothrop Stoddard, a historian with a Ph.D. from Harvard, were demanding that the U.S. government permanently bar what Stoddard referred to as "the truly alien hordes of the European east and south . . . [who were] a menace to the very existence of our race, ideals, and institutions."[124]

No one captured this anti-immigrant mood better than the journalist George Creel. A nationally known muckraking journalist, public relations specialist, and astute propagandist, Creel became a prominent advocate for restriction in the postwar years.[125] In a September 1921 article in *Collier's* magazine, for example, Creel described immigrants waiting to come to the United States as "swarming like flies at every European port of embarkation." Calling them "little more than human wreckage," Creel portrayed these Alpine and Mediterranean peoples in stark contrast to earlier immigrants who, he explained, "were Nordic—clean-blooded, strong limbed people" from northwestern Europe. He firmly rejected claims that large numbers of the earlier "tidal wave" of Alpine and Mediterranean people had assimilated. The Americanization of these people, he maintained, was thwarted by "certain fundamental differences between the Nordic stock and the Alpine and Mediterranean stocks."[126]

Nine months later, Creel returned to this topic in an even more incendiary piece simply titled "Close the Gates!" Arguing that "[t]he men and women who settled America—who *made* America—were pure Nordic stock," he railed against the new immigrants as a grave and growing threat to the nation. Depicting the immigrants who had arrived in the United States in the last twenty years as "slag in the melting pot," he reiterated this conviction that they could never become Americanized. Rather, he stated, they "coagulate in alien masses, clinging tenaciously to their language, their traditions, their customs, and their institutions." Restriction, he argued, was the only option for saving "the race and the republic."[127]

Adding fuel to this emotional bonfire were findings from the study of intelligence tests that the U.S. military conducted in 1917. These data on over 1.7 million recruits gave ethnic nationalists a new weapon, which they wielded to great effect in the struggle to severely restrict immigration from eastern and southern Europe. Developed by Robert Yerkes, Lewis Terman, and H. H. Goddard, three of the most prominent psychological researchers of the era, the Army Alpha test for literate recruits and the Army Beta test for the illiterate were the first mass intelligence tests. While they had only a modest influence on the war effort, these tests had a profound effect on the debate about immigration.[128]

In 1921, Yerkes and his colleagues published their findings, claiming that the scores on these intelligence tests revealed a clear racial hierarchy among the recruits, with Nordics leading all groups and recent immigrants and blacks demonstrating consistently low levels of intelligence. In later years, these findings and the methods that underlay them were vigorously challenged, in part because of the egregious cultural biases of the test makers, but at the time they bestowed the imprimatur of science on the growing anti-immigrant movement and they gave restrictionists additional evidence to push their policy agenda.[129]

Two years later, Carl C. Brigham, who had worked with Yerkes, published an even more influential book, *A Study of American Intelligence*, based on the Army intelligence tests. Using Yerkes' data and the racial theories of Madison Grant, Brigham flatly declared, "The intellectual superiority of our Nordic group over the Alpine, Mediterranean, and the Negro group has been demonstrated."[130] Building upon this conclusion, Brigham insisted that genetic, not environmental, factors explained differential outcomes. Even when his data pointed strongly toward other explanations, he found ways to dismiss them. For example, Brigham noted that the longer immigrants lived in the United States, the higher they scored on the intelligence tests. But rather than seeing this as evidence that Americanization education or socialization had "worked," Brigham argued, "The results of the psychological tests of foreign born individuals, classified according to length of residence, taken as typical of our foreign born population as a whole, indicate definitely that the average intelligence of succeeding waves of immigrants has become progressively lower."[131] For Brigham as with other proponents of ethnic nationalism, race triumphed over education at every point.[132]

The writings and speeches by such scientists as Brigham greatly bolstered the ongoing efforts to restrict eastern and southern European immigrants. By "proving" scientifically that most of these immigrants were members of intellectually inferior races and thus unable to truly Americanize, these academics made the political work of the restrictionists considerably easier.[133]

Since the 1890s, a number of politicians led by Senator Henry Cabot Lodge had pushed strongly for stringent requirements on people seeking entry to the United States. The initial goal of their efforts was legislation demanding that all new immigrants be able to read and write, a demand that after 1911 was bolstered by the conclusions of the U.S. Immigration Commission.[134] After facing a succession of vetoes from Presidents Cleveland (1897), Taft (1913), and Wilson (1915), in 1917 Congress passed a literacy requirement for new immigrants, this time with more than enough votes to override a veto. Unfortunately for the racial restrictionists, when the war ended this measure did not appreciably slow immigration.[135]

Therefore, they sought a new policy. Emboldened by intense anti-immigrant sentiment and the growing belief that Americanization education was for the most part a failure, the restrictionists called for entry quotas to stem the influx of immigrants from supposedly inferior races.[136] In May 1921, following overwhelming votes in the House and Senate, President Warren G. Harding signed into law a bill that temporarily limited immigration to 3 percent of the foreign-born population of each nationality in the United States as determined by the 1910 census. This law restricted European immigration to about 350,000 people annually, with the majority coming from northwestern Europe.[137]

Over the next three years, restrictionists lobbied to make this measure tougher and permanent. They sought to reduce the approximately 150,000 eastern and southern European immigrants who were still able to enter the United States under the provisions of the 1921 legislation. Madison Grant and other proponents of scientific racism played a major role in this effort and were in regular contact with Representative Albert Johnson (R-WA), who chaired the House Committee on Immigration and was a prime mover in the congressional push for more restrictive legislation. In addition to Grant, as early as 1920 Johnson commissioned Harry H. Laughlin, a leader in the American eugenics movement, to do a series of reports for the committee on the impact of immigration on the United States. The gist of Laughlin's widely disseminated studies was that the new immigrants were diluting the national racial stock. As he argued in testimony before the committee, unrestricted "immigration will tend to work not toward the improvement but toward the degeneration of the American people."[138]

By late 1923, pressure to firmly close the gates was intense. Johnson and the House Committee on Immigration returned to the fray by introducing new legislation that would admit only 2 percent of the foreign-born population of each nationality in the United States as determined by the 1890 census. Beyond reducing the percentage of immigrants, the use of 1890 as the baseline, which was prior to the great influx of eastern and southern European immigrants, ensured that the vast majority of post-1924 newcomers would be from northwestern Europe. As the U.S. commissioner of immigration stated, the new law "would encourage the immigration of the Nordic peoples, and restrict that of southern and eastern Europe."[139] In addition, the new legislation prohibited the entry of Asian immigrants and forbade those already in the United States from seeking citizenship.[140] An editorial in the staunchly restrictionist *Saturday Evening Post* applauded these changes, particularly the use of the 1890 census as the baseline. The editorial noted that in 1890 the country was still "comparatively homogeneous" and not yet plagued by the arrival of those racially "refractory strains which began to overwhelm us in the 1890's that bore in on us the fact that we had an immigration problem, and one not to be solved by the melting-pot process, in which we had come to put so much faith."[141] Albert Johnson echoed that sentiment, declaring, "The myth of the melting pot has been discredited."[142]

In a lengthy 1927 essay in the *New York Times*, Senator David A. Reed (R-PA), who had introduced restriction legislation akin to Johnson's, put a finer point on this argument, declaring in essence that Americanization education had utterly failed. Put simply, Reed argued that no amount of citizenship training, service to the country in wartime, or even naturalization could overcome the inherent flaws these newcomers brought with them from the old country. He concluded, "From all this has grown the conviction that it was best for America that our incoming immigrants should hereafter be of the same races as those of us who are already here, so that each year's immigration should so far as possible be a miniature America, resembling in national origins the persons who are already settled in our country."[143]

In Congress representatives Adolph Sabath (D-IL), Fiorello LaGuardia (R-NY), and Samuel Dickstein (D-NY) denounced the bill. They were joined by local political leaders from many urban areas, a few big city newspapers, and civic organizations from immigrant communities, all of which castigated the new bill as discriminatory and racist, but to no avail. By 1924, even the business community, which had traditionally been the most powerful supporter of unrestricted immigration, had given up the fight. With strong support from members of Congress from almost all parts of the country, Johnson's bill moved quickly through the House, and Senator David A. Reed pushed similar legislation through the Senate. In May 1924, President Coolidge signed the National Origins Act into law.[144]

A year earlier, in his State of the Union speech, Coolidge had called for the restriction of immigration because "America must be kept American."[145] What he meant was that the country had to maintain a solid Nordic majority to keep the demographic and cultural character of the country as stable as possible. With the passage of the National Origins

Act, large-scale immigration from eastern and southern Europe essentially ended. The ethnic nationalists had triumphed, or so it seemed.

CONCLUSION

In June 1915, an editorial in *Immigrants in America Review*, probably written by Frances Kellor, prophetically declared, "There is likely to sweep over this country at the close of the European war an intense interest in immigration which will materialize pretty clearly into two lines of action—the further exclusion of immigrants, and the nationalization of those already here and those to come."[146] For many Americans in the group that Kellor labeled the "ethnic restrictionists," the passage of the National Origins Act in 1924 signaled a complete triumph for their point of view. The new law codified their racist ideas about the inferiority of the immigrants, promised to maintain Nordic demographic dominance for decades to come, and implicitly acknowledged the futility of Americanization education. But ironically, this group's single-minded focus on restriction made this triumph less complete than they assumed. Ethnic nationalists had not accounted for three developments in Americanization education that were well under way prior to 1924 and were not curtailed either by exclusion policies or by racist assumptions about the intellectual and cultural inferiority of the immigrants.

Kellor recognized the first of these developments as early as 1915. Even with the successful closing of the gates to large numbers of new eastern and southern European immigrants, she argued, the vast number of these immigrants already residing in the United States would still need to be Americanized. As she put it, "with more than 13,000,000 foreign-born immigrants in this country, the nation should proceed with a national program of 'Americanization' regardless of further admission or exclusion of aliens."[147] Such education, even the avowedly assimilationist education advocated by people such as Ellwood Cubberley, implicitly advanced ideas of civic nationalism, which by its very nature meant there would be continuing challenges to whatever cultural and political hegemony the ethnic nationalists had achieved.

The second development belying a complete triumph of the racial restrictionists was that the educational structures of Americanization, which were deeply embedded in every level of public schooling and in the activities of many organizations that worked with adult immigrants, remained active well after the passage of the National Origins Act. While racial restrictionists routinely mocked these educational efforts, their criticism was based more on their disdain for the immigrants than on evidence that Americanization efforts were flawed educational endeavors. Even when the restrictionists' ideas seemed to have convinced a large segment of the nation about the threats the new immigrants posed, educators and their allies ignored the restrictionists' view about the uneducability of the immigrants and persisted in using the schools and other educational venues to Americanize immigrants and their children. Even assuming only modest success in the Americanization education programs, these programs would produce tens of thousands of new citizens who embraced to varying degrees the values of civic nationalism that they had been taught.

Finally, any conclusion about who won the struggle between civic and ethnic nationalism in the first half of the twentieth century has to factor in the response of the immigrants. Because they constituted a substantial proportion of the American population, particularly in major urban areas, the impact of their ideas and values on American society, politics, and education was huge, though it has been underestimated in most historical accounts of Americanization education. The next two chapters examine how Americanization education was implemented on the K–12 and adult levels and how immigrants responded to and reinterpreted these efforts.

2

AMERICANIZATION AND THE
PUBLIC SCHOOLS,
1890–1930

During the years that racial restrictionists and their opponents battled over whether large-scale immigration from eastern and southern Europe should continue, educators in public schools across the country worked literally day and night to Americanize the newcomers and their children. Regardless of whether these educators were assimilationists, cultural pluralists, or amalgamationists, they shared the belief that with proper education, the new immigrants could become good Americans. All agreed that, at a minimum, Americanization education on both K–12 and adult levels should result in immigrants learning English; gaining knowledge of important individuals and events in American history; embracing democratic principles, attitudes, and behaviors; and, for adult immigrants, becoming citizens.[1] These educational activities formed the core of Americanization efforts on both K–12 and adult education levels. As Frank Cody, who had directed the adult evening program of the Detroit Public Schools prior to becoming superintendent of the district, declared, public education would "weld the many peoples of any community into one body politic and create throughout the nation the unity and power that comes from common ideals, a common language, and a uniform interpretation of citizenship."[2]

While proponents of the different approaches to Americanization may have agreed on these basic principles, they differed greatly about the degree to which the immigrants should abandon or assert their previous cultures in the process of becoming Americans. For the most part these disagreements took place between proponents of assimilation and cultural pluralism. As noted in the previous chapter, amalgamationists paid less attention to curriculum issues than did the other two groups. But depending on which definition of the metaphorical melting pot one used (either as an instrument of assimilation or as the creator of a new, composite American race), their position on Americanization in education would likely lie in either the assimilationist or the cultural pluralist camp. As one speaker at the 1922 meeting of the National Education Association (NEA) conference explained, educators had to choose whether Americanization should rest on the belief "that the sooner the immigrant forgets his language, his racial culture, and pride in his ancestry, the better it will be for our country" or on the idea "that America will profit to the degree that the foreign-born immigrant endeavors to conserve the best of his old civilization so as to contribute it to the enrichment of our own."[3]

Since the 1970s, historians of education have argued that between 1890 and 1930, the first position completely dominated Americanization education on both the K–12 and adult education levels. Moreover, regardless of whether these scholars view Americanization education positively (e.g., as promoting national unity and social mobility) or negatively (e.g., as strengthening Anglo-Saxon cultural hegemony and social stratification), most of these historians share a number of assumptions. They largely agree that Americanization education was successful in getting immigrants and their children to abandon their Old World cultures in the process of becoming American; that Americanization education was relatively monolithic in its goals, methods, and stability over time; and that immigrants either passively acquiesced to these efforts or fought in vain to thwart them.[4]

This chapter, which focuses on the Americanization efforts in public schools, and the next chapter, which uses the Chicago Foreign Language Press Survey to gauge immigrants' responses to Americanization, complicates and, at times, challenges these assumptions. This chapter is divided into two large sections. The first looks at K–12 Americanization efforts mainly, but not exclusively, in the Chicago, Cleveland, and Detroit public schools. The second section examines the Americanization programs for adults in these and several other cities. Educators at the time recognized their work on the K–12 and adult education levels as two halves of the same project. A speaker at the 1904 annual meeting of the NEA declared, "As the public day school is the most effective means of Americanizing the children who come from foreign lands to our shores in such large numbers every year, so the public evening school should be made the institution which shall Americanize their parents by teaching them our language, our history, and the principles of our government."[5]

The chapter makes several main points about how educators in public schools promoted these goals. First, between 1890 and 1915, Americanization work on both the K–12 and adult education levels stressed three core Americanization aspects—teaching English, American history, and the knowledge and skills necessary to be citizens of a democracy. Second, during World War I and the immediate postwar years, Americanization education gained a sharper edge and a wider swath. Wartime fears and suspicions led many civic and educational leaders to promote "100 percent Americanism," a particularly aggressive form of assimilation that demanded unwavering cultural conformity. While this campaign had a powerful effect on some aspects of K–12 education—most important the elimination of German-language instruction in elementary schools and demands for more patriotic content in history and civics courses—its greatest impact was on adult education. In the latter effort, public school officials led the way in fashioning innovative, but at times highly coercive, programs for teaching adult immigrants English and encouraging their naturalization.[6] Although there were some exceptions, many of these adult courses went further than ever before in pushing the idea that the faster immigrants shed their Old World cultures, the better their assimilation would be.

Third, by the 1920s there was a growing perception that changes were needed in both K–12 and adult Americanization efforts. Much of the impetus for this reevaluation was due to the dramatic *decline* in the number of participants in the adult Americanization programs beginning in 1916 and continuing for the duration of the war. Related to that development was a serious backlash against the overly aggressive approach used in many Americanization programs. In the late 1910s and throughout the 1920s, a growing number of prominent academics, educators, politicians, and public intellectuals condemned the actions of the "100 percent Americanizers" and called for a new vision of American identity and culture that included greater recognition of the contributions that diverse individuals and groups had made to American history and culture.[7] These critiques that targeted both K–12 and adult education began a slow but ultimately successful campaign to reenvision the United States as a distinctly cosmopolitan nation.

Americanization Education on the K–12 Level

AMERICANIZATION AND K–12 CURRICULA, 1890–1915

In 1901, eight years before she became superintendent of the Chicago Public Schools, Ella Flagg Young declared, "It is the free public school that has made the child of foreign parentage strive to take on the habits of dress, speech, and thought that would identify him with the people whose ancestors were merged into this social and political society at an earlier date than were his."[8] At the time Young wrote this, public schools in the United States had been fulfilling this role for some seven decades. Indeed, almost since the creation of common schools, such educational leaders as Horace Mann described this new institution as vital for assimilating foreign-born children into American life.[9] For the most part, however, this effort amounted to little more than having teachers impart the basic common school curriculum, essentially teaching English, some Anglo-American literature, a smattering of U.S. geography and history, and basic civics.[10]

Beginning in the 1890s, as massive numbers of immigrants from eastern and southern Europe poured into urban areas, this Americanization mission became even more pronounced, especially for big-city public school systems in the Northeast and Midwest.[11] By this time, because of the confluence of a series of economic, political, and educational factors, including the takeover of these districts by progressive reformers, the school systems that immigrant children attended were among the best educational institutions in the country. They were among the wealthiest school systems in the nation, attracted the best-educated administrators and teachers, and offered the most innovative pedagogical programs, methods, and materials. These school systems worked diligently to get as many of these new students as possible into classrooms, a situation that helped make the process of Americanization more effective. In all, immigrants and the children of immigrants experienced something unique in American history: a situation in which an enormous influx of poor people, both children and adults, had access to one of the finest public services the country had to offer.[12]

Despite the unprecedented numbers and diversity of the new pupils, in the 1890s and early 1900s educators in large urban public school districts did not make major changes in the curriculum inherited from the common school era. The teaching of English, for example, remained largely a process of plunging non-English-speaking children into English-only classrooms, with teachers providing, at best, minimal support for the pupils to learn the new language. Some more enlightened school districts, such as those of Boston, Cleveland, Detroit, New York, and Philadelphia, created "steamer classes" to help mainly older immigrant children learn English. These classes sometimes lasted as long as six months and were akin, at least in purpose, to modern English as a Second Language courses, but they never reached more than a small fraction of students who needed them.[13]

Regardless of whether immigrant students had attended steamer classes or were immediately assigned to regular classes, all of them experienced an intense Anglo-American cultural immersion in the public schools. No matter how experienced these children were with formal schooling prior to coming to the United States, the initial impact of attending American public school classrooms was jarring, often deeply so. While many teachers were compassionate and caring, others treated their new charges harshly, at times deriding and denigrating their students' backgrounds, ridiculing (and, at times, changing) their foreign-sounding names, and mocking their heavily accented attempts to learn English.[14]

Whatever the teachers' attitudes were toward their students, almost every classroom activity either implicitly or explicitly advanced key aspects of Americanization noted above. For example, the reading programs for elementary students in Detroit, Cleveland, and Chicago immersed children in the western literary tradition (with a strong emphasis on Anglo-American literature and history) from their earliest years. As part of this process, Detroit educators introduced simplified "versions of classic myths and fairy tales" in the elementary grades. Suggested readings for first grade included several of Aesop's fables; the stories of Cinderella, Red Riding Hood, and Sleeping Beauty; some of Joel Chandler Harris's Uncle Remus tales; brief biographies of Columbus, Washington, and Lincoln; and poems by such writers as Henry Wadsworth Longfellow. For fourth grade, educators recommended stories from Homer's *Odyssey*, Washington Irving's "Rip Van Winkle," Howard Pyle's adventures of Robin Hood, and biographies of Magellan, De Soto, and William Penn.[15] As these examples indicate, teachers exposed elementary students to history mainly through biographies of important individuals.[16] Their introduction to chronological American history did not come until seventh grade.[17]

The reading program in Cleveland was similar to the one in Detroit. The Cleveland superintendent's annual report for 1907–1908 opens with a description of a school serving almost 950 pupils, in which "seventy-one per cent were foreign-born and belong to thirty-eight different races." In this school, reading in the primary grades stressed "fairy tales, myths, legends, folk lore, tales of chivalry, and historical stories." Older students were introduced to major works of Anglo-American literature ranging from Nathaniel Hawthorne to Shakespeare. The decision to concentrate solely on Anglo-American literature was quite deliberate. As one educational leader in Cleveland declared, "Though all peoples possess a literature of greater or less value, this is in large measure ignored, and the content of our school readers is limited in the main to selections from English and American authors."[18]

Educators in Chicago made comparable decisions, mixing literature and history in the elementary classroom in ways that both enhanced English-language learning and exposed the children to important aspects of American culture, geography, and history. As early as 1907, an article in *Educational Bi-Monthly*, a journal published by the Chicago Normal School, strongly urged elementary teachers to use American history as a central feature in "teaching English to foreigners." The author specifically noted the usefulness of biographical studies, stating, "Our small clients do not hear in their homes of George Washington, Benjamin Franklin, Abraham Lincoln, Daniel Boone, and John Kinzie. We must vivify our talks about these people so that the spirit of these men may be carried into the foreign households."[19]

Seven years later, a survey of history teaching in seventy-two elementary schools in Chicago—about 60 percent of which had large enrollments of children from immigrant families—demonstrated that little had changed in that time. Most of the history teaching continued to take place in the context of reading instruction, and material overwhelmingly focused on heroes from American history, combined with some civics instruction. For example, the authors of the report commended a story in the "First Primer" that described the annual Easter egg hunt in Washington, D.C., which, they noted, "locates definitely the seat of the Federal Government." Similarly, they praised the "First Reader" for introducing George Washington and the flag.[20] Biographies of famous historical figures (e.g., Columbus, Washington, and Lincoln) and the celebration of patriotic holidays continued to figure prominently in teaching history in all the early grades.[21] Only in the later grades did teachers move beyond biography to introduce and require regular recitations of "the flag salute, the civic creed, the Gettysburg Speech and patriotic poems."[22] The report also found that teachers used history for introducing civics. Beginning with lessons about neighborhoods and local government, teachers used an early version of what social studies educators would call the "expanding horizons" curriculum. Each successive year, elementary teachers in Chicago would teach lessons on increasingly distant governmental agencies, ending with the study of the federal government.[23]

As this overview describes, the primary vehicles for Americanization education in big-city public schools were units and lessons in English and history. But as the new century unfolded, other Americanization initiatives, often inspired by the ideas of progressive educators, assumed a larger role in this process. Many of these initiatives were linked to what progressive educators would eventually call teaching "the whole child," instead of simply attending to the child's intellect.[24] Based on this integrated notion of experience and education, such innovations as kindergartens, playgrounds, art and music classes, and vocational courses such as home economics entered the curriculum and transformed the nature and function of public schools.[25]

Americanizers were quick to see promise in "whole child" reforms, especially their potential for assimilating immigrant children into American culture.[26] Kindergartens, whose history in the United States began outside of public schools, typify how educators adapted innovative programs for Americanization purposes. Originally designed to encourage children from poor, urban families to develop positive character traits, kindergartens quickly became an important venue for Americanization.[27] In 1903, for example, a speaker at the NEA annual conference extolled the assimilationist potential of these programs, declaring, "The kindergarten age marks our earliest opportunity to catch the little Italian, the little German, Pole, Syrian, and the rest and begin to make good American citizens of them."[28] Early childhood educators from across the country promoted these ideas, describing kindergartens as vital for initial instruction in English and as excellent sites for encouraging such American values and behaviors as "helpfulness, cleanliness, order, [and] law."[29] Many educators believed that because young children were so malleable, kindergartens would encourage the rapid adoption of American attitudes and habits and thus become agents of Americanization in their homes and communities.[30] By 1897, Chicago, Cleveland, and Detroit all had thriving kindergarten programs in their public school systems.[31]

In 1909, for example, the U.S. Commission on Immigration found almost 9,700 children enrolled in Chicago's kindergartens. Given that attending kindergarten was voluntary, this was a substantial number of pupils, equaling about 25 percent of the enrollment in first grade, which was compulsory. Moreover, the commission found that in "the kindergartens the children of foreign parents are more numerous than those of native parents."[32] That trend dovetailed nicely with school board policy. As historian David Hogan argues, the Chicago Board of Education clearly regarded kindergartens "as an agency of Americanization." School leaders believed that these programs could effectively teach the English language, habits of self-discipline, "patriotic thought," and "good citizenship" to children from immigrant families.[33]

Kindergarten thrived in Cleveland as well. Between 1900 and 1910, kindergartens in the Forest City experienced an almost fourfold increase in enrollments, from about 1,400 to over 5,500 children, a rate considerably greater than that of the school system generally.[34] Similarly, by 1911, Detroit had kindergartens in about 90 percent of its elementary schools, and as in Chicago and Cleveland, they played an important role in teaching English and socializing children from immigrant families into important aspects of American life.[35]

Kindergartens weren't the only important educational innovation of this era that educators enlisted in the process of Americanization. Playgrounds, which like kindergartens began as philanthropic efforts eventually adopted by public schools, also became centers for Americanization efforts.[36] David Blaustein, a social worker who was active in the playground movement and eventually headed the Education Alliance in New York City, noted that beyond meeting the recreational needs of immigrant children, well-run playgrounds were also superb sites for teaching such American values and behaviors as following rules, fair play, and teamwork. Indeed, he saw organized playground games "in which representatives of all races and nationalities took part" as powerful symbols of how America unites people "in spite of differences in religion and language, in customs brought from the old country."[37]

Chicago was typical in adopting playgrounds, in part because of their perceived potential for educating and socializing immigrant children.[38] By 1916, the city boasted fifty-five municipal playgrounds and play parks and forty playgrounds attached to public schools, all of which eventually fell under the purview of the Chicago Board of Education. Chicago educators viewed them not only as safe and supervised places to play, but as places that would teach "morals," "social consciousness," and "citizenship."[39] Much of the Americanization that went on in playgrounds was subtle, for example, encouraging immigrant children to play such American games as baseball or basketball. But at times it was also heavy-handed, in that some Chicago "play parks" required children to speak only English while playing on the premises.[40]

In addition to kindergartens and playgrounds, courses in art and music also were pressed into service as vehicles of Americanization. In his study of Jewish immigrants in the New York public schools, Stephen Brumberg argues, "Just as an American sense of moral and ethical values had to be explicitly taught to the overwhelmingly immigrant school population, so too did conceptions of American beauty and 'taste.'"[41] Art classes in elementary schools clearly reinforced elements of Americanization by assigning students projects for Washington's and Lincoln's birthdays, Memorial Day, Halloween, and Thanksgiving, and by having children create Mother's Day and Valentine's Day cards.[42] Regarding the use of music for Americanization purposes, one educational leader in Detroit observed in 1916, "By building up a new sentiment and feeling with American music as a basis, the new seed will fall on the most promising of soil."[43]

Most of these efforts focused on elementary rather than secondary students. Unlike elementary schools, which were covered by compulsory school laws, at this time attendance in high schools was voluntary and often rested on such factors as whether families could afford to forgo the income teen-aged children could provide. Thus, in 1910, fewer than 15 percent of Americans age fourteen to seventeen were in high school, and only about a third of the age group attended in 1920.[44] These numbers tell only part of the story, since there were substantial differences in rates of high school attendance among various groups. Czechs and Jews, for example, sent considerably larger proportions of their children to high school than did Italians and Poles.[45]

Regardless of their background, the children of immigrants who did attend high school entered an institution that seamlessly continued the Americanization work begun on the elementary level. Prior to the 1930s, the great majority of courses taken by high school students were in academic subject areas (e.g., English and history). In 1914–1915, for example, academic courses accounted for almost 80 percent of all the classes taken by high school students nationwide; seven years later they still accounted for almost three-quarters of all courses taken.[46]

Many of these courses, particularly those in English, history, and civics, clearly encouraged Americanization by concentrating overwhelmingly on the works and deeds of white Anglo-Saxon Protestants. Literature courses concentrated on works from the Anglo-American canon. American history courses focused mainly on presidents, national politics, major pieces of legislation, and wars. History textbooks in this era were particularly monocultural in their discussion of the development of the United States.[47] Typical of these texts was the one required in twelfth-grade U.S. history classes in all of Cleveland's public high schools. Written by the liberal historians Charles Beard and Mary Beard, *History of the United States* did briefly acknowledge the contributions of some "foreign officers" of the American Revolution, including "Pulaski and Kosciusko," two Polish heroes of the war.[48] But when the Beards turned their discussion to recent immigrants, their tone was far from complimentary. They noted that these new arrivals "came from countries far removed from the language and traditions of England whence came the founders of America"; they reproached the immigrants for their failure to assimilate, due in large part to their crowding "into colonies of their own where they preserved their languages, their newspapers, and their old-world customs and views"; and they assailed the businessmen who lured these newcomers to the United States but "asked few questions about the effect of this 'alien invasion' upon the old America inherited from the fathers."[49] Rather than discussing any positive contribution these immigrants might have made to the country, in a later section of the book the Beards focused entirely on the problems immigrants had caused and on the movement to restrict new arrivals.[50]

In all, during this period, teachers in such big-city school systems as those of Chicago, Cleveland, and Detroit largely continued the educational approach to Americanization that originated in the common school era. This was particularly true on the elementary level, where teachers provided essentially the same curriculum to all children regardless of whether they were native- or foreign-born. The goal of this curriculum was to unite the nation around common language, culture, and political ideals. The teachers' goals were to provide these students with the knowledge and skills that would enable them not merely to survive but to thrive in the New World. In addition, such innovations as kindergartens, playgrounds, and art classes complemented and enhanced these basic components of Americanization. Was this curriculum effective in Americanizing the children of immigrants? There is evidence that public schools did that job quite well, but this success did not come without a price.

As early as 1908, Jane Addams spoke at the annual conference of the NEA and warned that the rapid Americanization of children from immigrant families in public schools was undermining traditional relationships between parents and children.[51] Two years later, Grace Abbott, director of the Immigrants' Protective League of Chicago, echoed these sentiments in a speech to the National Municipal League. Abbott stated that despite their good intentions, educators were "widening the gap between the parent and the child by the policy" they followed in the public schools. "In our zeal to teach patriotism we are often teaching disrespect for the history and tradition which the immigrant parent had a part in making and so for the parent himself."[52] Both Addams and Abbot argued that, rather than further exacerbating this problem, schools should try to bridge the growing cultural gap within immigrant families. They recommended that teachers bring aspects of their pupils' cultural background into the classroom and show the same respect they showed to American culture. Abbott explained that teachers must make "it clear that the story of the struggle for Italian nationalism is a thrilling one to us and the Bohemian leaders, because of their long fight for religious liberty, are heroes to Americans."[53] At the time, however, few educators were listening to these suggestions. Indeed, in August 1914, with the outbreak of war in Europe, prospects for a more pluralistic vision of American society and a broader vision of what public school curricula should impart to students seemed to disappear entirely.

A "UNIFORM BLEND OF AMERICANISM": K–12 SCHOOLS IN THE WAR AND POSTWAR ERA

The nation's entry into World War I profoundly altered the activities and, in some cases, policies in American public schools. Chicago school superintendent John Shoop observed in 1918, "Every phase of school work has been colored by the National Government's war purposes."[54] School leaders believed that the most important contribution they could make to the war effort was promoting national unity. As part of that effort, educators organized Junior Red Cross auxiliaries, got students active in Liberty Loan drives, encouraged art classes to create posters and banners supporting the war, and prepared young men for military service in physical education programs.[55] But these high-profile, mostly symbolic activities did not result in major educational changes.

However, two war-related decisions did have lasting consequences. First, educational leaders in districts across the country sought to bolster linguistic uniformity by banning the teaching of German in public elementary schools; and second, they ramped up efforts to infuse "100 percent Americanism" throughout civics and history courses. Using the assimilationist version of the melting pot, Peter Mortenson, who in 1919 succeeded Shoop as superintendent of the Chicago schools, stated, "The public school is, and must continue to be the great melting pot into which the foreign born must be cast, where, with a liberal flux of education, the whole can be fused into a uniform blend of Americanism."[56]

Bilingual programs teaching German and English to elementary school children had been operating in public schools since the late 1830s. During the second half of the nineteenth century, German immigrants, particularly in the Midwest, successfully used their growing political power to establish these programs in Chicago, Cincinnati, Cleveland, Indianapolis, Milwaukee, St. Louis, and other cities, as well as in many small towns and rural communities.[57] The Chicago German language program started in 1865 and by 1915 enrolled over 18,000 pupils in 112 schools, on the elementary level.[58] The Cleveland public schools began offering German language instruction in 1869. At its peak in 1905, over 19,000 students were taking German.[59]

Despite the obvious popularity of these programs and the substantial political clout wielded by large German communities in many major midwestern cities, following America's entry into World War I, the drive to eliminate German language programs was unstoppable. Chicago was typical. In the spring of 1917, as war fever gripped the nation, Chicago school board members plunged into the debate about eliminating German instruction in the elementary grades.[60] The campaign to change this policy touched on many of the cultural, political, and social themes sweeping the nation at the time, including nativism, hyperpatriotism, and demands for the rapid assimilation of immigrants. One supporter of the ban on German instruction told the Chicago school board that public schools should not be used to maintain immigrants' home languages. Rather, the school system should promote assimilation and be "a real melting pot, a veritable crucible . . . [so] that when a pupil or individual is put in, he will come out permeated with an intense love for our American institutions, and a keen desire to see perpetuated the ideals . . . upon which this nation was founded."[61]

Faced with enormous pressure to scrap German language instruction in elementary schools, in June 1918 the Chicago Board of Education officially voted to eliminate the program. The president of the school board explained the reasoning behind this decision, stating, "The conviction is becoming general that if the future citizen is to become thoroughly American, and if he is to catch the American spirit, he must become well grounded in our language and institutions."[62] The following year the new superintendent, Peter Mortensen, commented approvingly on the abolition of German, noting that children from at least fifty-seven different nationalities were in the Chicago schools and that educators had to ensure that all of them learned English.[63] Confronting similar pressures, Cleveland closed its program in 1918.[64] Other cities and towns across the country followed suit.[65] These actions were perhaps the most significant educational victories won by proponents of aggressive assimilation in this era.

In addition to these local efforts, in many states the movement to eliminate German led to even more stringent bans on teaching any foreign language in elementary schools (although many of these bans were probably motivated by the desire to end German instruction). By 1919, fifteen states had passed legislation prohibiting public schools from teaching regular school subjects ("the common branches of study") in any language other than English. Four years later, the number of states had jumped to thirty-four.[66] Of these new laws, the one from Nebraska was the most comprehensive, controversial, and consequential. The law stated, "No person, individually or as a teacher, shall in any private, denominational, parochial, or public school, teach any subject to any person in any language other than the English language."[67] This legislation led to the 1923 U.S. Supreme Court case *Meyer v. Nebraska*, which struck down the Nebraska law and thus enabled ethnic groups at least to maintain dual-language private and parochial schooling. Immigrant groups across the country hailed this decision as proof that their efforts to maintain their home languages were entirely compatible with the Constitution and with their Americanism.[68]

The second important educational policy that touched the lives of immigrants in the public schools was the reinvigoration of civic or citizenship education as a way of promoting national unity. Here also, Americanizing immigrants was an important subtext to these efforts.[69] As Detroit superintendent Charles Chadsey explained in 1918,

Few of us saw the necessity for the teaching of patriotism before our entry into the war. It was taken for granted that we knew everything we should know about our country. The first few months of the war proved that this assumption was unwarranted. . . . We began to see that real patriotism did not end with the singing of the Star Spangled Banner. The great numbers of foreigners who have come to this country have not been properly Americanized and did not understand the principles of democracy. A great field had been neglected by school and state alike. This condition is not alone true for Detroit but holds for any industrial city with a polyglot population.[70]

At the opening of the 1918–1919 school year, Chadsey declared, "Systematic teaching of patriotism and citizenship will be emphasized this year."[71]

Detroit was not alone in taking this initiative. In this era, attempts to bolster patriotism and civics education were among the most important curricular issues in the country, attracting attention not only from educators but from political and civic leaders as well. For example, prior to World War I, reciting the Pledge of Allegiance, which was written in the early 1890s, in part to help Americanize immigrants, was rarely required in public schools. During and especially immediately after the war, organizations like the American Legion campaigned with increasing success in getting the flag pledge to be a regular feature of the school day.[72] In addition, during this period states began mandating courses in citizenship and civics. In a 1921 talk at the NEA annual conference, Arthur Dunn, one of the nation's leading civic educators, reported, "Civic education has received a great impulse during the past five or six years. Since 1915 more than a third of the states have passed laws for its promotion."[73] This trend continued throughout the 1920s and into the early 1930s.[74] In 1921, for example, Illinois passed a law mandating that seventh- and eighth-graders in all public schools devote at least one hour per week to studying the Declaration of Independence and the federal and state constitutions.[75] A decade later, Michigan passed a similar law, which required all twelfth-graders to pass a one-semester civics course for high school graduation.[76] Writing in 1926, Lucie Schacht from the Chicago Normal School provided a rationale for this rush of new efforts in citizenship education, arguing, "It took the World War to awaken in us the consciousness that we were not—merely by pouring ingredients into a bowl—developing either in ourselves or among the immigrants the principles of our government."[77]

Important as these new laws, policies, and attitudes were, they do not appear to have substantially changed curriculum content, especially as the crisis atmosphere of the war dissipated. Even the Red scare of 1919–1920, which had dramatic repercussions on local politics in Chicago, Cleveland, and Detroit, seems to have had little influence on K–12 social studies curriculum.[78] For example, in a 1922 essay, Arthur Dondineau, the supervisor of social studies in Detroit, made an oblique reference to the Bolshevik Revolution, but only as one factor among many that pointed to the need for more engaging methods in "the teaching of citizenship."[79] In making that plea, Dondineau was not alone. Throughout the 1920s, many school leaders sought new ways for teaching history and citizenship. Indeed, educators in some leading school systems, influenced by progressive educators, sought to replace specific lessons in history and civics with more thematic units based on ideas from the new, vaguely defined subject known as "social studies." One Detroit educator described this new approach as emphasizing "citizenship training as against mastery of subject matter."[80] Yet reports about teaching social studies from this period showed that "traditional" history and civics content and pedagogy remained deeply embedded in practice, especially on the elementary level.[81]

Educators in Chicago, for example, introduced a variety of new units and lessons that clearly fit the social studies framework and focused on topics of immediate interest to the students.[82] But elementary teachers in Chicago also continued to teach a great deal of history and civics in lessons about patriotic holidays such as Washington's and Lincoln's birthdays, Memorial Day, and Thanksgiving; studies of important historical figures ranging from Samuel Adams to Thomas Edison; and excerpts from great documents and speeches that define American democracy.[83]

Similarly, the 1923 Detroit Public Schools *Course of Study in Social Science: Grades One to Six* clearly drew on new ideas about social studies in forthrightly defining civic instruction as a means to develop students' characters, which meant emphasizing cooperation, loyalty, and "group consciousness" as key components of citizenship.[84] Nevertheless, the materials recommended for lessons about citizenship were largely discipline-based in their content. First- and second-graders, for example, learned about Columbus, Pilgrims, Benjamin Franklin, Lincoln, and Washington. Teachers also were encouraged to teach about Memorial Day, Flag Day and Election Day. Progressively building on these lessons, by sixth grade all pupils were studying "traditional" American history.[85] Cleveland followed an almost identical pattern, introducing some new social studies elements to their still quite traditional history and civics curricula.[86]

While school leaders in Chicago, Cleveland, and Detroit sought to balance the competing demands of teaching disciplinary knowledge in a social studies framework, one aspect of the curriculum remained well above the fray. Regardless of where school leaders and teachers stood in this debate, many, if not most of them, rarely questioned the monocultural bias of the civics and history lessons they were teaching. Few educators at the time considered including people other than white Anglo-Saxon Protestants in the teaching of American history or in explicating lessons related to American citizenship.

TOWARD A MORE PLURALISTIC VISION
OF AMERICAN HISTORY AND CULTURE

Despite these trends, in the aftermath of the war, supporters of a culturally pluralistic approach to Americanization showed surprising resilience. At the same time that racial restrictionists were asserting that immigrants from eastern and southern Europe posed a serious threat to the Nordic character of the United States, and most public school curricula were overwhelmingly Anglo-American in their content, some educational and political leaders in New York and Chicago launched well-publicized campaigns against the pervasive "Anglo-Saxonism" in public schools. These critics demanded that educators recognize and honor the contributions diverse people and races had made in building this country.[87] These efforts, though only moderately successful, set the stage for a broader challenge to the assimilationist model of Americanization, a challenge that would continue into the 1930s and '40s.

Criticism of the monocultural curriculum in public schools had been building for some time. As noted in the previous chapter, academics such as John Dewey and social activists such as Grace Abbot and Jane Addams had been calling for a more culturally inclusive form of Americanization since the early years of the twentieth century. They were not alone in this effort. Over the decades, a growing number of politicians, journalists, and organizations linked to various immigrant communities such as the Ancient Order of Hibernians, the German American Alliance, and the Knights of Columbus also railed against "the cult of Anglo-Saxonism" in American public schools.[88] For example, as early as 1907, the president of the Ancient Order of Hibernians declared that in "all our current school histories and most others, in fact, the Anglo-Saxon has been glorified and exalted to the exclusion of others who did so much for this country, like the Irish and the Germans and the other countries." These groups demanded that schools pay additional attention to the role immigrants had played in the building of the United States. At a minimum they called on school leaders to include such heroes as the Irishman John Barry and the German Baron Friedrich Wilhelm von Steuben in lessons about the multiethnic character of the soldiers who fought on the American side in the Revolutionary War.[89]

Unfortunately for supporters of this more pluralistic vision of American history, in the early years of the twentieth century, Irish Americans and German Americans were the main supporters of these views. Both these groups strongly opposed the United States entering World War I on the side of Britain, and, consequently, their criticisms of the Anglo-Saxon bias in school curricula quickly disappeared under the avalanche of pro-war and anti-German sentiment in 1917 and 1918. After the war, however, calls for a more inclusive vision of American history and culture resurfaced. Two new developments explain this reemergence. First, many immigrant groups took pride in the large numbers of young men from their communities who had served loyally and bravely in the American armed forces during the war. Historian Nancy Gentile Ford estimates that some half a million men, representing nearly 18 percent of the U.S. military, were immigrants. These foreign-born soldiers and sailors, many of whom attended Americanization classes and became citizens while in the service, thought themselves every bit as American as their native-born comrades in arms.[90] The World War I veterans brought a new, more confident spirit to immigrant groups struggling to be recognized as people who were proud of their American identity *and* their ethnic background.

Second, immigrant groups were responding to the growing anti-immigrant sentiments stirred up by the campaign to restrict immigration. They increasingly denounced the ethnic nationalism of the restrictionists and called for a new vision of American identity that was based not on race, but rather on one's commitment to American ideals and values.[91] Indeed, in the late 1910s and throughout the 1920s, immigrant leaders frequently turned the tables on their nativist critics, arguing that because the immigrants did not use race, religion, or culture as the defining characteristics of true Americanism, they had a better understanding of what it meant to be an American than did the so-called 100 percent Americans.

A clear expression of these ideas as they applied to education appeared in 1920, when Edward McSweeney from the Knights of Columbus published a pamphlet denouncing the strong Anglo-Saxon bias in American history textbooks. McSweeney called for schools to teach a more accurate account of the nation's history that would demonstrate the "composite" character of the United States and highlight the diverse peoples and cultures that had shaped the nation.[92] Noting that all racial groups had made "substantial contributions" to American culture, he added, "Assimilation of the various races living in the United States is not, and cannot be synonymous with their anglicanization [sic]."[93] Another Knights of Columbus pamphlet published around this time declared, "*The achievements of many different races—Irish, German, Italian, French, Scandinavian, Slavik [sic], Polish, Spanish, etc. in founding, developing, and maintaining the institutions of this country are treated with contempt to the glory of England—the age-long, implacable foe of America*" (emphasis in the original).[94]

In August 1920, *Skandinaven*, a Norwegian newspaper in Chicago, echoed these sentiments in an impassioned editorial that mocked aggressive assimilationists as "two-hundred-percenters" who were "holier than the rest of us." Declaring that the time had come "to restore real Americanism at home," the editor argued that the current Anglo-centric view of American history and culture must be revised. While recognizing the "many good things" that had come from England, the article declared, "England alone is not the mother of America." Rather, "[a]ll the nations of Europe and Africa are the mothers of America. England, France, Germany, Norway, Sweden, Denmark, Africa—each and all sent us the best in brain and in brawn and in spirit; in literature, in music, in song, and in poetry; in ideals and in home life; they sent all that our forefathers had struggled for in generations past, and brought it over here and placed it on the sacred altar of American citizenship in order that here there would arise a citizen who should combine the wisdom and the virtues of all the nations."[95]

By 1922, these ideas had gained enough traction to be included in the annual conference of the National Education Association. In a report on the work of the Committee on the Teaching of Democracy, the committee chair praised the "well-organized attempt of the Knights of Columbus to emphasize in the teaching of United States history the loyal service rendered by Catholics to America and the contributions made to democracy by Catholics and Catholicism should be furthered by Protestant and Jewish agencies."[96] Yet it is unlikely that any school systems took steps to make changes along these lines.

However, one year later this cosmopolitan view of American history became a news leader as the Hearst newspapers claimed that British interests were conspiring to promote Anglo-Saxonism in American history textbooks. In 1923, administrators from the New York public schools and officials in the mayor's office conducted investigations into allegations that the textbooks used in the school system were unduly biased in favor of Great Britain. Due to the highly politicized nature of these investigations, the call for a more pluralistic approach to American history was lost in the process, although a number of textbooks were banned from the New York schools because of their alleged Anglo-Saxon bias.[97] But the growing political power of immigrant communities and their increasing anger about the racist campaign of restrictionists ensured that the issues would not disappear.

Indeed, four years later they resurfaced in Chicago in the mayoral re-election campaign of William Hale Thompson, who built his campaign around allegations that the British textbook conspiracy had reached into the heart of the Chicago public schools. He derided the Anglo-Saxonism of numerous textbooks and reminded voters, "All nationalities are entitled to a place in the sun, and our national heroes are the stars in the firmament of our patriotism."[98] Swept into office with strong support from the African American, German, Irish, and Italian communities, Thompson quickly orchestrated a "trial" of school superintendent William McAndrew, charging him with foisting treasonous, pro-British textbooks on impressionable Chicago schoolchildren. This was a classic Chicago political farce, and, in the end, it damaged Thompson more than it changed things in the schools.[99]

But, as historian Joseph Moreau astutely notes, more was going on here than politics as usual in Chicago. Rather, the textbook controversy was "a metaphor for contemporary debates over national diversity." Moreau points out that leaders of this campaign maintained that "the true threat to Americanism did not lie with recent immigrants in urban ghettos . . . but with representatives of America's long-established native stock who rejected the principles of the nation's Founders."[100]

Like the controversy in New York, the textbook debate in Chicago did little to alter policy or practice. The only change came in 1928, when a political crony of Mayor Thompson produced a sixteen-page pamphlet for Chicago history teachers that provided short biographies of ethnic heroes of the American Revolution, including Polish heroes Thaddeus Kosciusko and Casimir Pulaski, and the German hero Baron von Steuben.[101] Whether teachers used the pamphlet is anybody's guess.

While these political conflicts in New York and Chicago produced more smoke than fire, they did indicate the stirrings of a new social, political, and educational dynamic, which sought to change public school curricula as part of a broader effort to redefine what it meant to be a good American. Two unrelated developments provide some evidence of this emerging trend. In the mid-1920s, a young Quaker activist, Rachel Davis DuBois, began developing ideas about how to introduce a more pluralistic vision of American history into public schools. Inspired by the ideas of Jane Addams about the "cultural gifts" that immigrants had brought to America, DuBois began her influential career in "intercultural education." Taking a page from the playbook of the assimilationist Americanizers, DuBois sought to use schools to transform students into good American citizens, which she defined as citizens who recognized, respected, and learned from the diverse cultures that made up the United States.[102] Chapter 4 examines the work done by DuBois and other leaders of the intercultural education movement.

Second, developments in Detroit indicate at least some small steps toward a more sensitive stance in regard to immigrant cultures in the public schools. In 1921, Detroit superintendent Frank Cody, who in 1916 had called for the "elimination of the hyphen," made an apparent intellectual about-face in a speech to the NEA in which he contended, "A snobbish attitude of superiority—a failure to appreciate the culture and development of other peoples—has been too often the cause of failure in excessive

Americanization campaigns." Cody continued, "Let us acknowledge the excellence of the metal, flowing white hot to us from other great lands and races, and seek by intelligent effort to direct it into the American mold."[103] While curriculum materials published by Detroit's Department of Social Studies do not show that Cody's ideas quickly influenced policy and practice, a 1929 directive from the Detroit Department of Social Sciences does contain an interesting addition in the list of holiday celebrations that the school system authorized. School leaders planned special events for "Constitution, Armistice, Lincoln's Birthday, Washington's Birthday, Jefferson's Birthday, and Kosciusko Day."[104] By this time, Poles were one of the largest ethnic groups in Detroit.[105]

Despite the racism and reaction of the World War I years and the early 1920s, change was afoot. Recall that in 1919, the superintendent of the Chicago schools talked about public education as "the great melting pot" that would fuse the children of the foreign-born "into a uniform blend of Americanism."[106] Eight years later, however, Francis G. Blair, the superintendent of public instruction in Illinois, used his presidential speech to the NEA to call for something very different, declaring, "We do not want to melt out of these foreign elements those great qualities which contributed so much to the upbuilding of our republic."[107] The era that commenced with an intense campaign for cultural uniformity highlighted by the ban on German instruction ironically ended with the promise of a new and vigorous effort to reshape American education and culture along more cosmopolitan lines. As the next section demonstrates, these sentiments were gaining support in adult education as well.

Public Schools and the Americanization of Adult Immigrants

THE DEVELOPMENT OF ADULT EVENING AMERICANIZATION
PROGRAMS, 1890–1916

In his 1904 report to the Detroit Board of Education, board president Gilbert Johnson exuberantly described the district's evening school program, saying, "Our night schools are to the uneducated, especially the foreign-born, what food is to the starving."[108] Originally founded in the late nineteenth century to provide basic educational opportunities to people with day jobs, public-school evening programs eventually became the single most important institution providing Americanization classes to adult immigrants.[109] Indeed, by the turn of the century, immigrants comprised the majority of students attending night schools in many major cities, and in some cases classes in English for the foreign-born enrolled more students than all other night school classes combined.[110]

Almost from the beginning of the massive influx of eastern and southern European immigrants, newcomers sought out public-school evening programs to learn English and prepare for citizenship. In fact, as historian Edward G. Hartmann found, in "practically every case, these classes were organized upon the request of the immigrants themselves."[111] In 1910, for example, Italians in Cleveland petitioned the school board for night classes in which to learn English and a variety of other practical subjects.[112] These demands for the classes were accompanied by rising enrollments of eager students. An anonymous Detroit teacher, writing in 1904, described his night school classroom as pervaded by a sense of "ambition which all these people possess to become Americanized and to know the language of this country as soon as possible in order that they may better their condition in life." Their drive, he declared, "urges them on to do their best, and they enter upon their work zealously, diligently, and perseveringly."[113]

Evidence of these trends appeared in the early 1890s. In 1894, for example, the supervisor of evening schools in Chicago reported that enrollments in courses in English for foreign-born students had more than doubled in just five years, from about 5,400 to over 11,000. The supervisor not only saw such a demand as a desire to learn English, but also saw that the "Poles, Greeks, Italians, Assyrians, and Armenians—all the diverse nationalities which throng our city—are yearly gaining a clearer knowledge of our manners, customs and laws through the instrumentality of the Evening Schools."[114]

A decade later, 14,000 of the more than 17,000 night school students in Chicago were either foreign-born or had foreign-born parents. Six ethnic groups alone—Czechs (Bohemians), Germans, Italians, Poles, Russians (most likely Jews), and Swedes—accounted for 60 percent of all the students enrolled in the program. By 1911, almost 22,000 students with foreign-born backgrounds attended Chicago's evening schools, the vast majority of whom were enrolled in English courses on the elementary level.[115]

Writing in 1906–1907, the head of the evening division of the Cleveland Public Schools reported similar trends. In that year over 4,400 students enrolled in night school classes, almost 30 percent more than the previous year. The Cleveland evening schools served students from 33 different nationalities, but eight groups—in rank order Hungarians, Russians (most likely Jews), Czechs, "Americans," Poles, Germans, Austrians, and Italians— made up almost 82 percent of total enrollments, with immigrants exceeding Americans by a six-to-one margin.[116] Five years later, total enrollments in the evening division had climbed to almost 7,400 students, most of whom were taking elementary English classes.[117] By the 1913–1914 school year, more than 10,800 students were enrolled in night school courses. Almost 94 percent of these students were foreign-born, representing forty-three different nationalities. These students were overwhelmingly taking English classes.[118] In 1913, the supervisor of the Cleveland evening school program extolled the "earnestness and worthy purpose" of these students. He stated, "No class more eager to learn attends the public schools, day or evening, than the very recent arrivals from foreign countries." He added, "This class of newcomers need give native-born Americans no concern. They already realize much of what America means and are determined to know more."[119]

Part of the attraction of the Cleveland program was its widely touted citizenship course developed by local educators in 1913–1914. Offered in public schools, public libraries, and settlement houses, this course helped prepare immigrants for naturalization. Most students in these courses knew a reasonable amount of English and probably had filed their "Second Papers" (also known as Petitions for Naturalization). Immigrants often enrolled in such courses while they were waiting the required ninety days until a judge in open court would assess their knowledge of the U.S. government and their worthiness for exercising the franchise. This test was the major hurdle immigrants had to clear before they could take the oath of allegiance and receive a Certificate of Naturalization attesting to their American citizenship.[120]

The Cleveland course sought to train the "foreign-born population for good efficient and devoted American citizenship; not merely to prepare them to answer in a perfunctory manner questions asked at a Naturalization Hearing." Thus, the suggested curriculum included lessons about "the machinery of government" (federal, state, county, and city); the three branches of government; "American history by brief study of famous biographies"; patriotic holidays, songs, and poetry; and the naturalization process. Some teachers also prepared their students with mock naturalization hearings.[121]

Detroit was slower than Chicago and Cleveland in building its night school Americanization program, due in part to an ongoing political struggle over control of the school board in which night schools were an issue.[122] Nevertheless, in 1912, a report by the head of the Detroit evening program announced that the surge in enrollments "of foreigners desiring to learn English" was so large that it made "necessary the wiring and lighting of extra rooms for the accommodation of these students." The school system opened one new room each for Germans, Hungarians, Lithuanians, and Poles, and two new rooms for what the supervisor described as the "industrious" Hebrews.[123] Between 1910 and 1915, enrollments in the adult elementary program in Detroit's evening schools almost tripled, from just over 1,200 to about 3,500. As in Chicago and Cleveland, the great majority of students in the elementary program, over 80 percent in 1915, were foreign-born.[124] All these data suggest that in the pre–World War I years, adult immigrants were eager and enthusiastic seekers of Americanization education.

The rapid growth of night school attendance created three predominant administrative and educational problems for school leaders in these cities: finding qualified teachers, determining an effective curriculum, and maintaining attendance. Of these, hiring teachers proved to be the easiest to solve. Discussion in both Chicago and Detroit raised questions about whether night school teachers needed to speak the immigrants' languages to be effective, but educational leaders in both cities determined that such skill was unnecessary.[125] Thus, by 1914, both Chicago and Detroit were relying on regular, day school K–12 instructors to teach in the evening schools, a trend that a 1916 report by the U.S. Bureau of Education confirmed as occurring across the nation.[126]

The downside of this policy, however, was that it reduced opportunities for educators from immigrant communities who previously had been working in these programs. At least in Detroit, this was a deliberate Americanization effort. In 1915, the administrator of the evening school program stated that in order to ensure the quality of instruction about American ideals and political life, an "effort was made to eliminate the old idea of a Greek being necessary to teach Greek, and to place wide-awake, socially efficient American instructors in charge of these rooms. . . . Better attendance, better results, and greater Americanizing influence was felt in every one of the schools."[127]

The second problem, that of developing effective teaching methods and creating useful class materials, was in part linked to the use of day-school teachers for the evening program. Since many of these teachers came to the night schools directly from their elementary classrooms, they often employed the same methods and same materials for adults that they had used for children. This was especially true in the beginning English courses. A 1916 study of elementary English teaching in sixty-six Cleveland night schools found instructors using laughably inappropriate methods and materials, including stories about birds and babies and poetry for children. In one class the teacher assigned a group of weary steel workers the task of copying the sentences: "I am a yellow bird. I can sing. I can fly. I can sing to you."[128]

Other cities such as Chicago and Rochester, New York, sought to create more age-appropriate methods, introduce more relevant and practical materials, and create engaging courses for adult immigrants. For example, in 1907, teachers in the Chicago evening school program focused their classes on vocabulary building, specifically concentrating on "words which represent the pupil's ordinary experiences" and "conversations about incidents of current interest." Once the students mastered this material, teachers encouraged them to use their expanded vocabularies and English verbal skills to tell stories. Only after these lessons were learned did the teachers introduce "grammatical principles" with an eye toward "straightening out difficulties of expression."[129]

By 1911, evening school educators in the Windy City also were developing new highly practical courses and lessons centered on students' interests in naturalization. As one Chicago school leader explained, "Some attempts were made to bring about a more direct and purposeful teaching of some elementary ideas of citizenship to the immigrants." This involved lessons about the naturalization process, including how to take "First Papers" and "Second Papers," and "some discussion of the city, county, and state governmental activities with which the ordinary citizen comes most frequently into contact."[130]

Similarly, the director of the Rochester evening schools explained that the program was based on the simple idea that teachers should "[t]reat an adult like an adult." Just because the teachers were teaching elementary English did not mean that they should use the same materials and methods they used with children. The director observed, "The grown-up foreigner is not interested in talking about lions, tigers, and the other phenomena of childhood's primer. . . . He wants practical knowledge."[131]

Thus, like adult students in Chicago, immigrants in Rochester learned English by mastering basic words and phrases, identifying everyday objects, and role-playing common social situations (e.g., "Buying a Hat"). More advanced students read newspapers. They also learned basic American history, often through biographies of famous Americans, and they learned about civics and citizenship in classes on naturalization.[132] But these courses were the exception rather than the rule. Indeed, even in Chicago as late as August 1916, school board member Harry A. Lipsky reported that "adults are not satisfied with the course of study" in the city's night schools because "the teachers convey knowledge to them as they would to small children, and many are so discouraged that they drop their attendance in night school entirely."[133] That last point about dropouts highlighted a major problem that plagued evening Americanization courses across the country.

Educators in big cities regularly boasted of large enrollment increases in the evening school programs. However, they rarely discussed the fact that the number of students who faithfully attended the courses was modest. For example, Chicago school leaders reported total enrollments in the "Elementary and Foreign Classes" of about 17,600 in the 1912–1913 school year and almost 25,400 students in 1913–1914. But the average nightly attendance in these classes amounted to about 55 percent in 1912–1913 and less than 50 percent the following year.[134] In New York City, between 1911 and 1917, the average nightly attendance in the evening elementary schools amounted to only about 37 percent of enrollments.[135]

The 1916 study of the Cleveland evening school program mentioned above found even worse attrition. Conducted by Herbert A. Miller, a sociologist from Oberlin College, the study found that in the 1915–1916 school year, of the 7,000 students who enrolled in October, only 1,000 remained when the night school term ended in March.[136] Given these numbers, Miller blasted the program, declaring that "every year thousands of earnest and hopeful foreigners flock to the night schools in keen anticipation of learning English, and after a few weeks become discouraged and drop out because the teachers do not meet their needs."[137] Miller argued that teachers in the program did not understand the kinds of students they were working with and were using methods that had "not been intelligently adapted to the needs and abilities of the pupils." Specifically, he called for a progressive-style program akin to those being developed in Chicago and Rochester that stressed "the immediate, the concrete, and the practical."[138]

Cleveland's night school program was not alone in attracting such sting-
ing criticism. In August 1915, the *Detroit Free Press* editorialized about the
poor performance of the city's night schools in educating immigrants in
the city.[139] A year later, the author of a report on problems facing the huge
number of non-English-speakers in New York City (perhaps as many as
half a million people) expressed the same frustration: "Their only public
facilities for learning English are in the night-schools; well, we all know
what the night-schools are, their precarious standing, their lack of funds,
and the unintelligent and inelastic system that controls them." She concluded, "There is no need to say more."[140] In his 1920 study *The Schooling
of the Immigrant,* Frank V. Thompson affirmed at least part of this criticism. He had found that across the nation high rates of attrition from
night schools for immigrants were common. He wrote, "The most favor-
able figures indicate a retention of membership in evening schools not
usually over one-half; the average is less—about one-third."[141]

These pre–World War I night schools were at once promising and frus-
trating institutions. Beginning in the 1890s, foreign-born adults flocked
to them despite the strongly assimilationist character of most adult evening programs. Indeed, from the early 1890s to 1914, tens of thousands of
foreign-born students in cities across the country enrolled in classes to
learn English and prepare for citizenship. Unlike elementary school pupils, who were under a legal mandate to attend schools, these adult students were not compelled to enroll in Americanization classes.[142] But as
heartening as Americanizers might have viewed these growing enrollments, they had to be concerned about the high dropout rate. Yet even
that problem had something of a silver lining, for it appeared that students
quit the classes more because of the inadequacy of the programs than
because of the immigrants' lack of enthusiasm for them. The great problems facing these programs were their weak financial support, poor quality of instruction, and lack of attention to the unique pedagogical demands
of adult immigrant learners. All of these problems became national issues
after the outbreak of World War I.

ADULT AMERICANIZATION IN THE WORLD WAR I ERA:
DETROIT AS A CASE STUDY

Soon after Europe plunged into war in August 1914, many Americans became increasingly concerned about the political loyalties of immigrants
generally, but especially about the allegiances of adult immigrants in

defense industries. As sociologist Howard Hill pointed out, "War industries are largely dependent on alien labor; 57 per cent of the employees in the iron and steel industries east of the Mississippi, 61 per cent of the miners of soft coal, 72 per cent of workers in the four largest clothing manufacturing centers, and [over] 68 per cent of construction and maintenance workers on the railroads are foreign-born."[143] In 1915, a wave of strikes "among foreign-born colonies in munitions factories and elsewhere" swept the nation. In its wake, the National Americanization Committee (NAC) and the Committee for Immigrants in America (CIA) jointly stated that "the large number of unassimilated groups in our factories and towns" represents "a vast *social* problem involving our national unity, the preservation of a uniform ideal of citizenship, the maintenance of industrial peace, and the conservation of a social ideal based on the use of the English language, a regard for American citizenship and American standards of living."[144] For many business, civic, and educational leaders, the solution to this vast social problem was a nationwide educational campaign to Americanize adult immigrants.

Most supporters of this effort believed that public school evening programs were a necessary but not sufficient institution for making this campaign successful. "We must have the night schools and classes as speedily as possible," a joint report from the NAC and CIA explained. "But behind every [night school] that is established we must have the social force of the particular community, all its agencies, all its resources, all its civic sympathies, if the future of American citizenship is really to be assured." The committees concluded: "No educational department can carry the work through alone."[145]

This idea resonated with civic and educational leaders around the country. During and immediately following World War I, Americanizers in the great industrial cities of the Northeast and Midwest established coordinated educational and social networks linking various local agencies involved in Americanization work. These networks created one of the largest adult education efforts in American educational history, but they also supported some highly coercive and culturally chauvinistic educational programs. The Americanization program in Detroit was, in many ways, exemplary of these efforts. Indeed, by 1916, many people across the country pointed to the Motor City as *the* national leader in adult Americanization.[146]

Early in 1915, at a time when local educational politics in Detroit had lost much of their earlier bitterness, business, civic, and educational leaders in

Detroit turned their attention to the problem of Americanizing the huge number of foreigners in the city.[147] As noted earlier, the Detroit public schools had been offering evening Americanization courses for many years. However, given the enormous growth of the city in the early 1910s, enrollment in the night schools was paltry when compared to other industrial cities, like Chicago and Cleveland. The approximately 3,500 foreign-born students who signed up for the public schools' adult elementary English courses in 1914–1915 represented only a tiny fraction of Detroit's foreign-born population, which was over 157,000 people in 1910 and almost 290,000 in 1920.[148]

The anemic response to the problem of Americanizing this flood of immigrants convinced leaders from the Detroit Board of Commerce (BOC), the most prominent business organization in the city, to get deeply involved in Americanization work.[149] In true progressive educational fashion, early in 1915, the BOC launched its campaign by hiring an outside expert, Raymond E. Cole, from the New York–based CIA, to survey foreign-born Detroiters and recommend ways to improve their Americanization.[150]

Cole's report presented a series of suggestions for strengthening Americanization education initiatives in Detroit. He believed that education was the "greatest factor in the fusion of immigrant races," and, consequently, he devoted most of his attention to recommendations for improving Americanization education for adult immigrants.[151] Arguing that neither public nor private institutions alone could solve the problems of Americanization, Cole made his first and most important recommendation for Detroit to establish an overarching organization to "supplement and co-relate" the city's Americanization efforts. He believed that such an organization was vital for achieving greater unity and efficiency in the Americanization campaign.[152]

Like most major cities, Detroit had a diverse but largely uncoordinated set of Americanization education efforts offered by a wide variety of organizations. Beyond the public school evening program, Cole found factory schools operated by the Ford Motor Company, evening classes offered by the Young Men's Christian Association (YMCA), and programs for immigrants in public libraries. He believed that these organizations were as important and effective as anything going on in the public schools. He reported, for example, that in 1915 the English program in the Ford factory schools (which began operation in May 1914) enrolled some 1,700 students. He did not add, but the point was obvious, that enrollments in a program that served workers in just one corporation equaled almost 50 percent of the enrollment in the public school program, which ostensibly attracted students from the entire city.[153]

Cole, however, did not disparage Detroit's public-school evening programs. Rather, he argued that a series of factors had contributed to the lackluster performance of the night schools, notably "insufficient appropriations," inadequate publicity for the program, and the need to look beyond school buildings as the best venue for offering these courses. That last idea was based on the successful Americanization work done by organizations such as the YMCA.[154] Cole also urged Detroit educators to introduce "new methods of instruction . . . to meet the needs of the immigrants." In addition, he also recommended that the public schools inaugurate a "special training course of 'methods with immigrants'" for all evening-school teachers.[155]

The BOC enthusiastically embraced Cole's recommendations. Seeing this report as an opportunity to both inform and engage prominent Detroiters, the education committee of the BOC sent copies to various local civic leaders, along with a letter requesting their support for a broad-based Americanization campaign in the city. The leadership of this campaign would come from a newly formed organization, the Americanization Committee of the Detroit Board of Commerce (AC/BOC). While most of the early members of this committee belonged to the BOC, the group also included: Detroit's mayor; the assistant school superintendent in charge of the public schools evening program; the head of the Ford Motor Company's Sociological Department, which ran the Ford Americanization schools; the general secretary of the local YMCA; and a U.S. district court judge, who presided over naturalization hearings.[156] The AC/BOC set out to implement all of Cole's recommendations for improving Americanization education in the city.

The first of these efforts focused on the night schools. Buoyed by a promise from the school board to double its night school appropriation for the 1915–1916 school year, in the summer of 1915 the AC/BOC set out to boost enrollments and improve the quality of the Americanization courses in evening schools. Labeling the campaign "English First," members of the committee urged every company employing more than a hundred workers to help publicize night school programs and encourage non-English-speakers to register for the classes in English and citizenship when the schools opened in September.[157]

Esther Everett Lape, a consultant from the CIA, led the effort to publicize the new Americanization education programs. She arranged for posters to be printed and displayed in factories and public libraries around the city, convinced a local outdoor advertising company to donate space on five hundred billboards announcing the campaign, and got movie theaters in immigrant neighborhoods to show "slides" publicizing night school classes. In Polish sections of the city, Lape enlisted the aid of parish priests, convincing them to publicize the classes in their sermons on the two Sundays preceding the opening of the evening schools in mid-September. At her behest, the United Hebrew Charities distributed materials in Yiddish that encouraged Detroit's Jews to enroll in the Americanization classes. She also worked with editors from local foreign language newspapers to get the message out to their readers. The *Hungarian News*, the *Italian Tribune, Russian Life,* the [Italian] *Voce del Populo,* and many other foreign language newspapers were quite supportive of the campaign. The major English language newspapers also heartily endorsed the campaign. Finally, with aid from the Detroit Federation of Labor and the local Brewery Workers Union, Lape had eight hundred posters promoting night schools posted in what she described as "the most advantageous position of all," neighborhood saloons.[158]

On the Sunday before the night schools were scheduled to open, Lape arranged for Detroit-area Boy Scouts to distribute fliers at "all the foreign churches" in the city. "Every important mass or service was covered by the Scouts with handbills in the language used by the congregation," she explained. "In all, more than one hundred thousand bills were distributed."[159]

The campaign to boost enrollments was enormously successful. In his report on the progress of the night schools in 1915–1916, Assistant Superintendent Frank Cody exclaimed, "With record-breaking enrollments and attendance, the season of 1915–16 stands out as the red letter year in the history of Detroit Evening Schools." Enrollments soared from about 3,500 the previous year to nearly 7,900, an increase of 125 percent.[160]

While the publicity campaign unquestionably aided this effort, a number of other factors played an equal, if not a greater, role. Almost all these new policies and practices reflected recommendations from the Cole Report. First among these was offering classes in venues other than public schools, particularly in factories, a practice the YMCA had been using to good effect for several years. Educational leaders were convinced that if access to English and other Americanization classes became easier, larger numbers of immigrants would attend. This idea was borne out in a number of settings. In one instance, for example, the public schools sent ten teachers to a major manufacturing plant where over seven hundred workers had agreed to attend classes at the end of their shifts. Over the next few years, this idea of bringing classes into the factories became among the most important innovations in Americanization education, not only in Detroit but across the nation as well. It also became one of the most controversial.[161]

Second, the public night schools adopted the "Roberts system" for teaching English in all of their adult elementary English classes and established an "Institute for Teachers in Public Evening Schools," which provided a special methods course on using the Roberts system.[162] Created by Peter Roberts, head of the national YMCA's Americanization program, this system for teaching English contributed to the considerable success the organization had had in its Americanization efforts in part because it used a practical approach to English instruction and Americanization.[163] Roberts was an enthusiastic and very effective promoter of his English language program.[164] Indeed, by 1912, the YMCA estimated that its teachers had helped over 55,000 immigrants in three hundred different venues to learn English.[165] Based on the apparent success of the Roberts system, during World War I the U.S. military also adopted this system for teaching English to the approximately 289,000 foreign-born soldiers who, between 1918 and 1924, used their military service as a vehicle for naturalization.[166]

The Roberts system was similar to the Chicago and Rochester approaches discussed earlier in its focus on teaching words and phrases that were useful and practical. For example, the first course in the Roberts system relied on his primer, *English for Coming Americans*, which taught "foreigners a handy comprehensive vocabulary of shop, market, and street English in a short period of time by means of acting out the simple daily life of the individual."[167] The second course broadened and deepened the knowledge and skills of the first, working mainly on basic reading, writing, and grammar skills, while at the same time expanding the students' vocabulary.[168] The third course moved beyond just teaching English and introduced some substantial content about American history and life. Using a fairly sophisticated text, *Reader for Coming Americans*, Roberts introduced immigrants to American history, civics, and industry. The book contained some sixty short (three-to-four-page) chapters about such topics as the life of George Washington or the differences between absolute monarchies and democracies. Roberts saw each chapter as a means for imparting important Americanization content while at the same time enhancing English skills. He also wanted teachers to use these topics to stimulate conversations in English between teachers and students. Roberts described the book's message about American democracy, justice, and civil and religious liberty "as a 'gospel of good tidings' to millions of immigrants."[169]

The beauty of the Roberts system was its logical progression from basic elements of English to broad general knowledge about the history, economics, and politics of the United States. In some ways it was a comprehensive and highly practical Americanization curriculum based on the interests and needs of adults. It enabled teachers to step into classrooms and immediately begin teaching lessons that made sense to their students.

The third factor contributing to the success of the Detroit program was the addition of a new course in citizenship built around a free textbook provided by the Board of Commerce. Frank Cody described the course as one that "quickly acquainted the foreigners with the vital details of American local government and tried to instil American ideals, moral and political, into their minds." As with the Chicago course, this initiative sought to grab and maintain student attention by offering knowledge that appealed to students' interests and needs. Many of the one hundred evening sessions of the Detroit course focused on naturalization and included help for students in filling out the forms that were required in the process. Moreover, upon successful completion of the course, students earned a "Certificate of Citizenship," which courts recognized "as sufficient qualification for citizenship papers, provided the legal requirements of residence and eligibility have been met." Not surprisingly, the course proved to be quite popular.[170]

As important as these innovations were in boosting enrollments, another factor was also in play. Some employers coerced immigrant workers to take Americanization classes. The Ford Motor Company was the most notorious employer in this regard. From its inception in 1914, the Ford English program rested on compulsory attendance. One Ford manager explained, "If a man declines to go to school, the advantages of the training are carefully explained to him. If he still hesitates, he is laid off and given a chance for uninterrupted meditation and reconsideration. He seldom fails to change his mind."[171]

When the AC/BOC night school campaign began, a number of companies followed Ford's lead. For example, the Saxon Motor Company immediately made night school attendance a requirement for employment. Similarly, the Northway Company gave its employees three choices: 1) attend the English class offered at the factory; 2) attend a night school class; 3) "be laid off." One business leader responded to the AC/BOC query about the English First program by stating simply, "There is no place in our factory, in Detroit, or in this country, for men who are not trying to learn our language, and become good, useful citizens." A number of companies simply declared that they would employ only workers who spoke English; and others, such as the Packard Motor Company, announced an "Americans First" policy, stating that they would not promote noncitizens to "positions of importance in the organization."[172]

While historians have often focused on these examples of coercive Americanization, Ford and other companies were the exception, not the rule. The Cadillac Company, for example, encouraged its employees to attend night schools but did not punish those who failed to do so. The Solvay Process Company determined that incentives rather than penalties were the wisest course of action. It offered an hourly raise to workers who learned English.[173] According to Gregory Mason, a journalist who wrote an enthusiastic story about Americanization in the Motor City, most Detroit businesses followed some variation of this less onerous pattern. They "neither organized schools of their own nor made attendance on [sic] the night schools compulsory, but encouraged this attendance in every fair way in their power."[174] Indeed, historian Anne Brophy found that the AC/BOC failed "in convincing a large number of Detroit industrialists to make English and citizenship a job requirement either."[175]

Regardless of whether companies coerced or enticed workers into attending the night schools, it is likely that most students experienced a considerable degree of aggressive assimilation in their classes. The Ford Motor Company program, for example, was an all-encompassing effort to transform foreign workers into some version of an "ideal American." The program included not only mandatory attendance for the classes, but also home visits by agents from the Sociology Department who assessed the moral and physical characteristics of workers' living spaces and families.[176]

In the classroom, Ford educators also used the Roberts system for teaching English, but they embellished the program with their own particular brand of 100 percent Americanism. As one Ford spokesman put it, the "one great aim" of the Ford Schools was "to impress these men that they are, or should be, Americans, and that former racial, national, and linguistic differences are to be forgotten."[177] According to Gregory Mason, teachers in the Ford schools typically told students to "walk to the American blackboard, take a piece of American chalk and explain how the American workman walks to his American home and sits down with his American family to their good American dinner." Even Mason, a staunch Americanizer who was no friend of the hyphen, castigated the Ford program for its "grotesquely exaggerated patriotism".[178]

In the ensuing years, nothing has come to symbolize Ford's relentless push for assimilation better than the pageant that students from the English schools participated in when they "graduated" from the program. Indeed, the ceremony has become an enduring example of overly aggressive Americanization, most recently in *Middlesex*, Jeffrey Eugenides' Pulitzer Prize–winning novel about immigration and identity.[179]

Initially performed in an auditorium and later at a baseball field near a Ford plant, the graduates of the Ford School stepped onto a stage before an audience of family members and co-workers. The graduates first appeared wearing the clothes of their original homelands and slowly filed into a huge papier-mâché cauldron emblazoned with the words, "Ford English School Melting Pot." Atop this cauldron, teachers from the school stirred the numerous nationalities together using long ladles representing the nine months that the students had spent in class. Eventually, the men emerged from the cauldron, each dressed exactly alike in a dark, American-style suit and tie, and each waving a tiny American flag. The head of the Ford educational program summarized the meaning of the pageant, saying, "Into the pot 52 nationalities with their foreign clothes and baggage go and out of the pot after vigorous stirring by the teachers comes one nationality, viz. American." A sign hanging above the cauldron declared simply, "*E Pluribus Unum.*"[180]

The Ford program was at the extreme end of the spectrum in terms of its aggressive assimilation. Indeed, even before the company began forcing workers into Americanization classes, it had already set a distinctive standard for ruthlessness in its efforts to get workers to toe an assimilationist line. In January 1914, the company fired as many as nine hundred

Greek and Russian employees for missing work on the Eastern Orthodox Christmas, which was celebrated thirteen days after December 25th. One Ford official declared, "[I]f these men are to make their home in America, they should observe American holidays."[181]

While such extreme behavior was unusual, demands that immigrants give up their native culture as part of the Americanization process was common. Other adult English and citizenship programs, such as those sponsored by the Detroit Public Schools, were not mandatory, but they were equally committed to excising the hyphen. Writing in 1916, Frank Cody bluntly stated that getting immigrants to naturalize was not enough, because the immediate result was "a hyphenated America, a kind of dual citizen." Echoing Theodore Roosevelt and Woodrow Wilson, Cody called for additional education beyond English and citizenship classes to "eliminate the hyphen in thought and habit as well as before the law."[182]

There is not a great deal of evidence about how immigrants in Detroit responded to these often-coercive Americanization efforts and to the educational practices that sought to marginalize their cultural backgrounds. However, at least some leaders from the immigrant communities, including the editors of several local foreign-language newspapers, were generally supportive of the Americanization campaign despite its oft-stated assimilationist goals. On December 16, 1915, for example, two months into the campaign, the education committee of the BOC invited eight leaders of various immigrant groups, five of them newspaper editors, to a lunchtime meeting to discuss the ongoing Americanization initiative. The eight included representatives from the city's German, Italian, Lithuanian, Polish, and Russian communities. All of them supported the campaign; several even offered their "hearty" cooperation. While two of the editors, one from the *Polish Daily Record* and the other from *Russian Life*, criticized some of the teaching methods used in the classes, none opposed the campaign itself.[183] In August 1916, another group of immigrant leaders and newspaper editors—this time representing the Hungarians, Jews, and Russians—met with the committee and also pledged their support.[184]

With the exception of the *Polish Daily Record*, which eventually denounced the Americanization campaign as akin to attempts by the Russians to eradicate Polish culture, the relationship between the editors of Detroit's foreign language newspapers and the AC/BOC was both cordial and long-standing.[185] As late as 1929, leaders of the Americanization Committee of Detroit were still honoring "the Foreign Language Newspapers in Detroit for their generous and courteous support of our program."[186] Similarly, leaders of the ethnic communities and, as the next two chapters demonstrate, most of the foreign language newspapers in Chicago and Cleveland were equally, if not more, supportive of Americanization efforts in their cities, although they vigorously rejected efforts to strip immigrants of their native language and culture.

One reason for this support may have been fears of intimidation that many editors of foreign language newspapers felt in this era. Particularly after the United States entered the war, many ethnic newspapers fell under suspicion of being insufficiently patriotic. It is likely that some editors believed that providing support for local Americanization efforts was a sure way to demonstrate their loyalty. But, as will be discussed in chapter 3, many ethnic groups (e.g., Czechs, Lithuanians, Slovaks, and Poles) had strong reasons of their own to support the war and their own nuanced and instrumental views of why their readers should support Americanization efforts as well.[187]

In all, the Detroit Americanization initiative of 1915–1916 appeared to be a rousing success. The First National Conference on Americanization and Immigration, held in Philadelphia in January 1916, was abuzz with discussion of and praise for the Detroit program. One conference participant reported, "The Detroit delegation heard many tributes to the effectiveness of the pioneer work undertaken by the Detroit Board of Commerce and the Detroit Board of Education. Those at the conference heard speaker after speaker refer to the splendid impetus the movement has received in Detroit."[188]

Historian Edward Hartmann argued that members of the NAC saw the Detroit program, particularly its use of factories as venues for teaching English and citizenship, as a potential blueprint for successful Americanization efforts across the nation. Hartmann explained, "Now, as the result of the Detroit experiment, the Committee recognized that effective Americanization work among aliens inevitably meant active steps thorough the medium of the industrial plants of America, for here in this important economic area seemed to lie the real 'melting pot.'"[189]

Similarly, over the next year, the U.S. Chamber of Commerce in conjunction with the NAC began touting a program of "industrial Americanization" that was strongly influenced by the Detroit program.[190] The chairman of the AC/BOC of Detroit noted, "The Chamber of Commerce of the United States appointed a committee on immigration, and at various conventions and meetings held under the auspices of this committee, Detroit speakers and Detroit methods predominated."[191]

As a result of the conference, the Detroit model that linked the public schools and major corporations became the virtual center of the Americanization universe. In March 1916, a representative from the Chicago Association of Commerce visited Detroit to examine the city's educational program firsthand. As one Detroit Americanizer explained, business and educational leaders in the Windy City sought to "carry on [Americanization] work in Chicago along the lines originated in Detroit." The following year, Chicago celebrated the Fourth of July with a huge Americanization rally featuring parades, flag ceremonies, and a mixed chorus of Czechs, Croatians, Lithuanians, and Poles singing the national anthem.[192] Similarly, in April 1916, Los Angeles announced plans to restructure its night school program based on the Detroit model.[193] At the same time, the Americanization Committee of Pittsburgh also introduced the first of a series of initiatives that eventually led to an Americanization program remarkably similar to the one in Detroit.[194]

Even Cleveland, which was an early leader in Americanization education, now looked to the Motor City for guidance. Throughout 1916, the secretary of the AC/BOC made several trips to Cleveland, explaining to civic leaders there how Detroit had gotten major corporations and the public schools working together on Americanization. These consultations bore fruit early in 1917, beginning with the hiring of Frank Spaulding as superintendent of the Cleveland schools, as well as with Raymond E. Cole, who conducted the survey that launched the Detroit campaign, being tapped to lead Americanization efforts in the city. Both men immediately set out to make Cleveland renowned for its Americanization work, using Detroit as a model. Spaulding, for example, created a new Department of Educational Extension, whose mission was to carry out Americanization activities in the schools, factories, stores, and even the homes of the foreign-born. Cole worked directly with major corporations in the city, getting them to provide the kind of factory schools found in Detroit. He declared that the Detroit Board of Commerce "has led the nation in initiating and carrying on the most effective Americanization work through its industries."[195] Other industrial cities, including Akron, Boston, Buffalo, Cincinnati, Gary, Rochester, Syracuse, Wilkes-Barre, and Youngstown, revised their Americanization education programs along similar lines.[196] The results of all these efforts were impressive. Frank V.

Thompson reported that between 1914 and 1919, the chances of immigrants finding an Americanization program linked to public schools increased 40 percent nationwide.[197]

PEDAGOGY VS. PROFITS: THE FAILURE OF THE
AMERICANIZATION CAMPAIGN?

Yet as successful as these developments appear, significant problems with the Americanization campaign began appearing as early as 1917. For example, even as Americanizers in Detroit were basking in national acclaim, evening school enrollments in the city's Americanization courses were plummeting. Enrollments in the 1916–1917 school year dropped, falling from almost 7,900 in 1915–1916 to about 4,300 in 1916–1917.[198] In that same time period, Cleveland also registered declines, with enrollments in its evening elementary schools dropping from about 7,500 to some 4,700.[199] Worried about whether this development was unique to Cleveland, the director of that city's evening school program surveyed other major school systems around the country. He found that Chicago, Cincinnati, New York, Philadelphia, Pittsburgh, and St. Louis, as well as a number of other cities, had experienced similar declines "varying from ten to forty per cent."[200] For example, the number of foreign-born students in Boston's evening elementary school program plunged by more than half between 1913–1914 and 1916–1917, from about 11,500 students to over 5,600, the drop-off occurring steadily each year.[201] Philadelphia experienced the same trend in its evening elementary program, with a steady decline from about 8,500 students in 1914 to over 4,600 three years later.[202] In New York City, enrollment of foreign-born students in elementary evening courses fell from just over 55,000 in 1915–1916 to about 38,500 in 1916–1917, a 30 percent drop. The district superintendent in charge of the evening schools put much of the blame on the immigrants' lack of interest in the programs, declaring, "We have offered every opportunity free, we have thrown open our schools and bid them come; but they did not avail themselves of the opportunities nor did they desire to come."[203]

But other school leaders suggested a number of more plausible reasons for these enrollment declines. These included the dramatic reduction of new immigrants coming to the United States due to the war; the increased availability for work in defense-related industries; the proffering of overtime work, particularly night shifts; the breakdown in cooperation between factories and the public schools in providing classes (undoubtedly related to the two previous trends); the tendency among many foreign-born workers to focus on the immediate crisis in their embattled homelands, rather than on planning for their future in the United States; a resurgence of loyalty to their homelands due to the war; and workers spending more of their time and their additional wages on "various amusements and social activities."[204]

Other possible factors contributing to the dropout problem were the coercive nature of some programs and a lack of attention to the background culture of the students in many programs. As Anne Brophy notes, in the spring of 1918, even the Detroit Board of Commerce was commenting on these problems and urging Americanizers to focus on "ideas about brotherhood, respect, and immigrant gifts to America." The Detroiter, the official voice of the BOC, bluntly stated, "Coercive Americanization, like coercive loyalty, does not make for good citizenship."[205]

The problem of getting adult immigrants into the Americanization classes worsened after the country entered World War I. As the demands of war production grew, increasing numbers of people were able to find jobs, and substantial numbers of young men from immigrant communities (almost half a million) entered military service.[206] During this period the national unemployment rate dropped sharply, from 8.5 percent of the workforce in 1915 to 1.4 percent in 1918 and 1919.[207] In some cities, the correlation between this development and the decline in night school enrollments was striking. In April 1918, for example, the president of the New York City Board of Education told participants at a federally sponsored conference on Americanization and the war that his school system had reduced its English classes for foreigners by 40 percent from the previous year, due to lack of attendance.[208] Around that same time, the number of foreign-born students in the Boston Public Schools evening elementary program plunged to just 3,200, approximately 70 percent fewer than in 1913–1914. In November 1919, the Boston superintendent reported that of the twenty-one evening elementary schools operating in 1913–1914, only twelve were still open five years later.[209] As the historian Maxine Seller commented, "Ironically, the war itself, which had sparked the massive campaign for adult education, helped to defeat it."[210]

The failure to attract students was not due to a lack of effort or publicity on the part of the Americanizers. Soon after the nation entered the war, the U.S. Bureau of Education in collaboration with the NAC launched a series of conferences and institutes for educators and civic leaders that explained how to establish or improve Americanization programs. The bureau also produced a steady stream of syllabi, pamphlets, and posters designed to aid communities in their Americanization efforts. In addition, it published a number of important bulletins on immigrant education.[211] Similarly, the Committee on Immigrants of the U.S. Chamber of Commerce redoubled its efforts to promote "Industrial Americanization," which was designed to encourage foreign-born workers to attend night courses in Americanization offered by public school systems.[212]

Locally, supporters of Americanization were equally active in seeking to encourage students to register for night schools and other Americanization programs. In Detroit, the AC/BOC continued its extensive publicity campaigns for night and factory schools throughout the war years.[213] In Cleveland, on the heels of Wilson's declaration of war, local political leaders created the Cleveland Americanization Committee (CAC), headed by Raymond E. Cole. Using the Detroit program as its template, the CAC worked closely with the public schools to promote Americanization classes across the city. Supported by a substantial infusion of new funds, school leaders organized courses for immigrants "in public-school buildings, factories, parochial schools, churches, public libraries, hospitals, and, in fact every place within the city" where immigrants might be willing to attend class.[214] As in the Detroit campaign, the CAC advertised the program widely and convinced employers to encourage or pressure workers to attend the courses. Due to these efforts, Cleveland bucked the national trend of enrollment declines, albeit modestly. The campaign netted 1,241 more students than in the previous year. But even with that increase, the total equaled only about half of the more than 11,000 students who had registered for the elementary program in 1914–1915.[215]

Chicago, which had been extremely slow in developing a coordinated Americanization program for the city, finally took action after the United States entered the war. In 1918, the Chicago Association of Commerce created a Committee on Americanization (COA), which, like its counterparts in Cleveland and Detroit, pledged to work with the board of education in providing English and citizenship classes in factories and mills throughout the city.[216] As in Detroit, the COA campaign began with a large-scale publicity campaign to drum up support for the program. It claimed that within a year this effort had induced some 6,000 students to enroll in Americanization classes across the city.[217] However, most of these students must have attended programs outside the purview of the Chicago Public Schools, which in 1918 reported a substantial one-year drop in enrollments in classes for foreign-born students, from just over 7,500 in 1916–1917 to only about 3,700 students in 1917–1918. The slide in enrollments continued the following year as well.[218]

Ironically, the decline in enrollments in Americanization classes generally was related to the reliance on factory classes. This innovation, which was central to the transformation of Americanization education after 1914, became a liability once the United States entered the war. Employers quickly realized that they could not simultaneously satisfy the demands for increased war production and the demands for Americanizing workers. As orders for war materials spiked, it became increasingly difficult to offer Americanization classes, because of limits on both time and space. Indeed, in this period, some major corporations ended their factory schools altogether. On October 9, 1917, for example, Frank Cody dropped a bombshell at an AC/BOC meeting when he reported that "the Packard and Ford companies were about to abandon their schools."[219]

Actually, Ford did not completely abandon this effort, but it reduced the program drastically. Before the year was out, the company slashed the number of rooms devoted to English classes from twenty-two to three. Over the next few years, the program limped along, serving a small number of students, and in 1922 the company ended it completely. All told, the Ford program, which was then and has continued to be the most widely cited example of factory-based Americanization, enrolled about 14,000 students during its most active period, 1914–1917. Despite these impressive numbers, historians Allan Nevins and Frank Hill point out that of this total only about "1,500 received diplomas certifying that they had completed a full course of 72 lessons."[220] In other words, the Ford program appears to have been far less successful than its contemporary publicists or later historians have maintained.

The dispiriting announcements from Packard and Ford were just the beginning of the bad news for the AC/BOC. At its next meeting, representatives from several other major corporations reported that restructured workdays, demands for overtime, and lack of space made offering such classes difficult, if not impossible.[221] In its 1918–1919 annual report, the AC/BOC found that night school enrollments in Detroit were "not enough to make complete use of the facilities offered by the Board of Education."[222] Trends across the nation were similar. For example, writing in 1920, the acting superintendent of the Philadelphia Public Schools found that evening school enrollments in 1919 were only 16 percent of what they had been in 1914.[223]

These developments were so damaging to the Americanization campaign that in January 1918, Esther Everett Lape, who had been instrumental in launching the Detroit initiative, wrote, "I doubt if there is any audience in the country that needs to be convinced that we have made a bad job of Americanization, and have somehow or other bungled the whole matter of American citizenship."[224] One year later, even the indefatigable Americanizer Francis A. Kellor lamented the "failure of Americanization in the past years."[225] In August 1920, a writer for the pro-restrictionist *Saturday Evening Post* bluntly declared that "the events of the past few years have shown conclusively that [the United States] has not been able to assimilate most of the 10,000,000 aliens who emigrated to America in the ten years before the war."[226]

In a 1921 retrospective essay on Americanization, Frank Cody, then superintendent of the Detroit Public Schools, provided an equally gloomy assessment of the campaign in the Motor City. He noted that the enrollment declines, which began in Detroit in the fall of 1916, worsened after the United States entered the war, and in 1917 and 1918 the numbers "sank to almost nothing." He added that during these two years "Americanization work languished across the country," noting that he had heard from school leaders in half a dozen major cities that had substantial immigrant populations, and that "without exception they showed decreases in registration of adult foreigners in our schools."[227] One year later, speaking to the annual NEA conference, Cody went further and admitted that the highly touted factory school initiative in Detroit essentially had been a failure, with only about ten corporations having run successful programs. Even Ford Motor Company, which, as Cody noted, had run the "largest experiment in private conduct of factory classes," decided that they were "not worth the expense and effort." He concluded, "Our experience has led me to believe that it is almost as difficult to hold school successfully in an automobile or other factory as it would be to make automobiles successfully in a school."[228]

Whether the great Americanization campaign failed as badly as these commentators claimed remains an open question.[229] But regardless of the accuracy of these assessments, the perception of failure had profound consequences both politically and educationally. The more immediate consequence came in the debate about immigration restriction. Advocates of racial restriction pointed to the high attrition rate from these programs as evidence that eastern and southern European immigrants had neither the inclination nor the ability to become American citizens. An excellent example of that stance can be seen in a 1921 editorial from the *Saturday Evening Post* that fulminated against the new immigrants, declaring that most of them were biologically unfit for assimilation; that a "change of air, of scene, of job cannot change the fundamental facts of heredity, and it is on these that a race is built"; and that these people were utterly unlike earlier settlers whose "viking [sic] adventuring" brought them to America. The editorial concluded, "The trouble with our Americanization program is that a large part of our recent immigrants can never be Americans. They will always be Americanski—near-Americans with un-American ideas and ideals."[230]

These views had a powerful impact on the debate to end the immigration of southern and eastern European immigrants. Yet ironically, as the next two sections demonstrate, the prospect and then the reality of closing the door to new immigrants actually spurred aliens in the United States to naturalize in huge numbers, increased the demand for Americanization education, and, most surprisingly, strengthened the hand of advocates for a more inclusive, culturally pluralistic approach to Americanization.

POSTWAR TRENDS

Despite the dispiriting wartime developments and negative assessments of the Americanization campaign, once the Armistice was signed, night school enrollments revived. Cleveland, which substantially augmented its Americanization efforts during and immediately after the war, reported that over 9,400 students enrolled in its elementary night schools in 1920–1921.[231] Chicago, which also stepped up Americanization work in 1918 and 1919, registered over 12,300 students in its English classes for the foreign-born in 1921–1922. In April 1919, the *Chicago Daily Tribune* declared that "only an agile and determined immigrant possessed of overmastering devotion to the land of his birth can hope to escape Americanization by at least one of the many processes now being prepared for his special benefit, in addition to those which have surrounded him in the past."[232] That same year, Detroit reported almost 8,400 students in its "English for Foreigners" classes, an enrollment nine times greater than in 1919–1920.[233] In Boston, the number of foreign-born students in the evening elementary program more than doubled between 1919–1920 and 1920–1921, from a little over 2,100 students to over 4,800.[234]

A number of factors figured into these postwar enrollment increases. The Red scare of 1919–1920, which largely targeted foreign-born leftists and led to a sizable number of deportations, spurred new Americanization efforts across the country.[235] In Chicago, for example, educational leaders re-doubled their adult Americanization efforts as part of their campaign against Bolshevism.[236] Similarly, the depression of 1920–1921 created a situation where large numbers of unemployed workers had time to pursue schooling in the hope that new skills (e.g., greater knowledge of English) might help them find work.

But perhaps the most important factor leading to increased naturalization was the growing power of racial restrictionists. Beginning in 1921, opponents to immigration succeeded in passing a quota law that sharply reduced the number of eastern and southern European immigrants who could enter the country.[237] Over the next few years, as the push intensified to pass even tougher laws barring entry to these supposedly inferior races, increasing numbers of immigrants living in the country sought to make their status permanent. With the Americanization education infrastructure now well established in areas with large immigrant populations, the growing number of aliens seeking naturalization had easy access to programs that would prepare them for citizenship.

An excellent example of these developments can be seen in the effort to Americanize immigrant women in the post–World War I years. Both before and during the war, the percentages of women in traditional night school English classes were quite small, less than 10 percent of enrollments in classes in Detroit between 1914 and 1916, and only about a quarter of enrollments in Chicago's classes for the foreign-born from 1916 to 1919.[238] But in the postwar years, that trend began to change. For example, in the fall of 1918, the Americanization Society of Grand Rapids, Michigan, began what became a nationally recognized campaign to Americanize immigrant women in that city and specifically to get them to be active voters.[239] Similarly, in attempting to address the problems facing immigrant women, in 1919–1920, Detroit also introduced a program of "mothers' classes." As the head of the Detroit evening school program explained, "Perhaps the slowest to feel and show the effect of Americanizing influences is the foreign language-speaking woman, particularly the mother of children." Given the difficulties facing these women, school leaders established afternoon classes for them located in public schools and settlement houses in immigrant neighborhoods.[240] In addition, recognizing that teaching these students would need special preparation, educators in Detroit also established a ten-hour methods course in teaching "English for Foreigners" to prospective teachers of the mothers' classes.[241] These efforts appear to have paid off. In the 1921–1922 school year a third of the nearly 8,400 students enrolled in the "English for Foreigners" classes in Detroit were women.[242]

School leaders in Chicago also offered afternoon mothers' classes primarily devoted to English instruction in public schools. In addition, Chicago settlement houses also provided a number of educational opportunities for immigrant women. By 1920, seventeen settlements across the city were offering classes in English, as well as in cooking and sewing, to immigrant women. In the 1927–1928 school year, over "600 foreign-born mothers" in Cleveland enrolled in afternoon English classes.[243]

These developments were linked in part to the ratification of the Nineteenth Amendment giving women the right to vote; and, more important, the Cable Act of 1922, which declared that non-naturalized women who married U.S. citizens did not automatically gain U.S. citizenship through the marriage, thus requiring them to seek naturalization on their own, encouraged educators across the country to extend their programs to women.[244] Writing in 1922, Americanizers in Akron, Ohio, declared that in the previous year their city's "greatest [Americanization] achievement has been the development of women's classes, particularly in the homes." They announced that fifty-six such classes had been created in the last year.[245] Even small cities like Gardner, Massachusetts, boasted about the creation of mothers' classes in the post–World War I years.[246]

In Detroit, these factors also seemed to have influenced more women to enroll in citizenship classes. In 1921–1922, of the 1,333 students enrolled in these evening school citizenship classes, only six were women. Four years later, the number of women in these classes jumped to 194, equal to about 9 percent of the total enrollment.[247] During the same period, other organizations in Detroit, such as the YMCA and the International Institute, which was founded in 1919, also played a large role in promoting "women's Americanization" in the 1920s.[248]

All these developments helped boost enrollments during the 1920s. Moreover, during the post–World War I years, the number of naturalizations increased dramatically. Between 1910 and 1914, before Americanization became a concerted national enterprise, only about 354,000 people were naturalized. Over the next five years, however, as the Americanization campaign ramped up, the number of naturalizations rose to almost 636,000 and jumped again between 1920 and 1924 to over 825,000. Put another way, if we look specifically at the decade in which the Americanization education campaign was operating at full tilt, 1915–1924, the total number of naturalizations was over 1,461,000, which included almost 289,000 people who naturalized during or soon after they completed their military service. These numbers should have heartened Americanizers, but whether this substantial growth in naturalizations was directly related to the Americanization education campaign is difficult, if not impossible, to know.[249]

Undoubtedly the tremendous amount of publicity about Americanization in this period and the great increase in the availability of Americanization classes were factors in this increase of naturalizations, especially in the period 1925 to 1929, when huge numbers of people sought to naturalize in order to remain in the United States after the passage of the National Origins Act. Indeed, following the passage of the National Origins Act in 1924, the number of naturalizations skyrocketed. Between 1925 and 1929, some 956,000 additional immigrants naturalized, by far the largest five-year total of naturalizations to date. The Americanization education infrastructure that was put into place during the Americanization campaign undoubtedly supported this trend, but by the late 1920s, interest in these programs was on the wane, and their role in these developments went largely unnoticed. Given this longer perspective on the Americanization campaign, it is difficult to support the claim of many critics at the time and some historians since that the campaign of 1915 to 1924 was a massive failure. Nevertheless the perception of failure lingered, a development that had interesting educational ramifications in the late 1920s and the 1930s.

TOWARD A MORE PLURALISTIC VISION OF AMERICANIZATION

As noted earlier, the perception that the great Americanization campaign had failed emboldened racial restrictionists, who had been arguing for decades that no amount of education could transform immigrants from eastern and southern Europe into good Americans. Restrictionists, however, were not the only group to find their arguments strengthened by claims that the Americanization movement had failed. On the other side of the ideological spectrum, people who supported a culturally pluralistic approach to Americanization education used the perception that aggressive assimilation had failed in order to promote their ideas of how best to educate and integrate immigrants into American society.

In the 1920s, a growing number of American educators, public intellectuals, and social activists reinvigorated the ideas of Jane Addams and John Dewey as an alternative to the strongly assimilationist form of civic nationalism of the Americanization movement. Like liberal educators on the K–12 level, these individuals sought to make curricula in adult programs more sensitive to and representative of the contributions that diverse groups had made in American history. These intellectual and educational leaders advanced three interrelated arguments in support of these ideas. First, they maintained that coercive assimilationist programs contradicted the basic ideals of American democracy. Second, they charged that curricula centered only on Anglo-Saxon or Nordic contributions to American history and culture ignored the diverse character of people who built, shaped, and sustained the United States. Third, they maintained that by ignoring the cultural and historical backgrounds of the immigrants, the assimilationists had missed a superb opportunity to show their students how they fit into American history and culture and thus making their Americanization a more natural and effective process.

Of these criticisms, none was more passionately expressed than the argument that coercive Americanization programs such as the one at Ford Motor Company trampled on the very ideals it hoped to inspire. How, these critics asked, could the United States proclaim itself the protector of democracy, when companies like Ford made Americanization education compulsory for its immigrant employees? In 1920, for example, Boston school superintendent Frank V. Thompson denounced "the so-called 100-per-cent Americans" who used tactics that he described as akin to those of autocrats and Bolsheviks. "If Americanism is primarily a mode of thinking and feeling," he declared, "the compulsionist [sic] is forced to maintain the theory that habits of thinking and feeling can be manufactured by force and decree."[250] That same year, Smith College professor Julius Drachsler wrote in amazement that "America of all countries" should succumb to the idea of "compulsory citizenship." He argued that the Great War was caused by exactly those kinds of "national policies of coercion." Drachsler added, "It would seem the experience of Germany with Alsace-Lorraine and East Prussia, of Russian Czardom with Poles,

Jews and Finns, of the Ottoman Turks with Armenia, of the Hapsburgs with Slovak, Hungarian, Roumanian and Croatian, would be a solemn warning to America that compulsion breeds stubbornness, and that stubbornness contains the seeds of conflict and of hatred."[251] Two years later, in a speech to the NEA, Albert Shiels, who had recently resigned as superintendent of the Los Angeles Public Schools to join the faculty at Teachers College, blasted coercive naturalization programs as "un-American." He added that they "have failed lamentably in making loyal citizens."[252]

This last point led directly to the second critique, namely, that successful Americanization education on the adult and K–12 levels had to acknowledge and honor the cultural backgrounds and cultural gifts of the immigrants. The belief that immigrants were important contributors to American history and culture harked back to the pluralistic ideas that Jane Addams and John Dewey had voiced in their prewar speeches to the NEA. In the post–World War I years, these ideas found increasing resonance among a diverse group of educators. For example, in March 1920, an adult educator from Buffalo, New York, picked up this theme, declaring that Americanization "has little to do with melting pots, chauvinism and provinciality." Echoing Horace Kallen, the educator proclaimed, "Americanization reverberates the strains of a tremendous symphony in which all the varied contributions of the nations are blended in a harmony as inspiring as it is true, beautiful and good."[253]

Seven months later, in an address to administrators of the Americanization agencies in Ohio, the prominent Americanization educator and YMCA leader Peter Roberts urged educators to respect and attend to the cultural backgrounds of their immigrant students.[254] After noting the long struggle for liberty by the oppressed peoples in Europe, Roberts urged his listeners to "remember that [struggle] when we teach these men in our classes." He reminded his audience that democracy came to us from the Old World and that it "is not an American-born product." He argued that "the cosmopolitan heart of America" should be a model for international democracy, and he then added a ringing endorsement of civic nationalist ideas, declaring,

> . . . let us make the heart of America more cosmopolitan than it is today. Do not be afraid of the blood of the Latin, of the blood of the Iberian, of the blood of the Slav, coming into the melting

pot, saying, "It will vitiate the blood of America." Nothing of the kind, my friends. I have had experience all over the United States. I know whereof I speak. I say there is more need of Americanization for many Americans than there is need of Americanization among many of these foreign born.[255]

As important as these ideas were in revising native-born Americans' views of immigrants and their contributions to American history and life, some educators added a third criticism of assimilationist approaches to Americanization. These educators noted that by failing to link Americanization to the native cultures of immigrants, Americanizers were making a fundamental pedagogical error. In 1921, Garry C. Myers, a professor at the Cleveland School of Education, wrote that Americanizers should appeal to the immigrant by "suggesting to him that he has come from a land with heroes worthy of esteem; that he can and will develop into a good American citizen." Myers added, "Therefore one of the earliest steps in Americanization is for the immigrants to learn to read in English the simple biographies of great heroes of their own land, heroes who lived for great ideals who symbolized many things that are the best of what America stands for."[256]

Four years later, J. V. Breitwieser, a psychologist from Columbia University, made a similar suggestion, stating, "It is a well known pedagogical principle that real education consists in drawing out, in giving expression, in imitating adjustments from the point of view of the student rather than to get a mere imitational parrot-like response of dogmatic formulae." With that in mind, he noted, "Practically every nation has heroes that to its inhabitants represent some of our national principles." Thus, if teachers referred to these heroes when teaching about American ideals, they would not only honor the backgrounds of the students but would also be more educationally effective. As he put it, "George Washington is illuminated by the light of a knowledge of Garibaldi."[257]

Philip Davis from Boston University summed up these ideas by embedding them in a very different vision of Americanization than the one put forward by assimilationists. He stated that "Americanization is the process of assimilating on the part of the immigrants these basic principles of American Democracy enriched by the national and racial qualifications and traditions which the immigrants bring with them."[258]

As David Tyack and a number of other scholars recently have argued, during the 1920s these critics of aggressive Americanization became increasingly well known and influential.[259] This development was, as historian Diana Selig notes, due to a significant change in the national attitude about immigrants that emerged after the passage of the National Origins Act in 1924. She writes, "In a sense, the passage of the restrictions laws redirected debate from political to cultural terms, creating room for pluralism to take hold."[260]

Rejecting the coercive and chauvinistic aspects of the adult education programs of the World War I years, these critics argued that such efforts were incompatible with American ideals and values and, as important, ineffective and inefficient. They campaigned for a more culturally sensitive and cosmopolitan approach to Americanization, an approach that recognized the importance of teaching the shared ideals and values of American democracy while simultaneously acknowledging the great contributions immigrants made to American history and life.

One of the best indications of the influence of these ideas can be seen in the changing nature of the Detroit Americanization program. In her study of the Americanization Committee of Detroit, Anne Brophy found that, in the early 1920s, as business leaders' interest in Americanization began to wane, the movement in the Motor City gradually transformed from an aggressive assimilationist effort to a social welfare initiative. Beyond promoting Americanization classes, the committee's approach to Americanization "increasingly emphasized reciprocity and mutual respect between Americans and immigrants." Representatives of immigrant communities joined the committee's leadership at the same time that the committee began to hire native-language speakers to aid in providing social services to non-English-speaking clients. The committee still supported traditional Americanization courses, but even in this area, the courses sought to use "ethnic ties to encourage Americanization." Writing in 1928, a leader of the committee described its efforts as trying to preserve "all that is beautiful in the racial background of the men and women from the lands across the seas with whom we work as friend and advisor daily throughout the year."[261] Brophy describes this as taking an alternative approach to Americanization, in which "'America' was no longer the fixed standard to which the immigrant must adapt, but a dynamic, evolving *process* to which immigrants could contribute" (emphasis in the original).[262] The next two chapters examine the evolution of this new approach to Americanization education and its profound impact on how foreign- and native-born Americans viewed themselves and their country.

Conclusion

From the late nineteenth century through the 1920s, public schools were formidable agents of assimilation. The public school systems of Chicago, Cleveland, and Detroit immersed their students, both children and adults, in an educational regime dominated by Anglo-American culture. Whether one considers kindergartens, elementary schools, high schools, or adult evening classes, this culture permeated the curriculum. Americanization education centered on teaching English; familiarizing students with U.S. history, particularly stories about Washington, Lincoln, and other American heroes; and providing knowledge of democratic ideals and institutions. In teaching these subjects, educators put the ideas of assimilationist civic nationalism into practice. They believed that they were giving their students the knowledge and information needed to survive and hopefully thrive in the New World. These educators had little reason to refer to or teach about the home cultures of their students; they simply did not see that as part of their job.

Despite that attitude, by the late 1920s things began to change at least modestly. In response to a number of factors—including a growing number of academics, civic leaders, and public intellectuals calling for greater respect for and inclusion of the cultural backgrounds of immigrants; the growing political power of immigrant groups, particularly in large northeastern and midwestern cities; and the perception that aggressive assimilationist polices in the World War I years had failed to Americanize adult students—school leaders began seeking strategies for making the public school curriculum at least somewhat more inclusive. On both the K–12 and adult levels, these steps were small and often merely symbolic, but they pointed in the direction of larger changes to come.

As chapter 3 demonstrates, these pluralistic ideas clearly resonated with a growing number of Americans, particularly members of the vast and vibrant immigrant communities in the nation's great industrial cities. Inspired by what they believed were the most positive aspects of the Americanization movement, and supported by people espousing a more cosmopolitan vision of the country, leaders of the immigrant communities fashioned a new and broader approach to Americanization. This position, which I call patriotic pluralism, enabled them to become proud, knowledgeable, and committed American citizens while simultaneously asserting their distinct cultural and religious backgrounds. In promoting this perspective they helped to make the United States a more democratic and inclusive nation.[263]

3

AMERICANIZATION AND THE FOREIGN LANGUAGE PRESS, 1890–1930

Throughout the first three decades of the twentieth century, public schools in the United States were active and enthusiastic agents of the assimilationist form of Americanization. But each day when school was dismissed and the children of immigrants poured out of their classrooms, or when adult students headed home after their evening courses, they stepped into a very different educational milieu. In this era, virtually every great industrial city in the Northeast and Midwest had sprawling "colonies" of immigrants, largely composed of people from similar cultural and religious backgrounds. These neighborhoods were places where the languages, foods, holidays, and heroes of the Old World abounded. If the public schools were agencies of assimilation, then immigrant neighborhoods were the embodiment of cultural pluralism and ethnic diversity.

Both implicitly and explicitly, life in immigrant neighborhoods imparted some very different lessons than those taught in public schools about the character and composition of the United States. Whereas the schools either denigrated or ignored the cultural backgrounds of immigrants, in these neighborhoods the Old World cultures were vibrant and powerful, influencing the ideas, attitudes, and behaviors of countless numbers of people. The immigrant neighborhoods were home to a vast array of educational institutions other than public schools—churches, synagogues, theaters, fraternal organizations, political clubs, athletic societies, and musical groups, to name just a few. All these organizations and groups helped perpetuate the cultures that European immigrants brought with them across the Atlantic. Yet many of them also aided immigrants in adjusting to life in the New World, so much so that they often played an important role in Americanization.[1]

In an insightful essay, historian Maxine Seller argues that community-based organizations and groups in immigrant neighborhoods were so influential with regard to Americanization that, to a large extent, these newcomers Americanized themselves. She states, "Immigrant communities succeeded where American educators failed because they provided education planned and executed by immigrants themselves." Community-based organizations and institutions prepared immigrants for naturalization and the vicissitudes of American life using the immigrants' own languages, employed educational methods that "did not violate immigrant cultural traditions," and offered curricula that appealed to broader interests than simple assimilation. Of these organizations and institutions, "the single most influential educational force in the immigrant community, more influential than the Church, the labor movement, or any single organization was the foreign language press."[2]

The foreign language press *was* an enormous cultural and educational presence in immigrant communities during the first part of the twentieth century.[3] The number and reach of these papers were large and impressive. Joshua Fishman reports that in 1920 the United States had 140 daily foreign language newspapers with a total circulation of almost 2 million; 594 weeklies with over 3.6 million in circulation; and 109 monthlies with a circulation of 756,000. In addition, 111 newspapers and periodicals were printed in both English and a foreign language, with a total circulation of 422,000.[4] Virtually every ethnic group in the U.S.—even small ones such as Bulgarians and Latvians—published newspapers in their native languages.[5]

These papers linked the Old World to the New. They provided reports from the homeland, news about compatriots locally and throughout the United States, and announcements of cultural and religious events of interest to the community. But they also were a major source of information about how to negotiate and adapt to American life and culture. This latter function led many, if not most, foreign language newspapers to become bridges to Americanization, especially for adult immigrants.[6] As Edward H. Bierstadt, a particularly thoughtful commentator on Americanization in this era, declared in 1922, the foreign language press "is not only the most valuable medium of interpretation between the native and the foreign born, but it is practically the only medium."[7] Harry A. Lipsky, a member of the Chicago Board of Education, put it this way: "For all purposes, the foreign-language press is the one sympathetic, intelligent, and most trusted medium through which the foreign-born, old and young, may be approached and through which Americanization work can best be carried on."[8]

The newspapers did not carry out this educational function in isolation from the demands and pressures of the larger American cultural and political context. After the outbreak of World War I in 1914, local and national leaders of Americanization education campaigns recognized the power and influence of the foreign language press and actively recruited editors and publishers of these newspapers to become involved in efforts to unify the country.[9] As noted in the previous chapter, well into the 1920s, Americanizers in Detroit worked cordially with editors of a number of foreign language newspapers in support of Americanization education in the Motor City.[10]

Americanizers in Chicago also saw the editors of local foreign language newspapers as important contributors to their efforts. In 1919, for example, editors of several leading foreign language newspapers in the city joined with representatives of the Chicago Association of Commerce and the Board of Education to create a mutually agreed-upon definition of Americanization that called for "the development and possession by the individual, of intelligent pride, loyalty, love, and devotion to the government, institutions, and ideals of the United States, and the practical identification of his interests with those of the nation and its people."[11] One year later, a report on Chicago's Americanization campaign applauded the continuing contribution the foreign language press made to this initiative.[12] Early in 1922, the editor of Chicago's *Greek Star* also praised the foreign language press for its "noble service in acquainting new arrivals with American ideals." He added that most of the immigrant newspapers in the city had "proved valuable aids in the Americanization campaign."[13] Foreign language newspapers also played an important role in Americanization efforts in Cleveland and in other cities with large immigrant populations.[14] Yet as important as foreign language newspapers were in Americanization efforts, few historians of education have examined what these papers said about this process.[15]

Focusing on the 1890s to the late 1920s, this chapter investigates how newspapers, primarily those in the Chicago Foreign Language Press Survey (CFLPS), dealt with issues of Americanization, specifically with questions about assimilation, cultural pluralism, and amalgamation. The chapter argues that the relationship between the Americanization education movement and the editors and writers of foreign language newspapers was fluid and dynamic, rather than fixed and oppositional. Stating this does not imply that the power relationship between Americanizers and the immigrants was equally balanced. Clearly, native-born Americanizers set the educational agenda, specifically by determining the content of the Americanization curriculum—learning English; knowing important facts and ideas about American history; embracing American democratic ideals, values, attitudes, and behaviors; and becoming loyal American citizens. Nevertheless, editors and journalists from the foreign language press had considerable latitude in how they responded to, interpreted, and altered that curriculum in their papers.[16] More important, they determined how to teach key elements of the curriculum to their readers. In modern theoretical language, these writers co-constructed the Americanization curriculum.

In a number of ways, these newspaper editors and writers approached the process of Americanization like the best of progressive educators: they knew their communities well, literally spoke their language, employed culturally relevant examples and stories, focused on issues that were of immediate concern to their readers, and used this knowledge to educate their readers about how to become Americans and thrive in the United States. In the process of becoming "Americanization educators," perhaps the most important steps these journalists took were to directly challenge the ethnic nationalism of racial restriction and to tacitly and overtly reject all three of the extant civic nationalist options for participation in American life and culture—assimilation, cultural pluralism, and amalgamation. Instead, without explicitly naming it as such, they offered a new position that I refer to as patriotic pluralism.

Patriotic pluralism is akin to cultural pluralism, but with one major difference: the degree of emotional attachment that immigrants had for the United States and its defining democratic ideals. In his classic work *Culture and Democracy in the United States*, Horace Kallen described cultural pluralism as a mixture of immigrants' adhering to the common political ideals of this country while simultaneously maintaining their ethnic cultures. But due to the largely abstract and "external" character of American democratic ideals, Kallen argued, the spiritual life of immigrants, or, as he put it, their "intensest emotional life" would mainly come from their ethnic groups and their ancient traditions, *not* their Americanism. As the philosopher Michael Walzer explains, according to Kallen, immigrants would *not* get "the greatest part of their happiness from their [American] citizenship."[17] This chapter, by contrast, argues that Kallen seriously underestimated the degree of emotional attachment the immigrants had for the United States and American democracy. As articulated by the journalists writing in the Chicago Foreign Language Press Survey, immigrants avowed a deep devotion to the United States that was every bit as intense as their commitment to retaining aspects of their cultural and religious backgrounds.[18] Rather than seeing this marriage of patriotism and pluralism as contradictory, editors and writers in the CFLPS believed it represented the essence of American democracy.

The development and dissemination of this position rested on how well these newspapers educated their readers about the common ideals that united all Americans without underplaying how these ideals protected their right to be different. Like the public schoolteachers and adult educators discussed in the previous chapter, the foreign language press promoted devotion to the United States and American democracy, a willingness to defend the country in times of peril, respect for the law, civility in political discourse, active participation in political life, a commitment to equality, and respect for diverse points of view. But unlike most native-born Americanizers, the editors and writers of CFLPS newspapers notably emphasized the last two of these ideals, which enabled them to assert the immigrants' fundamental equality when confronting racial restrictionists and to proclaim the cosmopolitanism of the United States in response to the cultural chauvinism of the "100 percent Americans." The CFLPS newspapers did this while focusing on the same elements of Americanization education that public school leaders stressed, specifically learning English, understanding American history, and becoming knowledgeable citizens. But in every case, the CFLPS writers added a distinctive, pluralistic dimension to their teachings, a dimension that vitalized and revised Americanization education and, ultimately, America itself.

Language Issues

In October 1904, the Greek *Star*, sounding very much like the great nineteenth-century common-school reformer Horace Mann, proclaimed, "The Public Schools are the Bulwark of the Nation." Such praise for public schooling was common in many of the foreign language newspapers in Chicago in the late nineteenth and early twentieth centuries.[19]

In September 1907, *Dziennik Ludowy* (the *People's Daily*), a left-wing Polish newspaper, echoed these sentiments, stating, "The children of Polish workers should attend the public schools, schools from which they may benefit a great deal!"[20] In 1914, reacting to Edward A. Ross's accusation of widespread illiteracy among new immigrants, *L'Italia* declared, "We have a cure for illiteracy in our public schools, and in every immigrant family there is a passionate desire to embrace that opportunity."[21] Five years later, a journalist writing in the *Jewish Daily Courier* summed up these sentiments in the first of two articles both entitled "The Great and Free American Public School." Applauding the Chicago Public Schools (CPS) for teaching a common culture to all its students, the author declared, "[The public school] has taken the children of various groups, and has shown them those truths upon which they can all unite."[22]

One of the most fascinating aspects of the strong support that many immigrant editors and journalists gave to public education was their implicit endorsement of the Anglo-centric public school curriculum. This was particularly surprising because many of the immigrants who came to the United States in this era (e.g., Czechs, Greeks, Poles, Slovaks, Slovenians, and Ukrainians) emigrated from empires that had attempted, often ruthlessly, to replace local, regional, and national vernaculars with the language of the imperial regime.[23] As one Polish journalist explained, in Europe "sadistic persecutors closed parochial schools, smashed Polish presses, or tore out tongues because they had uttered Polish words."[24]

Why, then, did immigrants who had fought fiercely to preserve their native languages in Europe not agitate with equal passion against the generally monolingual policies of public schools in the United States?[25] Why didn't the public-school language policies provoke "school wars" similar to those over religious issues in the nineteenth century? The answers to these questions are numerous, including: the pragmatic recognition among immigrants that knowing English was vital to success in the United States, the peculiarities of language politics in cities with large German populations, and the ways in which immigrants used the freedoms of American democracy to try to maintain their cultural and linguistic heritage.[26]

There is abundant evidence that the foreign language newspapers in Chicago took a pragmatic perspective on language issues. Virtually all of the editors and journalists represented in the CFLPS argued that to succeed in the United States, children of immigrants and adult immigrants *had* to learn English. Typical was a 1911 editorial in *Narod Polski (Polish Nation)*, the official publication of the Polish Roman Catholic Union of America, one of the oldest Polish fraternal associations in the country, which stated, "All Poles are only newcomers here, the English language is necessary here outside of the home, therefore, our children attend public schools in order to learn as much English as is necessary for making a living."[27] A 1913 article in *Lietuva (Lithuania)* simply declared, "For Lithuanians, as well as other national groups, it is absolutely necessary that English be learned."[28] After noting approvingly the large number of foreign-born children attending public schools, a 1921 article in the Greek newspaper *Saloniki* turned to the problem of adults and declared, "It is the *duty* of every *immigrant* to learn English, in order to live more harmoniously in the community [emphases in the original]."[29]

As the article from *Saloniki* indicates, getting adults to be proficient in English was as important to immigrant leaders as having young people become fluent in the language. Beginning in the 1890s, in October or early November when evening school sessions began, papers throughout Chicago's immigrant communities ran editorials and articles urging readers to enroll in English classes. A 1910 piece in the Polish newspaper *Dziennik Zwiazkowy (Alliance Daily)*, the official voice of the Polish National Alliance (PNA), urged its readers to attend public-school evening classes to become "adept in the use of the English language, which is so necessary in this country."[30] Writing twelve years later, a commentator in a Serbian newspaper was even more blunt, telling readers, "There are no prospects for you until you learn the English language."[31] Such appeals were constant from 1890 to 1930, with no dramatic spike in number in World War I or the immediate postwar period, the time when Americanization campaigns were at their most aggressive.[32]

While the newspapers clearly encouraged their readers to learn English, this stance did not mean that they were willing to give up their native languages in the process. Indeed, many of the same articles and editorials that urged immigrants to learn English also called on them to preserve the languages of their respective motherlands. For example, immediately after encouraging Poles to learn English, the author of the 1911 article from *Narod Polski* quoted above elaborated: "This does not prevent the parents from teaching their children the Polish language, correcting them whenever they speak it improperly and encouraging them to speak it correctly."[33]

From this perspective, the great issue facing the immigrants was not whether they should learn English—virtually all agreed they must—but rather how to retain their native languages in the New World. Until 1917–1918, the immigrants had four main options for native language maintenance: dual-language programs in public elementary schools; the inclusion of foreign languages as electives in public high schools; dual-language instruction in parochial schools; and afternoon and weekend cultural and linguistic "heritage" schools.

If the desire to learn English provides evidence of the immigrants' pragmatism, the struggle over teaching foreign languages in public elementary schools demonstrates the importance of ethnic politics. As discussed in previous chapters, following America's entry into World War I, school boards across the country eliminated the first of these options for maintaining immigrants' native languages, dual-language programs in public school systems. In Chicago, one of the most interesting aspects of the campaign to end German classes in public elementary schools was the degree to which some of the largest and most important immigrant groups *supported* the elimination of this program in the CPS. As historian Jonathan Zimmerman argues, "Anglos threw the first punches, to be sure, but an enormous range of ethnic groups helped deliver the final blows."[34]

A confluence of international and local politics encouraged prominent immigrant groups to join with "100 percent" Americanizers in opposing the long-running German language program in the CPS. Czechs and Poles led this effort, in part because both groups had suffered from Germanization efforts in their homelands.[35] As early as July 1890, for example, the Czech newspaper *Svornost* sharply rebuked Germans who defended the German language program in Chicago, using a quote from no less an authority than Chancellor Otto von Bismarck to make its point. According to *Svornost*, after receiving a petition from Alsatians requesting that French be taught in their elementary schools, Bismarck replied, "The public schools must teach only one language—that is the language of the nation. To introduce into it another language would be against all reasonable educational principles." *Svornost* endorsed these "reasonable educational principles" and demanded that English be the *only* language of instruction in Chicago's elementary schools.[36]

In addition to these international factors, local ethnic and educational politics inflamed the controversy as well. Much of the anger registered by *Svornost* was due to staunch German opposition to requests for Czech dual-language programs in Chicago public schools. Consequently, the editor of *Svornost* reasoned that if not every immigrant group in Chicago had the right to establish dual-language elementary schools, then none should have that right.[37] Despite such arguments, over the next decade the substantial political power of Chicago's German community enabled Chicago's German language program not merely to survive but to thrive.[38] At the same time, Germans continued to adamantly oppose expanding the program to include other languages. In 1900, for example, German politicians succeeded in stopping Chicago's Czechs, Italians, and Poles from establishing dual-language programs in schools in their neighborhoods.[39]

Over the next fifteen years, controversy about German as a language of instruction on the elementary level continued, as did German opposition to demands of other ethnic groups for equal treatment. Not surprisingly, anger about the German program broadened and deepened, especially as the outbreak of war in Europe stirred up ancient hatreds and animosities.[40] In June 1915, for example, the main Czech newspaper in Chicago, *Denni Hlasatel* (the *Daily Herald*) published a scathing attack on German influence in Chicago public schools declaring, ". . . we Bohemians resent the teaching of the language of a nation that always has been our chief oppressor."[41] Four months later, as prominent politicians campaigned against "the hyphen," the paper editorialized that the only hyphenated group that posed a threat to the country was the Germans.[42]

After the United States entered the war and anti-German sentiment quickened, a number of immigrant groups in Chicago saw a golden opportunity to purge German influence in the CPS generally and to abolish the German language program specifically. Within days of Wilson's declaration of war, for example, Poles lashed out at a widely used spelling book that allegedly praised Kaiser Wilhelm. Eventually, Czechs, Greeks, and Italians called for ripping the offending page from the book and replacing it with pictures of Washington, Lincoln, or the American flag.[43] At the same time, Czechs and Poles campaigned to get the school board members to rename Bismarck School. When the board failed to respond to this demand, Czech and Polish newspapers vented their anger at Mayor William Hale Thompson, whom the papers noted had appointed the supposedly pro-German board members in the first place.[44]

The culmination of these anti-German efforts came in August 31, 1917, at a school board meeting where members passed a resolution introduced by Anton Czarnecki, a Polish American, that abolished the dual-language German elementary school program in the CPS. The resolution declared that no foreign language should be taught in elementary schools and that instead "the entire regular daily sessions be devoted by the pupils toward becoming proficient in our own American nation's language, history and citizenship."[45] This vote ended more than half a century of German language instruction in Chicago's public schools.

The complex nature of immigrant politics about the issue of German language instruction in public schools was not confined to Chicago. In Cleveland, opposition to the use of German as a language of instruction in elementary schools was long-standing. The school board curtailed the program in 1906, again in 1914, and finally ended all German language instruction in elementary schools in 1918. At the 1914 meeting where the school board considered this issue, Polish, Czech, and Greek speakers all announced their opposition to German in the public schools, in some cases, in terms quite similar to those that critics used in Chicago.[46]

Ironically, at roughly the same time that school boards across the nation were ending dual-language programs in public elementary schools, prospects for including immigrants' languages in public high schools were improving. In Chicago, the great breakthrough on this policy came during the administration of Superintendent Ella Flagg Young (1909–1915). Young had studied with John Dewey at the University of Chicago and, like her mentor, was sympathetic to ideas about bringing aspects of immigrant culture into public school curricula.[47] In 1911, she succeeded in getting the Chicago Board of Education to allow *high schools* throughout the city to teach such languages as Czech, Danish, Hebrew, Lithuanian, Norwegian, Polish, and Swedish, so long as sufficient numbers of students signed up for the courses.[48] Immigrant groups were jubilant. In February 1912, for example, Young described this new program to a large audience of Czechs who, according to *Denni Hlasatel*, regularly interrupted her "excellent speech" with "storms of applause."[49] Over the next two decades, including the period of intense agitation about Americanization, various high schools in Chicago continued to offer these languages as electives.[50] In some cases, students in these classes formed after-school clubs supported by the schools that promoted understanding of the Old World culture associated with the language community.[51]

Why didn't these courses provoke the same kind of vehement opposition as the elementary programs? One reason is that high schools had been offering modern languages for decades, and, as a consequence, these new courses easily fit into the traditional high school curriculum. Instead of taking French or Spanish, some students now could choose Czech or Polish. Unlike the bilingual schools, which taught various subjects in the children's native language, these high school programs focused on teaching second languages and introducing students to aspects of the culture of the country where the language was spoken. A second reason is that only a small number of young people attended high schools at this time, and thus access to these courses was limited. In 1910, nearly every elementary-school-aged child was enrolled in school in the United States, but fewer than 15 percent of Americans aged fourteen to seventeen were in high schools. A decade later, high schools enrolled fewer than a third of the age group.[52] Given the small number of high school students generally and the even smaller subset of these students opting for foreign language courses, the critical mass for controversy was never reached. Finally, these courses did not challenge the dominance of English or, as with the German programs, claim parity with English in the public schools. For public schools these high school programs were a win-win opportunity. They cost little educationally or financially, but they paid off in a big way politically. They demonstrated that school leaders were sensitive to the concerns of their constituents. Similarly, leaders of various ethnic communities saw these programs as important tools for helping their children retain aspects of their cultural background and as powerful symbols of their group's growing political clout in the community.[53]

An article that appeared at the start of the 1914–1915 school year in *Dziennik Zwiazkowy,* a staunchly nationalistic, secular paper, described the cultural problems facing Polish students in public schools and the hopes Polish leaders had for the high school language courses. While recognizing the legitimacy of public school Americanization programs, the writer worried that the process "washes every child with the same wave, washes away all of the child's characteristic attributes, and makes a typical American out of him." Given that situation, the author praised the fact that some Chicago high schools now were offering Polish as an elective. But the article ended on a sour note, signaling that the high hopes many immigrant leaders had for these courses might have been in vain. Polish high school students, the author noted, were not signing up for classes in the Polish language, a situation that was simply "shameful."[54]

The Poles were not alone in facing this problem. As Zimmerman has shown, none of the high school courses in immigrant languages that school boards approved before, during, or after World War I realized the great hopes of their supporters. Enrollments in these classes in Chicago and other cities with large immigrant communities remained consistently low. For example, six years after New York City added Hebrew as an elective, only 2,000 students, fewer than 2 percent of all the Jewish students in New York high schools, enrolled in these classes. Given such dismal results, it is not surprising that from the 1910s to the 1930s many foreign language newspapers expressed anger and frustration over this situation and repeatedly urged parents to register their students in these classes. For the most part, these pleas went unanswered.[55]

Zimmerman offers an astute insight into why the children of immigrants stayed away from these classes. Beyond the obvious power of American Anglo-centric culture and the desire of many of these young people to be as American as possible, Zimmerman argues that differences between the languages taught in school and the ones spoken at home were crucial in this trend. The majority of the newcomers were poor, many had been peasants, and most of them spoke local or regional dialects from places like Calabria or Galicia, not the sophisticated vernacular spoken by educated urban elites. Moreover, when these immigrants came to America, they quickly added English words to their native dialects, thus creating a patois that was even further removed from the literary language of their homelands. Unfortunately for supporters of these new high school courses, students who enrolled in them found themselves learning a version of their "native" language that was quite different from what they heard around the dinner table. The result was that these courses became battlegrounds over culture and social class *within* the immigrant communities. In addition, rather than bringing the children of immigrants closer to their parents, as activists such as Jane Addams had argued, these classes often deepened tensions within the home. Just as learning English in public schools distanced the children of immigrants from their non-English-speaking parents, so learning their homeland's *literary* language in school widened the gap between the first and second generation, but in a particularly poignant way.[56]

At the same time that immigrants were wrestling with these issues in public schools, they were also struggling with similar questions about language and Americanization in dual-language parochial schools, the third educational option immigrants used to preserve their language and culture in America. Although most of the children from eastern and southern European immigrant families attended public schools, sizable numbers of children—a majority among certain groups—attended parochial schools, many of which offered dual-language programs.[57] These dual-language schools operated mainly on the elementary level and had three important goals: inculcating religious doctrine, maintaining the language and culture of the homeland, and preparing students for life in the United States.[58]

The problem for Catholic schools, which were by far the majority of these kinds of institutions, was that propagating the faith was the only goal that everyone involved in Catholic education fully shared and endorsed. The other two—retaining ethnic languages and culture and inculcating aspects of Americanization—were highly problematic, in large part because of deep disagreements among church leaders about the nature of Catholic education in the United States. These disagreements were part of the broader debate about whether the Catholic church in the United States would be, in Bishop John Ireland's words, an "American Church" or a collection of distinctly ethnic Catholic churches.[59] In education, church and lay leaders weighed the relative merits of two models of Catholic schooling, what historian Timothy Walch calls "American Catholic schools" that were modeled after public schools in their focus on assimilation or "ethnic parish schools" that were often bilingual and bicultural institutions.[60]

Between 1890 and 1930, dual-language, ethnic parish schools flourished for some large immigrant groups in cities such as Chicago, Cleveland, and Detroit. For example, during the first few decades of the twentieth century, a large majority of Polish children in Chicago attended Polish-language Catholic schools.[61] In addition to the Poles, in Chicago, sizable numbers of Czechs, Lithuanians, Hungarians, Slovaks, and Slovenes also attended dual-language Catholic schools.[62] Similarly, in Cleveland in 1916, thirty of the fifty-two Catholic schools in the city offered dual-language programs in Polish, German, Czech, Slovak, Slovenian, and Hungarian. At the same time, the Lutheran church in Cleveland supported a number of dual-language German and Slovak parochial schools.[63] Detroit also had a substantial number of Polish parochial schools.[64]

Popular as these schools were, however, they often came under fire from critics both within and outside the Catholic community. Prior to

World War I, newspapers serving several of Chicago's immigrant communities criticized the educational quality of these schools, particularly their insufficient instruction in English and other subjects necessary for fully participating in American life. In 1905, for example, *Lietuva* condemned the "Polanized priests" who ran schools in Lithuanian neighborhoods, arguing that their educational priorities (teaching prayer and catechism) meant that "not enough time is spent on general education such as English grammar, Lithuanian grammar, American history, geography, and other important educational subjects, which form a very good foundation for those who are planning to attend high school and university."[65] In September 1911, the editor of *Dziennik Zwiazkowy* also blasted the clergy who, "for its own selfish advantage, would like to force Polish children into the parochial schools even if these schools are inferior [to public schools]."[66]

As concerns about national unity and assimilation grew during the 1910s, opponents of immigration often targeted dual-language parochial schools as breeding places for un-Americanism. Writing in December 1913, Edward A. Ross, for example, decried parish schools for segregating students by nationality and for their teaching of the "mother tongue" almost to the exclusion of teaching English. As a consequence of these policies, he argued, "American-born children are leaving school not only unable to read and write English, but scarcely able to speak it. The foreign-speech school, while it binds the young to their parents, to their people, and to the old country, cuts them off from America." Due to the prevalence of such institutions, Ross concluded, "those optimists who imagine that assimilation of the immigrant is proceeding unhindered are living in a fool's paradise."[67]

With the outbreak of World War I, condemnation of these schools became sharper and more frequent. Although criticism initially focused on German Lutheran schools, by 1918 some states began promoting English-only policies for all parochial schools.[68] Responding to these developments, in February 1919 *Narod Polski* denounced Americanizers who, it claimed, were trying to impose a "Prussian system of denationalization" on immigrants. Rhetorically asking what had happened to America's commitment to freedom and justice, the paper declared, "If American chauvinists were allowed to throw the Polish language out of parochial schools, then tomorrow they will be allowed to throw out from these same schools the Catholic religion." The paper insisted that parents who send their children to these schools want them "to be equal to Americans in everything, fulfilling all duties in patriotism and speech." The article concluded, "We comprehend Americanization in this manner; teach everyone to write, read, and speak the English language; acquaint everyone with the statutes, principles and ideals of the United States; demand from all respect of laws and the sacrificing of one's personal self for his country in time of need, but along with all of this not to tear away by force . . . any other language which he has a knowledge of, or wishes to acquire."[69]

Despite such powerful sentiments and the fervent efforts by some groups to maintain dual-language parochial schools, by the 1920s these programs were on the wane. Even the 1923 U.S. Supreme Court decision *Meyer v. Nebraska*, which affirmed constitutional protection for these schools, did not halt the gradual disappearance of many of them. Two main factors contributed to this decline. First, in the case of Catholics, the rise to power in the 1910s and 1920s of a group of American-born bishops who favored assimilation and oversaw most of the large, urban dioceses in the United States marked a major turning point for the ethnic parish schools. Second was the declining enthusiasm for such schools among second- and third-generation immigrants.[70]

Typical of the American-born bishops was George Mundelein of Chicago, who, as one historian observed, "aligned himself with the '100 percent' attitude toward ethnic assimilation in America" and in 1916 mandated that English be the primary language of instruction in all Catholic schools in the Windy City.[71] Despite strong resistance from some immigrants, most notably Poles, this policy took root in Chicago and urban dioceses as well.[72]

The second factor affecting the policies of Catholic (and non-Catholic) dual-language schools was that American-born children from various immigrant groups were becoming less enthusiastic about such education. Concerned about the quality of these schools vis-à-vis English-only parochial schools or local public schools, these second- and third-generation Americans were far less enthusiastic about this option than were their parents or grandparents.[73] As a 1920 article in a left-wing Polish newspaper in Baltimore argued, the reason that Poles were not leaders in "any field of intellectual work" was their commitment to the dual-language "parochial school which does not encourage further study, but on the contrary blocks a child's mind, deprives him of learning, trains factory slaves *a priori* condemned to become prey of capitalistic demagoguery."[74]

Supporters of these schools angrily denounced such arguments, and in some neighborhoods dual-language parochial schools continued to thrive throughout the 1920s.[75] But disenchantment with these schools was rising. As Walch notes, many members of "the new generation did not object to an Americanized curriculum; in fact they welcomed it." Facing such pressure and the mandates of assimilationist bishops, Catholic educators gradually revised the mission of their dual-language schools to fit the American context. Other groups, such as Lutherans, did the same. Practically, this meant relegating the teaching of homeland languages to religious classes or even to extracurricular activities. Eventually, some of these schools simply eliminated their second-language programs altogether.[76]

These developments were important factors in the creation of weekday after-school programs, weekend schools, and summer educational offerings, the fourth approach used by immigrant groups to pass on their culture and language. This approach underlines the distinct way that many immigrants dealt with Americanization. Groups such as the Czechs, Greeks, and Jews that sent large numbers of children to public schools pioneered these programs, seeing them as especially crucial for maintaining and inculcating their cultural and religious heritage into the younger generation.

As early as 1879, for example, leaders of Chicago's Jewish community established a Hebrew school specifically for these purposes.[77] In the twentieth century, such schools became a fixture of Jewish education, particularly in the fast-growing Conservative and Reform movements that eventually dominated Jewish life in the United States.[78] Similarly, in 1905, the editor of the Greek *Star* called for establishing after-school programs to enhance the education that young Greeks were getting in public schools. The editor explained, "The Greek-American youth with his racial and religious traditions and with his American education crowned with his knowledge of the Greek language will be a model citizen of this great Republic."[79]

The Czech community in Chicago also ran Saturday and Sunday programs inspired by the same ideas.[80] Writing in 1917, amid the wartime Americanization campaign, the editor of *Denni Hlasatel* echoed the *Star*, arguing that "Czech schools" complemented and enhanced the education provided by public schools. In doing so, they produced better Americans, because their students would introduce the finest aspects of Czech culture into American life. As the editor explained, "Yes, we want to become good Americans; we want to show our gratitude for the kind reception accorded to us; we want to show our appreciation by offering the best within the abilities of our people. . . . The Czech school is the link between us and this country."[81] One year later, a lengthy editorial in the *Jewish Daily Courier* nicely captured the idea that retaining vital aspects of the immigrants' Old World experience enhanced American life. Drawing on the more culturally pluralistic interpretation of Zangwill's famous metaphor, the editor declared, "The powerful flame under the melting pot brings out the finer characteristics in all the nationalities that live in America, and the interplay of the different character traits—each nationality manifesting in its own way its love for America—makes the whole very interesting."[82]

This quote offers a glimpse into a central idea of patriotic pluralism. Groups that sent large percentages of their children to public schools and generally accepted the assimilationist agenda of that institution nevertheless believed that their communities had to provide additional "cultural" education for their children to ensure the survival and cohesion of their group in the United States. Beyond seeing such education as necessary for preserving their languages and traditions, community leaders also saw these afternoon and weekend heritage schools as providing an important value-added component to American culture by enabling their children to proudly bring knowledge of the art, culture, and wisdom of their group into the national mainstream.

While Czechs, Jews, and Greeks were the most enthusiastic users of afternoon and weekend language and culture schools, other groups, including Croatians, Hungarians, Poles, Russians, Serbs, and Ukrainians, also established these kinds of institutions wherever communities were large enough to sustain them.[83] For example, as early as 1888, the Ukrainian community of Shenandoah, Pennsylvania, founded a "heritage school" to keep Old World traditions and the language alive. Like other immigrant groups, the Ukrainians believed that such schools would complement what their children learned in public schools. In 1895, after noting "America's public schools are the most important institution in the nation," the editor of the Ukrainian newspaper *Svoboda (Freedom)* urged parents to send their children to American schools but also to enroll them in

Ukrainian heritage schools.[84] Almost three decades later, Chicago's *Russkii Viestnik* (*Russian Herald*) made a similar argument when promoting the Russian schools in the community.[85]

These programs were not necessarily the first choice for immigrant groups seeking to pass on their language and culture to the next generation, but they proved to be durable educational institutions. Part of the reason for their resiliency is that they had one distinct advantage over other programs, namely, that they faced little or no pressure from outside the community in determining the curriculum they would offer. Unlike second language initiatives in either elementary or secondary public schools, the afternoon and weekend schools were free from external oversight, particularly from the state. Additionally, unlike parochial day schools, they did not face pressures to reduce the language and cultural content they offered in order to be more competitive in the educational marketplace. Finally, they did not seek to displace public school programs.

In all, on the issue of language, the major immigrant groups in Chicago carefully walked a fine line between assimilation and cultural pluralism. Proud of their cultural and linguistic backgrounds, yet eager to play a full and equal role in American life, they sought to balance the necessity for learning English with their desire to pursue their own linguistic, cultural, and religious aspirations.[86] As sociologist Michael Olneck argues, these immigrants did not seek "to enlist [public] schools in programs of cultural and linguistic separatism or to use schools to challenge singularity of English as the national language. Rather, immigrants have largely sought to utilize the schools to acquire the skills, knowledge and linguistic repertoire necessary for successful integration into American society." He concludes, "When they have sought the incorporation of languages into the curriculum, this has been primarily to secure recognition of their legitimate place in the system of American ethnic groups or to provide them with the means to acquire cultural and linguistic repertoires to participate in that system."[87] Maintaining these positions amid the anti-German and subsequent anti–foreign language campaigns during World War I and the postwar years was difficult indeed. But the immigrants' varied language-maintenance strategies and, as the next sections show, the instruction provided by foreign language newspaper themselves enabled many of them to maintain important aspects of their Old World culture and impart them to their children.

Reading Themselves into American History

Nowhere can the attempt to balance immigrants' cultural backgrounds with Americanization be seen more clearly than in how Chicago's foreign language newspapers taught their readers about American history. Articles and editorials about topics in American history were common in most of these newspapers. The editors clearly believed that they had an obligation to educate their readers about the great events that had shaped the United States, the heroes and heroines involved in these events, and the ideals and values these people and the nation embodied. But teaching about these aspects of American history, writers in the foreign language press offered a distinctly different vision of the nation's growth and development from the one told in public schools and adult evening schools across the country. Unlike the traditional American history narrative that was dominated by the achievements of Anglo-Saxons, these newspapers offered a more expansive view of the country's past. They recognized that people from diverse backgrounds had made significant, at times pivotal, contributions to the nation. This new narrative did not seek to supplant the great figures of American history or to challenge the overwhelmingly positive tone of the national story. Rather the editors and writers for the foreign language press sought to supplement the traditional story with an expanded cast of characters.[88]

Notably, this new interpretation of American history gained strength during the period of aggressive Americanization, particularly during World War I, when huge numbers of immigrants took up arms to defend the country. Furthermore, in the midst of the postwar debate about limiting immigration, foreign language newspapers used this new interpretation to attack the racist views of restrictionists who portrayed the country's history and character as exclusively Anglo-Saxon or Nordic.

In teaching American history, foreign language newspapers followed a pattern set by many schoolteachers who used the annual cycle of patriotic holidays as occasions to introduce and explain major figures, events, and documents of the nation's past. Over the course of the year, the newspapers offered a broad historical overview of American history, including the voyages of exploration (Columbus Day), the colonial era (Thanksgiving), the Revolution and early national period (Washington's Birthday and the Fourth of July), the Civil War (Lincoln's Birthday and Decoration Day [Memorial Day]), and, after World War I, America's rise to international prominence (Armistice Day [Veterans Day]). In almost every case, the editors and writers of the foreign language press found ways to simultaneously teach American history and weave people from their homelands into this grand historical narrative.

As in schoolhouse histories, the story of the United States that the ethnic newspapers told began with the voyages of an Italian sailor. Not surprisingly, Italians used Columbus as evidence of their long-standing links to America and as a source of what at the time was called racial pride. Typical was a Columbus Day tribute written in October 1930 by an Italian journalist who waxed poetic about "the great Genoese, whose gigantic figure shines with an eternal light in the cycle of history and of whose example of mastery and glory our race can well be proud of."[89]

Italians were not alone in using this story to read themselves into American history, although other groups at times were less careful about the historical accuracy of their claims. In 1892, for example, during the celebration of the four hundredth anniversary of Columbus's first voyage, a prominent rabbi in New York offered a special prayer not only for the Great Mariner but also "for the two Jews" who supposedly "had accompanied him on his voyage."[90] Similarly, a Croatian writer suggested that sailors from the Dalmatian littoral had been part of Columbus's crew.[91] Other groups, such as Norwegians and Poles, also used the Columbus story to establish their participation in the voyages of exploration and discovery, but they did so by claiming that sailors from their homelands had preceded Columbus to the New World.[92]

Whether they were historically accurate or historically imaginative, these stories represented efforts by immigrants to revise American history in ways that legitimated their presence in the United States. The writers of these articles sought to demonstrate to their readers that people just like them had been important actors in the American story from its very beginning. In doing so they were challenging the traditional American historical narrative, which, after Columbus and the voyages of exploration, was largely the story of Britons and their American descendants. The writers for the foreign language press did not deny the enormous and lasting impact of British culture on American history and life, but they insisted that the development of the country was not the work of one group of people alone.

The Chicago foreign language press taught this lesson repeatedly in its articles and editorials. In their discussions of colonial America, for example, writers for the foreign language press described contributions made by people from their homelands as early as the 1600s. Not long after the Columbus Day celebrations in 1927, a Swedish newspaper reminded its readers that Swedes had been living in North America since 1638. Similarly, Jews celebrated the 1654 arrival in New Amsterdam of their coreligionists. Poles pointed to a prominent Polish family that settled in New Jersey in 1662. Germans commemorated the arrival in 1683 of a sizable number of immigrants from the Rhine Valley led by Franz Daniel Schaefer, known as Pastorius. They proudly noted that Schaefer, who helped found Germantown, Pennsylvania, was the first person in the colonies to publish a denunciation of slavery. Lithuanians claimed that in 1691 a Latvian prince led a group of Lithuanians to the New World, where they founded a colony on the Hudson River.[93]

Many of these stories stressed how much the newcomers resembled the Pilgrims, particularly their flight from Old World persecution to New World freedom. Consequently, of all the American holidays, Thanksgiving had particular resonance for immigrants, because they identified themselves so strongly with the story it embodied. Many of them saw themselves as modern-day Pilgrims who sought religious and cultural freedom in the New World. After describing a traditional Thanksgiving dinner, the editor of *Dziennik Zwiazkowy* declared, "This is a beautiful and inspiring custom."[94]

Throughout the year, the theme of finding freedom in the New World was common in many of the articles and editorials about American history. But it was especially prevalent in discussions of Washington and the American Revolution, and Lincoln and the Civil War. Across the nationalities, the newspapers in the CFLPS regularly ran stories explaining to their readers how central these men were in shaping America. In addition, many of the foreign language newspapers expanded on these traditional lessons in U.S. history by describing how people from their homelands had rallied to these American heroes in their time of need. Such stories underscored the idea that "foreigners" had stood shoulder to shoulder with native-born Americans in the bloody struggles to secure and expand freedom. When paired with discussions about the Fourth of July and Decoration Day (originally a holiday commemorating fallen soldiers in the Civil War), the stories about Washington and Lincoln became powerful tools for teaching American history and democratic values, stories that were simultaneously patriotic and pluralistic.

An editorial about George Washington that appeared in the Polish newspaper *Dziennik Chicagoski* (*Chicago Daily News*) on February 21, 1891, captures the spirit of these efforts. Noting the upcoming holiday, the editor explained that because "we wish to give our readers an opportunity to recall the heroic deeds of this great man, we are publishing his biography in today's issue." Apologetically, the editor added, "Because our space is limited, we will present only the most important facts concerning this great American." This brief biography of Washington (it was 2,000 words long!) described Washington as "the greatest of the world's great men" and covered major events in Washington's military and political careers.[95]

Regardless of which immigrant newspaper told Washington's story, one of the most important points that all of them made was that Washington and his fellow revolutionaries had challenged and defeated a powerful and overbearing king. Immigrants who had suffered under the tyranny of absolute monarchs in Europe saw Washington as an inspiration. Unlike native-born Americans, they had firsthand understanding of monarchy and aristocracy, a fact that made them appreciate Washington in a very personal way. As an editorial in the *Greek Star* explained, "Long before they take out their first naturalization papers, the great majority of our immigrants learn to know and to revere the name of George Washington. He is perhaps more real to them than to native Americans, for the immigrant can better appreciate all that the name of Washington stands for."[96] A writer for the Slovak paper *Osadne Hlasy* (*Immigrant Voices*) elaborated on this idea, noting the differences between conditions under "the Hapsburg reign of terror" and life "in this land of liberty." The writer reminded readers that Slovaks, like all Americans, owed a large debt to "the greatest man in history, George Washington, for we also enjoy the right earned for us by Washington, the right of freedom under the protection of the Stars and Stripes."[97]

In seeing Washington and other American revolutionaries as opponents of monarchical and aristocratic rule, writers for the foreign language press also taught their readers that American democracy rested on the belief that all men were created equal. Here again, the distinction between the Old World and the New was stark and clear for many immigrants. As World War I raged, the editor of *Dziennik Zwiazkowy* wrote on Washington's Birthday that Poles "should honor and love him who fought that today we might be free among the free and equal among the equal."[98]

The Fourth of July holiday provided editors and writers of the foreign language press with numerous opportunities to educate their readers about these ideas in ways that were easy for them to understand. Writing on July 3, 1911, for example, the editor of *Dziennik Zwiazkowy* discussed American independence by noting how "sacred and significant" that word was for Poles, because more than a century earlier their country had lost its independence "completely." The editor urged Poles "to take an active part in tomorrow's festivities, and [rejoice] in the fact that years ago the people of this hospitable land had overthrown the unwelcome lords and became masters of their own destiny."[99] The implicit hope in this editorial was that someday Poles, like colonial Americans, would overthrow the imperial regimes that had destroyed their country.

These writings reflect the development of a dynamic relationship between the demands of Americanizers that immigrants be knowledgeable about U.S. history and politics and the response of the newcomers who applied this content in ways that linked the New World to the Old. A superb example of this process can be found in the preamble of the constitution of a local chapter of the Polish National Alliance. Beginning with reference to the conquest and division of Poland in the late eighteenth century, the authors of the document describe how loyal Poles chose exile over "cruel bondage" and "sought refuge under the guidance of Kosciuszko and Pulaski in the free land of Washington and settling here found Hospitality and Equal Rights." The preamble referred to these immigrants as "valiant pilgrims" who created the Polish National Alliance "for the purpose of forming a more perfect union of the Polish people in this country." This is a deeply American document, steeped in the history and language of colonial America, the Revolution, and the U.S. Constitution. Yet it is also profoundly Polish, maintaining that among the goals of the PNA was "preserving the mother tongue as well as the national culture and customs" and working toward the restoration of a Polish state in Europe.[100]

When the United States entered World War I, the comparisons between the American War of Independence and the current struggle to free nations then under the heel of Germany and Austria-Hungary increasingly became a consistent part of Fourth of July editorials and articles. Typical was a 1918 editorial in *Lietuva*, which began with a detailed discussion of the Declaration of Independence that quoted a large section of the famous second paragraph. The editorial concluded with an appeal for an independent Lithuania that echoed the final words of the Declaration: "To achieve this end, we Lithuanians, along with other liberty-loving people, shall not begrudge either our fortunes or our lives, until the flame of liberty brightens the whole world."[101]

As noted earlier, not only did many foreign language newspapers in Chicago see the Revolution as an inspiring symbol of democracy's triumph over tyranny, a number of these papers also saw it as a struggle in which people from their homelands had played important roles. Frequently, writers for the foreign language newspapers used stories about Washington's Birthday and the Fourth of July to extol the exploits of their heroes of the Revolution, as well. As early as 1906, for example, *Dziennik Chicagoski* published a Washington's Birthday article noting that "[Poles] take pride in the knowledge that by the side of Washington at critical times, stood the Poles Thaddeus Kosciusko and Casimir Pulaski who fought staunchly for freedom."[102] Similarly, on July 3, 1911, *Dziennik Zwiazkowy* editorialized about the importance of Kosciusko to the American victory at Saratoga. The editor added, "The Poles should be proud of this country, for they have contributed toward its independence."[103] Lithuanians, who also claimed Kosciusko as one of their own, argued that along with him "many Lithuanians from New York fought side by side with the brave soldiers of George Washington against the tyrannical rule of the British king."[104]

German newspapers also frequently featured articles about their compatriots who had fought in the Revolutionary War. Following the explosion of anti-German sentiment after the United States entered World War I, these articles stressed the important contributions that Germans had made to the American cause during the Revolution and the long-standing loyalty Germans had shown to the United States. Writing on March 11, 1917, for example, the *Illinois Staats Zeitung (Illinois State Gazette)* pointed to such German participants in the Revolutionary War as Maria Ludwig (Molly Pitcher), the heroine of the Battle of Monmouth, and Baron von Steuben, who "raised the tattered Colonial soldiers to be useful fighters for the Independence of America." The author of the article declared, "Washington's letter of thanks to Baron Von Steuben is the best proof of how groundless and malicious the present critics are against the German Americans."[105] Years after the war, German papers continued to stress how important their compatriots had been to the early development of the United States.[106]

Even groups that did not have representatives from their homelands involved in the Revolutionary War found ways to either read themselves back into early American history or identify themselves with key events in that history. For example, Greeks described the United States as the flowering of Greek civilization. As early as 1904, Greek newspapers were reminding their readers that the roots of American democracy lie in ancient Greece.[107] As a 1919 article in *Saloniki* entitled "The Fourth of July Should Also Be a Greek Holiday" explained, "Liberty is the greatest gift of humanity—a gift of Greece. Ancient Greece fought for freedom of the people and her fight is now being carried on by America."[108] In 1927, Peter Lambros, editor of the *Greek Star*, summed up these ideas in an Armistice Day essay, declaring, "Notwithstanding the fact that it was Columbus, an Italian, who discovered America, this country is known as the true daughter of ancient Greece, for it has adopted and developed Greek civilization to the point of perfection."[109]

Not all of these articles and editorials were paeans to the perfection of the American democracy. The most telling criticisms of the early years of the American republic focused on the hypocrisy of the founders over the issue of slavery. As a 1919 article in *Dziennik Zwiazkowy* argued, despite their reverence for the Declaration of Independence, it was impossible for Poles to ignore the fact "that the Declaration was written by a slaveholder, Thomas Jefferson; that the general of the American armies who became president of the Constitutional Convention and first President, was a slaveholder, George Washington."[110] Two months later, an editorial in the *Jewish Daily Courier* simply described slavery as "the sin of the fathers of this country.."[111] The Russian newspaper *Rassviet (The Dawn)* described slavery as a "cancerous growth" that metastasized for over two centuries until Lincoln destroyed it.[112]

Lincoln's Birthday and Decoration Day provided the foreign language press with the opportunity to teach its readers about the Civil War, the ending of slavery, and the preservation of the Union. While editors and writers for the foreign language newspapers admired and respected Washington, they revered Lincoln. His humble beginnings, steadfastness amid adversity, opposition to slavery, and even the great sorrow that seemed etched in his face had powerful appeals to many immigrants.[113] In April 1890, for example, on the thirty-fifth anniversary of Lincoln's assassination, the German paper *Illinois Staats Zeitung* recalled the particular devotion Germans had for the martyred president. "The heart of the Germans beating most affectionately for Lincoln is," the author wrote, "at the same time, the best American heart."[114]

A long, detailed 1909 editorial about Lincoln's life that appeared in the Norwegian newspaper *Skandinaven* praised Washington, but noted that unlike the first president, Lincoln was more a man of people. "We can feel his great, warm heart had room for all the woe and sadness in the country; he attracts us; the blood surges through our veins more quickly as we behold his face, and our eyes grow moist as we watch the varied scenes of his life passing by."[115] Fifteen years later, an article in *Polonia* made a similar point, stating that "at the height of his glory, [Lincoln] remained a simple and common man. The poor and forsaken had a friend in him, and his whole life, from the time when his mother caressed him in her arms till his martyrdom, was and is a best example of [an] American citizen.[116]

Perhaps the most revealing evidence of the immigrants' reverence for Lincoln can be found in their desire to link him with their own histories and heroes. Seeking to teach their readers about Lincoln and the Civil War in terms they would easily understand, the writers for the foreign language press also found ways to make Lincoln one of their own. During the World War I years, for example, the Polish newspaper *Dziennik Zwiazkowy* repeatedly reminded its readers that Lincoln and Thaddeus Kosciusko were born on the same day. Following his exploits in the American Revolution, Kosciusko had led a failed rebellion against Russian domination in Poland, thus making him a hero to Poles on both sides of the Atlantic and providing a powerful link between their national aspirations in Europe and their emerging American identity.[117]

A 1917 writer in *Dziennik Zwiazkowy* further strengthened these Polish and American ties by explaining that, in his will, Kosciusko requested that the large tracts of land he received for his service in the Revolutionary War be used to help end slavery. "Kosciusko's executor was supposed to have been Jefferson," the author stated, "but actually, it was Abraham Lincoln, for it was he who rescued the Negroes from slavery, although it was necessary to spill blood to do so."[118]

Several days before the celebration of Lincoln's Birthday in 1924, Peter Lambros gave an extensive speech comparing Lincoln to the great Athenian leader Pericles. Focusing on the similarities between the "Gettysburg Address" and Pericles' famous "Funeral Oration," Lambros wrote, "Pericles believed that *demou kratos*, the rule of the people, was the noblest idea ever conceived by human thought. This noble idea was never again so well expressed until Lincoln said, "Government by the people shall not perish from the earth."[119] In a piece on Lincoln's Birthday celebration in 1918, a writer for the left-wing Jewish paper, the *Daily World*, praised Lincoln extensively and compared him to Moses, although the author also argued that as great as Lincoln was, he was no Karl Marx.[120] Russians compared him to Czar Alexander II, who freed the serfs and, like Lincoln, died at the hands of an assassin.[121]

A number of immigrant groups had sizable numbers of soldiers who served in the Civil War, thus making Decoration Day a very special day for them. As with the Revolution, immigrant groups were eager to demonstrate that their compatriots had rallied to the nation's defense during this vital struggle. For example, many of the Germans who migrated to the United States in the 1850s were ardent abolitionists, and an estimated 177,000 of them fought on the Union side during the war.[122] Chicago's German community regularly honored these Civil War veterans. In August 1900, for example, the *Illinois Staats Zeitung* reported on a huge celebration in which German American and other civic leaders paid tribute to a thousand German veterans of the Civil War whose comrades, one speaker declared, "gave their blood for the preservation of two great ideals"—the salvation of the Union and the abolition of slavery.[123]

Czechs also fought and died for the Union cause. Following Decoration Day ceremonies in 1891, *Svornost* declared, "When the first shots in defense of this Union of ours were heard, it was again the inflammable heart of the Slavic race, which answered and hundreds of Bohemians took up arms in defense of the freedom of this land."[124] Twenty-two years later, another Decoration Day article, this time in *Denni Hlasatel*, provided one of the best examples of how a foreign language newspaper used the commemoration of fallen soldiers in the Civil War to present a patriotic yet pluralistic perspective on American history: "Our hearts burn with ardent love for two countries," one speaker declaimed, "and thus we think with pride of those Bohemians who, in going to war, followed their patriotism as Americans, their American conviction."[125]

Other groups such as Jews, Poles, and Swedes, who claimed only small numbers of Civil War veterans, nevertheless pointed to them as evidence of their participation in this key juncture of American history. Jews, for example, extolled a company of Jewish soldiers that served in the mostly German Eighty-Second Regiment of Illinois Volunteers.[126] In a 1911 Decoration Day article, *Dziennik Zwiazkowy* declared, "There were not very many Poles at that time in America, but those who happened to be here contributed also their share of blood and hardship, to prove to the world Lincoln's saying, 'that a country founded on democratic principles is a reality not a Utopian dream.'"[127]

The entry of the United States into World War I provided the nation's vast immigrant communities the opportunity to *make* American history, rather than read themselves into it via their ancestors. Soon many immigrants themselves were among the honored fallen and were mourned nationally as Decoration Day changed to the more inclusive Memorial Day. As Nancy Gentile Ford states, "During the First World War, the U.S. government drafted into military service nearly half a million immigrants of forty-six different nationalities, creating an army with over 18 percent of its soldiers born in foreign countries." This percentage does not include the large number of second-generation "immigrants" who grew up in non-English-speaking homes. The American Expeditionary Force included large numbers of Armenians, Czechs, Greeks, Jews, Lithuanians, Poles, and Slovaks.[128] They acquitted themselves nobly and well. Writing in March 1919, even George Creel, who soon would become a leading advocate of immigration restriction, admitted that the records of the U.S. War Department show that "Americans of foreign birth and descent have written the story of their valor on every page."[129] Memorial Day gave all these groups the opportunity both to grieve for their "fallen warriors" and to strongly affirm their Americanism.[130]

Following the end of World War I, the commemoration of Armistice Day provided another opportunity to honor participants in World War I. Like Memorial Day, Armistice Day enabled immigrant groups that had few or no links to the Revolution or the Civil War to join those that did and to acknowledge the losses they all had suffered in defense of the country. In mid-November 1922, the *Chicago Tribune* reprinted an editorial from the *Greek Star* that echoed these themes. The editorial, which was probably written to commemorate Armistice Day, began by declaring, "Our love for Greece, the Mediterranean country where the warm sun first shone on us, is great indeed"; but it concluded by noting how glorious it was "to be able to say that we too may share in the pride of calling Washington, Lincoln, and Franklin our own!"[131]

This combination of devotion to the United States, pride in one's ethnic background, and the sense that these were not mutually exclusive categories is a defining feature of patriotic pluralism. When the editors, journalists, and other authors in the Chicago foreign language press taught their readers about American history, they were clearly doing so from both a patriotic and a pluralistic point of view. Like the history lessons in public schools and evening classes, these writers provided immigrants with vital knowledge about their adopted country, explained important political ideals that inspired the nation, and in general offered information that was both necessary and useful for understanding life in the United States.

But, unlike what was taught in public schools or evening classes, which rarely dwelled on how such material related to the immigrants, the foreign language newspapers presented these lessons in ways designed to resonate with their readers. Using readily understandable examples and stories of people like them who had helped make American history, these articles and editorials gave the immigrants a sense of ownership of these topics. These journalistic educators did their work so well that, by the 1920s, even groups that had no direct links to the early years of the nation began using the term "our" to describe the founding fathers.[132]

For the most part, these efforts were *not* a direct response to the great Americanization campaign during World War I and the immediate postwar years. Indeed many of the articles and editorials about American history predated the Americanization campaign by a decade or more, and they continued to be published on a regular basis throughout the 1920s, long after that campaign had wound down. Rather, these articles and editorials represented a new and distinct form of Americanization that immigrant leaders developed over several decades. Like native-born Americanizers, the editors and writers of Chicago's foreign language press sought to make immigrants familiar with the nation's past and its heroes. Similarly, they encouraged their readers to embrace the democratic political ideals upon which the nation was founded. But unlike native-born Americanizers, contributors to these newspapers rejected the idea that Anglo-Saxons alone had shaped the development of the United States. In modern terms, they saw the making of American history as a multicultural project in which individuals from a diverse array of backgrounds played important roles.

As Jonathan Zimmerman accurately has noted, this view of American history in which "each 'race' gets to have its heroes sung" did not challenge the triumphalist character of the country's conventional historical narrative. It simply enlarged the cast of characters.[133] Yet missing from that critique is a sense of the context in which these early advocates of a multi-cultural vision of American history operated. In this era, indeed well into the 1930s, these immigrants faced a relentless nativist campaign, which argued that people from eastern and southern Europe were members of inferior races and thus were congenitally incapable of becoming Americans. Moreover, nativists argued the newcomers had contributed nothing of importance to American history and culture; indeed, they threatened to destroy the nation.[134] Considered from within that context, the efforts by foreign language newspapers to acknowledge the contributions that immigrants like them had made to American history was, in its way, revolutionary. It was a direct attack on an ethnic nationalist interpretation of American history and the racist attitudes perpetuated by that interpretation. By demanding recognition of the diverse contributors to American history, writers in the foreign language press were advancing a vision in which one's commitment to democratic ideals, rather than one's racial background, was the defining feature of Americanism.

This effort was part of a larger process seeking to reshape the country along civic nationalist lines. As Henry Louis Gates wrote, upon discovering that one of his forefathers was a free black soldier who fought on the American side in the Revolutionary War, "Of course, it is perfectly irrelevant, in one sense, what one's ancestors did two centuries ago; but re-imagining our past, as Americans, can sometimes help us to re-imagine our future."[135] This was precisely what these writers for the foreign language press were trying to do.

American Citizens Proud of Their Cultural Heritage

In addition to learning English and becoming knowledgeable about American heroes and history, the other vital component of Americanization was naturalizing and embracing the democratic ideals that defined the nation. Of the three core aspects of Americanization, becoming an American citizen was perhaps the most emotionally charged, because it demanded an unmistakable break with an immigrant's past. Newcomers could learn English, but that did not stop them from speaking their home language or teaching that language to their children; and they could become knowledgeable in American history without forgetting their homeland's past. However, since the founding of the republic, immigrants wishing to become American citizens had to take an oath of allegiance explicitly renouncing their loyalty to any foreign power.[136] As significant and difficult as that step may have been for many immigrants, the leading foreign language newspapers in Chicago nevertheless strongly supported naturalization. Moreover, these papers routinely published editorials and articles that taught their readers about American democratic ideals and values, and, once the immigrants had naturalized, the papers strongly urged readers to play an active role in American politics.

As with the two other elements of Americanization supported by the newspapers, the foreign language press addressed this political dimension of Americanization in ways that were outwardly similar but inwardly varied from what native-born Americanizers might have expected. Perhaps more than with any other aspect of Americanization, the immigrant newspapers were determined to adapt to political life in the United States *on their own terms.* This meant reconciling their commitment to American citizenship with their devotion to their native land and culture, a challenging but ultimately successful project.

Part of the reason many of the newspapers were such staunch supporters of naturalization is that most immigrants who came to the United States between 1890 and 1918 originated from the great autocratic empires that ruled Europe at this time—Austria-Hungary, Germany, Ottoman Turkey, and Russia. In other words, many of the immigrants did not have independent homelands to renounce. Moreover, the imperial regimes that ruled these homelands were often brutally oppressive in their attempts to force linguistic, cultural, and, at times, religious uniformity in their realms. Some education historians have found that the premigration cultures of immigrant groups strongly influenced how they responded to schooling in the United States, which in turn led to differences in educational achievement and attainment.[137] Similarly, I argue that immigrants' attitudes about Americanization, particularly those aspects of Americanization related to citizenship and civic education, were shaped by their political experiences in their home countries.

While Jews were the most frequent and obvious victims of persecution throughout Europe, many other groups of immigrants from this era also had suffered at the hands of various imperial powers.[138] The Czechs and Slovaks chafed under the German and Austro-Hungarian "yoke" for many years; the Croats languished first under the Turks and then the Austro-Hungarians; the Carpatho-Russians (also known as Ruthenians or Rusyns) bore for centuries the rule of the Hapsburgs; the Greeks and Serbs had endured hundreds of years of Turkish rule; Lithuanians and Ukrainians were long-suffering subjects of the Russian czars; and, in the late eighteenth century, the Poles saw their country dismembered by Austria, Prussia, and Russia.[139] In every case, immigrants from these groups welcomed the cultural, linguistic, and religious freedom they found in the United States, and many relished the opportunity to become U.S. citizens.[140]

These premigration experiences had a profound influence on how Chicago's foreign language newspapers and their readers responded to Americanization. Indeed, when discussing issues of citizenship and politics, many of the foreign language newspapers in Chicago explicitly compared their painful experiences in Europe to the promise of a better life in the United States.[141] Writing in 1891, for example, the editor of the Polish paper *Dziennik Chicagoski* declared, "Those who have lived in bondage can seek freedom here. Here they breathe freely, and rest in peace, and here, with pride, they become citizens of a free country, which is not ruled either by the Czar or knout."[142] A 1906 editorial in the Greek newspaper the *Star* made the same point. Recalling the bitter history of Greece under Turkish rule, the writer applauded "America the great," where Greeks "were becoming American not only through naturalization but also through devotion and love for what America stands for—liberty, equality, and justice for all."[143]

More than two decades later, a contributor to the Jewish *Reform Advocate* reiterated these sentiments, declaring, "Reviled, hunted, and persecuted even to death for centuries by all the world, the Jew comes to America where he is accorded freedom, protection, and the same rights as are granted to people of other creeds."[144] Jewish newspapers across the country also played a pivotal educational role in preparing their readers for citizenship in the United States. As Ronald Sanders explains in his study of the most prominent Yiddish newspaper in the United States, the *Jewish Daily Forward*, "the work of the paper was to escort the Jewish immigrant out of the world of the Eastern European ghetto that he had just left, lead him into modern society, teach him the thought and politics of Western democracy, and above all make him an American."[145] The same could be said of all the major foreign language newspapers in Chicago.

Given these attitudes, the editors and journalists writing for the foreign language press in Chicago needed little goading from Americanizers to encourage their readers to become citizens.[146] In May 1918, *Denni Hlasatel* reprinted a speech by a Czech religious leader who observed that "after the Civil War, when freedom was established, men and women from all the oppressed European countries flocked to the shores of America, where they found a 'government of the people, by the people and for the people' as President Lincoln defined it." Noting that the United States had no dictators or monarchs, he concluded, "There is no higher title which could be bestowed on man or woman than that of American citizen."[147]

Eleven years later, a leader from the Greek community echoed and elaborated on these ideas, stating,

> Americanization is a great privilege and a great honor. It is the best "ization" in the world. It grants freedom in religious beliefs, freedom to love your mother country, freedom to function according to your habit and customs, to use your language, to maintain your church, protected by the laws of the land; freedom to celebrate your racial and religious holidays, but, on the other hand, in wearing the honored toga of Americanization, one must be a loyal and true citizen of this greatest Republic. Being a loyal and true citizen, it unfolds before you untold possibilities and potentialities and it urges you to reach (if you are qualified), the highest offices in the country, without racial or religious discrimination or bias being used against you.[148]

This speech is an excellent example of civic nationalism generally and patriotic pluralism specifically. The speaker extolled American democratic ideals, supported the common political culture, and was deeply patriotic. Yet, much of his patriotism derived from the fact that important aspects of American democratic life and thought—freedom of religion, freedom of assembly, and the freedom to maintain one's language and culture—protected the rights of minorities to be different. In essence the speaker rejected the mutually exclusive choice that advocates of assimilation or cultural pluralism offered the immigrants. Rather, he chose both American and Greek heritage, arguing that they mutually supported one another. Becoming an American citizen enhanced the opportunity to maintain cherished traditions and customs.[149]

In encouraging their readers to become American citizens, the editors and writers for nearly all the major newspapers in the CFLPS articulated a similarly hybrid view of Americanization, specifically stating that becoming an American citizen benefited not only the individual and the United States, but the ethnic group as well. It was additive, not subtractive.[150] In this vein, the writers routinely argued that becoming an American citizen was not a betrayal of their motherland, but rather a new way to aid her. As *Narod Polski* declared in 1909, "He who is not yet a citizen of this country, let him try and get papers as soon as possible. This will help him personally and will help all of us and the Polish cause."[151]

Two years later, a long editorial in *Dziennik Zwiazkowy* sharply rebuked Poles who had not yet become naturalized, stating, "The negligence of the Poles about accepting American citizenship is absolutely incredible. . . . Being a citizen of the United States does not in the least prevent us from loving our mother country or from working for her interests, and by becoming citizens of the United States we can accomplish a great deal for Poland through the influence we can exert on this nation's policies."[152]

Other major foreign language newspapers in Chicago used similar arguments to get their readers to naturalize. As early as 1889, for example, *L'Italia* bluntly stated, "Everyone is urged to become a citizen, because Italians will have more power than they now have."[153] A quarter of a century later the paper still maintained that stance.[154]

This instrumental argument was based on the simple political truth that the more immigrants from their group naturalized, the stronger their group would be in American politics. While prominent Americanizers such as Theodore Roosevelt and Woodrow Wilson repeatedly told immigrants that they must see themselves as individual Americans and not as members of hyphenated voting blocs, the Chicago foreign language newspapers largely ignored that advice. Unquestionably, these papers urged their readers to vote as their civic and patriotic duty, but they also routinely encouraged them to go to polls specifically to support candidates from their group. In a representative example of this position, a 1918 article in the Polish paper *Dziennik Zwiazkowy* forthrightly declared, "All Poles in Chicago should stand undivided in their support of Polish-American candidates."[155]

The newspapers were politically savvy enough to recognize that if other ethnic groups in Chicago were going to take them seriously, they had to unify their voters, get them to mark their ballots for the "right" candidates, and maximize turnout. Given the need to increase the number of voters they could get to the polls, it is hardly surprising that so many foreign language newspapers routinely promoted citizenship classes for their readers and naturalization as soon as possible.[156] In other words, even when these groups entered the political process mainly to support candidates from their group, they were simultaneously taking a major step toward Americanization.

Related to these efforts were similar initiatives to get immigrant women to naturalize and vote.[157] Many, though not all, of the major foreign language newspapers in Chicago strongly supported the campaign for women's suffrage.[158] In 1913, when women in Illinois gained the right to vote in presidential and local elections, a flurry of editorials and articles in foreign language papers strongly encouraged women to register and exercise the franchise.[159] For example, in March of 1914, just prior to the first Chicago election in which women could vote, an editorial in the *Jewish Daily Courier* hailed the fact that almost 220,000 women already had registered. The editor predicted that their votes would determine the election.[160] Throughout the war years, newspapers from wide range of perspectives, including the conservative Polish paper *Narod Polski,* the left-wing Lithuanian paper *Naujienos (The News),* and the Croatian Socialist paper *Radnicka Straza (The Worker's Sentinel),* which quoted Abigail Adams in support of its position, all enthusiastically encouraged women from their respective immigrant groups to vote and to continue their struggle for equal rights. All of them backed the Nineteenth Amendment.[161] Following the passage of the amendment, *Narod Polski* applauded this victory and urged Polish women to "[l]earn the laws of the United States, register in the proper time, vote on election day. Those who are not citizens should take out their naturalization papers. If your husband is not a citizen, prevail upon him to take out his citizenship papers."[162]

Europe's plunge into war in August 1914 provided yet another naturalization argument for many editors and writers in Chicago's foreign language newspapers. Newspapers serving such groups as Croatians, Czechs, Poles, and Slovaks, whose homelands were part of either the Austro-Hungarian or German empires, repeatedly urged their readers to obtain American citizenship to avoid conscription into the armies of their oppressors. In July 1915, for example, *Denni Hlasatel* urgently called on all Czechs and Slovaks to immediately become American citizens, stating, "It is impossible to stress sufficiently the importance of every Bohemian getting rid of his Austrian allegiance as soon as possible."[163]

America's entry into the war created an important new avenue to citizenship—military service. Following the passage of what became known as the "Act of May 9, 1918," which created special provisions for the naturalization of aliens who served in the U.S. military, there was an enormous surge of foreign-born soldiers and sailors seeking citizenship. As Nancy Gentile Ford has shown, many of these soldiers and sailors prepared for naturalization by taking English and citizenship courses that were offered during basic training.[164] In a 1919 report about these new citizens, Raymond F. Crist, director of citizenship in the Bureau of Naturalization, affirmed the quality of these programs and the depth of foreign-born soldiers' patriotism, stating, "The names upon the role of honor of the nation that were cabled back by the American Expeditionary Forces in France give emphatic testimony to the loyalty of the foreign born." He continued, "The alien-born soldier has returned to America an educated and transformed individual. He is an American in all the senses."[165]

This surge of new citizens dramatically increased the number of people who naturalized during and immediately after the war. Specifically, of the 151,000 immigrants who naturalized in 1918, 42 percent came from the armed forces. The following year, 59 percent of the more than 217,000 immigrants who became citizens came from the military. In 1920, of the almost 178,000 immigrants who naturalized, 29 percent were soldiers or sailors. As late as 1921, about 10 percent of the approximately 181,000 people who naturalized that year still came from the armed forces.[166]

Military service was not the only impetus in seeking citizenship in the postwar period. In fact, the 1920s proved to be a considerably more bountiful decade for naturalization than the 1910s. Between 1910 and 1919, the annual average for naturalizations was about 99,000. Between 1920 and 1929, the annual average jumped to over 178,000, an almost 80 percent increase.[167] While many factors contributed to this postwar increase, it is likely that the growing threat of immigration restriction played a significant role in encouraging people to apply for citizenship. As early as 1921, after the passage of the first law specifically reducing new immigration from southern and eastern Europe, immigrants from those areas recognized that the "golden door" was closing, and American citizenship became increasingly more valuable. This was particularly true for immigrants with families still living abroad, because the 1921 law allowed citizens to bring family members to the United States regardless of the quotas.[168]

Given these developments, during the 1920s, many of Chicago's foreign language newspapers renewed their efforts to get readers to naturalize. As in the prewar years, these pleas often combined staunch declarations of loyalty to the United States with appeals for ethnic solidarity.

Typical was a 1929 editorial in the Polish newspaper *Dziennik Zjednocze-nia*, which unambiguously declared, "We adhere to the belief that the interests of Poland will be served best if we become good citizens of the United States, properly discharge the duties we owe it, and raise the stan-dard of the Poles."[169]

Announcements about new courses and reinvigorated public school naturalization programs were widespread during this period. In addition, some institutions that worked closely with immigrant groups created new programs to encourage and aid naturalization. In 1919, for example, the National Catholic War Council began a "program for citizenship," which rested on the idea "that immigrants who come to this country to stay for any great length of time should assume their part of the common burdens of society by becoming citizens and seeking to perform the tasks of citi-zenship intelligently." The council urged all immigrants to learn the ba-sics of democratic thought and become patriotic citizens. In regard to teaching the immigrants American history, the council appears to have taken the advice of critics of aggressive assimilation who urged educators to use "European patriots such as Lafayette, Kosciusko, and Pulaski" to inspire their students to become Americans.[170]

Throughout the 1920s many of the major immigrant groups in Chicago set up or expanded programs to facilitate naturalization. At times these programs worked with public schools, but more often they were grassroots initiatives sponsored by organizations in the immigrant communities themselves.[171] By all accounts, these efforts were quite successful. *Dzien-nik Zjednoczenia* noted in 1928 that, "Polish Naturalization Schools in Chicago are filled with prospective candidates for citizenship."[172]

Not content merely to promote citizenship classes and encourage read-ers to naturalize, some of the foreign language newspapers also ran infor-mational articles about American government and civics. For example, in 1908, the *Greek Star* published an exhaustive 4,000-word essay on "The Federal Constitution of the United States of America," with a wealth of information on American government, politics, and history.[173] Similar ar-ticles ran at various times in the Czech paper *Denni Hlasatel*, the Croa-tian paper *Jugoslavia*, the *Jewish Daily Courier*, the Lithuanian paper *Lietuva*, the Polish newspapers *Dziennik Chicagoski* and *Polonia*, the Greek newspaper *Saloniki*, and the Hungarian *Magyar Tribune*.[174] These articles combined with those on American history to provide readers with a considerable amount of information about democratic politics.

All these efforts had an impact. As historian Reed Ueda argues, "When the flow of immigrants decreased in 1924, the proportion of naturalized foreign-born from eastern and southern Europe climbed until it equaled or exceeded the proportion of naturalized newcomers from northern and western Europe. By 1950, for example, nearly 80 percent of foreign-born Italians had secured citizenship compared with 75 percent of immigrants from the United Kingdom."[175]

Given the strong support for naturalization evinced by leading foreign language newspapers in Chicago, it is not surprising that such organizations as the Chicago Association of Commerce and the Chicago Board of Education saw the papers as reliable allies in their quest to assimilate immigrants. As noted earlier, Americanizers in Akron, Cleveland, Detroit, and Pittsburgh also praised local foreign language newspapers for their support of Americanization campaigns in these cities. But this "alignment" does not indicate that the foreign language papers were simply tools of the Americanizers. As the content of the articles and editorials shows, the immigrants took a nuanced and distinctive approach to Americanization that was quite different from the blunt prescriptions of the aggressive Americanizers. While such leaders as Woodrow Wilson were telling immigrants, "You cannot become thorough Americans if you think of yourselves in groups,"[176] the editors and writers for the Chicago foreign language newspapers insisted that immigrants could be good Americans even as they held firm to important aspects of their home culture. In terms of naturalization, the leading foreign language newspapers in Chicago strongly urged their readers to be loyal, knowledgeable, and patriotic American citizens, but they also emphasized that as citizens they had far more power to protect, sustain, and promote their ethnic group than if they remained politically tied to the land of their birth. Moreover, the papers repeatedly argued that because of the freedoms guaranteed by the U.S. Constitution, a person could be both a proud American citizen and still cherish one's native culture and homeland.

As Warner Sollors has observed, one particularly powerful, albeit sexist, metaphor that immigrants and others used to describe this "both/and" stance portrayed an immigrant's native country as his mother, and America as his bride.[177] From this perspective, they argued, it was just as absurd for 100 percent Americanizers to demand that immigrants reject their homelands when they naturalized as it would be to ask husbands to forsake their mothers upon taking their marriage vows. Clearly, the natures of the love immigrants had for their native countries and for America were as different as a man's love for his mother and his wife. Equally as clear, these newspapers maintained, a man could and should love them both.

This was a useful and, at times, compelling metaphor. In 1925, a writer for the *Magyar Tribune* recalled a heated exchange in which a leader of the Hungarian community used the mother–bride example in a particularly effective way at a 1910 meeting of the Chicago Board of Education. Following an appeal to the board for a bilingual night school for Hungarian immigrants, a board member objected, stating that Hungarians were too attached to their homeland. Upon hearing this criticism, the Hungarian leader turned to the board member and asked, If someone told you to disown your mother, would you do it? After the board member failed to come up with a suitable response, the board voted to approve the school.[178]

During the national Americanization campaign of the World War I years, immigrants and their supporters reiterated and embellished this metaphor to challenge 100 percent Americanizers' demands for total assimilation. In June 1916, for example, a Danish newspaper in Chicago applauded a recent speech given by William Jennings Bryan at the Norwegian National Festival in Brooklyn, New York. Bryan praised his audience for "the fact that you still love the land of your birth," adding that such affection for one's homeland "does not lessen our nation's confidence in you as citizens of the United States." He continued: "One of the best ways to decide whether a man will make a good husband, is to find out if he has been a loyal son. A man who doesn't love his mother, is not apt to be an exemplary husband. So I feel that one who doesn't have in his heart a love of the land in which he first saw the light, cannot add much to our strength or to our citizenship."[179]

By 1920, even the director of the Americanization of the U.S. Bureau of Education used a variation on this theme to argue for a more culturally sensitive approach to Americanization. "We cannot crush out of men's hearts the love they hold for the childhood homes," he declared, "Nor would we do so if we could. The heart which could so easily and quickly forget the land of its birth could never love with a deep devotion the land of its adoption."[180] As late as October 1937, an Americanization educator in Cleveland used this metaphor in a radio address that was reprinted in one of that city's Slovenian newspapers. Noting the Slovenians' eagerness to Americanize, the teacher explained that even as they became U.S. citizens, Slovenians still loved their homeland: "They call their home country their mother; however America is their bride."[181]

As with learning English and American history, this nuanced stance toward naturalization taken by the Chicago foreign language newspapers demonstrates how skillfully these papers negotiated the demands of Americanizers for naturalization and political allegiance on the one hand, and the desire to maintain their cultural distinctiveness on the other. A 1907 article in the *Greek Star* nicely captured this approach when it encouraged its readers to become citizens. It stated, "We owe it to ourselves, we owe it to the future happiness of the Greek people of America to become real Americans and adopt the best and finest things that America has to offer, while, at the same time, we maintain and preserve the best and finest things in our Greek culture and heritage."[182]

But beyond simply balancing aspects of Americanization with elements of cultural pluralism, Chicago's foreign language newspapers promoted naturalization as an essential step toward gaining or augmenting the political power of their groups. The papers argued that once immigrants were naturalized, their votes would help their compatriots play a larger and more influential role in American politics. Gaining this position of strength, political leaders from their communities could better defend their cultural differences and promote their political interests. As a 1914 article in *Narod Polski* bluntly put it, "The vote is our weapon."[183] In short, the Chicago foreign language newspapers, aided by civic leaders from their communities, prepared and encouraged immigrants to enter the freewheeling, pluralistic political struggles that gripped the city, state, and nation in these years.[184] Political leaders from the immigrant communities were effective and influential in these efforts not only in Chicago, but across the country.[185]

For example, historian John Bodnar points out that in the post–World War I years, immigrant groups in Cleveland were "simply too numerous and, therefore, too powerful" for establishment politicians to ignore. As early as 1921, pressure from Catholic and other groups in the city prevailed on the mayor to use the police to "suppress" a Ku Klux Klan (KKK) rally. In 1929, the city introduced a two-month-long series of free intercultural and international music concerts at Gordon Park that featured performances by musicians from at least seven different ethnic groups, including African Americans, Czechs, Italians, Poles and Slovaks. But by far the most enduring example of immigrants' emerging political and cultural power in the Forest City was the creation of a series of Cultural Gardens along a mile-long, park-like boulevard on the east side of town that commemorated the contribution major immigrant groups made to western civilization generally and American history specifically. Bodnar describes the leaders of this effort as "members of the professional classes inside and outside the ethnic communities who favored notions of pluralism and tolerance over the aggressive Americanism that proved so powerful in the 1920s."[186]

At the same time, in Detroit and Michigan, a coalition of immigrant and religious groups demonstrated their growing political clout by successfully defeating two statewide referenda, one in 1920 and the other in 1924, to abolish all parochial schools in the state. The second of these referenda was strongly backed by the KKK, which boasted that its Michigan chapter was the largest in the nation. These two elections, which took place prior to the U.S. Supreme Court decision, *Pierce v. the Society of Sisters,* convincingly highlighted the power of immigrant voters, especially in Detroit and Wayne County, which provided overwhelming majorities against the referenda.[187]

In becoming politically active, the immigrants and their children deepened their Americanization by participating in the nation's democratic processes and institutions. But even as the assimilative process that Thomas Archdeacon describes as moving from immigrants to ethnics continued, these groups did not necessarily abandon their European background.[188] Indeed, many of these groups also showed considerable consistency and solidarity in terms of their voting behaviors. In 1961, for example, nearly four decades after the great Americanization campaign sought to eliminate "hyphenated" voters, Robert Dahl's influential study in New Haven, Connecticut, found remarkable consistency in ethnic voting patterns. Dahl noted that "in spite of growing assimilation, ethnic factors continued to make themselves felt with astonishing tenacity." Several years later, political scientist Michael Parenti also reported the surprising consistency and longevity of distinctive voting patterns among many of the groups that came to the U.S. in the early twentieth century. Parenti observed, "Ethnics can thus sometimes behave politically as ethnics while remaining firmly American." He added, "It may be said that minorities have injected a new meaning into a national motto originally addressed to the fusion of thirteen separate states, *e pluribus unum,*

a supreme allegiance to, and political participation in, the commonality
of the Union, with the reserved right to remain distinct unassimilated entities in certain limited cultural, social and identificational respects."[189]
The Chicago foreign language press of the 1910s and 1920s would have
heartily agreed.

Restriction and the Struggle for Civic Nationalism

During the 1920s, the combination of idealism and instrumentalism
that had inspired Chicago's foreign language newspapers to enthusiastically support naturalization and general political engagement was put to
its severest test by the racial restrictionists. In the years immediately following World War I, racial restrictionists gained power across the country, in large part by sowing fears about a renewed "invasion" of immigrants. Declaring themselves the defenders of America's Anglo-Saxon
or Nordic character, racial restrictionists reviled eastern and southern
European immigrants as members of inferior and congenitally un-
American races. On that premise, they sought to end immigration of
these people almost entirely. Ironically, the efforts by restrictionists encouraged both greater naturalization by immigrants and stimulated increasing numbers of foreign-born citizens to become politically active.
Specifically, large numbers of immigrants mobilized and launched a vigorous intellectual and political counterattack that articulated a powerful
vision of American civic nationalism. As John Higham explained, "emerging from the ethnic turmoil of the 1920s, a common process drove people
in many ethnic enclaves to redefine themselves in more open and inclusive ways. Although their immediate experience was often painful and
disillusioning, in the end they were rebuilding and extending the tradition
of American universalism."[190]

In the early 1890s, well before the influx of new immigrants had reached
its peak, major foreign language newspapers in Chicago were reporting
on efforts by nativists to severely restrict the number of immigrants arriving from eastern and southern Europe. In 1892, for example, the Polish
newspaper *Dziennik Chicagoski* ran a lengthy exposé about a recent surge
of anti-immigrant/pro-restriction editorials in English language newspapers across the country. Typical was an editorial in the Portland *Orego-
nian* that called for a ten-year ban on new immigration, declaring, "We
want pure Americans—not half-breed citizens." Quoting a number of

such editorials, *Dziennik Chicagoski* derided the claims that hordes of disease-ridden paupers and criminals were invading American cities and undermining "Anglo-Saxon ambition and industrialism."[191]

Writers for the foreign language press in Chicago expressed little doubt about what nativists meant by "pure Americans." As the Czech paper *Svornost* explained, these "Know-Nothings" believed that the only real Americans were those "whose ancestors laid the foundation of Jamestown or arrived on the shores of America in the 'Mayflower.'"[192] From that perspective, it did not matter whether the immigrants learned English, studied American history, adopted democratic ideals and values, or even naturalized. They would never be true Americans. If, as the nativists maintained, the United States was an Anglo-Saxon nation, the eastern and southern European newcomers would always be "half-breed citizens." For the next three decades, immigrants struggled against this rising tide of racial restriction by forcefully articulating their commitment to civic nationalism and arguing that restricting immigrants because of race contradicted the country's most cherished ideals.

Between 1890 and 1915, newcomers from eastern and southern Europe battled a wide range of anti-immigrant initiatives. Politically, they struggled against relentless efforts to restrict immigration mainly through proposed federal legislation that demanded literacy tests for all newcomers, which newspapers serving the immigrant communities in Chicago regarded as little more than smoke screens obscuring the racist attitudes of nativist politicians.[193] The newspapers also vigorously challenged what they saw as a growing smear campaign against immigrants in the English language press that supported these legislative efforts. For example, in early 1914, after the *Century Magazine* published several articles by University of Wisconsin professor E. A. Ross disparaging virtually all of the recent immigrant groups, the Chicago paper *L'Italia* denounced the essays as "reeking with racial prejudice and religious rancor." While acknowledging that the country had every right to restrict entry of "the criminal, the diseased and the depraved," *L'Italia* declared, "Professor Ross however seems to argue in favor of complete exclusion of immigration, especially from southern and eastern Europe, and in support of his theory he descends to depths of racial prejudice, religious bigotry and palpable misrepresentation."[194]

The following year, in an impassioned Decoration Day speech, R. J. Psenka, editor of the Czech newspaper *Svornost*, also addressed the underlying racism of the current anti-immigrant agitation. Asking, "What is the substance of 'being an American'?" Psenka exclaimed,

> If "being an American" depends on a long line of ancestors set-tled in this country, then we, immigrants and children of im-migrants, can never become Americans. But if "being an Amer-ican" consists of appreciating the precious heritage of personal and spiritual liberty left to us by the great founders of this na-tion, such as Thomas Paine, Benjamin Franklin, and George Washington, of maintaining the American principles of equal-ity and progressiveness, then it may be said that the average Bohemian-American is a much better American than the ma-jority of Americans who were born in this country and have a long line of ancestors who lived in this country, and who only too often let the immigrants defend the principles of American liberty against those who are trying to abolish it.[195]

This is a classic example of civic nationalism, declaring that the most defining factor of a true American was a person's depth of commitment to American political ideals and loyalty to the country, not, as a growing number of restrictionists were arguing, a person's racial or religious back-ground. Over the next decade, these kinds of arguments, including state-ments that immigrants often understand American ideals better than native-born restrictionists, became increasingly common in the Chicago foreign language press.

With the beginning of World War I, overt *racial* attacks on immigrants lessened amid the boisterous assimilationist campaign to get immigrants to shed their premigration culture and become "100 percent Americans." Unlike the restrictionists, assimilationists such as Theodore Roosevelt and Woodrow Wilson argued that once immigrants disavowed the "hy-phen," they could and should be considered Americans. The staunchly assimilationist *Chicago Tribune* echoed this theme, declaring, "The United States cannot long be composed of Poles, Swedes, Bohemians, Germans, Canadians, Italians, etc. It must come around to being com-posed of Americans."[196] As the previous section on citizenship has shown, writers for the foreign language press unquestionably agreed that immi-grants should become good Americans, but they vigorously rejected de-mands that they abandon their homelands and native cultures in the process.[197]

When the United States entered World War I, many foreign-born communities in the country found a new way to express this "both/and" idea as they cheered the tens of thousands of young men from their communities who enlisted in the armed forces and purchased millions of dollars of war bonds. Part of the reason for their enthusiasm was that numerous groups, including Czechs, Lithuanians, Poles, Slovaks, and Ukrainians, not only believed that it was their patriotic duty to support the United States but also hoped that an Allied victory would liberate their homelands.[198] Other groups such as Italians, Russians, and, late in the war, Greeks, whose countries were battling the Central Powers, also applauded America's entry into the war on the Allied side.[199] Thus, even as huge numbers of immigrants put their lives on the line in the U.S. military and naturalized by the thousands while serving, they sought to balance their American patriotism with love for their former homelands.

Dziennik Zwiazkowy editorialized on May 10, 1917, "The Poles are enlisting in the American Army because by fighting for America they are also fighting for Poland."[200] Five months later, an editorial in *Denni Hlasatel* made the same argument. "Our foremost duty now is to prove ourselves loyal and grateful to our new homeland and to repay it for the benefits it has granted us," the editor declared. He added, "We must help the United States to win this war which she entered not only to preserve her own freedom, but also to liberate the small nations from oppression, among whom we Czechs and Slovaks are numbered."[201] In a Cleveland parade supporting the war effort, Czechs carried two banners, the first stating, "We are Americans through and through by the spirit of our nation," and the second declaring, "America do not be discouraged. We have been fighting these tyrants for three hundred years."[202]

At least one English language newspaper, the *Chicago Evening Post*, applauded the American patriotism of these Polish and Czech soldiers and acknowledged their complex motivations for serving in the military. The editor of the *Post* declared that these sons of Chicago "whose background is in the plains of Poland or the mountains of Bohemia are springing to arms with a double inspiration." The editorial continued, "They fight not for one land, but for two. They fight not alone for America, but for the freedom of the world."[203] One year later, the editor of the *Jewish Daily Courier* also commented that Czechs and Poles seamlessly had united their love of America with their commitment to their homelands. He viewed these trends as powerful examples that American patriotism could be enriched by the diversity of its people. "America is now learning its most important lesson," he declared, "that it is not at all necessary for the liberty, security, and prosperity of America to fuse all the nationalities here to a point where they will lose their identity entirely. On the contrary, it is much better that they should treasure dearly the inheritance which they brought with them from the old world—their language, their songs, and the beautiful traditions of their past."[204]

In August 1918, an editorial in *Dziennik Zwiazkowy* reiterated that position. According to the editor, it was not the homogenizing melting pot that made Americans, but rather "the love of liberty, the love of ideals, the love of a great country of freedom and honor for its traditions and past [that] have united the spirits of many nationalities, of which America can be proud. And America is proud of its brave citizen-sons who, although of various descents, are fighting on the fields of France as one under the spirit of Americanism, even those who were not originally born here. What more does America need, what more can it desire?"[205]

Unfortunately for the immigrants, in the immediate postwar years, it appeared that many Americans had no interest in learning the lesson that the *Jewish Daily Courier* believed the war had taught, nor did they graciously acknowledge the sacrifices or even the Americanism that the editor of *Dziennik Zwiazkowy* avowed. As the economy faltered, as the Red scare dominated headlines, and as rumors flew that millions of impoverished refugees were waiting on European docks for ships to carry them to America, the prewar fears and disdain that many native-born Americans had about immigrants resurfaced.[206] In the early 1920s, concerns voiced by racial restrictionists about whether immigrants from eastern and southern Europe had assimilated, or ever could assimilate, gained renewed traction. Some critics even turned the complex motives that led many immigrant groups to support the war into a reason to bar their compatriots from entering the United States. Writing in 1921, George Creel, who two years earlier had praised America's immigrant soldiers, now argued that despite their service in the U.S. military, their hearts still belonged to their homelands. He maintained that the Treaty of Versailles had stirred up nationalistic sentiments among immigrants in the United States to such a degree that loyalty to America was now "a bad second in many foreign blocks, the lands of their birth having reclaimed their allegiance."[207]

During this era, Creel was a powerful voice in what became a thunderous chorus demanding restriction. The result was a flurry of new legislation designed to drastically reduce the number of people coming to the United States from eastern and southern Europe. In December 1920, while debating one such piece of legislation that called for a two-year suspension of immigration to the United States, an Ohio congressman stated bluntly that if the bill was not passed, then "our country [would] soon be full of foreign cripples and undesirable people."[208] The most troubling part of these new bills was that supporters largely based their ideas on "scientific" racial hierarchies that characterized immigrants from eastern and southern Europe as inherently less intelligent, less moral, and less capable of self-government than Americans who had descended from Anglo-Saxon or Nordic stock. As a 1924 *New York Times* editorial declared, immigration restriction was necessary for "[p]reserving the American Race."[209] Immigrant leaders deplored these ideas and their effect on immigration policy, namely, racial admission quotas that favored newcomers from northwestern Europe while slashing the number of southern and eastern Europeans to almost zero.

Given their loyalty and sacrifices during the war, immigrant groups that originated from proscribed regions were shocked and angered by these efforts. In March 1920, for example, the Italian Chamber of Commerce in Chicago sent a resolution to Congress vehemently protesting the quotas, which allowed large numbers of Germans to immigrate to the United States but blocked most Italians. The organization was outraged that this legislation would enable people who had been America's enemies in the Great War to immigrate to this country, while refusing to allow people who had been America's allies the same privilege.[210]

Over the next four years, these concerns grew as restrictionists sought ever more drastic ways to reduce the number of eastern and southern Europeans coming to the country (e.g., basing the quotas on the census of 1890, when very few people from those regions had come to the United States, rather than that of 1910, when a substantial number of them had immigrated).[211] By 1923, Chicago's foreign language newspapers increasingly reported on and editorialized about the racist nature of the legislation. In December 1923, for example, the *Chicago Chronicle*, a Jewish paper, blasted what the paper's editor termed "viciously efficacious" legislation whose purpose "is quite obviously calculated to exclude immigrants from countries from which most of our Jewish influx is coming." The editor continued, "No true American Jew wants to have legislation enacted which embodies special favoritism to those of his own blood, but neither does he want it specially doctored to react against them."[212]

Four months later, as the National Origins Act was moving through Congress, the Italian Chamber of Commerce in Chicago made exactly the same points in a letter to members of the Senate Immigration Committee. Noting that if the intention of the legislation was simply to "raise the standards of would-be immigrants" without discriminating against any race, the Italian Chamber of Commerce was "in thorough accord and sympathy." But that was not what the organization saw in the legislation. Rather, the authors declared, "In restricting the quota of immigrants from Italy to a minimum and increasing that of the Nordic race to a maximum, the American nation will brand millions of its citizens as belonging to an inferior race." The basis of this brand of inferiority was the restrictionists' belief that "the Italian immigrant is not absorbed into American life, that he is un-American and even anti-American in spirit, ideals, and aspirations—in short that he is un-assimilable."[213]

Virtually all the eastern and southern European groups in Chicago recoiled from what they saw as the racism underlying the National Origins Act.[214] On March 4, 1924, a large group of "[n]ative-born Americans, Irish, Jews, Poles, Italians, Lithuanians, Czechoslovakians, and representatives of other nationalities" crowded into the Chicago City Council chambers and urged local politicians to protest the restrictive legislation. Jane Addams addressed the crowd and denounced the bill as discriminatory and hateful. Following her speech, an Irish American district court judge recounted the importance of immigrants in American history and to loud applause declared that "the principles of our founding fathers . . . prove that the present anti-immigration bill is a blow at American ideals, and is a dastardly act which should be condemned." The council members approved a resolution deploring the bill and agreed to send a delegation to Washington to lobby against it.[215] At the same time, the Detroit City Council and the Americanization Committee of the Detroit Board of Commerce both passed similar resolutions.[216]

Undoubtedly, many native-born restrictionists would have viewed a gathering of immigrants invoking "our founding fathers" as absurd, but as early as 1915 editors and writers for foreign language newspapers had argued that the racial premise behind many of the attacks on immigrants contradicted the most basic ideals that defined the nation—indeed, the very ideals that Americanizers were encouraging immigrants to embrace. Consequently, these writers frequently asserted that immigrants both understood and internalized these ideals better than many native-born Americans.[217]

In April 1924, as Congress was debating the National Origins Act, a group of young Poles reiterated that point in an appeal to Congress to defeat the Act. After noting their sacrifices and service during the war, they denounced "self-styled 100% Americans" for questioning their loyalty to this country. "We have no apologies to make about our Americanism and resent the imputation that we are less desirable American citizens because we have not sprung from the Nordics or Anglo-Saxons." They concluded that Congress should end its efforts to restrict eastern and southern Europeans from entry into the United States and should instead focus on "the Americanization of un-American Americans."[218]

Despite such pleas and the strenuous efforts of a small number of congressional opponents of the bill, including Emanuel Cellar (D-NY), Robert H. Clancy (R-MI), Samuel Dickstein (D-NY), Fiorello LaGuardia (R-NY), and Adolph Sabath (D-IL), the House and Senate passed the National Origins Act by large margins and President Coolidge signed it in late May 1924.[219] Over the next few years, racial restrictionists continued to introduce legislation that allowed even fewer immigrants from eastern and southern Europe. In August 1926, for example, the *Jewish Daily Forward* reported that a new plan before Congress would cut the total number of immigrants allowed in the United States from over 161,000 to 150,000. According to the *Jewish Daily Forward*, Senator David A. Reed (R-PA), one of the architects of the 1924 National Origins Act, declared that this new plan would further ensure that "the majority of immigrants" would be "'Nordics,' or 'Anglo-Saxons.'"[220] The foreign language press in Chicago routinely railed against these measures, asserting time and again that "all men are created equal" and that what mattered most about being a good American was one's commitment to the nation's democratic creed, not one's cultural, racial, or religious background, but to no avail.[221]

As powerful as these pleas for civic nationalism were, the commitment that some foreign language papers evinced to democracy, equality, tolerance, and minority rights seemed to apply to the United States, but not to their homelands. For example, Polish newspapers in Chicago did not demand that their reborn homeland offer the same equal rights protection for its Jewish, Lithuanian, or Ukrainian minorities that Polish Americans were claiming for themselves in the United States. Moreover, these papers uniformly failed to denounce Polish pogroms against Jews or injustices done to Lithuanians and Ukrainians in the immediate post–World War I years. Indeed, at times, many of these papers defended Poland's anti-Semitic actions in editorials and articles that were themselves ferociously anti-Semitic.[222] As chapter 4 argues, during the 1930s this moral and political tension between civic nationalism at home and ethnic nationalism abroad was increasingly put to the test, especially for German Americans, Italian Americans, and Polish Americans, whose homelands by this time had descended into totalitarian or authoritarian nightmares.

In addition to this moral and political double standard regarding their homelands, Gary Gerstle has pointed out that the European immigrants' embrace of civic nationalism also cloaked a fair amount of hypocrisy in regard to non-European Americans. An egregious example of this hypocrisy reared its head when two of the fiercest congressional opponents of racial restriction, Adolph Sabath and Samuel Dickstein, supported the portion of the National Origins Act that forbade entry to all Asians and denied citizenship to Japanese immigrants no matter how long they had been in the United States. These politicians were civic nationalists in regard to eastern and southern European immigrants, but ethnic nationalists in regard to Asians.[223]

The other area of hypocrisy concerned African Americans. Given the racial nature of the debate about immigration restriction and the civic nationalist stance that many writers for the Chicago foreign language press took regarding restriction (i.e., that one's commitment to American ideals and values, not racial background, should determine a person's Americanism), it would seem that these writers would have been supportive of black efforts to gain civil rights. In general, however, writers for the Chicago foreign language papers, or the WPA workers who decided on what to include in the CFLPS, generally ignored black–white issues in this era.

This is not to say that politicians from immigrant communities such as Congressman Sabath or the editors and writers of the Chicago foreign language newspapers were completely silent on the betrayal of civic nationalism in regard to African Americans. During his long career in Congress, for example, Sabath strongly supported equal rights for blacks.[224] Moreover, on a relatively small number of occasions when the papers in the CFLPS covered or commented on black–white relations, they often did so from a civic nationalistic perspective.

In the early 1900s, for example, a number of foreign language newspapers in Chicago denounced lynching as a horrific contradiction to the democratic ideals that America claimed to represent. In an editorial deploring the 1903 Kishinev pogrom against Jews in Russia, *Svenska Nyheter* (the *Swedish*

News), argued that Americans should also condemn the lynching of blacks in the United States, which was equally odious. Similarly, the Greek *Star* described lynching as a "stain upon the brightness of American civilization."[225] In 1912, the *Daily Jewish Courier* echoed these sentiments but put lynching in the larger context of the denial of blacks' "natural rights" in most areas of American life.[226] In his study of Italian immigrants in Chicago, which included an extensive reading of *L'Italia*, Thomas Guglielmo argues that in the first two decades of the twentieth century, "*L'Italia* carried stories almost weekly about brutal killings of African Americans in the South and elsewhere, in which the newspaper often condemned the United States for its rank hypocrisy and bankrupt "Civilita Americana" (American Civilization)."[227] In a similar vein, in an angry Independence Day article, the left-wing Croatian newspaper *Radnik* decried the betrayal of America's revolutionary ideals, specifically noting, "There is no doubt that the Negroes of today, even after the war which was fought for their liberation are maltreated and oppressed economically and socially."[228] As late as 1930, the editor of the Norwegian newspaper *Scandia* fiercely condemned lynching and indignantly observed that the people who committed these crimes "considered themselves one-hundred-per-cent Americans."[229]

In this period, the *Jewish Daily Courier* appears to have devoted more attention to black–white relations than other papers in the CFLPS, perhaps due to the editor's belief that the plight of blacks in America was akin to that of Jews in Europe. In April 1914, for example, the paper explicitly made that comparison in condemning the arson attack on a home owned by a black family in Oak Park, Illinois, as a "despicable" act of "race hatred." The author then observed, "A sad occurrence of this nature reminds us of Poland, where the Polish aristocracy are burning Jewish homes in order to get them out of their neighborhoods and villages."[230] Three years later, in May 1917, the paper also denounced attacks on blacks in East St. Louis, Illinois, attacks that were precursors to the ghastly race riot that took place in that city two months later.[231]

When in July of 1919 a bloody race riot exploded in Chicago, the *Courier* ran a lengthy editorial condemning the violence. Although the editorial was, at times, patronizing toward African Americans, it ended with a powerful statement of civic nationalism that drew on biblical precepts about the "sin of the fathers being visited upon their children" and the democratic guarantee of equal rights for all. "The great slave dealers in America," the editor wrote, "who, for a hundred years, imported Negroes for economic exploitation, thereby committed an injustice not only against themselves and their slaves, but also against their grandchildren." He added, "We can rectify this mistake only by solving the Negro problem in an equitable fashion. This means that the Negro must be given all the rights guaranteed in the Constitution of the United States. . . . Only then will America have domestic harmony between Negro and White."[232] The *Courier* was not the only foreign language paper to sympathize with blacks after the riot. Guglielmo notes that *L'Italia* also supported the black community after the 1919 riot and repeated its condemnation of American "hypocrisy when it came to issues of race and color."[233]

While such support for blacks was not common in the Chicago foreign language press, at times immigrant groups clearly saw their interests aligned with those of African Americans. Following the resurgence of the KKK in the 1920s, for example, some Chicago foreign language newspapers made common cause with African Americans in their opposition to that strongly restrictionist, anti-black, anti-Catholic, and anti-Semitic organization. As the Hungarian newspaper the *Magyar Tribune*, editorialized in 1924, "The Catholics, the Jews and the Colored people, regardless of whether they are immigrants or not, are the Klan's natural enemies."[234]

Similarly, three years later, when white students from a Gary, Indiana, high school walked out in protest to the presence of black students in the school, the editor of the Russian newspaper *Rassviet* blasted the walk-out as a reflection of the KKK's power in that state. The editor was incensed by the hypocrisy of civic leaders in Gary, who, on Lincoln's Birthday "will praise in their speeches the great things done by Abraham Lincoln, the liberator of the Negro slaves, [but] will think in their hearts about the best way of depriving the descendants of these slaves of the right to be taught in the schools that were open to all other children born in the United States." The editor concluded, "If so-called one-hundred-per-cent patriots have their way in this case, they may soon try to expel out of the American schools all "foreigners," such as Germans, Russians, Poles, etc."[235]

A striking aspect of this editorial and the one cited earlier from *Scandia* is that both papers use the phrases "one-hundred-per-cent Americans" or "one-hundred-per-cent patriots" to pejoratively describe the people who were depriving blacks of their inalienable rights. These were, of course, the same phrases that editors in the foreign language press used to mock the racial restrictionists who were vilifying immigrants at this time. Implicit in that usage was the civic nationalist message that immigrants who embraced the idea that all men are created equal were better Americans than racists who could trace their lineage to *Mayflower*. The editorial in *Russviet*, went even further in taking a civic nationalist stance by arguing that as long as blacks were denied their basic civil rights, the rights of all minorities, including the foreign-born, were at risk.

The civic nationalist arguments that appeared in the Chicago foreign language press had deep American roots. Indeed, Abraham Lincoln used similar arguments to defend immigrants and reassert his belief that the denial of political equality for blacks could lead to loss of rights for other minorities. Speaking in Chicago on July 10, 1858, Lincoln recalled the recent July Fourth holiday and the "iron men" of the Revolutionary generation, whom he described as the fathers and grandfathers of the country. But he then reminded his audience that as he spoke, perhaps half the people then living in the United States were descended from immigrants who arrived in this country *after* the Revolution and thus had no direct link to the founders. As he put it,

> If they look back through this history to trace their connection with those days by blood, they find they have none, they cannot carry themselves back into that glorious epoch and make themselves feel that they are part of us, but when they look through that old Declaration of Independence they find that those old men say that "We hold these truths to be self-evident, that all men are created equal," and then they feel that that moral sentiment taught in that day evidences their relation to those men, that it is the father of all moral principles in them, and that they have a right to claim it as though they were blood of the blood, and flesh of the flesh of the men who wrote that Declaration and so they are. That is the electric cord in that Declaration that links the hearts of patriotic and liberty loving men together, that will link those patriotic hearts as long as the love of freedom exists in the minds of men throughout the world.

Lincoln then turned to the issue of slavery, arguing that the Declaration of Independence implied the political equality of all races. Once people started making exceptions to that principle, he explained, the inevitable consequence was a justification for slavery. As he put it, "whether it come from the mouth of a King, an excuse for enslaving the people of his country, or from the mouth of men of one race as a reason for enslaving the men of another race, it is all the same old serpent, and I hold that if that course of argumentation that is made for the purpose of convincing the public mind that we should not care about this, should be granted, it does not stop with the negro."[236]

Six decades later, these ideas resonated in the Chicago foreign language newspapers. Like Lincoln, the editors and writers for these papers were not immune to the racial bigotry of their time, but at their best, they promoted an agenda that sought to advance civic nationalism by demanding, as did African Americans, that this country live up to its most cherished ideals, most important its commitment to equality.

For many years, scholars have pointed to the stark differences in the historical experiences of immigrants and African Americans, differences rooted in what anthropologist John Ogbu has described as membership in either voluntary or involuntary minority groups. Specifically, as voluntary minorities, European immigrants generally experienced America as a land of freedom and opportunity, and they were, for the most part, strongly encouraged to assimilate. On the other hand, slavery, Jim Crow, and the denial of "true assimilation" have marked the experience of black Americans, who were involuntary immigrants.[237] Yet, despite these great differences, when confronted with the ethnic nationalism of the racial restrictionist, the editors and writers of the Chicago foreign language press responded with arguments strikingly similar to those that such African American leaders as Frederick Douglass and W. E. B. DuBois had been making for decades.[238] Like these black leaders, the writers for the Chicago foreign language newspapers argued that the egalitarian ideals touted by native-born Americans were belied by claims of Anglo-Saxon or Nordic supremacy, and that "outsiders" often have had a more profound understanding of these ideals than people whose ancestors came over on the *Mayflower*. In 1903, DuBois stated that "there are to-day no truer exponents of the pure human spirit of the Declaration of Independence than the American Negroes." Fourteen years later, M. E. Ravage, a Jewish immigrant from Romania, echoed that idea in regard to European immigrants, declaring,

> When I hear all around me the foolish prattle about the new
> immigration—"the scum of Europe," as it is called—that is in-

vading and making itself master of this country, I cannot help saying to myself that Americans have forgotten America. . . . The more I think upon the subject the more I become persuaded that the relation of the teacher and taught as between those who were born here and those who came here must be reversed. It is the free American who needs to be instructed by the benighted races in the uplifting word that America speaks to all the world. Only from the humble immigrant, it appears to me, can he learn just what America stands for in the family of nations.[239]

With such arguments European immigrants joined African Americans and other minorities in changing the way *all* Americans thought about equality, freedom, and national identity. As Langston Hughes wrote in his powerful poem "Let America Be America Again," outsiders, whether they were blacks, immigrants, or the poor, believed fervently in this country's democratic creed and sought to make America "the dream the dreamer dreamed."[240] The next chapter argues that these ideas helped shape this country's response not only to the great totalitarian threats from abroad, but also to the unfulfilled promise of American democracy. Looking back on this era, Gary Gerstle argues that the surge of civic nationalism in the first few decades of the twentieth century drew from the "same taproot" that eventually yielded the ideas of "a Gunnar Myrdal and the integrationist dream of a Martin Luther King Jr."[241] As reflected in the Chicago foreign language press, European immigrants played a vital role in that process.

Conclusion

The picture of Americanization that emerges from the newspapers of the CFLPS does not fit any of the usual categories that people then or scholars later have used to describe the relationship between immigrants and American society. Insofar as assimilation is concerned, the editors and writers of the newspapers reviewed in this chapter clearly opposed "100 per cent" Americanization, which demanded "absolute forgetfulness" of the immigrants' Old World languages and cultural heritages.[242] But this stance does not imply that the CFLPS writers were strong supporters of cultural pluralism, or at least the form of cultural pluralism that sought to maintain immigrant communities separate and distinct from the rest of

American society. While the editors and writers for the Chicago foreign language press fought fiercely to retain important aspects of their Old World cultures—their languages, religious beliefs, pride in their homelands and heroes, and recognition of the contributions their people had made to western civilization and American history—they did so as staunch Americans. The third approach to Americanization, amalgamation, did not fare any better with the editors and writers for the Chicago foreign language newspapers than did assimilation or cultural pluralism. Indeed, when they wrote about the melting pot, most were wary of both uses of the term, wanting their people neither to melt into some sort of Anglo-Saxon mold nor to disappear into an entirely new mixed American race.

But rejecting these conventional approaches did not mean these writers rejected Americanization. Rather, the Chicago foreign language press promoted a new version of Americanization—patriotic pluralism. Beginning as early as the 1890s, major Chicago foreign language newspapers repeatedly presented a perspective on Americanization that combined a deep, patriotic commitment to this country with pride in the immigrants' native cultures. The CFLPS writers wanted both the *unum* and the *pluribus*. And, because so many of them had experienced cultural, linguistic, and religious persecution in Europe at the hands of imperial despots, they quickly recognized that the best way to defend their cultural distinctiveness was to become patriotic Americans committed to defending democracy. They saw the nation's common democratic heritage as the essence of the *unum*, and simultaneously as the source of protection for the *pluribus*. As John Higham once noted, "A multiethnic society can avoid tyranny only through a shared culture and a set of rules that all of its groups accept."[243] Taking that perspective, writers for the Chicago foreign language press saw no contradiction between being patriotic Americans and being proud of their native culture and traditions.

Consequently, over the years, these editors and journalists undertook a sophisticated educational effort in which they taught their readers about the ideals and values that hold this country together while simultaneously reminding them that their cultural differences were worthy of respect and could enrich their adopted country. As an Italian writer stated in 1928, "Americanization does not mean to forget the best and noblest traditions of our motherland; it means, instead, to jealously retain the best and sanest of the Italian tradition, and at the same time to absorb the best of the life of our adopted motherland."[244] In other words, the people writing for these newspapers strongly endorsed Americanization, but they redefined the term to suit this new vision and in the process promoted a new, more inclusive vision of the United States.[245]

Perhaps the most important aspect of this redefined version of Americanization emerged out of the struggle against the racial restrictionists. By defending their Americanism against nativists who argued that the new immigrants were racially unfit for American citizenship, the editors and other contributors to the Chicago foreign language press strongly asserted that the only valid definition of an American was one that rested on the depth of a person's commitment to the nation's democratic ideals, not on one's bloodline. These immigrant writers were obviously basing much of that stance on self-interest, but at the same time they also were actively embracing and extending the inclusiveness and universalism of the American democratic creed. Contrary to the lamentations about the perceived failure of Americanization, from this perspective, Americanization was a great and important success.

In taking a civic nationalist stance on racial restriction and in advocating a more inclusive vision of Americanization education, these editors and writers were participating in a broader cultural trend. As political scientist Eric Kaufmann argues, beginning in the late 1920s ideas about "cosmopolitan Americanism" began to significantly influence American culture.[246] Historian Diana Selig sees similar trends occurring in anthropology and educational psychology, which opened the way for educators to acknowledge the richness of immigrants' backgrounds and to see the possibilities of such programs as intercultural education.[247] In short, during the late 1920s, the patriotic and pluralistic form of Americanization touted by the Chicago foreign language press became part of a larger set of intellectual and educational trends that strengthened the civic nationalist character of this country. These trends broadened and deepened in the 1930s and 1940s.

4

"THEY HAVE NEVER BEEN— THEY ARE NOT NOW— HALF-HEARTED AMERICANS": AMERICANIZATION EDUCATION, 1930-1955

In 1940, several months after the fall of France, Gerhart Saenger, a psychologist and recent immigrant to the United States, published a grim but insightful essay on the problems of minorities in modern nation-states. "Wherever we turn," he wrote, "we hear the cry for national, racial, or cultural unity. The demand of the hour is to conform or to die." But he added that racial and religious politics in some countries had made it all but impossible for certain minorities to conform. "In fact," he declared, "their very existence may be regarded as a threat to the welfare of the group with whom fate has placed them." These groups, Saenger warned, faced the prospect of mass extermination. While noting that such attitudes were defining features of the race-based dictatorships throughout Europe, Saenger also was deeply concerned about how democratic societies would address the problem of majority rule and minority rights in this new and frightening era.[1]

In the 1930s and 1940s, many American political and educational leaders shared these fears, with growing concern about the spread of ethnic nationalism in all parts of the world. Their concerns centered on the same kinds of questions about ethnic and civic nationalism that had animated the Americanization debates of the 1910s and 1920s: What determines a person's national identity? What is required for assimilation? Can minority groups maintain distinctive aspects of their original culture and/or religion and still be seen as loyal members of modern nation-states? Are some groups unassimilable because of inherent racial characteristics? As racial purity and national identity came to dominate political developments in countries around the world, the answers to these questions had profound and often ghastly consequences for people who found themselves on the wrong side of violent ethnic nationalist regimes.

During the 1930s and early 1940s, the United States avoided the most horrifying aspects of this movement toward ethnic nationalism, but this period in American history was nevertheless marked by a fierce resurgence of nativism. Critics of the eastern and southern European immigrants once again raised questions about whether these people could genuinely assimilate into American society. Clearly, the apparent triumph of racial restriction in 1924 did not end the debate about what defines an American and what kind of country the United States should be. Not surprisingly, questions about the effectiveness of Americanization education continued as well.

Unfortunately, most scholars who have studied immigration in the first half of the twentieth century end their discussions of Americanization education before or in 1930.[2] Yet in 1930, about 12 percent of the U.S. population, approximately 14 million people, were foreign-born and over one-third of these people were not naturalized. Moreover, another 26 million Americans had at least one foreign-born parent.[3] During the Great Depression and World War II, as concerns grew about assimilation, naturalization, and the loyalty of various immigrant groups, many national leaders again turned to Americanization as a way to unify the country. Indeed, these efforts were so substantial that they made the 1930s and early 1940s among the most important periods in the history of Americanization education.

This chapter looks at Americanization programs on both the adult and K–12 levels. It examines the revival of nativism during the Depression years; the rarely discussed adult Americanization education campaign in the late 1930s and early 1940s; the response of foreign language newspapers in Chicago and Cleveland to nativism in the United States and racist, totalitarian regimes in Europe; and the development of intercultural education programs on the K–12 level, a movement that promoted inclusive ideas about American history and culture that were strikingly similar to the patriotic pluralism espoused by the foreign language press. In a number of ways, these educational efforts, particularly in the period between 1938 and 1948, greatly strengthened the nation's commitment to civic nationalism and helped beat back the rise of ethnic nationalism domestically and globally. This period also marked the culmination of Americanization education for the immigrants who came to the United States in the first half of the twentieth century.

Successful Americanization involved more than merely integrating into American society; it also involved changing the way Americans in general conceived of this country. Beginning in the late 1930s and continuing through most of the 1940s, educators on the adult and K–12 levels, foreign language newspaper editors and journalists, and such intellectual and educational leaders from immigrant communities as Louis Adamic, Franz Boas, Leonard Covello, Norman Drachler, Bruno Lasker, and Hilda Taba advanced a robust, patriotically pluralist vision of civic nationalism. This vision characterized the United States as a country composed of different and, at times, quarrelsome groups, but groups that nevertheless were united by their commitment to the United States and its democratic ideals. While this vision had attracted only a few prominent advocates in the 1910s and 1920s, by the late 1930s it had become increasingly popular. Indeed, during World War II, it characterized how many people conceived of this country. The prominent role that immigrant educators, intellectuals, and journalists played in these developments indicates that M. E. Ravage's 1917 argument about the need to reverse the educational relationship between immigrants and native-born Americans had, to some degree, come to pass.[4] These Americanized immigrants pioneered a new, pluralistic understanding of America that would eventually become part of the intellectual and cultural mainstream.

Ethnic Nationalism Resurgent, 1930–1941

In the 1930s and early 1940s, the movement toward civic nationalism and a greater appreciation of cultural pluralism in the United States was neither easy nor assured. In fact, in many ways, conditions could not have been worse for these ideas to thrive. Following World War I, the "problem of minorities" became an increasingly urgent and politically volatile issue in both Europe and the United States. In Europe, the attempt to build ethnically homogeneous states from the ruins of the Austro-Hungarian, German, and Ottoman empires inadvertently created a massive new problem, namely, large numbers of ethnic and religious minorities living within the new nations. As the historian Mark Mazower points out, "Versailles had given sixty million people a state of their own, but it turned another twenty-five million into minorities." These minorities included not only groups that had no states of their own, such as Jews, Roma (Gypsies), Ukrainians, and European Muslims, but also large numbers of Germans and Hungarians who found themselves citizens of states dominated by other ethnic groups. All these minorities presented problems for the new nations of Europe, which struggled to solve them, not necessarily in peaceful ways.[5]

Things worsened during the 1930s as the global economic depression spread misery and unemployment throughout much of Europe. The economic crisis contributed to the rise of new authoritarian and totalitarian movements, many of which were based on the fierce ethnic nationalist principles that had first taken root in Fascist Italy and Nazi Germany. These new ethnic nationalist movements gradually gained power throughout eastern and southern Europe and frequently focused their wrath on minority groups within their borders. By the late 1930s, in addition to Germany and Italy, Hungary, Poland, Romania, and Spain all had dictatorial governments that crushed civil liberties and left minorities defenseless against increasingly racialized laws and policies. This retreat from democracy was so powerful in central and eastern Europe that some commentators predicted that dictatorial regimes advocating ideas of racial purity were the wave of the future. Mazower observed, "Triumphant in 1918, [democracy in eastern and central Europe] was virtually extinct twenty years on."[6] By the mid-1930s, the propositions that all men were created equal and that the duty of the state was to protect the rights of minority groups were in full retreat throughout the European heartland. Civic nationalism appeared to be a dying political proposition.

At the same time in the United States, a similarly poisonous combination of economic collapse, widespread unemployment, wavering faith in democracy, and the scapegoating of minorities was increasingly apparent. Indeed, beginning in the mid-1930s, many educational and civic leaders in the United States watched the rise of totalitarianism in Europe with growing fears that the contagion could spread across the Atlantic.[7] As early as 1936, for example, Louis Adamic, a Slovenian immigrant who became a leading proponent of patriotic pluralism in this era, published an article in *Harper's*, decrying homegrown "fascistic fanatics" who were targeting the foreign-born as the cause of the nation's problems.[8] Noting that such mainstream organizations as the American Federation of Labor and the U.S. Chamber of Commerce were actively contributing to such "alien-hatred," Adamic concluded that these actions and attitudes were "threatening to inflict upon . . . [the United States] certain characteristics of European fascist states."[9]

In August 1940, the elite Educational Policies Commission of the National Education Association (NEA) presented an even darker assessment in a brief essay, *Education and the Defense of American Democracy.* "The picture which the world presents to the friends of democracy is ominous and terrifying," the educational leaders wrote. "Totalitarianism, with its scorn of the doctrine of human brotherhood, its mockery of democratic principles of equality among men, its denial of the dignity of the individual human being, its derision of the ideal of peace among nations, its glorification of war as man's noblest pursuit, its conversion of the citizen into a pawn of the state, its inculcation of the sentiments of national and racial bigotry, its elevation of dictatorship into a moral and religious principle—totalitarianism, the military state in its contemporary form, holds Europe in thrall and casts its lengthening shadow over the whole earth."[10]

In seeking to counter the growing popularity of these ideas in the United States during the 1930s, the educators, politicians, and immigrant leaders who defended civic nationalism faced an uncertain and divided American public. Tremors from the ethnic nationalist and totalitarian earthquakes in Europe reverberated throughout the United States. Amid the deepening economic catastrophe, such groups as the Ku Klux Klan (KKK) increasingly railed against blacks, Catholics, immigrants, and Jews, seeing them as corruptors of the American way of life. Joining the KKK in these stands were such new organizations as the pro-Nazi German American Bund and the Silver Shirts, an organization whose name deliberately evoked Hitler's Waffen SS. Both the Bund and the Silver Shirts openly espoused the racist ideology of Nazi Germany.[11]

In a number of important ways, however, the ethnic nationalist ideology espoused by the Klan, the Bund, and the Silver Shirts was less a European import than a reassertion of ideas that the racial restrictionists had used since the 1920s. Indeed, during the 1920s and 1930s, European groups espousing the racist doctrines of Nordic supremacy drew heavily from American sources. Adolf Hitler, for example, praised the 1924 National Origins Act in *Mein Kampf,* noting that "the American union" was the only country in the world that had taken positive steps toward creating what he called a "folkish state" (i.e., an ethnic nationalist state in which citizenship was based on bloodlines rather than on assimilation).[12] Once the Nazis consolidated their takeover of Germany, they publicly acknowledged their ideological debt to American racial theorists, honoring such prominent leaders of the racial restriction movement as Lothrop Stoddard and Harry H. Laughlin. Laughlin, for example, accepted an honorary degree from the University of Heidelberg in 1936, which applauded his efforts to establish the "scientific" principles that supported German conceptions of racial supremacy and inferiority.[13]

Thus, the German American Bund and the Silver Shirts were not really espousing a new or distinctly European idea when positing a clear racial hierarchy with Nordics as the master race, although they did use the symbols and tactics of the Nazi movement in Germany to promote it. Like the racial restrictionists, these groups argued that Nordics had built the country and were ordained to rule it, an idea that Stoddard advanced in his 1927 book *Re-Forging America.*[14] Moreover, these groups sought to minimize, if not completely eradicate, the influence of supposedly inferior and unassimilable races in American politics and culture. For a while in the 1930s, these ideas gained traction in the United States, due in part to the apparent success the Nazis had in returning Germany to its position as one of the most powerful nations in the world.[15] In addition, in 1939 and 1940, following the swift and overwhelming German victories at the start of World War II, it appeared that Nazi doctrines of racial superiority and inferiority were poised to become the reigning political ideology in the world. But as later sections of this chapter demonstrate, these victories of ethnic nationalism in Europe also helped inspire a powerful countermovement in the United States, one that engaged in a life-and-death struggle to ensure the survival of civic nationalism and democracy.

While the most extreme ideas about European racial hierarchies thrived mainly on the fringes of American politics, deeply ingrained prejudices about immigrants and opposition to immigration itself remained widespread in the United States during the Depression decade. The fear and distrust of foreigners that had animated the efforts of racial restrictionists still lingered in all parts of the country. In 1930, for example, President Herbert Hoover provided a vivid example of anti-immigrant sentiment when he angrily responded to criticism from fellow Republican Fiorello LaGuardia, the Italian-born mayor of New York City, saying, "[G]o back to Italy where you belong and advise Mussolini on how to make good honest citizens in Italy." Hoover added, "The Italians are predominantly our murderers and bootleggers . . . like a lot of other foreign spawn, you do not appreciate the country which supports and tolerates you."[16]

Such anti-immigrant attitudes hardened as the national economic crisis worsened. In the early 1930s, increasing numbers of journalists and politicians claimed that immigrants were exacerbating the problems of the Depression by taking jobs that should have gone to "real Americans." Due to such fears, Roper polls of public opinion in the 1930s routinely found strong opposition to any efforts to allow more immigrants into the United States, particularly if these efforts involved relaxing the quotas established in the 1924 National Origins Act.[17] As historian Salvatore LaGumina argues, in the Depression years "nativism continued to be an integral part of the American body politic," and "immigration issues, far from being either ignored or regarded as unique, autonomous problems, were considered inseparable from pressing national problems."[18]

Typical of these nativist attitudes was a series of anti-immigrant articles that appeared in the *Saturday Evening Post* in 1935 and 1936. At this time, the *Saturday Evening Post* was one of the mostly widely read periodicals in the nation, with about three million subscribers.[19] In the first of these articles, the well-known journalist Isaac F. Marcosson railed against immigrants in language that echoed the rhetoric of the racial restrictionists in the 1920s. Beginning by noting that the man convicted in the Lindbergh kidnapping was an illegal immigrant, Marcosson denounced virtually all newcomers, legal and illegal, as usurpers of American jobs, criminals, welfare freeloaders, agents provocateurs from the Soviet Union, or simply "terrorists and other undesirables."[20] Marcosson sought guidance on immigration issues from Harry H. Laughlin, and he approvingly quoted Laughlin's succinct analysis of the situation. "The whole problem revolves around the racial make-up and the hereditary stuff of the American people," Laughlin declared. After noting that governmental programs for immigrants were draining scarce resources from American society, Laughlin added, "This dollar cost is trifling compared with the damage which low-grade immigrants practically dumped on America have done to the human breeding stock of future Americans."[21]

Two weeks later Congressman Martin Dies (D-TX), also writing in the *Saturday Evening Post*, added his voice to this issue, claiming that the massive unemployment of the Depression was directly attributable to the flood of immigrants that inundated the United States between 1890 and 1924. Dies declared, "If the nation had awakened at that time [the 1890s] to the perils of its immigration policy and promptly ex-cluded the 20,000,000 or more of aliens that since have entered the competitive ranks of labor, agriculture and business, it is reasonable to believe that the unemployment problem would never have assumed such serious and unprecedented proportions in this country."[22] Two months later, an editorial in the *National Republic*, a staunchly right-wing magazine, specifically endorsed Dies' solution for ending the na-tion's unemployment problem by "permanently exclud[ing] new immi-grants from every country" and immediately deporting the "3,500,000 aliens in our midst."[23]

In the January 25, 1936, edition of the *Saturday Evening Post*, journalist Raymond G. Carroll revived the ethnic nationalist complaint that these immigrants were unassimilable. After wandering through various ethnic neighborhoods in New York City, Carroll threw up his hands in despair at these "unbroken units of foreign people picked up in bulk over there and set down over here in exactly the same environment." He continued, "They cling to old customs, to native foods, drinks and dress, and strive together in attempts to re-create pale wraiths of the homelands." Most damning, however, was Carroll's assessment of their Americanization. "Many of these aliens stay foreign into the second and third generations. Americanism is a mask put on for Election Day, job hunting, and relief getting. Their bodies are here, their minds are overseas."[24]

Articles such as these hit a nerve among many Americans and members of Congress. Given the continuing high rates of unemployment (in 1935, some states still reported that nearly 20 percent of eligible workers were out of work), the possibility that aliens were getting jobs or relief work while native-born Americans went without was a highly volatile issue.[25] This was especially true when people looked at such federal relief pro-grams as the Works Progress Administration (WPA; later, the Works Proj-ects Administration). At roughly the same time that these anti-immigrant articles appeared in the *Saturday Evening Post*, the editor of *Liberty Mag-azine*, published by Robert McCormick, the owner of the *Chicago Tri-bune*, denounced the huge numbers of "unnaturalized foreigners on our relief rolls." The American Legion also weighed in on this issue, calling on the federal government to "employ only American citizens on relief projects."[26] Members of Congress quickly responded to these demands by mandating that relief programs such as the WPA employ only American citizens.[27]

In short, during most of the 1930s, anti-immigrant sentiment became increasingly prevalent across the United States. At the same time, anti-Semitic and anti-Catholic attitudes quickened throughout the country.[28] One of the best examples of the resurgence of such ethnic nationalism appeared in a 1939 report on immigration commissioned and published by the New York State Chamber of Commerce. Written by the indefatigable Harry H. Laughlin, the study reasserted all the derogatory ideas about new-stock immigrants, including comparing them historically to the barbarians whose interbreeding with native Romans contributed to the fall of the empire. With such fears in mind, Laughlin called on the U.S. government to further limit new immigration by allowing entry of "only such immigrants as are assimilable, in numbers and quality, to the predominating native white stocks of the United States."[29] In addition, as historian Zoe Burkholder has found, soon after the New York Chamber of Commerce published this report, the organization called on state legislators to slash New York's education budget by 25 percent, abolish all public high schools, and compel educators to concentrate solely on teaching basic literacy. Throughout the 1930s, many other local Chambers of Commerce regularly demanded severe cuts in public school budgets, but the demands of the New York chamber stand out for the distinctly racist, anti-immigrant premise the organization used to support its position.[30] The stance taken by the chamber in this case reflected the views of racial restrictionists in regard to the ability of education to "make" Americans. This push for massive cuts in public school budgets indicates, once again, that racial restrictionists believed that the education of immigrants was literally a waste of time and money.

Clearly, during the 1930s and early 1940s a sizable portion of the American public espoused, or at least condoned, nativist attitudes, and a substantial number held anti-Semitic and anti-Catholic attitudes as well. Perhaps the most widely circulated example of this revival of nativism came in a July 3, 1941, article by Westbrook Pegler, the most prominent nationally syndicated newspaper columnist in the country at this time. In the essay, Pegler reprised the xenophobic rhetoric of the 1920s in a blistering attack on European immigrants, whose Americanization he declared was "insincere" or "incomplete." Attributing the fall of France to that country's lax immigration policies, Pegler declared that European immigrants in the United States, regardless of whether they had naturalized, were a potential "fifth column" that posed a palpable threat to the nation.

To deal with this threat, he advocated creating a distinct, subordinate form of citizenship for all naturalized Americans, a status that would forbid them from holding any political office or taking leadership in any labor union. Pegler declared, "True, that would create a B class of citizenship, but I see no objection to that, in view of our experience, and especially in view of the doubtful quality of much of the immigration which has swept in here, much of it under pretext, since the scourge began abroad."[31]

Such attitudes about European immigrants and growing fears that some foreign-born groups, specifically Italians, Germans, and Russians, might undermine national security ultimately led to the passage of the Alien Registration Act in June 1940. The Act made it "unlawful to knowingly or willfully advocate, abet, advise, or teach the duty, necessity, desirability, or propriety of overthrowing or destroying any government in the United States by force or violence." In addition, the Act required that all alien residents in the United States over the age of fourteen register with the federal government and be fingerprinted.[32] By the end of the year, between 4.7 and 4.9 million aliens had been registered. These included over a million people from Italy and Germany (over 661,000 and 364,000 respectively) and an additional 375,000 from the Soviet Union.[33]

Despite fears about non-naturalized European immigrants, following the Japanese attack on Pearl Harbor and America's declaration of war against all the Axis powers it was the small Japanese American community on the West Coast—not the large Italian and German American communities in the Midwest and East—that bore the brunt of the new wave of wartime hysteria. The internment of the Japanese Americans stands as one of the most profoundly undemocratic actions taken by the United States during the "Good War." Similar to the federal policies that segregated blacks and whites in the armed forces, the internment directly contradicted the civic nationalist ideals that the nation was defending. Moreover, unlike most of the attacks on eastern and southern European immigrants in this era, these actions reflected another long-standing aspect of American ethnic nationalism that defined people's rights and dignity primarily by the color of their skin.[34]

Ultimately, however, the nation's experience in World War II, particularly the confrontation with Nazi Germany and its pervasive racist ideology, inspired challenges to all aspects of American ethnic nationalism. Indeed, in response to the rising tide of racism of the 1930s and 1940s, a tide that threatened this country both at home and abroad, a strong countervailing movement in defense of civic nationalism developed in the United States. Unlike the assimilationist vision of civic nationalism that characterized the World War I years, the form of civic nationalism that arose in the late 1930s and early 1940s was akin to the politically and educationally inclusive ideas of patriotic pluralism described in chapter 3. During the Depression and war years, a growing number of prominent civic nationalists argued vigorously that America's cultural, racial, and religious diversity was a distinct and powerful source of national strength.[35] In direct response to racial fear-mongers, they praised the deep and abiding patriotism of the new Americans.[36]

An excellent example of this stance can be found in the response by the liberal journalist I. F. Stone to Pegler's call for a "B class" of citizenship for naturalized Americans. Characterizing Pegler's views as akin to those of the Third Reich, Stone defended the American "melting pot state" in which "men are bound together by ties stronger than blood." He continued: "No idea is better suited to unite all Americans at home and to appeal to oppressed people abroad than the idea we have had since 1776. We need no better. We need only infuse the idea with new vitality by living more truly in accordance with it."[37]

While Stone was specifically decrying attacks on European immigrants, his vision, like that of many civic nationalists of this era, was both broad and compelling. By the early 1940s, this vision began to play a central role in defining the United States. Americanization education contributed to the growing strength and acceptance of this form of civic nationalism not only through teachings in formal classes for adult immigrants, which paid far more attention to the cultural backgrounds of the immigrants than ever before, but also in the writings of the foreign language press; through the works of leading immigrant intellectuals whose books, articles, and speeches were increasingly gaining a national audience; and through the adoption of intercultural education programs in many K–12 school districts, programs that offered a distinctly patriotic and pluralistic vision of American history and culture. The rest of this chapter examines each of these developments in turn.

Adult Americanization, 1930–1945

In late October 1936, as the presidential campaign was drawing to a close, Franklin Roosevelt returned to his home state of New York to rally his supporters. On October 28, he gave two back-to-back speeches in New York City. Not surprisingly, given the city's huge immigrant population, Roosevelt used these speeches to reflect on the contribution immigrants had made to the United States and the great strength that he found in the nation's cultural diversity. The first of these speeches was appropriately given at a ceremony commemorating the fiftieth anniversary of the dedication of the Statue of Liberty. Describing the millions of immigrants who first glimpsed the statue as they entered the New York Harbor, Roosevelt declared, "They came to us speaking many tongues—but a single language, the universal language of human aspirations." He added, "They not only found freedom in the New World, but by their effort and devotion they made the New World's freedom safer, richer, more far-reaching, more capable of growth."

In addition, unlike his cousin Theodore, Franklin Roosevelt made a point of commending immigrants "who have left their native land to join us [and who] may still retain here their affection for some of the things they left behind—old customs, old language, old friends." While he strongly praised members of the second generation who had adopted "the new language" and "new customs" of the United States, his inclusive stance regarding newcomers who retained their Old World heritage was dramatically different, not only from the positions taken by previous presidents, but also from the attitudes of nativists who still feared and maligned these immigrants.[38]

Roosevelt expanded on this theme in his next speech at Roosevelt Park (named after his mother) in lower Manhattan. Echoing Randolph Bourne, the president observed that many immigrants who had settled in this neighborhood "wove into the pattern of American life some of the color, some of the richness of the cultures from which they came." Then, as if directly challenging the racial restrictionists who had ridiculed immigrants' ability to become true Americans, he declared, "We gave them freedom. I am proud—America is proud—of what they have given to us." He continued, "They have never been—they are not now—half-hearted Americans. In Americanization classes and in night schools they have burned the midnight oil to be worthy of their new allegiance."[39]

These speeches are striking because never before had someone of such national prominence so warmly praised the new immigrants for their cultural diversity while simultaneously defending their Americanism. At a time when violent ethnic nationalism was reshaping the face of

Europe, and many Americans were readily expressing anti-immigrant, anti-Semitic, and anti-Catholic sentiments, Roosevelt strongly reaffirmed this country's civic nationalist creed. Moreover, he also acknowledged the important role that Americanization education had played in what he termed "the great process out of which we have welded our American citizenship."[40]

For Roosevelt, these statements were not just late-in-the-campaign rhetoric. Rather, they reflected two important aspects of his administration's education policy. The first was the unprecedented financial and material support that the federal government gave to adult education programs, particularly those involved in Americanization education. Almost from its inception, the WPA, the New Deal's most ambitious relief program, provided funding for educators teaching citizenship and English classes. This support broke new ground in how Americanization education was delivered and in helping hundreds of thousands of immigrants prepare to become American citizens. Second, during the 1930s and 1940s, at least some of these federally sponsored English and citizenship classes adopted a kinder and gentler approach to Americanization education, often celebrating the diverse backgrounds of these "Americans in the making" rather than demanding that immigrants cut their ties to their native cultures.[41] In taking this stance, members of the Roosevelt administration may simply have been motivated by political opportunism, recognizing that support for more culturally sensitive Americanization education was a small price to pay for ensuring the loyalty of many new-stock immigrants to the Democratic Party. But there is also evidence that many supporters of federal naturalization education programs agreed with criticism of the heavy-handed Americanization efforts of the past and sought to do things differently this time around.

In regard to financial and material support, within two years of taking power, New Deal administrators provided money to help shore up beleaguered adult Americanization programs in public schools. In the early 1930s, the situation facing adult evening school classes, like so many other public school programs, was dire. As the full force of the Depression bore down on these schools, educational leaders slashed funding for evening programs in their desperate attempt to balance school budgets.[42] A 1933 study conducted by the National Education Association found that in the previous two years almost 43 percent of cities cut funding for night school programs, and over a third specifically cut adult American-ization classes.[43]

But unlike K–12 education, which received only modest financial aid from Washington during the 1930s, New Deal leaders readily provided funds to support adult education programs.[44] Indeed, as early as February 1934, federal relief organizations were supporting teachers in adult evening schools. Eventually, adult education became the largest educational pro-gram supported by the WPA.[45] Between 1935 and 1940, the WPA supported over 40,000 adult education teachers who taught almost two million stu-dents. The budget for these efforts averaged $20–25 million annually.[46] Much of this money went directly to Americanization programs. For ex-ample, in Cleveland in 1941–1942, over 60 percent of the 6,400 students in WPA-supported adult education programs were in citizenship classes.[47]

Leaders of the WPA were interested in adult Americanization educa-tion for a variety of reasons. As in all WPA projects, the primary objective was putting people to work. In this case, that meant getting unemployed teachers back into classrooms. But what made adult education so popular among WPA leaders was that once in the classroom, these teachers ideally would provide knowledge and skills to the unemployed that would in turn help them get jobs. As major corporations increasingly banned nonciti-zens from employment, and as Congress passed new legislation barring aliens from relief programs (while at the same time making citizenship easier to acquire by reducing naturalization fees), the WPA saw an obvi-ous target of opportunity.[48]

In 1936, the U.S. Commissioner of Immigration and Naturalization es-timated that there were about "four and a half million people of foreign birth in this country who are aliens in the technical sense, that is, persons who have not yet become citizens."[49] Over the next few years, the WPA ratcheted up its efforts to get these people naturalized. By the early 1940s, the WPA collaborated on Americanization programs with the U.S. Office of Education (USOE) and the Immigration and Naturalization Service (INS).[50] At the same time, various nongovernmental organizations, in-cluding the Young Men's Christian Association (YMCA), the Foreign Language Information Service, the Immigrants' Protective League, the National Catholic Welfare Conference, and the National Council of Jew-ish Women, all of which had long histories of working with immigrants, stepped up their citizenship education efforts.[51] In addition, such labor unions as the International Ladies' Garment Workers' Union and the United Mine Workers established English and citizenship classes.[52]

Two pieces of federal legislation passed in 1940, both of which were precipitated by the growing likelihood that America would be drawn into World War II, contributed to the expansion of these efforts. The first was the Alien Registration Act of 1940, which, as noted earlier, mandated that the federal government register all aliens in the United States. The second was the Nationality Act of 1940, which gave the commissioner of the Immigration and Naturalization Service supervisory authority over naturalizations nationwide. It also codified the steps individuals had to follow to become citizens and mandated a uniform examination for all applicants that would assess the applicants' ability to speak English and determine whether they understood and had an "attachment to the fundamental principles of the Constitution of the United States."[53] This last aspect of the Act, standardizing the naturalization examination, gradually supplanted the various and idiosyncratic ways in which citizenship tests had been given for decades.[54]

These new laws provided a golden opportunity for the federal government to promote Americanization and expand its efforts in this area.[55] For example, following the mass registration of aliens in 1940, the INS provided "names of candidates for naturalization" to local public schools and, in the summer and fall of 1942, sent "approximately two and one-half million letters of invitation to attend citizenship classes" offered by public schools and the WPA.[56] This was not, however, a one-way street. As historian Mark Van Pelt points out, one of the "unanticipated consequences" of this law "was that 1.7 million of those registered had indicated that they wanted to become American citizens."[57]

This eagerness for naturalization was due to a number of related factors. Specifically, the likelihood of war led huge numbers of non-naturalized immigrants to recognize that this was a particularly propitious time to seek citizenship. Fearing the loss of jobs or relief benefits, facing the prospect that Americans might once again target "enemy aliens" in wartime, they sought protection in naturalization. Moreover, as one commentator noted, non-naturalized people from such countries as Germany and Italy recognized "the fact that extreme political ideologies abroad made American citizenship more meaningful than ever."[58]

In June 1941, upon realizing that a flood of applicants for naturalization was looming, President Roosevelt set aside $14 million in WPA funds (worth approximately $180 million in 2004 dollars) to support a newly created federal agency, the National Citizenship Education Program (NCEP) that would support Americanization education nationwide. William F. Russell, dean of Teachers College, Columbia University, headed up the NCEP during its influential but brief (two-year) existence. Essentially, the NCEP was an umbrella organization that coordinated the Americanization efforts of the WPA, which provided salaries for teachers and supervisors of evening school programs, and the INS, which produced curriculum materials, and with local school districts, which provided classrooms and other forms of logistical support.[59] As Russell explained in October 1941, the mandate for the NCEP was to aid the INS and "local boards of education in making available to applicants for naturalization, facilities to prepare them for citizenship duties and responsibilities." To do this, the NCEP would provide aid for teaching and supervising Americanization classes; creating new teaching materials (ranging from textbooks to lesson plans); "organizing pre-service and in-service training programs for teachers"; "furnishing clerical and stenographic assistance"; and aiding nongovernmental agencies that were teaching "English and the principles of our form of government."[60] The funds for the NCEP were "intended to provide, on the basis of a year's work, 11,000 additional teachers to reach approximately 990,000 foreign-born students." In less than a year, forty-five states had requested aid from NCEP, and by March 1942, the program was supporting about 6,000 teachers who were working with an estimated 650,000 students.[61]

While the NCEP was clearly a broad-based effort, Van Pelt argues that Russell, during his stint as director, focused primarily on improving the quality of textbooks—a problem that had plagued Americanization programs for decades.[62] As noted in chapter 2, many of the materials that teachers used in English and citizenship classes were simply recycled from elementary schools and consequently often were totally inadequate for adult learners. Moreover, even materials written specifically for adults frequently neglected many practical topics that at least some leading adult educators thought immigrants needed to understand as they negotiated their way through the naturalization process and their integration into American society. Russell set out to change that situation.

Within a month of the creation of the NCEP, he commissioned educators at the University of Chicago to prepare a series of textbooks that would address important aspects of adult Americanization education.

Featuring such titles as *On the Way to Democracy, The Rights of the People,* and *Our Constitution Today,* these books were clearly designed to prepare older students for naturalization. Moreover, the books in the Chicago series came in three-volume sets, which, like those in the Peter Roberts program discussed in chapter 2, were designed to move students into increasingly sophisticated reading levels. Similarly, Russell hired a number of well-known authors, including the University of Wisconsin historian Merle Curti, to prepare another series of books on American history. These books also came in sets with differentiated reading levels. In addition, NCEP staffers working at the University of Maryland prepared books for instructors about how to teach English to non-native speakers and how to teach basic literacy. Finally, educators at the University of Michigan prepared guides for teachers working in citizenship classes and began, but never finished, a proposed twenty-eight-volume series about the cultures of various ethnic groups in the United States.[63] All of these books represented a new approach to Americanization education, not so much in terms of content (although the proposed ethnic culture series *was* quite distinctive), but mainly in regard to the attention that NCEP leaders paid to educational methods and audience.

An excellent example of this new approach to Americanization textbooks can be seen in *Citizenship Education,* a teacher's guide published by the Illinois unit of the NCEP in 1941. One of the most interesting aspects of the guide was the degree to which it appeared to have been influenced by ideas popularized by progressive educators, specifically by trying to move beyond traditional subject areas and include material that students would find immediately interesting and useful. This trend was hardly surprising, given William Russell's background at Teachers College, home to many of the nation's leading proponents of progressive ideas. Consequently, the guide began by urging teachers to recognize that applicants for naturalization needed not only basic instruction about American democracy and history, but also information about such topics as how to deal with a consumer economy, maintain good health, and strengthen the home. NCEP educators believed that useful knowledge about such everyday situations would make citizenship classes more relevant, meaningful, and interesting.[64]

Besides expanding the range of topics included in the NCEP's version of Americanization, the guide also drew on progressive educational ideas by encouraging teachers to use more active and engaging methods for teaching. The introduction to *Citizenship Education* explicitly criticized earlier programs for their frequent "use of the inadequate question and answer method." Rather, the NCEP guide recommended that teachers engage students in discussions about a range of issues: how "good family government" might be "the same as national and state governments"; why "the individual worker often . . . needs the strength of organization" [i.e., a labor union] in dealing with employers; and the freedoms one has in a democracy. In addition, the guide suggested such activities as mock trials to explain the judicial system and recommended field trips to "a city council meeting, a court session, [and/or] the mayor's office," for students to understand local government. Two of the most intriguing suggestions for class activities were the recommendations that teachers should either explain or lead a class discussion about "the contributions of each nationality group toward the securing of our freedom" and asking members of the class "why they came to America," in order to demonstrate how each class member fit into the broad sweep of American history.[65] These last two recommendations provide a glimpse into the other significant change in Americanization education that was encouraged by federal intervention in this process: the shift in attitude regarding how educators in these programs approached the cultural background of the immigrants.

This new approach to Americanization was part of an important social and educational change that was occurring in the late 1930s and early 1940s. Led by a growing number of educators, politicians, and public intellectuals, this shift directly challenged ethnic nationalist attitudes about the educability of immigrants, disparaged ideas of Nordic supremacy, and sought to redefine the relationship between immigrants and "mainstream" American culture along civic nationalist lines. Rejecting the aggressive assimilationist approach of the World War I years, these racial liberals, as historian Diana Selig calls them, advocated a version of Americanization that combined a strong commitment to American ideals and values with recognition of the "cultural gifts" that immigrants brought to the United States. Selig argues that the idea of cultural gifts "represented a process of exchange in which groups would share traditions in order to create a larger, richer culture that would incorporate people from diverse backgrounds, encourage civic participation, and bring minorities into the democratic system."[66] This stance echoed the ideas about cultural pluralism that Jane Addams, John Dewey, and other scholars and activists had advocated in the 1910s and 1920s. These ideas also were strikingly similar to the vision of patriotic pluralism articulated by the foreign language newspapers in Chicago during the same period. In the 1930s and 1940s, as a number of key figures in the Roosevelt administration endorsed these ideas, racial liberals campaigned to change American attitudes about race, immigration, culture, and inclusion, and they sought to bring these ideas to bear on both adult and K–12 education.[67]

Indicative of this trend is a 1939 *New York Times* editorial that clearly advocated a more culturally inclusive approach to Americanization education. In 1924, the *Times* had supported the National Origins Act, but fifteen years later, the paper made a dramatic about-face and now applauded the contributions immigrants had made and were making to American life and culture. Commenting that foreign-born citizens were often "more American than many of the native-born," the editorial praised both Americanization education programs and the growing appreciation of the cultural riches that immigrants brought to our shores. "Our adult education classes are helping to educate the newcomers," the editorial declared, "but we should not forget that they have helped to educate us. 'Americanization' no longer means a dogmatic hammering of ideas into people's heads." Praising the "cultural gifts and the inherited abilities which immigrants have brought us and continue to bring us," the *Times* concluded, "We have drawn on the cultural and racial riches of half the world to make America. Remembering this will help save us from the infection of destructive and disruptive doctrines."[68]

During the late 1930s, educators who supported these changes were introducing them into citizenship classes and other Americanization efforts across the country. One of the best examples of this shift toward a more culturally sensitive approach to Americanization education can be found in a 1937 evaluation of the WPA Americanization program in Schuylkill County, Pennsylvania, conducted by Carl A. Marsden, a professor at New York University. After observing teachers throughout the county, Marsden declared that the "program of Americanization aims at more than the mere elimination of illiteracy and the procurement of citizenship papers." Noting that the classes he observed included students from Poland, Czechoslovakia, Russia, Germany, Italy, and Ireland, Marsden reported that the program "strives to preserve for America the cultural heritage of the varied nationality groups that comprise our citizenry." Moreover, he pointed out that this program explicitly "recognizes that those groups have a positive contribution to make to the enrichment of our own culture. The program, therefore, constantly glorifies the contributions of each nationality group and has succeeded, at least partially, in fostering an appreciation of and tolerance of one group for the other."[69] In these efforts, Americanism was being redefined as both a devotion to America's democratic principles and a commitment to respect, indeed honor, the nation's cultural diversity.

This respect for cultural diversity in classrooms was not the only WPA initiative that indicated a significant shift in attitudes about the ethnic backgrounds of immigrants. As noted earlier, the Chicago Foreign Language Press Survey, the Cleveland Foreign Language Press Digest, and the Cleveland Comments on Current Events collection were all supported by WPA funds. In addition, the WPA's "American Folk Life" oral history project included interviews with eastern and southern European immigrants. Similarly, the Federal Writers' Project began (but never completed) local studies of various immigrant communities as part of what was called the *Composite America* series. Finally, during the 1930s, the WPA provided financial support for the construction of several of Cleveland's Cultural Gardens, which remain to this day a tribute to the city's immigrant and multicultural heritage.[70]

Other federal agencies also supported educational initiatives designed to show the multiracial and multiethnic nature of American history and culture. One of the most prominent of these efforts was the Federal Radio Project, which in the late 1930s produced a series of twenty-six half-hour programs titled "Americans All—Immigrants All." Broadcast on the CBS Radio Network, each of these programs highlighted the contributions of different immigrant groups. According to historian Nicholas Montalto, "Americans All—Immigrants All" was "one of the most successful educational programs (at least from the viewpoint of audience popularity)" in the history of educational radio. Building on the popularity of the shows, the U.S. Office of Education sent out 25,000 brochures promoting the series to high school principals across the country. In addition, the USOE offered a "listener aid" to provide additional information about the various groups showcased on the weekly programs.[71]

Following the country's entry into World War II, the USOE sought to employ these views of American diversity in its support of renewed Americanization efforts. In 1942, for example, the USOE published *Helping the Foreign-Born Achieve Citizenship*, which began by declaring that the methods used for Americanization during this war would be decidedly different from those used during World War I. Apparently heeding the criticism that educators had directed against the aggressive assimilationist efforts of the "100 percent" Americanizers during World War I, Mildred J. Wiese, author of the pamphlet, stated, "Those of us who were familiar with the problems of the foreign-born during the last World War think back with embarrassment and dismay to the way in which many fine citizens were treated because of their foreign accents, their ancestry, or the action of their kin overseas." She called for greater sensitivity to cultural differences of students in English and citizenship classes and offered advice on how to implement these ideas.[72]

Clearly, much of the impetus for this new approach was the nature of the enemy in World War II. As historian Richard Weiss has argued, "[t]endencies toward greater ethnic democracy in the United States were strengthened by the need to contrast American freedom to Nazi tyranny. The identification of totalitarianism with the ruthless suppression of ethnic minorities resulted in a counteridentification of democracy with minority group encouragement and tolerance."[73] In directly opposing the ethnic nationalism of Nazi Germany, Fascist Italy, and imperial Japan, many educators realized that the United States could not maintain national unity by adopting the authoritarian educational methods of its foes. Challenging the blind obedience and cultural uniformity demanded by totalitarian regimes, some leading American educators proclaimed an educational vision akin to patriotic pluralism, specifically calling on Americans to unite around the core democratic values of the nation and simultaneously embrace the diversity of the American people as a true expression of those values. As the United States moved toward war, civic and educational leaders vigorously advanced these ideas rhetorically and, more important, in policy and practice.

One of the finest examples of this stance is a short book, *The Education of Free Men in American Democracy,* published in 1941 by the Educational Policies Commission of the NEA, perhaps the most influential group of educators in the country. George Counts, a prominent professor of education at Columbia's Teachers College, wrote the book, which was an educational call to arms. Describing the perilous situation facing democracy after the fall of France, Counts argued that educators had to reexamine and reinforce democratic ideals with their students. For Counts, a core value that educators had to promote was that "racial, cultural, and political minorities should be tolerated, respected, and valued." Counts declared that democracy "rejects completely the totalitarian theory that the health of society is to be measured in terms of the extent of conformity and acquiescence." He added, "Differences derived from diverse ancestry, life conditions, or personal aptitude or conviction should be employed, not to found rival and hostile groups, but rather to enrich the common good."[74]

Writing in 1945, Victor Morey, an education specialist in the INS Office of Research and Educational Service, looked back on how these new perspectives had changed the nature and content of citizenship classes for adults. While noting that some aspects of the World War I era Americanization efforts were quite positive (i.e., "instruction of the foreign-born in history and government"), he denounced the effort "to make everyone a 100 percent American," especially the insistence that immigrants "should discard all old-world cultural traditions, customs, and habits and adopt a completely new set of standards." Like the critics of these practices in the 1920s, Morey argued that such attitudes and the coercive policies and practices that often accompanied them were pedagogically counterproductive. As he put it, "[b]y 1925 considerable evidence had been collected to prove the undesirability of such mechanical preparation for citizenship."[75]

Morey maintained that by the mid-1940s a broader and more culturally sensitive approach to citizenship education *had* taken root. This approach still focused on teaching American history and democratic government, but, Morey observed, "there was an increased willingness, however, to search the culture of the foreign-born for those aspects of it that would make a real contribution to the American way of living."[76]

To what extent did the extensive federal involvement and the advocacy of more culturally sensitive ideas about Americanization relate to educational policy and practice in the early 1930s and early 1940s? The Chicago Public School system, which worked closely with the WPA, INS, NCEP, and USOE in this period, provides an excellent site for assessing changes in Americanization education. As noted in chapter 2, in the 1910s and 1920s the Windy City had been somewhat slow in developing its Americanization initiatives, but by the 1930s, the Chicago Public Schools (CPS) were running one of the most comprehensive programs in the nation. Their efforts included offering traditional English and citizenship classes in evening schools citywide and two day-school programs. The first of these was the Dante School, which provided a broad range of classes to about 300 foreign-born adults, most of whom were taking elementary classes in order to move into adult high school programs. The second day-school program taught Americanization classes to almost 9,000 adult immigrants in 1937–1938 in public school buildings, "park centers, library buildings, settlements, Y.W.C.A. and Y.M.C.A. buildings, industrial plants, church and office buildings."[77] This second program was, according to one Chicago educational leader, "supplemented," "by the W.P.A. division of citizenship and naturalization."[78]

In the 1938–1939 school year, the CPS/WPA programs provided Americanization classes in 160 locations around Chicago. At the time, the WPA was supporting about 45 percent of the 146 teachers who regularly taught citizenship and English classes. According to the Chicago superintendent's report for that year, "approximately 8,800 persons, representing 35 national groups, attended these classes," and, between January and June of 1939, "1,659 students secured the final certificate of naturalization."[79]

Regardless of which program students were attending, educational leaders in Chicago extolled their commitment to becoming Americans and lauded their efforts to realize their goal of citizenship. "They are probably the most enthusiastic, interested, and loyal classes in the evening schools," one Chicago administrator declared.[80] This assessment echoes the appraisals made by evening school administrators in the early years of the twentieth century. But many of these immigrants who managed to make it to the United States between 1936 and 1940 were quite different from previous immigrants. Most of the early immigrants were from poor, rural backgrounds and were barely educated. In contrast, many of the immigrants in the late 1930s were well-educated, middle-class, and urbanites. As the Chicago school administrator cited above noted, in "many instances these foreign-born people have had an excellent education in their native countries, even including degrees in the learned professions."[81]

In response to these new immigrants, some Chicago educators gradually reshaped the curriculum. They focused less on basic skills and knowledge and more on improving the newcomers' "facility in English," presenting "a great deal of American history and theory of government." Paralleling the culturally sensitive stance of the WPA programs discussed above, at least some Americanization educators in Chicago took a similar stance in their efforts, for example, teaching about the contribution immigrants had made to American history and culture. Describing a class of students from a dozen different nationalities, a Chicago administrator declared, "In their oral work they tell stories of the home lands and vie with one another in amicable fashion to portray the fine achievements and characteristics of the countries of their birth. They see how much each country has contributed to the greatness of the United States and learn thereby tolerance and understanding."[82]

By the 1940–1941 school year, the Chicago Public Schools and the WPA were offering 330 Americanization classes to about 15,000 students in a host of different venues across the city. This dramatic increase in enrollments, up over 70 percent from 1938 to 1939, was likely due to the passage of the Alien Registration Act of 1940. While noting that there were many reasons for immigrants to enroll in these classes, including their knowledge of the "hardships and suffering which their relatives and friends have endured in their native lands," one Chicago administrator frankly admitted, "The registration and fingerprinting of aliens has also stimulated the foreign-born to become naturalized."[83]

To meet this rush of new students, the Chicago Public Schools reached out for help from the WPA, the INS, the Immigrants' Protective League, the Illinois State Committee on Naturalization and Citizenship, and other groups. The Illinois Society of Colonial Dames, for example, sponsored a pageant for students in these classes at the Chicago Historical Society. Entitled "The Making of an American," this event was unlike the well-known Americanization pageant conducted by the Ford Motor Company earlier in the century, which portrayed America as gaining nothing from the cultural backgrounds of the immigrants. The Ford pageant clearly asserted that America was better off when immigrants completely jettisoned their cultural backgrounds. The Chicago pageant, on the other hand, took a different stand. As one evening school administrator noted, this pageant "dramatized in a beautiful way the building of America through the combined efforts of native and foreign-born people."[84]

Enrollments in naturalization classes continued to be strong in the 1941–1942 school year, during which some 15,000 students took courses at 148 different sites throughout the city. Students opting for these classes experienced a somewhat different approach to citizenship education than in the past. For example, teachers in Chicago's WPA naturalization classes were using such NCEP textbooks as *On the Way to Democracy* and *Our Constitution Today* with their students, textbooks specifically designed for adult learners. Moreover, even though Chicago's Americanization teachers strongly promoted patriotism among their students, unlike during the World War I era their emphasis in these wartime efforts was not demonstrating the superiority of Anglo-Saxon culture. Rather, they stressed the blessings of pluralistic democracy, which they argued helped to "facilitate the merging of foreign and native cultures."[85]

Cleveland's experience with the WPA and the NCEP was quite similar to that of Chicago. By 1937, in addition to its regular public school evening program, numerous organizations offered English and citizenship courses at different venues across the city. The foreign language newspapers in the city repeatedly urged their readers to take advantage of these courses, especially after the passage of federal legislation restricting WPA jobs and other forms of relief to American citizens. The introduction of WPA-supported Americanization courses drew particular praise in the Czech, German, Hungarian, Polish, and Slovak newspapers in the city. These papers enthusiastically promoted citizenship courses, applauded the growing number of students attending them, and celebrated newly naturalized people from their communities.[86] In early 1938, for example, the Polish newspaper *Wiadomosci Codzienne (Polish Daily News)* observed, "For the past two years WPA has conducted classes in reading, writing, and American history for the benefit of immigrants. Due to this instruction many aliens passed their citizenship examinations and became naturalized citizens."[87] The same year, the Czech paper the *American* praised the WPA citizenship classes and commented that the "classes are becoming very popular among the foreign-speaking groups here."[88]

Four years later, a Cleveland public school administrator looked back with considerable satisfaction on these efforts, noting, "The Cleveland Board of Education has been the local sponsor of the adult education section of the WPA since its inception." By that time, almost two-thirds of the 6,400 adult education students in WPA-supported programs in Cleveland were immigrants taking classes under the auspices of the NCEP. These students attended classes in thirteen public school buildings, "as well as numerous branch libraries, settlement houses, and churches."[89]

Foreign language newspapers in Cleveland continued to extol WPA and NCEP support for citizenship classes into the 1940s. For example, when Senator Robert Rice Reynolds (D-NC), an anti-immigrant isolationist, condemned the NCEP, the Cleveland Hungarian newspaper *Szabadsag (Liberty)* strongly denounced Reynolds.[90] Similarly, the German paper *Waechter und Anzeiger (The Sentinel and Advertiser)*, praised the NCEP specifically for teaching immigrants the importance of the Bill of Rights as part of their citizenship education.[91] In the Jewish newspaper *Yidishe Welt (Jewish World)*, the very fact that the U.S. government was encouraging aliens to naturalize at the same time that the fascist nations of Europe were stripping Jews and other minorities of their citizenship intensified that paper's support for the WPA and NCEP efforts. In September 1941, the paper urged Jewish aliens to take these classes to prepare themselves for the honor of being an American citizen.[92]

With the closing of the WPA in late 1943, federal Americanization education efforts wound down, although the INS continued to supply the textbooks and other educational materials created by the NCEP to Americanization programs around the country.[93] But, even as the federal government withdrew its support, local school districts and such organizations as settlement houses, the YMCA, and ethnic fraternal organizations that had been involved in these kinds of educational activities since the turn of the century stepped up their Americanization programs. In addition, as noted earlier, new organizations such as labor unions were also supporting naturalization classes for their members in the 1930s and 1940s.[94] After World War II, this campaign continued and even quickened when a large number of war refugees began arriving in the United States.[95] Writing in 1947, an adult educator in Detroit described these new students as mostly young, literate, and "educationally hungry." Four years later, Chicago reported that some 7,400 foreign-born adults were attending citizenship classes in over 100 sites throughout the city.[96] These efforts continued into the 1950s.

This rarely acknowledged Americanization campaign of the 1930s and 1940s was in many respects similar to the more famous Americanization crusade of the World War I years. Based in part on similar wartime fears about the potential disloyalty of unnaturalized immigrants, this later campaign was designed to educate and naturalize as many aliens as possible in a short period of time. Similarly, this campaign brought together a wide variety of organizations, both public and private, and enlisted them in an effort to unite the nation. In addition, as in the World War I era, government leaders once again called for and participated in grand public displays of Americanism. In 1940, a Congressional resolution proclaimed that the third Sunday in May was to be "I Am an American Day," which celebrated newly naturalized citizens and native-born Americans who had reached voting age. Sponsors of "I Am an American Day" hoped that it would eventually be "as widely celebrated a holiday as the 4th of July."[97]

Despite the similarities to the Americanization campaign of the 1910s and 1920s, this campaign differed in four dramatic ways from its predecessor. First, while President Woodrow Wilson, former President Theodore Roosevelt, and the U.S. Office of Education were all deeply committed to Americanization in the World War I years, the federal role in that effort was modest. In the 1930s and 1940s, however, Franklin Roosevelt supported Americanization education both rhetorically and financially by providing substantial funding and important services to the WPA and local public school Americanization efforts. This support was boosted by the creation of the NCEP, which provided additional funds for teachers and also created a new, up-to-date set of textbooks and other educational materials.

Second, this later effort was aided enormously by the Alien Registration Act of 1940, which forced non-naturalized immigrants to register with the federal government and, consequently, provided them with a powerful reason for seeking citizenship. Moreover, once these immigrants were registered, it was much easier for school districts and other Americanization education programs to find them and urge them to attend naturalization classes. In general, these Americanization agencies found a willing audience, especially among "enemy aliens." Italians and Germans were among the leading groups seeking naturalization in this period.[98]

Third, this campaign differed from the previous one in its approach to Americanization. Rejecting the aggressive assimilationist stance of earlier Americanizers, many leaders and educators of the World War II era campaign extolled the cultural gifts that immigrants brought to the United States or spoke about the blending of races and cultures in America in ways that evoked Israel Zangwill's vision of the melting pot. This more culturally sensitive approach was, in large part, a direct response to the worldwide rise of violent ethnic nationalism, which was cutting a bloody swath across Asia, and Europe at this time. But more was involved than just the expression of an American contrarianism. During World War I, when critics of aggressive Americanization described efforts to strip immigrants of their cultural backgrounds as akin to the Germanization or Magyarization policies of our enemies, these critics were either dismissed outright or labeled as un-American. This time around, leading Americanizers explicitly stated that they did not want to repeat the errors of the past and sought instead to recognize and respect cultural diversity.

In many ways, Franklin Roosevelt and key members of his administration were central to this shift away from aggressive assimilation, due largely to the inclusive rhetoric they often used when speaking to or about immigrants. For example, on April 21, 1938, in a speech delivered to the Daughters of the American Revolution, a group not known for its pro-immigrant sentiments, Roosevelt famously chided his audience by declaring, "Remember, remember always that all of us, and you and I especially, are descended from immigrants and revolutionists."[99]

In October 1940, in a more somber mood, Roosevelt used a New York *Herald Tribune* forum entitled "Saving Democracy" to describe the relationship between the American form of government and the diverse groups of people that made up the United States. Reacting to propaganda spread by various totalitarian regimes (and their vocal supporters within the United States) that America was an "effete, degenerate democracy" due to its "hybrid, mongrel and undynamic" population, he defended the variegated nature of the American people, placing special emphasis on the positive and vital role that immigrants had played in American history. He then added, "It is the very mingling of races dedicated to common ideals which creates and recreates our vitality."[100] This was a powerful reassertion of civic nationalism at a time when this political and social ideal was in retreat across most of the world.

In May of the following year, Secretary of the Interior Harold Ickes reiterated these civic nationalist sentiments in an "I Am an American Day" speech before a crowd estimated at 750,000 people in New York's Central Park.[101] While most of his speech was a denunciation of Nazism, Fascism, and Communism, at one point Ickes contrasted American democracy to totalitarian systems by asking rhetorically, "What constitutes an American?" He answered stating, "Not color nor race nor religion. Not the pedigree of his family nor the place of his birth." Rather, in a ringing assertion of civic nationalism, he declared, "An American is one who loves justice and believes in the dignity of man. . . . An American is one in whose heart is engraved the immortal second sentence of the Declaration of Independence."[102] While Ickes was clearly spelling out the differences between the United States and its totalitarian adversaries, he also was taking sides in the long-running battle between civic and ethnic nationalists within this country.

The fourth and last important difference between this "Americanization campaign" and the earlier one concerns the number of naturalizations that occurred during the time of these campaigns. While it is impossible to *directly* attribute the increase in naturalizations to these campaigns, they were certainly an important factor in making aliens aware of the opportunity to naturalize, particularly by encouraging them to take that step, and by providing an educational infrastructure that large numbers of prospective citizens could use. Moreover, prominent leaders and supporters of the 1930s and 1940s initiative took a less culturally aggressive stance in their approach to Americanization. They often praised the cultural gifts that newcomers had brought to the United States, arguing that immigrants enriched this country.

Whether these factors or others had encouraged people to naturalize, the fact is that between 1935 and 1944, the number of people who became citizens was enormous. Indeed the number was far greater than at any other time in the first half of the twentieth century. Specifically, between 1915 and 1924, the dates that bracket the earlier Americanization campaign, approximately 1,462,000 people naturalized. Two decades later, between 1935 and 1944, which correspond to the second large-scale Americanization effort, almost 2,320,000 people became citizens. Put another way, more people naturalized in just three years, 1942–1944, than in the entire decade from 1910 to 1919 (1,031,000 compared to 991,000). Writing in the late 1940s, one observer commented that the number of naturalizations since 1940 "is the largest number in any similar period since records have been kept, despite the fact that the naturalization potential was the lowest."[103] From a broader perspective, the decade of the 1940s witnessed the largest number of naturalizations (about 2,156,000) of any decade in the twentieth century until the 1990s.[104]

The Foreign Language Press and the Rise of Ethnic Nationalism, 1930–1942

How did the new Americans and their American-born children respond to the great domestic and international challenges of the 1930s and 1940s, particularly as these challenges refocused attention on issues of Americanization and national identity? As in chapter 3, the foreign language press collections assembled by the WPA provide evidence that can help in answering that question. During the 1930s and early 1940s, foreign language newspapers remained the most important adult education agency in immigrant communities. While there were fewer foreign language newspapers published during the Depression and war years than the 1910s and 1920s, historian Richard Polenberg still found that in 1940, at least "237 foreign-language periodicals were being published in New York City, 96 in Chicago, 38 in Pittsburgh, 25 in Los Angeles, and 22 in Detroit." Cleveland had at least a dozen foreign language newspapers in the late 1930s and early 1940s, most of which were dailies.[105] Reporting on and interpreting the great events of this era, the foreign language press both reflected and shaped the attitudes and ideas of its readers.

The WPA collections of articles and editorials from the Chicago and Cleveland foreign language press, which cover most of the years from 1930 to 1942, provide a superb view into how editors, journalists, and other leaders from immigrant and ethnic communities reacted to such issues as the revitalization of nativism, the place of immigrants and their children in American society, and the efforts by immigrant leaders to maintain their commitment to patriotic pluralism.[106] In many ways the newspapers' responses to these issues were consistent with and quite similar to the stances expressed by the Chicago foreign language newspapers during the 1910s and 1920s. But during the Depression and World War II years, a new issue emerged that both overshadowed and influenced all the others: the rise of militant ethnically nationalistic dictatorships in many of the countries that these immigrants had once called home. Nothing created a greater challenge to these immigrants' commitment to democracy and civic nationalism—key elements of Americanization—than did these developments in Europe. How the editors and writers for the Chicago and Cleveland foreign language newspapers wrestled with this development and how they determined where their ideological and political allegiance lay illuminates a vital part of the story of Americanization in the first half of the twentieth century.

Before turning to a discussion of how developments in Europe influenced ideas about Americanization, it is important to examine how the papers dealt with the issues of ethnic nationalism, national identity, and democratic politics in the American context. As shown earlier, in some ways, the resurgence of nativism in the United States in the 1930s was akin to the rise of ethnic nationalism in many of the immigrants' home countries. The reassertion of nativism here reminded the foreign-born and their children that a sizable number of Americans still did not regard immigrants, even ones who had naturalized, as full members of American society.[107] During this period, the editors and journalists writing for the foreign language newspapers in Chicago and Cleveland devoted considerable time and energy to denouncing the mainstream newspapers, magazines, films, and radio broadcasts that seemed to legitimate anti-immigrant prejudices and encourage politicians who supported policies based on those prejudices.

Typical of these denunciations was a February 1933 editorial in a Swedish newspaper from Chicago, which assailed the *Saturday Evening Post* for its unrelenting slurs against immigrants. The Swedish paper rejected the claim by the *Post's* editor that immigrants who had come to the United States after 1890 were responsible for increasing crime, raising the cost of public education, contributing to unemployment, forcing high taxes, and supporting the actions of "communists, anarchists, and other revolutionary elements" in the United States. Indeed, after declaring that immigrants had contributed enormously to the greatness of their adopted country, the editor concluded that, "immigration has been a blessing to America."[108]

Many editors of foreign language newspapers in Chicago and Cleveland focused their wrath on Texas congressman Martin Dies who, as noted earlier, argued that immigrants were undermining the American economy and political system. By the late 1930s, Dies was perhaps the most visible and vocal anti-immigrant member of the House of Representatives. Responding to his support for "anti-immigrant" legislation, a September 1938 editorial in the Cleveland Hungarian newspaper *Szabadsag* used the language of the American democratic creed to belittle the congressman as a "fake Democrat and fake patriot."[109] Two months later, the editor of the Polish daily *Wiadomosci Codzienne* summed up his views of the congressman, stating that Dies "has a peculiar phobia. He hates all the foreigners in this country."[110]

Reacting to the threats posed by anti-immigrant organizations, journalists, and politicians, the Chicago and Cleveland foreign language newspapers reprised many of the arguments about American history and the character of this country that had been used in the 1920s. These writers repeatedly denounced the racial bigotry of "one hundred per cent Americans" or "Nordics" and strongly reasserted their belief in civic nationalism. A June 1935 editorial in *Otthon (Home)*, a Hungarian newspaper in Chicago, angrily denounced attacks on the foreign-born from "hundred-per-cent Americans," declaring, "These patriotic demagogues shut their eyes to historical facts. This country was not made great by those who came over on the Mayflower and their descendents only."[111]

In May 1937, an article in *Enakopravnost (Equality)*, a Slovenian newspaper in Cleveland, drove home the same point, reporting with great enthusiasm on a speech by Walter G. O'Donnell, a professor from John Carroll University. O'Donnell stated that, "No racial group, Nordic or otherwise, has any grounds for assuming an arrogant attitude, in derogation of the rightful claims of other racial groups to equality of opportunity."[112] Other foreign language newspapers in both Chicago and Cleveland expressed similar sentiments throughout this period.[113]

As in the 1910s and 1920s, one of the most common responses that writers for the Chicago and Cleveland foreign language newspapers made were repeated assertions that the United States was historically a cosmopolitan country that had been created and enriched by people from diverse backgrounds. Writing just before Columbus Day in 1930, a journalist for *Sandara (Concord)*, a Lithuanian newspaper in Chicago, echoed Israel Zangwill, declaring, "Although colonial [America] was populated chiefly by the British, today no single nationality constitutes a majority." The article continued, stating that the American "population now is a conglomeration of all the nationalities under the sun . . . [and] a new and distinct nationality is slowly but surely being formed by means of the great American melting pot—the new American nationality."[114]

In a similar vein, in November 1937, *Rodina (Family)*, the Carpatho-Russian paper in Cleveland, ran a series of articles deploring the narrowness of Nordic and Anglo-Saxon conceptions of American culture. The final article asserted, "To preach that there is already an American art or an American music is erroneous." Moreover, the article continued, it is "the 'recent' Americans who hold the treasure bag from which will come the greatest American art. America will need to turn primarily to the Slav, the Latin, the Teuton, not to mention the Negro, within its borders, for this art."[115]

Perhaps no one in Cleveland at the time captured these cosmopolitan sentiments better than Walter O'Donnell, who, in January 1937, was quoted at length in the Cleveland Romanian newspaper *America*. The John Carroll University professor denounced recent verbal attacks on foreign-born and black Americans, attacks that blamed these groups for such developments as political "corruption and bossism." Rejecting such racial scapegoating and declaring that cosmopolitanism was a historically grounded

American reality, O'Donnell declared, "All men regardless of race, color, or creed are brothers under the skin." He added, "American society is made up of various races, nationalities, and creeds. . . . All have a part to play in the vast scheme of American life."[116]

As these articles and editorials indicate, during this period the foreign language newspapers in Cleveland and Chicago conducted a substantial educational project that included presenting readers with a broadly inclusive vision of American history and culture. This vision reflected their ideas about the multifaceted character of the American nation. As noted in the previous section, key political leaders, educators, and even some leading English language newspapers were promoting a very similar point of view.

As part of this presentation of a broader view of American national identity, the Chicago and Cleveland foreign language newspapers continued to read their ethnic groups back into American history to demonstrate that they were as American as their Anglo-Saxon critics. Moreover, these papers frequently focused attention on their group's participation in America's wars, on their ethnic heroes (e.g., Pulaski, Kosciusko, DeKalb, or von Steuben), and, given the still painful memories of World War I, on the members of their communities who had served and died in that struggle.[117] Typical of these pieces was a 1938 Memorial Day editorial in the Polish paper *Wiadomosci Codzienne*. After discussing the meaning of the Memorial Day holiday, the editor declared, "We Poles participate in these ceremonies, as much of our blood has been shed for America." Reminding his readers of the Polish soldiers who had fallen in the Revolutionary War and the Civil War, "and the thousands upon thousands of Polish Americans who died in the World War," the editor concluded simply, "This is our country."[118] With their defense of civic nationalism in the face of nativist attacks, or their revision of U.S. history to highlight the multiracial and religiously diverse character of the nation, the editors and writers for these newspapers demonstrated a strong commitment to patriotic pluralism well into the 1930s.

Writing in the introduction to the 1937 German section of the CFLND, Richard Brenne, editor of the *Waechter und Anzeiger* provided an excellent example of this stance, arguing, "The affection which [German Americans] retain for the land of their birth or their parents as well as for its traditions, customs, and language in no way tends to diminish the loyalty which they owe and willingly give to the land of their adoption. . . . In defense of the constitution, for the preservation of liberty and the rights of man, Americans of German descent will stand firm and unafraid as of yore."[119] The editors and writers from almost every ethnic group represented in the CFLND used similar terms to describe their commitment to the United States and their pride in the distinctive cultural background their people had brought to America.[120]

However, during the late 1930s and early 1940s, these dual commitments, which defined the form of Americanization that these groups had embraced, were severely tested. Many of their home countries became bastions of brutal authoritarian or totalitarian regimes that rested on the doctrine of Germany for the Germans, Poland for the Poles, and Romania for Romanians. These regimes proclaimed the primacy of "blood and soil" and had nothing but contempt for democracy, democratic politics, the rights of minorities, or the richness of racially and religiously pluralistic societies. Above all, these regimes rejected civic nationalism, the political idea that the editors and journalists writing for the Chicago and Cleveland foreign language press so frequently invoked in their long struggle with American nativists. By the late 1930s it was clear that the greatest political problem facing immigrant communities was how to balance their commitment to American democratic ideals with their devotion to homelands that increasingly rejected those ideals.

Given that situation, how did leaders and opinion shapers of immigrant communities in the United States respond to these developments abroad? Was patriotic pluralism still a viable option in a world where aligning with one's homeland meant forsaking fundamental American democratic ideals and values? If immigrants were naturalizing and participating in political campaigns in part to advance the political goals of their specific group, how would they react to situations in which those goals seemed to promote the interests of their homeland over those of the United States? The answers to these questions played a major role in shaping the Americanization of immigrants who naturalized in the late 1930s and 1940s. As important, the answers give insight into the degree to which Americanization had taken root in these immigrants.

The remainder of this section draws on materials in the two Cleveland newspaper collections—the CFLND and Comments on Current Events (COCE)—largely because these collections cover January 1937 to December 1938 and May 1941 to July 1942, periods in which issues about democracy versus dictatorship and civic versus ethnic nationalism became paramount in the immigrant communities, as they did in the United States generally. The responses to the growing tension between the democratic ideals that the writers for Cleveland foreign language papers espoused and the undemocratic actions that governments in many of their homelands conducted can be grouped into two broad categories. First were papers that consistently defended democracy, denounced the dictatorial trends and actions in their homelands, and called for either American action or, at least, great vigilance in response to the growing threat of totalitarian and authoritarian regimes. Second were papers that also declared their allegiance to American democratic principles but either rationalized or blatantly supported the actions of dictatorial regimes despite their clear rejection of democracy.

The newspapers in Cleveland that responded quickly and forcefully in condemning the race-based dictatorships in Europe included the Jewish newspaper *Yidishe Welt*, which consistently decried the collapse of democracy in Europe and the torrent of anti-Semitism sweeping across the continent; left-wing papers such as *Enakopravnost*, a Slovenian daily that saw Fascism and Nazism as grievous threats to workers' movements; and newspapers serving Carpatho-Rusyns, Czechs, Hungarians, Lithuanians, Romanians, Slovaks, and Slovenes, whose homelands, by the late 1930s, increasingly were either controlled by dictatorial regimes or threatened with takeovers by such regimes. While these papers varied in their reasons for opposing the rise of dictatorships in Europe, in denouncing these regimes all the writers sounded similar themes reasserting their commitment to democratic ideals and values, especially those related to liberty, equality, and respect for minorities. They all applied principles that were central to their Americanization, and they used arguments that they had sharpened in their long struggle with nativists and racial restrictionists in the United States to denounce similar political movements in their homelands.

No foreign language newspaper in Cleveland was more vocal in support of this stance than the *Yidishe Welt*. In *The Origins of Totalitarianism*, Hannah Arendt argues that anti-Semitism was central to the rise of Nazism and most of the other dictatorial regimes that dominated Europe in the late 1930s and early 1940s.[121] Thus, it was not surprising that American Jewish leaders generally and editors of Yiddish newspapers specifically were among the first people in the United States to sound the alarm about the growing dangers of totalitarianism in Europe.[122] Indeed, over a decade before Arendt wrote her classic study, an editorial in the *Yidishe Welt* anticipated her argument, stating, "Among Jews and non-Jews in liberal spheres it is often said that the attack on Jews is always the beginning of attacks on other minorities and on the fundamental principles of democracy."[123]

The Jewish community in Cleveland was a national leader in opposing not just anti-Semitism but also the antidemocratic movements that threatened the United States and the remaining democracies in Europe.[124] Not surprisingly, the *Yidishe Welt* concentrated much of its reporting and editorializing on the triumph of militant ethnic nationalism in central and eastern Europe and the subsequent loss of civil liberties for minorities across the region. As early as 1935, Germany had enacted the Nuremberg Laws, which made "purity of German blood" a legal category and stripped Jews of their citizenship on racial grounds. As historian Lucy Dawidowicz explains, "citizenship was not a matter of individual rights but derived from membership in the Volk."[125] This was a brutally clear application of ethnic nationalism, and by 1938 dictatorial regimes in Hungary, Poland, and Romania all followed Germany's lead in using the doctrine of racial purity as a justification for stripping Jews of their civil rights and, in some cases, their citizenship.[126] The movement toward such disenfranchisement was punctuated by the passage of increasingly onerous laws, violence, and terror.[127] Writing in October 1938, Leon Wiesenfeld, a columnist for the *Yidishe Welt* who penned the most comprehensive and urgent columns on the deteriorating situation of European Jewry, stated prophetically, "The Jewish people are now facing the greatest catastrophe in history."[128] Not surprisingly, American Jews embraced democracy, pluralism, and civic nationalism more strongly than ever.[129]

The plight of the Jews in Europe stood out as the most egregious example of the evils perpetrated by resurgent ethnic nationalists, but during the late 1930s other groups in Europe—usually minorities in countries created after World War I—also faced growing persecution, restriction of their civil rights, and violence. While the League of Nations supposedly guaranteed minority rights in pluralistic countries such as Poland (where fully a third of the population was not ethnically Polish), the league utterly failed to live up to its commitments. Not only did the Polish government aggressively persecute Jews, but it also directed its wrath at its large Ukrainian and Lithuanian communities. For example, during the interwar period, in an effort to strip Ukrainians of their cultural heritage, the

Polish government closed thousands of Ukrainian language schools.[130] The Lithuanian minority in Poland faced similar violations of their civil rights. Writing in February 1937, the editor of Cleveland's Lithuanian newspaper *Dirva (Fertile Field)* declared, "The League of Nations agreed to allow Poland to govern the acquired land [surrounding and including Vilnius] only on the condition that Poland would recognize the minority rights of Lithuanians, such as freedom of speech, press, and education. Poland is now working to abolish all these rights and make the acquired land completely Polish."[131]

Poland was not alone in persecuting minorities. Some half a million Slovenes lived in Italy, and, following the Nazi takeover of Austria, many more fell under the control of the Third Reich. In March 1937, *Ameriska Domovina (American Home)*, a centrist Slovenian newspaper in Cleveland declared, "Our people under the Italians today are in the same suppressed condition as their ancestors were under the Turkish rule centuries ago."[132] One month later, the editor of *Enakopravnost*, the leftist Slovenian paper, also denounced efforts by Italians to wipe out Slovenian culture. As one article put it, the Fascists "took away all of the Slovenian schools, burned all national homes, destroyed all economic organizations, and jailed or drove away all intelligent Slovenes and Croats. To crown their cruelties they forced Slovenes to drink castor oil, spat into their faces and tortured them in many ways."[133] In his introduction to the Slovenian section of the CFLND, the publisher of *Enakopravnost* warned ominously, "How these Slovene minorities will retain their nationality in view of the repression practiced by the governments of Hitler and Mussolini cannot be said."[134]

In a similar vein, a writer for the Carpatho-Rusyn newspaper *Rodina* condemned Czechoslovakia for repressing its Carpatho-Rusyn minority. Describing the rise of a "full Slovakian dictatorship" in their homeland, a writer in *Rodina* declared that the process of "Slovakianizing our race in Carpatho-Russia is gaining daily."[135] Two months later, Cleveland's Hungarian newspaper *Szabadsag* editorialized that the fascist regime in Romania was not only adopting ideas of racial superiority but was also "depriving the Hungarian minorities [in Romania] of their religious freedom by brutal force, forgery, and lies."[136] But the Hungarian government itself came under fire from the Czech newspaper *Svet-American*, which argued that Hungarians "do not allow the slightest autonomy of minorities in matters of press and society." The editor complained, for example, that the Hungarian government was forcing Slovak children to "attend purely Hungarian schools."[137] As such intolerance increased, writers for the Cleveland papers routinely defended their compatriots who were being persecuted in ethnic nationalist regimes that were gaining strength across Europe. Yet, for the most part, the Cleveland foreign language newspapers *did not* identify with or support their home country's lack of tolerance for minorities. In fact, many of them negatively contrasted their home country's ethnic nationalism to the pluralism and inclusiveness of the United States.

As a writer for *Szabadsag* argued, unlike the ethnically nationalistic countries of Europe, the "American nation, chief representative of all the nations of the world, embraces all the great who flock here from everywhere with great joy, regardless of creed or color."[138] Similarly, at the 1938 celebration of Romanian Independence Day, a leader of the Cleveland Romanian community declared, "We, of foreign birth in America, appreciate the full meaning of the term independence." He explained, "We walk here as free men. We can express our views. . . . We must never forsake this tradition but improve it. America is America because of the foreign born. We must stress democracy."[139]

That newspapers representing such stateless minority groups as Carpatho-Rusyns, Jews, and Slovenes would take such a position is quite understandable, but perhaps the most notable newspapers sounding early warnings about the political nightmare that was descending upon Europe were those serving the Hungarian and Romanian communities in Cleveland, *Szabadsag* and *America*. By the late 1930s, both Hungary and Romania were home to powerful anti-Semitic, ethnic nationalist organizations (the Arrow Cross in Hungary and the Iron Guard in Romania). Both countries had governments that were increasingly fascist and were well on their way to becoming important military allies of Nazi Germany.[140] Given that situation, *Szabadsag* and *America* easily could have hailed the rise to power of their ethnic nationalist compatriots in the old country. Yet, throughout 1937 and 1938, both papers regularly denounced Hitler, Mussolini, and the racist, antidemocratic movements in Hungary and Romania. In addition, they condemned anti-Semitic laws and policies in their homelands and lashed out at such American anti-Semites as Father Charles Coughlin. The newspaper editorials also called for the investigation and deportation of aliens who supported fascism, Nazism, and communism, and cheered the antitotalitarian speeches delivered by such prominent national and international leaders as Harold Ickes, Fiorello LaGuardia, Thomas Mann, and Franklin Roosevelt.[141] In March 1938, an editorial in *America* summed up this antitotalitarian stance quite simply: "If they follow what happens in Europe, where the dictators have wiped out entirely the civil rights of the people, the Roumanians of America should make a comparison between what would have happened to them if they were now in their homeland."[142]

In wrestling with the tension between the two central features of the patriotic pluralist form of Americanization education (i.e., a commitment to the democratic ideals of the United States coupled with pride in their European cultural heritage), these newspapers had little difficulty in asserting their Americanism over the demands for racial loyalty that ethnic nationalists in their home countries were making. They seemed to recognize that the "blood and soil" movements, which by the late 1930s dominated much of Europe, would lead to war and unprecedented bloodshed in their homelands and across the continent. The editor of *Szabadsag* prophetically declared in February 1938, "Let everyone open his eyes and see the terrible danger." He concluded, "If the world will not destroy Hitler's Nazi government . . . then Hitler will destroy Europe's civilization, the freedom of peoples, and independence of nations, and the lives of tens and hundreds of millions."[143]

While these newspapers took positions that clearly reaffirmed their Americanization and the universality of American democratic ideals, three other newspapers abstracted in the CFLND—the German *Waechter und Anzeiger*, the Polish *Wiadomosci Codzienne*, and the Italian *La Voce del Popolo Italiano (The Voice of the Italian People)*—had much more trouble balancing their avowed commitment to democracy with developments in their homelands.[144] For most of 1937 and 1938, the editors and writers of these papers frequently expressed loyalty to the democratic principles of the United States, but they were less eager to apply these principles to the ethnic nationalist regimes in their former homelands. Indeed, the editors and writers for these papers, particularly *Wiadomosci Codzienne* and *La Voce del Popolo Italiano*, frequently turned a blind eye to antidemocratic developments in their native lands, rationalized these developments in ways that tried to mitigate their dictatorial content, or actively supported these actions.

During this period, the editor and writers for the *Waechter und Anzeiger* struggled mightily to resolve the tension between their pride in Germany

for regaining its status as a world power and their growing dismay at its si-
multaneous transformation into a racist, totalitarian state. With the dread-
ful experience of German Americans in World War I still fresh in their
memories (e.g., two former editors of the *Waechter und Anzeiger* had been
interned as enemy aliens during the Great War), German Americans in
the 1930s and early 1940s knew they had to tread carefully around these
issues.[145] But this effort was made more difficult by the vehemently pro-
Nazi stand of the German American Bund, which despite its modest
membership attracted considerable national attention in the late 1930s. As
historian Ronald Bayor observed, "[p]ressed by Jews to denounce the Nazis' anti-Semitism but loath to attack anything German, the German
Americans, hesitating, found themselves faced with anti-Nazi boycotts
and growing hostility from the American public as Nazi organizations
made inroads in their community."[146]

The *Waechter und Anzeiger* wrestled fiercely with these often-
contradictory positions. For example, writers for the paper applauded German economic accomplishments, supported the Nazi efforts to bring all
Germans under one government (e.g., editorializing in favor of the *an-
schluss* with Austria and efforts to bring the Sudeten Germans into the
Reich), and argued persistently that the United States should avoid being
duped again by the British into entering any future war with Germany.[147]
The paper also reported on and, at times, advertised the varied activities
of the German American Bund in Cleveland and wrote positively about
various efforts by the German consul in Cleveland to strengthen the ties
between people of German ancestry in America and their compatriots in
the Fatherland.[148]

An excellent example of this German nationalist stance was the paper's
strong support for a student exchange program announced in January
1937 that involved over two hundred high school students, a hundred from
Berlin and a hundred from the Cleveland area.[149] Jewish organizations
and the *Yidishe Welt* vigorously denounced the program for its implicit
legitimization of Nazi racist educational policies that had forced Jewish
students, teachers, and administrators out of German public schools and
mandated a curriculum in those schools that was virulently anti-Semitic.[150]
Rabbi Abba Hillel Silver, Cleveland's most nationally renowned Jewish
leader, condemned the exchange, declaring that the Nazi regime "has, in
its own country, destroyed ideals of tolerance, good will, and freedom of
thought." Lashing out at the concept of Aryan superiority, Silver added, "I

would advise the German students to notice how [the United States] has
grown and prospered in spite of the fact that it was built by people of all
races, beliefs, and colors."[151] Despite such criticism, the exchange took
place with strong support from Cleveland's civic and educational leaders.
The *Waechter und Anzeiger* heartily endorsed the program and ran enthusiastic articles about it.[152]

Such positions might make it appear that Richard Brenne, editor of the
Waechter und Anzeiger, was unconcerned with the totalitarian character
of the Third Reich and indifferent to the malevolent ethnic nationalism
that was reshaping German political and social life. But things were not
that simple. While Brenne clearly was proud of his German heritage and
was pleased to see Germany rise from the ashes of World War I, he balanced these sentiments with a deep commitment to American democratic ideals and growing fears about the racist Nazi state. As a June 1938
editorial put it, "We are proud of Germany's accomplishments, but . . .
[we] prefer to follow the example of our forefathers and the pioneers to the
glory of the Stars and Stripes."[153]

The paper did more than just assert loyalty to the United States and its
democratic ideals. According to the *Yidishe Welt,* in 1933, the *Waechter
und Anzeiger* signed an agreement with the Jewish newspaper to "fight
Nazi influence in Cleveland," an agreement that apparently was still in
force in the late 1930s.[154] Despite disagreeing with the Jewish community
over such issues as the student exchange, the *Waechter und Anzeiger* frequently demonstrated that it was strongly committed to pluralistic democracy and was outraged by the increasing barbarism of the Nazi regime.
For example, in April 1937 the *Waechter und Anzeiger* decried the loss of
religious freedom in Nazi Germany, noting that German Americans consider such freedom as "inalienable rights." Quoting from a German language paper in Omaha, Nebraska, the editorial concluded, "We won't be
in a position to defend our old fatherland . . . if these liberties are not preserved for the German nation."[155]

One year later, the paper vigorously denounced the German American
Bund, particularly its violent attacks on anti-Nazi individuals and organizations. Concerned that many Americans saw the Bund as a potential
Nazi fifth column (especially given the Bund's ethnic nationalist belief
that loyalty to one's "German character" superseded one's loyalty to the
United States), the paper argued that if a new war broke out, the backlash
against German Americans would make "the World War persecutions

look like child's play."[156] The day after that editorial appeared, the *Yidishe Welt* applauded the anti-Nazi editorial in the *Waechter und Anzeiger*.[157] In a similar vein, three days later, the editor of the Hungarian newspaper *Szabadsag* declared, "This paper [the *Waechter und Anzeiger*] is our brother, not only because it is anti-Nazi, but because we are united in American democracy."[158]

As with many individuals and organizations, the single most important incident shaping the *Waechter und Anzeiger's* stance regarding Nazism was *Kristallnacht*, the bloody rampage against German Jews that took place on November 9 and 10, 1938. In these two days of violence and terror, over one hundred Jews were murdered, synagogues throughout Germany were burned, and some 30,000 Jewish men were sent to concentration camps.[159] One week after the pogrom, the *Waechter und Anzeiger* denounced these events in a powerful editorial, entitled "The German Name Disgraced." Arguing that the vast majority of German Americans were horrified by what had just occurred in Germany, the editor declared that the actions of the Nazis were "so horrendous" as to shock the civilized world. He continued: "We know from countless phone calls and from personal exchanges with our readers who have come to us in the editorial office in dismay, that the people of the German-American community condemn these monstrous incidents with all vehemence and are ashamed that the German people could have become so depraved." Strongly supporting President Roosevelt in his condemnation of the Nazi regime, the editor added, "The German-American people will not be intimidated by threats from fanatics back in our old home country, and will remain true to the flag of American democracy and humanity."[160]

For the *Waechter und Anzeiger*, the tension between pride in the resurgence of Germany and devotion to American democratic values was, by late November 1938, clearly decided in favor of the latter. Rejecting the antidemocratic policies of the Nazi regime, disgusted by the ethnic nationalist claims of Aryan supremacy, outraged by the Nazi persecution of the Jews, and fearful that another war with Germany would result in renewed attacks on German Americans, the *Waechter und Anzeiger* reaffirmed its Americanism and urged its readers to do the same. As a December 12, 1941, editorial declared, the paper "repeatedly warned of the follies of the German American Volksbund and has steadily denounced the racial prejudice in Germany."[161] In taking this stance, the *Waechter und Anzeiger* appears to have mirrored the feelings of the German Americans not only in Cleveland but in other parts of the country as well. Historian Timothy Holian argues that in the 1930s, "[f]or the most part, the German language press came out solidly and vocally against Nazi Germany and its policies, expressing opposition to developments in Germany." In addition, Holian notes that these papers were consistent in "reiterating their position of unquestioned loyalty to the United States and its interests."[162]

Cleveland's Polish newspaper, the *Wiadomosci Codzienne*, however, handled similar tensions quite differently, strongly supporting a wide array of antidemocratic actions taken by the Polish government in the late 1930s. Perhaps due to its editor's deep devotion to the reborn Polish state, the abstracts of *Wiadomosci Codzienne* articles and editorials in the CFLND never criticized Poland's turn toward fascism in the mid-1930s, its violence against Jews and its increasingly anti-Semitic legal code, or its mistreatment of other minorities, such as Lithuanians and Ukrainians.[163] Indeed, unlike the *Waechter and Anzeiger, America*, and *Szabadsag*, which deplored the rise of ethnic nationalism and increasingly dictatorial rule in their homelands, throughout 1937 and 1938 the *Wiadomosci Codzienne* resolutely defended their homelands' descent into dictatorship and repeatedly lashed out at critics of Poland for supposedly undermining the nascent Polish state. While the paper still extolled American democratic principles, urged its readers to become citizens, and reminded Poles to be thankful for the freedoms and rights guaranteed by U.S. Constitution, it did not apply these principles to developments in Poland.[164]

Nowhere was this failure to assess events in Poland according to fundamental democratic standards more glaring than in regard to Poland's treatment of its large Jewish minority.[165] Fierce and unrelenting anti-Semitism was one of the most notable aspects of the *Wiadomosci Codzienne* editorials, columns, and articles abstracted in the CFLND. Indeed, no other paper in the CFLND came close to the level of anti-Semitism of the *Wiadomosci Codzienne*. In January 1937, for example, the paper applauded the Polish parliament for banning Jews from service in the Polish military.[166] Two months later, an editorial approvingly quoted the vice-marshal of the Polish Senate, who called on all Jews to leave Poland.[167] In May, another editorial specifically urged Polish Jews to move en masse to Madagascar. A signed column the same day defended anti-Semitic riots in Poland as simply reactions to the fact that there were too many Jews in the country.[168] Two months later, yet another editorial supported the denial of national culture funds to Jews in Poland because "Jews are a minority group and have a psychology which makes them indifferent to Polish struggles and ideals."[169] While the Jews were not the only minority group in Poland that the *Wiadomosci Codzienne* disparaged, the paper reserved most of its vitriol for them.[170]

What makes these stands so fascinating is that at the same time that the *Wiadomosci Codzienne* was either dismissing or defending the persecution of minorities in Poland, it was taking a totally opposite stance in regard to blacks in the United States. For example, the paper described lynching as "a plague in America," defended the Scottsboro Boys, excoriated "the appalling racial prejudice in the South," and decried U.S. Senator Theodore Bilbo's proposed legislation to deport blacks to Africa as "a cruel and disgraceful injustice."[171] In this last instance, the editor of the paper apparently did not seem to recognize that he was repudiating a policy regarding blacks in the United States that he had endorsed regarding Jews in Poland.

The *Wiadomosci Codzienne* was not the only foreign language paper in Cleveland to denounce lynching and support civil rights for African Americans, at various times, *Enakopravnost*, *Szabadsag*, the *Waechter und Anzeiger*, and the *Yidishe Welt* all took similar stands.[172] But the *Wiadomosci Codzienne* had the distinction of being the only paper in this group that *consistently failed* to apply these democratic principles of racial and political equality to its Old World homeland.

In fact, even when confronted with the apparent contradiction between supporting minority rights for blacks in the United States while condoning outrages against Jews and other minorities in Poland, the *Wiadomosci Codzienne* stood its ground. In June 1938, an article in *Wiadomosci Codzienne* responded to an un-named English language newspaper that had asked what the great Polish and American hero Thaddeus Kosciusko might say "about the present day persecution of Jews in Poland." The writer for the *Wiadomosci Codzienne* responded by dismissing the problems of Jews in Poland entirely, stating, "We answer that if Jews were persecuted in Poland the German and Austrian Jews [who were trying to enter Poland] wouldn't be so anxious to seek asylum there."[173] What the writer failed to acknowledge was that three months earlier, the Polish government had made it all but impossible for even *Polish* Jews who had lived abroad to enter Poland, let alone German or Austrian Jewish refugees.[174]

It took the invasion of Poland by Germany and the Soviet Union in September 1939 to shock the *Wiadomosci Codzienne* into recognizing that the gravest threat to the Polish state was not its "unassimilated" minority groups, but rather its totalitarian neighbors. As in the World War I era, the interests of Polish Americans in seeking the restoration of a Polish state eventually paralleled the interests of the United States in the war against the Axis powers. Once Germany took over all of Poland in 1941, *Wiadomosci Codzienne* began moderating many of its earlier positions regarding the lack of democracy and the anti-Semitism in the prewar Polish state. Indeed, during this period the paper went so far as to describe both Poles and Jews as victims of Nazi oppression.[175] Whether this stance was simply a matter of political expediency or a sincere repudiation of its earlier views is impossible to say, but from this point on the editorials and articles from the *Wiadomosci Codzienne* in the COCE collection seem as committed to the defense of civic nationalism, freedom, and democracy as those in all the other foreign language newspapers at this time.

In a number of ways, the positions taken by Cleveland's Italian community followed a similar trajectory to that of the *Wiadomosci Codzienne*. Throughout all of 1937 and 1938, *La Voce del Popolo Italiano* (often referred to simply as *La Voce*) not only resolutely defended Italian domestic and foreign policies but also routinely extolled the Fascist regime that had ruled Italy since 1922. In taking this stand, *La Voce* was not alone among Italian language papers in the United States. Scholars estimate that between 60 and 90 percent of all Italian language newspapers in the United States were pro-Fascist, at least until Italy declared war on France and Britain in September 1940.[176]

In taking this pro-Fascist stance, *La Voce* did not reject the ideals and values of Americanization. Indeed, in July 1937, the paper published a powerful piece by Leonard J. Melaragno, a local Italian American attorney, who described Americanization as living "in conformity with the greatest ideals of humanity and progress." Urging his readers to learn English, know "the laws of this country," and become "informed about the spirit of the constitution," particularly its "principles of universal fraternity," he called on "Italians who form a part of America's great cosmopolitan group seek to earn the privilege of being citizens." He added, "There is not true Americanism without the right to take part in the political and economic life of this republic, in which freedom of speech, of religious belief, and of party declaration are enjoyed."[177] This speech was just one example where *La Voce*, like all the other foreign language papers in the CFLND, encouraged its readers to naturalize and described such national holidays as the Fourth of July as opportunities to celebrate the freedoms safeguarded by democracy.[178]

But these assertions of Americanism paled before the consistent reiteration of editorials, columns, and articles about the glories of Fascism, the greatness of Mussolini, and the perfidious nature of anyone, particularly writers for the English language press, who questioned the Fascist regime.[179] Led by the prolific columnist J. V. Rapone, *La Voce* enthusiastically supported Italy's invasion of Ethiopia and hailed the Munich accord, claiming that it was necessary to protect the minority rights of Sudeten Germans, while at the same time, and without any sense of hypocrisy, he defended the introduction of anti-Semitic racial laws in Italy.[180]

A number of scholars have sought to explain this enthusiasm for Mussolini and Fascism among Italian Americans. John Patrick Diggins, Thomas Guglielmo, and Stefano Luconi, for example, all note that in the 1920s and early 1930s Mussolini was lionized by large numbers of Americans, not just those of Italian descent. These scholars argue that Italian Americans took great pride in the fact that many leading Americans and indeed many people around the world were hailing Mussolini as a great leader who had helped make Italy an emerging world power. As Guglielmo observes, Italian Americans now had a contemporary hero to point to in their battle with the racial restrictionists who still insisted that Italians were members of an inferior race. In addition to these factors, Luconi argues, many Italian language newspapers in the United States were, to some extent, actually supported by the Italian government, which offered a range of financial inducements for the papers to take a pro-Fascist stand.[181]

Whatever led many Italian Americans to enthuse about Mussolini and the modernization of Italy under Fascist rule, this ardor began to dissipate after September 1, 1939, when Europe plunged into war.[182] In Cleveland, for example, on June 13, 1940, three days after Italy had declared war on France and Great Britain, the leader of the local chapter of the Sons of Italy wrote a letter to the editor of the *Cleveland Press* stating that members of his organization were "stunned" and dismayed by Italy's action. The leader continued, "But now that such a thing has happened we as Americans stand shoulder to shoulder with other Americans, in assuming the responsibilities of upholding and safeguarding our form of government. Our motto has been and will be 'America first and above all.'"[183] As with the German and Polish communities, events abroad led

Italian leaders to undertake a profoundly important reexamination of their commitments and identity. What emerged was a reinvigorated commitment to American democratic ideals.

The most eloquent indication of this shift in attitudes came on September 15, 1941, at the dedication of the Italian cultural garden in Rockefeller Park on Cleveland's east side. At this event, Alexander DeMaioribus, a prominent local Italian American politician, gave a ringing endorsement of civic nationalism, declaring that a person does not become an American "by virtue of any blood strain or any heritage except the heritage of freedom. We Americans are brothers in a common political faith whose fundamental concept is that all government is justified only as conserving the rights and dignities of the individual."[184]

By late 1941, virtually every foreign language newspaper in Cleveland was saying much the same thing. For European immigrants, the horrors of the war that Germany, Italy, and Japan had loosed compelled huge numbers of first- and second-generation immigrants to assert with fierce determination their devotion to the United States and its democratic heritage. At the same time, the newspaper editorials and articles in the COCE collection increasingly supported President Roosevelt's moves against the Axis powers. Endorsements of these decisions came not only from those papers serving Carpatho-Rusyns, Czechs, Jews, Poles, and Slovenes, whose European compatriots had fallen under the yoke of Nazi tyranny, but also such groups as the Hungarians, Romanians, and Slovaks, whose countries by early 1941 were allied with the Axis powers.[185] These papers routinely called on all ethnic groups in the United States to rally around the president and support his efforts to strengthen the U.S. military and to provide substantial war materials to Great Britain. In May 1941, for example, the editor of the Czech newspaper *Svet-American (The World-American)* wrote, "We cannot look on inactively, while the dictators, like a forest fire, over run one country after another. It would be suicide for us to wait until the armed bandit hordes of the 20th century press on to the thresholds of our homes."[186] Five months later, the Slovak paper *Hlas (Voice)* simply declared, "Enslaved Europe supplies a tragic preview of the fate that awaits America if Germany is not defeated."[187]

Given this stance, it is not surprising that these papers also condemned the powerful group of isolationists who maintained that America must avoid war at all costs.[188] Almost every paper in the COCE collection regarded isolationists as Nazi or Fascist pawns, and they lashed out at them with particular fury. Focusing specifically on such people as Charles A. Lindbergh, Westbrook Pegler, Senator Gerald Nye (R-ND), Senator Burton K. Wheeler (D-MT), and Father Charles Coughlin, the papers blasted isolationists as "adherents of Hitlerism in America" and, most important, as agents of discord and disloyalty.[189] Indeed, by mid-1941, isolationists had replaced nativists as the primary political target of most newspapers in the CFLND.[190]

For example, one day after Lindbergh's widely covered September 16, 1941, speech in Des Moines, Iowa, in which he accused American Jews of trying to manipulate the United States into war with Germany, the Slovak paper *Hlas* declared, "Charles Lindbergh, once the glorified idol of our country, has become the most zealous leader of the fifth column."[191] Similarly, a writer in *Szabadsag* noted that stirring up racial and religious hatred was a typical Nazi tactic to divide and conquer. The writer declared that "Lindbergh and his associates" were indeed trying to "incite people against each other; first, the Gentiles against the Jews; then the atheists against the Christians; unorganized labor against the organized; and, finally, war-spirited youth against the gray-haired oldsters."[192]

At the same time, the editor of the Slovenian newspaper *Enakopravnost* analyzed Westbrook Pegler's call for a subordinate citizenship status for naturalized immigrants, discussed earlier in precisely the same way, stating, "Unwittingly Mr. Pegler has stumbled upon the methods the Nazis hope to use for the disintegration of America." Putting these efforts in the context of ethnic and civic nationalism, the editor explained that Nazis "hope to encourage Americans to think in terms of their differences of racial origin rather than their heritage of a common democratic tradition. They hope to use the melting pot for a witch brew of mutual hatred and suspicion."[193] Even the *Wiadomosci Codzienne* warned its readers in February 1942 that the Germans were "attempting to stir up racial hatred in America, especially against the Negroes and Jews. Their purpose is to create discord and thereby make it easier to defeat this country."[194]

This stance led to more than just rhetorical support for national unity and greater tolerance of diversity. Indeed, a number of Cleveland foreign language newspapers saw the war against Nazism and fascism as an opportunity to educate Americans about the necessity of bringing this country closer to the ideals that define it. Their argument was simple. Given the ghastly consequences of the policies that ethnic nationalist regimes in Europe had unleashed, the United States had to dedicate itself to eradicating all aspects of ethnic nationalism and religious bigotry here at home.[195] In October 1941, the *Waechter und Anzeiger* published an editorial that put these arguments in a historical context:

> We do not have to go back very far to remind ourselves of no-torious cases of intolerance by short-sighted, fanatic, and narrow-minded groups. Impetuous times always give the know-nothings, the Ku Klux Klan, and similar fanatics a wel-come opportunity to fish in troubled waters. Politicians ex-ploit such trends for their own selfish purposes; obstinate na-tivists loathe all those whose ancestors did not come over on the *Mayflower*. It usually begins with the baiting of a particu-lar race or those of a different faith, but most of the time de-teriorates into an assault against all foreign-born and all aliens. . . . Today it is the Negro, tomorrow the Jews, the fol-lowing day the Catholic against whom the outcry is directed—and all of a sudden, all citizens of German, Italian, Welsh, or Slavic descent—all whom the mean souls do not consider 100 percent Americans—are thoroughly damned.

The editorial concluded, "In times like these when whole nations display on their banners the most flagrant intolerance as their national principle, our land owes it to itself to demonstrate that 130,000,000 people of differ-ent races and classes can—in a spirit of mutual respect and understanding—live freely side by side."[196]

This editorial echoes the writings of the editors of the Chicago foreign language newspapers from the 1910s and 1920s, as well as evoking the statements of Abraham Lincoln, M. E. Ravage, and Langston Hughes cited in the previous chapter. Moreover, it anticipates German clergyman Martin Niemöller's famous postwar poem "First they came for the Com-munists." The *Waechter und Anzeiger* editorial is as powerful an expres-sion of civic nationalism and Americanism as one can find in this era.

These writings brought together some of the major themes that had marked immigrants' struggles against nativists and racial restrictionists and the immigrants' efforts to fashion a new and more nuanced version of Americanization. In addition, these eloquent rhetorical appeals to civic nationalism were coupled with a material display of patriotism of the highest order, as millions of young men and women with new-stock im-migrant background aided the war effort through both military and civilian service. Writing in the *New York Times* in 1942, Louis Adamic, who by this time was perhaps the nation's leading commentator on immigrants and their children, lashed out at "alien-baiters" like Westbrook Pegler who had questioned the loyalty of immigrants to their adopted country. Adamic pointed out, "Over one third of the men in the Army have names such as Kadlubowski, Aaltonen, Levy, Suchy, Blotnik, Terbovec, Vlavianos, Schlesinger, and Romello."[197]

In many ways, the World War II experience completed the Americanization of the European immigrants who came to the United States before 1924. Despite nativist carping about their Americanism, the immigrants and children of immigrants who served in the military or worked in the defense plants proved to be as patriotic as any group in American history. Indeed, these people, who represented scores of different nationalities and came from dozens of different homelands, some of which were at war with the United States, were instrumental in defeating the Axis powers. In doing so, they took their place beside the heroes of the Revolution and the Civil War as exemplars of devotion to this country in perilous times. There was no doubt about their Americanization.

Acknowledging this, however, does not imply that they became ersatz Anglo-Saxons or that they melted into an indistinguishable American mass. Many remained patriotic pluralists. As historian Deborah Dash Moore argues in her book on Jewish soldiers in World War II, their experiences in the military made them "both more American and more Jewish."[198] Similarly, historian Joseph Wytrwal argues that Polish Americans, who staunchly supported the war effort, came away from this struggle with a greater sense of their Americanism combined with renewed pride in their Polish heritage. A good indication of this stance came in May 1944 when 3,000 "Americans of Polish descent" met in Buffalo, New York, to create the Polish American Congress, whose purpose was to express their "undivided service, love and attachment" to the United States and to give their "full support and aid to the Polish nation."[199] As historian June Granatir Alexander argues, Slovak Americans and other first- and second-generation immigrants also came through World War II with a strong sense of being "both proud ethnic and patriotic Americans." Indeed, decades later, immigrants and their native-born descendants were still constructing their sense of American identity along "both/and" lines.[200]

Part of the reason for this persistence is that, unlike during the years following World War I, when assertions of patriotic pluralism were confined largely to immigrant communities, during and after World War II this stance became an iconic part of American culture broadly conceived. One vehicle for this development was a new genre of Hollywood films featuring multicultural combat platoons. The first of these films was *Bataan*, which appeared in 1943. Set in the Philippines during the Japanese invasion of that country, the movie told the story of thirteen American and Filipino soldiers who tried heroically to slow the advance of the enemy. The American members of the platoon included six white Anglo-Saxon Protestants, who themselves were quite geographically diverse. But in addition to these soldiers were an African American, an Irishman, a Jew, a Mexican (played by Desi Arnaz), and a Pole. They were a fractious, unruly group, but when it counted, in the final battle they stood together, fought together, and died together, as Americans.[201]

The combat platoon film was one of the great cultural and educational contributions of World War II. The message of these films was straightforward and reflected the ideas that writers in the foreign language press had been arguing for decades. Despite the great differences among the diverse peoples who make up the United States, when the nation and its democratic ideals and institutions are threatened, Americans will unite and ultimately triumph. As the philosopher Richard Rorty observed, the great question of the "platoon movies" was, "What do our differences matter compared with our commonality as fellow Americans?"[202] The platoon films were not the only venue for this message. John Hersey's enormously popular novel *A Bell for Adano*, which won a Pulitzer Prize in 1945, explicitly celebrated the diverse character of the American military and the role that GIs from immigrant backgrounds played as liberators of their ancestral homelands and promoters of democracy.[203] In addition to changing attitudes about American diversity in fiction and film, another great cultural and educational contribution of the World War II years was intercultural education, a movement that brought ideas about unity and diversity to tens of thousands of students in schools across the nation.

Americanization Revised: Intercultural Education, 1930–1955

In the spring of 1933, Louis Adamic, a Slovenian immigrant and former editor of a Slovenian newspaper in New York, began a seven-week journey through "the great industrial centers" of the Mid-Atlantic and Midwest regions to meet and talk with "second-generation" Americans. This journey played a crucial role in Adamic becoming, over the next decade, perhaps the best-known and most influential supporter of an important educational movement devoted to reenvisioning American history and culture along patriotic pluralistic lines.[204] What Adamic discovered in his travels were young people that he described as members of a new lost generation— American-born children of European immigrants who did not feel entirely at home in the United States or comfortable in the European traditions of their parents.[205]

In response, Adamic called for a "great educational-cultural" movement in which public school educators would teach an inclusive vision of American history. This new approach to history would give "these millions of New Americans a knowledge of and pride in their own heritage" and would lessen "anti-'foreign' prejudice" at the same time.[206] In calling on public schools to lead this effort, Adamic was, in essence, advocating an updated Americanization education campaign that would help second-generation, American-born young people recognize their historical and cultural connections to this country. As important, the campaign would "Americanize" the descendants of old-stock immigrants by teaching them that people from diverse backgrounds had made great contributions to this country's history and life.[207]

Six months after Adamic's article appeared, James Marshall, whom Mayor Fiorello LaGuardia had recently appointed to the New York school board, delivered a speech that echoed the Adamic essay. Marshall declared, "The best way to create a unified people is not by suppressing any part of them, but by teaching respect for each other." Noting that "we are all sons and daughters of immigrants, even the sons and daughters of the American Revolution," Marshall denounced resurgent nativism and urged educators to directly confront anti-immigrant bigotry. Specifically, he called for a more accurate picture of American history that highlighted not only great Americans from British backgrounds, but also the "tens of thousands of people contemptuously called 'Dagos,' 'Hunkeys,' 'Greasers,' 'Kikes,' 'Polacks,' 'Litvaks,' 'Niggers,' and even 'Micks,' who gave up their lives" in building the country. He concluded: "Only in such a way, by giving the schools a broad cultural outlook and a sympathetic viewpoint, can we hope to break down chauvinism, the chauvinism of dominant and of minority groups alike. In this way we shall enrich the American culture, we shall create a more homogenous people and we shall strengthen democracy by destroying the curse of race hatreds."[208] Several weeks later, *Rassviet,* the Russian language newspaper in Chicago, quoted Marshall at length and applauded his vision.[209]

At the same time that Adamic, Marshall, and the editor of *Rassviet* were calling for dramatic curricular reforms, other educators were making similar demands. Indeed, several months before the Adamic article appeared, Rachel Davis DuBois, a Quaker educational activist, established what became known as the Bureau for Intercultural Education in New York City. The mission of the Bureau was to get public schools to supplement traditional curricula with programs, units, and lessons about the "cultural gifts" that immigrants and other groups had contributed to American history and life and to promote anti-prejudice education. That same year, the prestigious American Historical Association added its voice to this chorus when its Commission on the Social Studies in the Schools concluded that K–12 educators should teach "understanding and mutual toleration among the diverse races, religions, and cultural groups which compose the American nation." The Commission also urged K–12 educators to actively battle against racial and religious bigotry.[210]

These developments and others like them marked the beginning of an important campaign for curriculum reform in many school systems across the country. Known as the campaign for intercultural or intergroup education, this initiative attracted a small army of consultants, school administrators, and K–12 teachers who had been inspired by the ideas of such reformers as Adamic, Marshall, and DuBois. Seeking to reshape public school curricula along more inclusive and culturally pluralistic lines, these educational reformers and their supporters in such mainstream educational organizations as the American Council on Education, the American Youth Commission, and the National Council for the Social Studies introduced a stunning change in curriculum policy in a number of major cities across the country.[211]

As Adamic had urged, these efforts sought to teach both minority and majority children a new version of American history and culture. This version was guided by ideas strikingly similar to the patriotic pluralist form of Americanization advanced by the foreign language press. Indeed, DuBois described her work in similar terms, noting that intercultural education offered "a gentler form of Americanization that preserved distinctive cultural traditions."[212]

Writing in 1942, Marion Edman, an administrator in the Detroit Public Schools and a national leader of the intercultural education initiative, also described the movement as fulfilling the legacy of the Americanization education campaign. Echoing DuBois, she argued that like its predecessor, this form of Americanization sought to strengthen national unity by inculcating democratic ideas and values. But unlike the earlier movement, this new intercultural approach did so by recognizing and respecting "the rich heritage [that immigrants] brought with them from foreign shores" and sought "to interweave this complex heritage into the pattern of American life."[213]

Over the past few years, the development of intercultural education has been the subject of a flurry of new historical research.[214] One of the main contributions that this new research makes is showing how promising intercultural education seemed in the late 1930s and the World War II years. As one observer wrote in 1946, "[i]ntercultural education is the shining new hope for resolving the group and race tensions that beset our country."[215] This section sketches the early development of intercultural education and then briefly examines intercultural initiatives in the public schools of Cleveland and Detroit during the 1940s.[216]

Intercultural education both mirrored and advanced a pivotal shift in the struggle for civic nationalism in education during World War II and the postwar era. It marked the culmination of the Americanization education movement on the K–12 level, but in ways that assimilationist Americanizers could have not have imagined. Rather than demanding that new immigrants become Americans by shedding their Old World backgrounds, intercultural education encouraged second- and third-generation Americans to integrate into the nation's political and cultural mainstream while retaining important aspects of their Old World heritage. In addition, the movement explicitly advanced a larger and more difficult civic nationalist project: the quest for civil rights for African Americans. From the very beginning of the intercultural education movement, such leaders as Rachel Davis DuBois had worked closely with black educators to transform public school curricula along more pluralistic lines that included materials about African Americans as well as about immigrants in what was being taught in school. Proponents of intercultural initiatives were among the first to lead an educational movement that directly linked efforts by European immigrants to break down barriers blocking their access to American life to similar efforts by African Americans.

In the 1930s and 1940s, four factors combined to make intercultural education possible and to establish it as a prominent national movement. First, as discussed earlier, unlike the World War I era, when educational and political leaders sought to unify the nation by demanding cultural conformity, in the 1930s and early 1940s increasing numbers of academics, journalists, public intellectuals, school leaders, and social activists described American diversity as one of the nation's greatest strengths. From that perspective, they sought to unify the country by stressing at once a commitment to the country's common democratic heritage and the conviction that this heritage honored and respected diversity.[217] In addition, by the early 1940s, many of these individuals and the organizations that they represented explicitly denounced race hatred as a tool of Nazi and Fascist regimes that sought to divide and defeat the United States as part of their quest for world domination. Second, prominent political leaders, including Franklin Roosevelt and key members of his administration, enacted policies and created programs that reflected these new ideas on unity and diversity, most notably in the WPA-supported Americanization campaign. Like many educational and social activists of this period, these political leaders also argued that ethnic, racial, and religious hatreds were threats to national security.

Third, during the Depression and war years, a growing number of immigrant intellectuals and educators—including Louis Adamic, Franz Boas, Leonard Covello, Norman Drachler, Bruno Lasker, and Hilda Taba—played increasingly important roles in promoting these ideas on the K–12 level. These leaders effectively introduced educational reforms that advanced a civic nationalist interpretation of American history and culture, and a powerful critique of "scientific" racism. Many of them sought to make school curricula more inclusive by recognizing the important contributions that groups other than Anglo-Saxons had made to American civilization. In essence, these immigrant intellectuals brought into the academic and educational mainstream ideas that foreign language newspapers had been articulating for decades.[218] Similarly, Boas and Lasker were particularly effective in rebutting ideas about racial superiority and inferiority, demonstrating that there was nothing "scientific" about scientific racism and that race hatred was learned, not innate.[219]

A key part of these efforts was a vigorous challenge to the widely held belief that race and intelligence were highly correlated, a belief that played a powerful role in the passing of the National Origins Act of 1924.

At the time, a small but vocal group of intellectuals, including William Chandler Bagley, John Dewey, and Walter Lippmann, denounced the racial and educational determinism of these ideas, but their arguments gained little traction. However, in the 1930s, a renewed attack on scientific racism bore fruit, most notably when Carl C. Brigham, one of the nation's leading scientific racists, "recanted" his argument that there was "a biological hierarchy of European groups (Nordic, Alpine, Mediterranean)." Throughout the 1930s and 1940s, Boas—and, following his death in 1942, his students—expanded this critique by vigorously attacking the idea that there was a similar hierarchy for whites, blacks, and other racial groups. Due to these challenges, ideas about racial hierarchies in intelligence lost ground in the 1930s and 1940s, although they remained an insidious part of popular culture and influenced public school programs for decades to come.[220]

Fourth, during this period, efforts to revise public school curricula along pluralistic lines were facilitated by the pioneering work on intercultural education that Rachel Davis DuBois had begun more than a decade earlier.[221] In a number of ways, DuBois brought together all of the factors discussed above and inspired a genuinely new curriculum reform campaign. Beginning in the 1920s, she developed a broad vision of intercultural education. Like John Dewey, who greatly influenced her, DuBois believed that "our American culture is not a finished and static thing," but rather was evolving and expanding as new groups brought their "cultural gifts" to the New World.[222] In a 1942 pamphlet commissioned by the U.S. Office of Education, *National Unity through Intercultural Education*, she argued that a key goal of intercultural education was teaching young people that American culture was "stronger and more beautiful through the very diversity of its blended elements."[223] As Diana Selig points out, DuBois was fond of saying that the composite American was "Indian-Scotch-Irish-French-Jewish-English-German-Negro-Oriental-Italian-Russian."[224] Working against the growing threat of ethnic nationalism at home and abroad, DuBois staunchly advocated a vision of patriotic pluralism for American education.

Intercultural education's rise to national prominence began with DuBois's efforts in New York City. Her first success in the city came in the spring of 1935, when she introduced a program of intercultural assemblies and discussion groups at Covello's Benjamin Franklin High School. Covello was delighted with the program, and he spread the word about the fine work DuBois had done at his school. Consequently, DuBois quickly earned the reputation as an effective curriculum reformer.[225] It was not surprising, therefore, that three years later, the New York City Board of Education responded to the horrors of *Kristallnacht* in Germany and a spate of anti-Semitic incidents near several local high schools by declaring "that in every public school in the city of New York, assemblies be devoted to the promulgation of American ideals of democracy, tolerance and freedom for all men: that these assemblies be devoted to making the children of our nation aware of the contributions of all races and nationalities to the growth and development of American democracy."[226]

Soon after, a sizable number of major school systems also adopted some form of intercultural education, and by 1940 a group of other educators, including Hilda Taba, an Estonian immigrant who, like DuBois, had received a Ph.D. from Teachers College, and curriculum reformers like William Van Til were also promoting intercultural programs across the country.[227] Taba, for example, served as the director of the Center for Intergroup Education at the University of Chicago, which was affiliated with the American Council on Education (ACE). During the late 1940s, Taba and the center became widely known for workshops sponsored by the University of Chicago that introduced K–12 teachers to intercultural ideas, methods, and materials.[228]

Much of this newfound popularity was due to concerns about national unity during wartime. Following the attack on Pearl Harbor, demands for intercultural education increased dramatically. School districts looked for new ways to teach their students about the democratic ideals and values that were under assault and to promote unity through units and lessons on racial, religious, and ethnic tolerance. For urban school systems with large immigrant and growing African American populations, such education was especially urgent, as racial and ethnic tensions created by the war increasingly spilled over into classrooms and playgrounds.

In 1946, for example, a survey done by the National Education Association found that over 90 percent of the 376 urban school superintendents who replied to a questionnaire about intercultural education believed that public schools should "deliberately and systematically build attitudes and understanding necessary to improve racial and group tolerance."[229] By this time, in addition to New York City, such cities as Springfield (Massachusetts), Pittsburgh, Cincinnati, San Diego, and Santa Barbara were operating intercultural education programs.[230] Of the major cities that adopted intercultural programs, Cleveland and Detroit quickly became national leaders. The Chicago Public School system lagged behind Cleveland and Detroit in this area, but its experiences with intercultural education, brief though they were, paralleled those of the other cities.

In a 1940 article praising Cleveland's creation of the nation's first Council for American Unity, the author argued that it was no accident that this group was formed in the Forest City. The reason was simple: "Cleveland has always demonstrated that it is possible to enjoy the feeling of full-fledged Americanism without stifling the cultural aspirations of the various ethnic groups whose immediate origin is not Anglo-Saxon American."[231] The same argument could be made regarding Cleveland's leadership in intercultural education. The city's rich tradition of respecting the cultural backgrounds of its large and vibrant immigrant communities and, as noted earlier, the strong commitment to American ideals expressed in the Cleveland foreign language newspapers, made it particularly open to these educational ideas that were so akin to patriotic pluralism.[232]

In addition, intercultural education helped Cleveland educational leaders address a number of emerging problems. Foremost among these was the dramatic rise in high school enrollments during the Depression. Due to the collapse of the youth labor market, huge numbers of poor and working-class students, who in good economic times would have dropped out for available jobs, either returned to or remained in high school. Nationally, the percentage of those aged fourteen to seventeen years in public schools in the United States jumped from just over 50 percent of the age group in 1930 to almost 73 percent in 1940. While these numbers fell during World War II, by 1950 more than three-quarters of the age group was in high school.[233] In Cleveland, high school enrollments rose from just under 29,000 in 1929–1930 to almost 40,000 in 1939–1940, an increase of nearly 38 percent.[234] Records do not indicate how many of these new high school students were from immigrant families. But given the large percentages of elementary pupils from immigrant families in the 1920s, it is reasonable to assume that a substantial proportion of the new high school students were first- or second-generation Americans.[235]

At the same time that new students were pouring into Cleveland high schools, the district also was experiencing a modest up-tick of non-native children enrolling in the system. Despite the severe restraints on immigration to the United States, between 1936 and 1940 over 308,000 new immigrants came to this country, many of them fleeing persecution and violence in Europe. In Cleveland, educational leaders responded to "refugee children and evacuees" with a more culturally sensitive form of Americanization.[236] As with the large number of second-generation students, intercultural education seemed like the perfect program for helping both sets of young people to integrate into American society.

Perhaps most important, Cleveland's civic and educational leaders also hoped that intercultural education would help reduce racial conflict between blacks and whites. Between 1930 and 1950, Cleveland's black population more than doubled, from about 72,000 people (7.9 percent of the population) to over 152,00 (10.4 percent of the population).[237] As the black population increased, racial tensions grew apace.

The best overview of intercultural education in the Forest City came from Allen Y. King, the director of social studies for the Cleveland Public Schools. Writing in the *Report of the Superintendent of Schools, 1943–1944*, King provided a lengthy and detailed discussion of how intercultural ideas had been implemented in the social studies curriculum. Placing the Cleveland program in the context of a nation at war, King began by praising the amazing array of cultures in the city, while at the same time noting that such cultural richness "imposes upon us the task of building unity with this diversity."[238] Fighting bigotry was a central part of this project. King argued, "Race hatreds and group intolerance are not consistent with the ideals of a nation based upon freedom, equality, and justice for all; their growth threatens our survival as free individuals and as a democratic people."[239]

Cleveland approached this project by weaving intercultural ideas, themes, and content throughout the social studies curriculum. In the elementary grades, for example, this meant exploring the "biographies of men and women who have contributed to civilization, . . . the basic principles of living together harmoniously, . . . [and] providing opportunities for satisfying experiences in democratic living." The biographical lessons included studying people from many "races and nationalities in our population." As King put it, besides teaching about the lives of traditional American heroes, "[s]pecial attention is also directed to the contributions individuals and groups of differing national and racial origins have made to our way of life."[240]

As significant as this change on the elementary level was, the most dramatic shifts in social studies occurred in the junior and senior high schools. For example, the Cleveland program required *all* seventh-and eighth-graders to take social studies classes that contained a unit called "America: A Nation of Immigrants." In these classes, King estimated that teachers spent between a quarter and a third of a semester studying "the various national and racial strains in the population." The course concentrated on why people immigrated, the challenges they faced once they got here, the "culture, arts, and traditions" that different groups brought with them, and great Americans who came from these groups. King pointed out that a key objective of the unit was for students to recognize that the "heritage of each group has enriched American life and all groups have contributed to America by what they have done since they arrived."[241] In other words, the hope expressed by the Chicago and Cleveland foreign language newspapers for a more inclusive form of American history appeared to have been realized in these changes.

At the senior high school level the social studies curricular changes were equally revolutionary. For example, twelfth-graders studied America's composite population in a course titled, "The American People: Building Understanding between Various Racial and National Groups in Our Population." One of the main goals of this course was to expose the "myth of racial superiority," a myth King noted had been "discredited by reference to the findings of anthropology." This course, King explained, made "a direct attack upon the problems and tensions in intergroup relations." He also noted that many teachers of these twelfth-grade classes included a unit on "The Negro in the Life of Our City and Nation." In all, "The American People" course strongly promoted the antiprejudice-education project that such people as Rachel Davis DuBois and Franz Boas had been advocating in the 1930s and early 1940s.[242]

By 1945, nine Cleveland schools were participating in a national intercultural (the term Cleveland used was "intergroup") initiative sponsored by the American Council on Education. Directed by Hilda Taba, this initiative began with four school systems—Cleveland, Milwaukee, Pittsburgh, and South Bend—and by late 1947 was operating in eighteen systems across the country. All told, at that time, seven of the ten largest school systems in the country had some sort of intercultural program under way, most of them linked to Taba's University of Chicago center.[243]

During the 1930s, Detroit also struggled with a huge increase in high school enrollments that included large numbers of second-generation Americans, and the public schools continued Americanization work with a small number of new immigrants before World War II, and a larger influx of foreign-born children after the war.[244] As in Cleveland, the largest challenge for the Motor City was the dramatic increase in the African American population, from about 120,000 people in 1930 (7.6 percent of the population) to over 300,000 (16.2 percent of the population) in 1940.[245] Clashes between blacks and whites, many of them first- or second-generation immigrants, became common. In June 1943, the city exploded in a race riot that left thirty-four people dead (most of them African Americans) and property damage in the millions of dollars.[246] Civic leaders almost immediately turned to the public schools as the primary institution to address racial problems in the city.

Within days of the end of the riot, a group of social and educational activists formed the Committee on Inter-racial Understanding in the Schools (CIUS). CIUS represented over forty generally liberal community and educational organizations that pressed school leaders to introduce a program that would attack racial and religious prejudice.[247] Three months later, the superintendent of schools created the Administrative Committee on Intercultural Education (ACIE). Chaired by Assistant Superintendent Paul Rankin, the mission of the ACIE was to act "as a clearing house for intercultural and interracial education as they related to curriculum, community, education and teacher training."[248]

Both committees quickly reached out to national leaders of the intercultural education movement. In the fall of 1943, the CIUS brought Rachel Davis DuBois to Detroit to speak and make recommendations. One year later, the ACIE signed a five-year agreement with DuBois's Bureau for Intercultural Education to create a system-wide intercultural education program. To support this effort the Bureau sent a flurry of prominent consultants, including Margaret Mead, Hilda Taba, and William Van Til to Detroit.[249]

Drawing on these experts and on suggestions from various local educators and groups, the ACIE began implementing intercultural education in the Detroit schools. A key step in this effort was gaining unqualified support for the intercultural education initiative from the school board. The board complied on January 9, 1945, adopting a policy statement drafted by the ACIE declaring that materials and experiences that promote "understanding and good will between groups that differ in race, creed, national origin, or economic status" should be "woven into regular curriculum."[250] To implement this plan, the board called for an extensive in-service program to aid teachers in bringing intercultural ideas and materials into their classrooms.

Perhaps the best example of the work done by the ACIE in its first year of operation was the publication of *Building One Nation Indivisible*, a ninety-four-page guide designed to help teachers introduce intercultural content and methods in major subject areas. Over a thousand copies of the book were distributed throughout the system. It provided a strong philosophical rationale for intercultural education that stressed three key points. First, it declared that there are "essential democratic loyalties and beliefs . . . which all Americans should have in common." Second, it argued that the majority *cannot* "make total conformity to the dominant culture pattern or membership in the dominant race a requirement for full and equal participation in the political, social, and economic advantages of American democracy." And finally, the book emphasized that members of "religious and ethnic minorities" should be free to "practice and perpetuate" those aspects of their culture that "do not conflict with essential democratic principles" or assimilate into the larger culture, as they wished. Like the writers in the foreign language press, the authors of *Building One Nation Indivisible* believed that truly democratic education had to encourage and sustain all three of these elements.[251]

Building One Nation Indivisible also provided basic information to realize these goals. It discussed how to create a classroom climate that supported both unity and diversity, gave pointers on leading discussions of sensitive issues, and suggested materials for use in class. Many of the recommendations of the program fit the "heroes and holidays" approach to intercultural education, but two lengthy sections (accounting for almost a quarter of the book) offered teachers substantial amounts of information about the immigrant and black experiences in America, and thoughtful methods for including this material in English and social studies classes.

The section on immigrants provides a good example of how the authors hoped *Building One Nation Indivisible* would encourage both unity and diversity. Written by Norman Drachler, a Detroit teacher who was the child of Ukrainian Jewish immigrants, this section described how to include materials on immigrants and African Americans into social studies classes primarily on the high school level. The section on immigrants began by noting the "study of immigration demonstrates clearly that the problems of minority groups have been present since the early days of this Republic."

These problems extended beyond the basic difficulties of moving to a new country or to new parts of the country. The section also included information about attacks on immigrants from such racist and antidemocratic groups as the Ku Klux Klan and the Silver Shirts. Moreover, the section argued that teachers should stress how, despite such opposition, the vast majority of immigrants made great contributions to American life. As evidence of this last point, the section included lists of famous immigrants and their contributions to the United States. The section also included advice on methods that would both help students break down prejudices about different ethnic, racial, and religious groups and enable them to relate their knowledge to new groups. Thus, it ended with a discussion of how blacks moving to cities like Detroit were experiencing many of the difficulties and challenges that earlier groups of immigrants had faced.[252]

In addition to providing teachers with new materials and methods, the ACIE created a network of intercultural education committees in almost every school in the system to further this initiative. The network provided a mechanism to disseminate news and materials about intercultural education to teachers throughout the district.[253] One of the primary responsibilities of these committees was encouraging teachers to participate in the numerous in-service programs that the ACIE developed in conjunction with the bureau, the CIUS, Wayne University (which operated its own intercultural education project), and a local philanthropic foundation.[254] These in-service activities included lectures, workshops at local colleges and universities, weeklong summer institutes, university courses, and "traveling" workshops that offered one-day programs at schools throughout the district. These activities sought to familiarize teachers with intercultural education and to aid them in preparing class materials for teaching intercultural topics.[255]

Beyond setting up these in-service programs, the ACIE made a strong effort to chronicle the intercultural ideas and materials that Detroit teachers used in their classrooms. As early as November 1944, the committee was regularly sending a bulletin, "Best Practices in Intercultural Education," to all the teachers in the district. The goal was to get teachers to integrate intercultural materials into their regular curriculum and to describe innovative teaching strategies. By 1946, these materials were so extensive that the school system published *Promising Practices in Intergroup Education*, a pamphlet that described how intercultural education was being implemented in classrooms around the city. The following year the Bureau for Intercultural Education in New York revised and republished the pamphlet for a national audience.[256]

Promising Practices in Intergroup Education provides a marvelous glimpse into the kinds of methods and materials Detroit teachers used in this program. The pamphlet compiled reports on intercultural instruction from teachers in 152 schools throughout the city. The authors then categorized these different approaches and evaluated the "advantages" and "drawbacks" of each. Some of the approaches were well known and widely used in Detroit and across the country. For example, the most common approach, "reported by practically every school," examined the contributions that diverse peoples made to the United States. Most teachers used biographies of prominent individuals from different minority groups, and they introduced pupils to different cultural aspects of various groups.[257] Also widely used was "The Study of Prejudice Approach," in which students investigated such topics as stereotyping, segregation, and scapegoating.[258] Both of these approaches were core aspects of DuBois's program of intercultural reforms, and both were recommended in the earlier ACIE publication *One Nation Indivisible*.

Other approaches broke new ground. Foremost among these was "The Ideals vs. Practice Approach" that explored the contrast between "what America stands for, and what some Americans actually practice, in dealing with minorities." Used in courses for older students, this approach examined "the inequalities which now exist in this country for people of various racial, religious, and national groups—inequalities of opportunity for employment, education, housing, recreation, health, and civil rights."[259]

Given the nativism, anti-Semitism, and anti-Catholicism of the 1930s, this approach to intercultural education certainly could well have explored the experiences of European immigrants. But the examples of lessons that highlighted the mismatches between American ideals and American reality all focused on the treatment of African Americans. As noted earlier, prior to the 1940s, most intercultural programs focused mainly on immigrants, despite efforts by DuBois and other proponents of intercultural education to include materials about African Americans in intercultural curricula. But following the race riots in Detroit, civic and educational leaders there and in other cities increasingly focused intercultural programs on issues related to blacks. Paul Rankin, chair of the ACIE, declared in November 1943, "Although intercultural problems will be considered, this Committee will give special attention just now to the promotion of interracial understanding."[260]

"The Ideals vs. Practice Approach" provided teachers with an excellent opportunity to address racial issues. Teachers who used this strategy got their students to investigate such topics as restrictive covenants (which the U.S. Supreme Court struck down in 1948, due to a lawsuit filed by a Detroit teacher); "Problems of Negroes Today"; and the activities of the Ku Klux Klan.[261] By their very nature, these topics compelled students to examine white racism, Jim Crow laws, and the pervasive discrimination confronting black people in the United States.

In all, *Promising Practices in Intergroup Education* provided a comprehensive look into the varied approaches, units, and lessons that Detroit teachers used in their classrooms. The pamphlet seems to indicate that, by 1946, this dramatic curriculum reform was a well-established and thriving part of the Detroit Public Schools. The effort appeared to be quite popular in Detroit and was well regarded by outside observers. For example, in April 1944, an official from the National Association for the Advancement of Colored People came to Detroit to examine race relations in the schools and came away "very pleasantly surprised" by the intercultural activities that she saw. Indeed, she declared that the system was "much to be commended" for its efforts in this area.[262] On the other hand, some Detroiters dismissed intercultural education as mere "window dressing," noting accurately that the school system was hardly a model of racial equality (e.g., the number of black teachers in the system was woefully small compared to the size of the black community; and the majority of black children were attending the oldest, most dilapidated schools in the city). Yet the program continued to get strong support from outside groups such as the liberal CIUS and the district's ACIE.[263] Moreover, as racial tensions in Detroit and other major cities grew, and as Americans became aware of the horrifying consequences that racial hatred had produced in the Holocaust, the need for educational programs addressing issues of race and culture seemed ever more urgent. But by the late 1940s, enthusiasm for intercultural education was fading.[264]

In 1949, for example, Allen King issued a report on how Cleveland students learned about current events. One would assume that the study of such events would have presented numerous opportunities for the discussion of issues related to intercultural education (e.g., the influx of European immigrants after World War II, Truman's desegregation of the U.S.

military, or Jackie Robinson breaking of the color barrier in Major League Baseball). But King did not include a single example that highlighted intercultural themes, and the words *intercultural* or *intergroup* did not appear anywhere in the report.[265]

Detroit was moving in the same direction. In October 1948, for example, members of the Administrative Committee on Intercultural Education changed its name to the Coordinating Committee on Democratic Human Relations, indicating a new, less specific mission.[266] This move was reflected in the schools. A brief article written by several teachers at a Detroit high school described the work of that school's "Committee on Democratic Human Relations" largely in terms of teaching students how to get along with each other, with only modest attention paid to substantive coursework on intercultural issues.[267]

By 1950, even the word *intercultural* disappeared from Detroit's annual superintendent's reports, replaced by the phrase "Democratic Human Relations." At the same time, the amount of coverage of intercultural efforts declined steadily in the annual reports. What little the reports did say about the program indicated that it had shifted its focus away from presenting additional material about the history and cultural contributions of diverse groups toward a more psychological approach that dealt with changing individual behaviors in regard to people from diverse backgrounds.[268]

By 1955, the national campaign for intercultural education was defunct. Historians have identified a number of factors that contributed to the decline and disappearance of this curriculum reform movement, including: the "red-baiting" of leftist and liberal educators during the McCarthy era, which often targeted strong supporters of intercultural education; a postwar resurgence of ethnic nationalism that led to the McCarran-Walters Act (which reaffirmed the racist quota system of the National Origins Act); the loss of leadership among supporters of intercultural education, as prominent supporters such as Hilda Taba moved on to new projects and areas of interest; and the increasingly psychological emphasis of antiprejudice initiatives that, as Zoe Burkholder argues, eventually transformed these efforts into little more than lessons on good manners.[269]

Two other factors, one political and the other pedagogical, also played a role in the demise of intercultural education. Politically, the Cold War undercut key components of intercultural education, specifically its link to national security issues and wartime patriotism. Intercultural education thrived during World War II and the immediate postwar years, in large part because its basic ideas about unity and diversity dovetailed with the nation's efforts to defeat the Axis powers and to repudiate ethnically nationalist ideas of racial superiority and inferiority. While the Soviet Union was an equally vicious totalitarian regime that murdered and brutalized tens of millions of people, racism was not central to Communist ideology, as it was to Nazism. Thus, the Cold War between the United States and the Soviet Union was not one of civic versus ethnic nationalism, but between democracy and dictatorship. From that perspective, the decision by Detroit educators and others across the country to shift their terminology from intercultural education to "Democratic Human Relations" may have been a shrewd political move.

Pedagogically, however, this move created a serious problem for supporters of intercultural education. In many ways, intercultural education ran against the tide of curriculum development in the 1930s and 1940s in that it sought to add new content to such discipline-based courses as history and literature. The problem with this approach was that during these years, large numbers of educational leaders sought to diminish discipline-based content regardless of how intercultural such content may have been. Instead, these educators hoped to get students involved in courses that were supposedly relevant and useful and required little or no background knowledge.[270] By replacing intercultural education, which had a clear vision of the new content students should learn, with lessons in human relations, educators could easily introduce fewer discipline-based educational experiences under the guise of teaching about democracy. For example, the "Human Relations" section of the 1954–1955 annual report of the Detroit superintendent, which gave a brief history of democratic human relations education in Detroit, concluded that in the approach now being used, more "attention is being directed toward developing good interpersonal relations, between student–student, teacher–student, teacher–principal, and school–community."[271] This was so vague as to be meaningless.

Whatever one might say about intercultural education, it clearly was about disciplinary content. Its supporters sought to broaden history and literature curricula by weaving stories of non-Anglo-Saxon heroes and heroines into the great American narrative and by recognizing the artistic, cultural, linguistic, political, and military contributions that people from all races, colors, and religions had made to this country. The disappearance of a movement that promoted such curricular inclusiveness was a profound educational loss. But rather than lament the fate of this promising reform effort, it is important to recognize that the very existence of intercultural education programs in many big-city school systems during the 1940s was a remarkable and important development, and that the achievements of these programs were significant.

In light of the long struggle European immigrants waged against ethnic nationalism and for recognition as true Americans, intercultural education was unquestionably a major breakthrough. During World War II and at least as late as 1948, intercultural education programs helped promote a national vision of the United States as a country composed of disparate groups that were united in their devotion to democracy and their love of country. This was exactly the stance that academic and cultural critics of aggressive assimilation had been making since the World War I era and was strikingly similar to the stance taken by the foreign language press in Chicago and Cleveland. Specifically, intercultural education advanced two core components of the patriotic pluralism that the foreign language newspapers espoused: debunking scientific racism, which was central to American ethnic nationalism and racial restriction, and recognizing that diverse people had made important contributions to American history and culture.

Equally striking was that many of the leaders of the intercultural education movement were themselves immigrants (e.g., Adamic, Boas, Covello, Drachler, and Taba). Even in the early 1930s, it was almost unimaginable that immigrants could lead a successful educational reform movement whose goal was the transformation of traditional Anglo-Saxon-dominated curricula. Yet by the late 1930s and extending well into the 1940s, these immigrant civic and educational leaders and their native-born American allies implemented such reforms in school systems ranging from New York to Los Angeles. These leaders were living proof of the power of Americanization education, but as the foreign language press had long argued, a form of Americanization education that recognized and respected the cultural differences and cultural contributions of diverse groups.

In addition, intercultural educators in the late 1940s increasingly used ideas and approaches developed to teach students about racial equality and the contributions of European immigrants to create new curricula that focused on issues related to African Americans, including units that attacked white racism and highlighted black contributions to American

history and life. With these efforts intercultural educators provided opportunities for blacks and the descendants of European immigrants to unite
in pressuring public schools to live up to their civic nationalist creed.

Perhaps nothing better illustrates the legacy of intercultural education
than the career of Norman Drachler. As noted earlier, Drachler wrote the
section about European immigrants for the 1944 intercultural education
manual *Building One Nation Indivisible,* which was used in Detroit. His
commitment to intercultural education ran deep. He was a Ukrainian Jew
whose family once was saved from a pogrom by Christian neighbors. In
1966, Drachler became the superintendent of the Detroit Public Schools.
Beyond dramatically increasing the number of black administrators and
teachers in Detroit, he was determined to rid the school system of American history textbooks that either ignored the role blacks had played in the
development of this country or contained racist characterizations of the
few blacks who actually were discussed in the texts.[272] Two decades earlier, when the Detroit schools were implementing intercultural programs,
the ACIE and the Detroit Urban League had called on publishers to revise racially biased textbooks, but to no avail.[273]

This time things worked out quite differently. Working closely with
Richard Henry, a militant black leader who once had kept his son out of
school in protest against racist history textbooks, Drachler banned the
books from the Detroit system and successfully forced publishers to substantially revise their American history textbooks along more intercultural
lines.[274] Historian Joseph Moreau has described this effort as one of the
great successes of the civil rights movement in the late 1960s.[275]

Conclusion

In 1942, a young Slovenian immigrant gave a high school commencement
speech in Cleveland that captured the essence of Americanization. Seven
years earlier she had come to the United States from a part of Slovenia that
was under Italian control. In her speech, she began by describing how the
Fascist regime had closed Slovenian periodicals, tried to suppress the Slovenian language, and threatened the very survival of Slovenian culture.
Much of this student's early education had been steeped in Fascist ideology, but her speech drew on classic themes in American history and the
promise of civic nationalism that was intrinsic to these themes.

Not surprisingly, she devoted considerable attention to the role of education in her process of Americanization. "What does America mean to

me?" she asked rhetorically. "It means schools where you are given every opportunity for self-expression and self-government." She described her delight at public libraries where people could "actually choose a book on any subject" and read newspapers with diverse political points of view. She then declared, "To me America means a country where people like my mother, just an ordinary person, recently arrived from a foreign country, can go to school and learn to read and write the English language. She has learned the history of the country, and last January 5th passed the examination for citizenship perfectly."

In a passage reminiscent of Lincoln's reference to the "electric cord" that joined immigrant Americans to the founders of this country, the student stated that though she was not fortunate enough to be descended from passengers on the *Mayflower* or people who had fought in the Revolution, she still felt that she was a true American. "I was not born to that privilege," she declared, "but I claim it now."[276]

As important as formal schooling and public libraries were to this young woman's Americanization, one could easily imagine other influences on her as well. For example, it is likely that when she returned home, a copy of either the centrist Slovenian newspaper *Ameriska Domovina* or the leftist paper *Enakopravnost* awaited her. In either paper, she would have found articles supporting Americanization while at the same time strongly encouraging her to use the freedoms that this country provides to sustain cherished aspects of her Slovenian heritage. She would have heard Slovenian spoken in the church she attended, and she could have joined any number of Slovenian clubs and organizations. In addition, she likely knew that six months before she gave her commencement speech, Louis Adamic, perhaps the most famous Slovenian in the United States and a strong supporter of "unity within diversity," had dined at the White House with Franklin Roosevelt and Winston Churchill. She had indeed come to a new world.[277]

In a number of ways, Americanization education in the 1930s and 1940s remained quite similar to earlier efforts. The basic requirements of learning English, knowing U.S. history, committing to the democratic ideals and values of the country, and becoming citizens remained core elements of the process. Yet, as this chapter argues, in one significant area, Americanization education in the 1930s and 1940s was markedly different from what had come before. Now it acknowledged that immigrants could be good Americans while retaining important aspects of their Old World heritage. Editors and writers in the foreign language newspapers of Chicago had been articulating this point of view for decades, and the Cleveland foreign language press reiterated it in the late 1930s and early 1940s. What had changed in the Depression and war years was that this stance moved from the periphery of American educational culture to the center.

During the New Deal and World War II years, educators who worked with adult students in WPA courses, curriculum writers who produced new textbooks for the U.S. Office of Education, and teachers in Chicago and Cleveland who taught in public evening school programs, all participated in a concerted effort to recognize the "cultural gifts" that immigrants had brought to America. On the K–12 level, educators in such large urban school systems as New York, Detroit, and Cleveland implemented intercultural programs that advanced ideas about racial equality, cultural pluralism, and civic nationalism under the broad goal of promoting national unity and patriotism in wartime. Intercultural educators taught lessons debunking racial superiority and inferiority and presented students with a new, inclusive interpretation of U.S. history and culture, all of which were strikingly similar to the vision foreign language newspapers had been advocating since the early 1900s. That these ideas were taught on both the adult and K–12 levels in school systems across the country would have been almost unimaginable in the 1910s and 1920s.

A variety of factors coalesced in the Depression and war years to bring about these dramatic changes. Most important was the rise of ethnic nationalism, both at home and abroad. Stoked by the economic collapse and the rise of fascism and Nazism, during the 1930s the United States was roiled by intense anti-immigrant (as well as anti-Semitic and anti-Catholic) sentiments and the reassertion of ideas about Nordic or Anglo-Saxon superiority. But unlike the 1920s, the Depression years witnessed a powerful political and educational backlash against these developments, a backlash that reached beyond immigrant neighborhoods and the foreign language press that previously had borne the brunt of the battles against American ethnic nationalism. Now such prominent political leaders as Franklin Roosevelt and Fiorello LaGuardia frequently inveighed against nativism and other forms of racial and religious bigotry and extolled the patriotism of the diverse peoples who made up this country. Moreover, as the United States moved toward war, political, cultural, and educational leaders increasingly argued that unlike the racist totalitarian regimes of Europe and

Asia, the United States was defined by its democratic traditions *and* its pride in the racial and religious diversity that democracy sustained and protected. Defending pluralism had become patriotic.

Nowhere was that change felt more strongly than in the foreign language press. As national leaders extolled unity and diversity, writers for the Chicago and Cleveland foreign language press promoted these same ideas to their readers. Indeed, in Chicago, editors and writers in the CFLPS newspapers reiterated the same ideas of patriotic pluralism that they had advocated since the turn of the twentieth century. Similarly, by the early 1940s, all the Cleveland foreign language newspapers regularly proclaimed their patriotism, their commitment to the nation's democratic ideals, their rejection of racism and religious bigotry, their willingness to fight against the very homelands their immigrant ancestors had left, *and* their pride in their ethnic backgrounds.

Adding strength to this trend, during the 1930s and 1940s an array of immigrant intellectuals and educators crossed the boundaries between immigrant neighborhoods and the national stage. They enthusiastically proclaimed a message of racial equality and unity within diversity. They highlighted the similarities between racism in the United States and Nazi ideology, defined Nordic supremacists as un-American, and reminded their fellow citizens of the cultural richness that immigrants and other minorities added to American civilization. In doing so they changed America as much as America changed them. As historian Philip Gleason argues, "cultural pluralism in all its ambiguities and complexities is the crucial legacy of World War II in respect to American identity."[278]

These developments signaled the ultimate success of Americanization education for European immigrants. Throughout the first half of the twentieth century, these immigrants and their native-born children consistently had sought to Americanize. But just as consistently they viewed this process as a negotiated exchange rather than as acquiescence to Anglo-Saxon cultural hegemony. Beyond that, these efforts also advanced a strong and capacious trend toward civic nationalism and demanded increased respect for racial and cultural diversity.

These arguments complicate the most popular current interpretation of Americanization, which maintains that rather than producing people committed to civic nationalism, Americanization actually stimulated the rise of a new form of ethnic nationalism defined by "whiteness."[279] Drawing on earlier works by such scholars as W. E. B. DuBois and Gunnar Myrdal, these historians argue, to use Myrdal's words, that for many European immigrants "the development of prejudice against Negroes is usually one of their first lessons in Americanization."[280] A number of scholars see the Depression and World War II years as the pivotal period in which first- and second-generation Americans in northern cities asserted their whiteness and thus completed their Americanization.[281] As one writer puts it, "white supremacy made possible the Americanization of the immigrant."[282]

These characterizations of Americanization as whitening the immigrants generally view the process as one of socialization or acculturation, rather than formal education. As historian David Roediger explains, "whitening is a process in social history in which countless quotidian activities informed popular and expert understanding of the race of new immigrants, as well as new immigrants' understanding of race."[283]

But because these whiteness scholars mainly view Americanization as a process of acculturating, their discussions of education on either the K–12 or the adult level are often perfunctory.[284] There is little doubt that public education was deeply involved in establishing and maintaining racial hierarchies in the United States. Whether one considers the separate and grotesquely unequal conditions of education in the South, the increasingly separate and unequal conditions developing in this era in the North, the development of curriculum tracks in high schools, or the racist characterization of blacks in American history textbooks, there is ample evidence of such practices.[285]

Yet, at the same time that schools were implicitly and explicitly teaching white ethnic nationalism, Americanization efforts in K–12 and adult classes offered a counternarrative of civic nationalism that challenged the racism in this country. As this and preceding chapters have shown, teaching immigrants and their children that the political and social identity of this country is based on ideas of democracy, equality, and freedom was among the most important aspects of Americanization education. These themes recur in elementary and secondary social studies programs, in adult day and evening classes, and in the pages of foreign language newspapers. They underlie the biographies of Washington and Lincoln that teachers on every level used to describe the character of the country. At their best, educators used these stories to inspire their students to become the spiritual heirs of these heroes of American history in terms of their commitment to democracy and their belief in the ideal that "all men are created equal." As in all efforts to use education to construct and transmit a national identity across the generations, there is, as political scientist David Miller acknowledges, an element of myth in these stories, but they are myths that help people acknowledge what they should aspire to as citizens and what standards should be used to recognize "defects in our practices and institutions that have allowed us to fall short."[286]

Nowhere were these efforts to define the United States as an inclusive, civic nationalist country argued with more passion and commitment than in the Americanizing efforts of the writers for the foreign language newspapers in Chicago and Cleveland. In their redefinition of American history as a story with diverse participants, in teaching their readers about basic democratic ideals and values, and in their demand that the United States live up to its civic nationalist creed, the editors and writers of the Chicago and Cleveland foreign language newspapers offered a vision of the United States at its best. By arguing that "being American" must be defined by people's commitment to the democratic ideals of the country, *not* by their race, religion, or cultural background, the editors and writers of these papers implicitly and, at times, explicitly challenged white ethnic nationalism. This was especially true in the late 1930s and early 1940s, as Americanizers, editors, writers for foreign language newspapers, and other educators sought to differentiate the United States from its racist foes.

This view of Americanization meant that in embracing their adopted country, in Americanizing, eastern and southern European immigrants and their descendants inherited an ever-present, historically rooted set of moral and political choices regarding, among other things, black/white relations in the United States. The immigrants and their children could acculturate to the racial hierarchies of the era and align themselves with white ethnic nationalists, or they could draw on their Americanization education and support efforts to make the United States a more civic nationalist country. As historian Eric Arnesen argues, identifying oneself as "white" did not necessarily mean endorsing "white supremacy." A person could "possess all the privileges and 'pleasures' of whiteness and hold to political opinions that formally oppose slavery, black subordination and the like."[287] By describing the meaning of America as rooted in the ideals and values of democracy, Americanization education as it appeared in the foreign language newspapers in Chicago, the WPA citizenship classes, and intercultural education in public schools sharpened and clarified these choices.

In the last chapter of *An American Dilemma*, Myrdal made a similar point by again mentioning Americanization. In this case, however, he was not referring to European immigrants but rather to the South, which, he declared, "has become rapidly 'Americanized' during the last generation."[288] Obviously, in this instance, Myrdal was not using the term "Americanized" to describe European immigrants adopting racist attitudes about blacks and becoming white ethnic nationalists. Rather, in this section of the study, he identified Americanization as the process of embracing the civic nationalist essence of the American democratic creed. Writing during World War II, Myrdal noted that American war propaganda was awash "with reminders of the great cause of democracy and the equality of peoples, which is the main issue in the War America is waging against nazism, fascism, and Japanese imperialism." And, because the war was being fought to defend these principles of civic nationalism, Myrdal asked how a "conservative white Southerner" could deal with the "split in his moral personality" as a patriotic American who supported a civic nationalist war and as a white ethnic nationalist who endorsed Jim Crow.[289]

This question did not apply to conservative white southerners alone. Over the rest of the twentieth century, all Americans, native-born and naturalized, collectively and individually had to wrestle with the same questions about the kind of country they wanted the United States to be. Given its firm grounding in civic nationalism, Americanization education cast a clear and powerful light on the path its advocates hoped the nation would take.

CONCLUSION

In late September 2001, Gregory Rodriguez, a senior fellow at the New America Foundation, published an essay in the *New York Times* in which he speculated about the impact the recent terrorist attacks might have on Americans' sense of national identity. Rodriguez began with a critique of assimilationist efforts in the early twentieth century, describing them as "a process of subtraction" in which "newcomers displayed their loyalty by discarding the language and customs of their native lands." He added, "Immigrants were criticized for congregating and finding mutual support." Building on these assumptions, Rodriguez observed, "Not until the 1960's was it permissible for immigrants to adhere to their cultural heritage."[1] More recently echoing these same ideas, James A. Banks, a leading proponent of multicultural education, declared, "In the past, schools in the United States embraced an assimilationist or mainstream approach to citizenship education. Schools tried to make students effective citizens of the nation-state by alienating them from their home and community cultures and assimilating them into the mainstream society."[2] In both of these cases, the authors were articulating conventional assumptions about how immigrants in the early twentieth century became Americans. They implied that campaigns to Americanize immigrants were little more than examples of cultural imperialism in which immigrants were essentially passive victims.

Many early-twentieth-century Americanizers did demand that eastern and southern European immigrants forsake their Old World cultures and abandon the "foreign" neighborhoods that sustained these cultures. However, this book demonstrates that Americanization education was a far richer and decidedly more complex educational and social process than the conventional rendition portrays. Indeed, rather than seeing Americanization education as a largely coercive, benighted enterprise, I argue that such education—in all its varied forms—substantially contributed to making the United States a more inclusive, more democratic, and ultimately more pluralistic nation. Moreover, immigrants played a substantial role in this process.

This argument rests on viewing Americanization education in its historical context in three specific ways: assessing such education in comparison to its most powerful ideological rival, the belief that most of the new-stock immigrants were racially incapable of learning to become Americans; broadening the range of actors who shaped Americanization education, particularly by including the contributions immigrants themselves made to this process; and examining how Americanization education changed over time. I'll discuss each of these contextual moves in turn.

First, Americanization education, even in its most aggressively assimilationist incarnation, advanced the belief that immigrants—regardless of their race, religion, creed, or culture—*could* learn to become good and true Americans. This inclusive stance stood in stark contrast to the powerful strain of nativism that gripped much of the country in the first half of the twentieth century. Proponents of nativist doctrines vociferously maintained that the United States was an "Anglo-Saxon" or "Nordic" nation. Consequently, they claimed that most of the new immigrants could never Americanize, because they came from "inferior races." Unlike some historians who find strong similarities between the assimilationist and exclusionist attitudes about immigrants, I see these stands as different in kind, not in degree.

Well into the 1950s, civic nationalists who maintained that education could transform immigrants into good Americans fought fiercely with ethnic nationalists who believed that such education was useless. The latter belief propelled nativists' demands that resulted in legislation banning virtually all immigration from eastern and southern Europe. Over the years, this struggle between civic and ethnic nationalists profoundly influenced Americanization education. Most important, it placed civic nationalist educators—regardless of whether they were assimilationists, cultural pluralists, or amalgamationists—on the same side. They all responded to the immigrant "invasion" by supporting educational programs designed for inclusion, rather than legislation bent on exclusion. Despite the varied Americanization goals and agendas these civic nationalist groups advocated, all of them believed in the power of education to transform people's hearts and minds, and all shared an inclusive vision of American life and culture. Their differences were in degree, not in kind.

This perspective complicates and challenges the notion that Americanization education was a monolithic cultural juggernaut bent on destroying all traces of the Old World cultures that immigrants had brought to this country. Rather, it maintains that during the first half of the twentieth century several different types of Americanization education contended with one another, each promoting a different approach to national unity built upon the basic ideals of civic nationalism and American democracy.

Unquestionably, during the 1910s and 1920s (particularly during World War I and the immediate postwar years), the assimilationist approach greatly influenced Americanization programs in the Chicago, Cleveland, and Detroit public schools at both the adult and the K–12 levels. Educational leaders in these school systems were quite explicit about their determination to immerse immigrant students in a curriculum dominated by Anglo-American history, civics, and literature. These educators paid scant attention to the cultural backgrounds of the immigrants. While many historians of education have described and criticized these assimilationist policies and practices, it is important to recognize that for all its cultural insensitivity, this approach still strongly advanced the fundamental civic nationalist idea that schools could teach and immigrants could learn how to become Americans. Educators who promoted assimilation believed that they were providing their students with the knowledge and skills they would need to survive and thrive in the New World. They were not wrong in that belief—just narrow.

By the mid-1920s a growing number of critics, both native and foreign-born, were making precisely that point, arguing that the assimilationist approach, especially in its most coercive and jingoistic form, was tactically and pedagogically flawed. These critics urged educators to implement other approaches to Americanization education, approaches that respected the cultural backgrounds of the immigrants and applauded the contributions they made to this country, past and present.

The second major point supporting this contextualized view of Americanization was that these critics were not lonely voices in the intellectual and cultural wilderness. Rather, during the late 1920s and continuing into the 1930s and 1940s, supporters of a more culturally inclusive version of Americanization education became increasingly influential in debates about curriculum policy and practice.

No group was more deeply involved in promoting an alternative view of Americanization than the editors and writers of the Chicago and Cleveland foreign language newspapers. Specifically, the articles and editorials presented in the three Work Projects Administration (WPA) collections that this study draws on convincingly demonstrate that writers for these papers were strongly in favor of Americanization, but also that they were determined to Americanize on their *own* terms. These community leaders paid close attention to the educational implications of assimilation, cultural pluralism, and amalgamation, and they ultimately found all of them wanting. Instead, they asserted a distinctive version of Americanization education, patriotic pluralism, that combined the most important elements of assimilationist Americanization with key elements of cultural pluralism.

One of the most striking things about the Chicago and Cleveland foreign language newspapers is how heartily most of them supported the basic demands that all those involved in the Americanization movement were making, regardless of whether they were discussing K–12 or adult education. The editors and writers of these papers strongly urged their readers to learn English, to become knowledgeable about American history, to understand and embrace American democratic ideals and values, and to become loyal citizens of this country. Indeed, these journalists regularly used their newspapers to explicitly instruct readers about American history, government, and politics and to urge noncitizens to naturalize.

This stance toward Americanization was neither cynical nor halfhearted. The devotion to the United States that these editors and writers expressed was consistently passionate and patriotic. The reason for this is simple. Most of the immigrants who came to the United States between 1890 and 1930 originated from the great autocratic empires of Europe and Eurasia. These empires granted few, if any, political or human rights and often engaged in brutal efforts to suppress the cultures and religions of subject peoples. In other words, these immigrants understood political and religious oppression all too well, and they fervently embraced the rights and freedoms that the United States offered.

However, their love for this country did not imply that these immigrant leaders accepted the idea that to become good Americans they had to abandon those aspects of their Old World cultures that they held most dear. Rejecting this particular aspect of assimilationist Americanization, editors and writers for these papers taught their readers that key aspects of the American political system—aspects that they learned about in naturalization courses or civics classes—were tools that immigrants and their descendants could use to protect and sustain their cultural distinctiveness. For example, these editors and writers pointed out that the basic freedoms articulated in the Bill of the Rights—the freedoms of the press, assembly, and religion—guaranteed immigrants' right to be different. In fact, the rights provided in the Constitution protected ethnic newspapers, parochial schools, after-school and weekend "heritage" programs, lodges, clubs, and civic organizations, essentially all of the institutions that the immigrants created to maintain aspects of their Old World heritage and to advance their New World aspirations. These immigrants did not need permission to adhere to their Old World backgrounds, nor did they have to wait until the 1960s to claim these rights. As editorials and articles from as far back as the early 1900s demonstrate, the writers for these papers believed that by embracing fundamental democratic ideals, by Americanizing, immigrants and their children could be proudly American *and* proudly ethnic. They viewed the process of Americanization as additive, not subtractive.

Nowhere was this stand more clearly evident than in the newspapers' discussions of American history. In numerous articles and editorials about American history, the writers for these papers repeatedly read their groups into the American national experience. Some writers noted, for example, that people from their homelands or cultural backgrounds had been in America since colonial times. Others hailed heroes from their homelands who had played important roles in the history of *this* country. Regardless of how they approached this subject, the editors and writers for the Chicago and Cleveland foreign language press sought to broaden the traditional American historical narrative, making it both more accurate and more inclusive. These writers promoted an expansive vision of Americanization and American national identity, a vision that celebrated patriotism and pluralism simultaneously.

The third key point supporting this revised interpretation of Americanization education is that in the 1930s and 1940s demands for a more culturally sensitive approach to Americanization education and a more capacious definition of American national identity gained greater traction and broader influence. In response to the upsurge of ethnic nationalism (both in Europe and the United States) and renewed anti-immigrant sentiment that thrived during the Depression years, growing numbers of political, cultural, and educational leaders (including a sizable number of immigrant academics, educators, and public intellectuals) reasserted their commitment to the civic nationalist ideals of this country. In doing so, they echoed the calls for a more culturally sensitive approach to Americanization education, recognizing that such an approach offered a clear alternative to the cultural and racial uniformity demanded by the authoritarian and totalitarian regimes that were ascendant across Europe in these years.

During the 1930s and early 1940s, the foreign language newspapers in Chicago and Cleveland provide vivid examples of how immigrants in these cities negotiated their complex American identities in the face of rapidly changing international events. All the Cleveland newspapers, for example, were fixated on the rise of ethnically nationalistic, authoritarian, and totalitarian regimes in eastern and southern Europe. Significantly, most of these papers demonstrated their Americanization by evaluating events in their homelands from an American democratic perspective, relentlessly condemning the descent into tyranny of their homelands and ignoring calls for ethnic solidarity. Most important, by late 1940, all of the CFLND newspapers, including those serving the German, Hungarian, Italian, and Romanian communities, strongly supported the United States as it moved toward war against these Axis powers. All of these developments had a profound influence on trends that were already taking shape in Americanization education on both the adult and the K–12 levels.

These changes were most visible in the large-scale Americanization campaign for adult immigrants that the WPA launched in the late 1930s and early 1940s. Like the better-known campaign of the World War I years, this Americanization campaign was spurred in part by fears about the loyalty of "enemy aliens" if the United States went to war with their homelands. Yet, in other respects, this was a very different initiative. For example, many of its leaders disparaged the excesses of the World War I campaign and urged educators to recognize, respect, and draw on the cultural backgrounds of the immigrants in the process of Americanization. At the same time, national political leaders, including most notably Franklin Roosevelt, applauded the contribution immigrants made to this country and reminded Americans that cultural diversity was one of this country's greatest strengths. These arguments resonated in immigrant communities of the 1930s and 1940s, exemplified by the largest surge in naturalizations in American history up to that point. During World War II, these ideas became central to the war effort, as national leaders increasingly defined the struggle as one between democracy and dictatorship, between civic and ethnic nationalism, and between pluralism and racism.

Paralleling these developments in adult education, on the K–12 level, intercultural education programs, which began as a culturally inclusive Americanization effort, flourished during the 1940s in the public schools of many of this country's great cities. To a large extent, intercultural education echoed the Americanizing ideas that foreign language newspapers had been articulating for years. But beyond introducing more inclusive curricula about European immigrants, by strongly promoting a civic nationalist perspective on American identity and by directly attacking ideas of Nordic supremacy (which guided both Nazism abroad and nativism at home), intercultural education helped lay the groundwork for the more difficult and challenging educational battles that supporters of the civil rights movement would wage against white ethnic nationalism in the 1950s and 1960s.

In all, this contextualized view of Americanization education in the first half of the twentieth century differs greatly from the conventional account of aggressive assimilationists forcing largely passive immigrants to abandon their Old World heritage as the price of entry into American society. Rather than a campaign that promoted cultural imperialism, Americanization education was a long, negotiated process between Americanizers and immigrants in which both sides gained as they increasingly sought and found common ground.

In this process, immigrants played a much larger and more active role than historians of education have traditionally maintained. Their influence helped change the nature and content of Americanization education by demanding that educators become more sensitive to diversity and respectful of the contributions immigrants had made to American history and culture. Considered from its modest beginnings in the 1890s to its final acts during World War II and the immediate postwar years, the Americanization of the European immigrants was a triumph of American education broadly conceived. At its best, Americanization education in these decades embodied the animating genius of this country in its pursuit of inclusion, its adaptation to new groups and cultures, and its quest for a more perfect union.

Today the United States is confronting another flood of immigrants, this time from virtually every country in the world. Once again questions about identity, loyalty, and culture are being hotly debated on the national scene.

In many of these debates, a small but vocal group of restrictionists are reviving arguments about unassimilable immigrants and invoking the 1924 National Origins Act as a model for current immigration policy.[3] With the reappearance of these questions and the passions they provoke, it is vital to remember that a century ago substantial numbers of Americans responded with fear and dismay at the "invasion" of the eastern and southern European immigrants, with many critics claiming that these newcomers could never truly become part of this country. Yet now when we look back on these immigrants, their devotion to this country is unquestioned, and their place in American history is as sure as that of people whose ancestors arrived here on the *Mayflower* or fought at Bunker Hill.

This great transformation, however, did not occur by happenstance or simply because the gravitational pull of American culture was impossible to resist. The Americanization of these earlier immigrants and their children was due to deliberate, widespread educational efforts on the part of native-born Americanizers and the immigrants themselves. Whether situated in K–12 classrooms, adult evening school programs, or in the pages of foreign language newspapers, these Americanization efforts focused on subjects essential for national unity, specifically on promoting a common language, teaching a common history, and inspiring a deep allegiance to this country and its democratic form of government. As represented in the Chicago and Cleveland foreign language newspapers, the immigrants learned these lessons well, put their distinctive stamp on them, and retaught them to native-born Americans in ways that broadened inclusiveness and enriched the culture of this country.

In other words, we have a historical model of how to do this well. Thinking additively, this model recognizes that teaching immigrants and their children the things we hold in common is as vital for preserving diversity as it is for ensuring unity.

NOTES

TABLES

ACKNOWLEDGMENTS

INDEX

NOTES

Abbreviations

ARCHIVED PAPERS

ACD   Americanization Committee of Detroit Papers, Bentley Historical Library, Ann Arbor, MI

AJA   American Jewish Archives, Cincinnati, OH

AJT   Arthur J. Tuttle Papers, Bentley Historical Library, Ann Arbor, MI

CAG   Chester A. Graham Papers, Bentley Historical Library, Ann Arbor, MI

GT   Graham Taylor Papers, Newberry Library, Chicago, IL

MHF   May Hope Francis Papers, Western Reserve Historical Society, Cleveland, OH

RFB   R. Freeman Butts Papers, Hoover Institution, Stanford, CA

WRHS   Western Reserve Historical Society, Cleveland, OH

WVT   William Van Til Papers, Hoover Institution, Stanford, CA

NEWSPAPER COLLECTIONS

CFLPS   *Chicago Foreign Language Press Survey*, Harold Washington Library, Chicago, IL. The WPA employees who created this collection used Roman numerals and alphabetic characters to index the various categories of articles and editorials in the collection. These Roman numeral/alphabetic index codes were common across every ethnic group. In citing the CFLPS articles and editorials, I identify the title of the article or editorial, the name of the newspaper, the date of publication, and the language it originally appeared in. I also include the primary Roman numeral/alphabetic index code that WPA employees listed for this article and editorial.

CFLND   *Cleveland Foreign Language Newspaper Digest*, Cleveland Public Library, 325 Superior Ave., NE, Cleveland, OH. There are nine bound volumes in this collection, five for 1937 and four for 1938. The researchers who translated the newspapers in this collection gave each article or editorial an abstract number. In citing the articles and editorials, I cite the name and date of the newspaper (no article or editorial titles are provided), the volume number in which the article or editorial is located, the abstract number of the article or editorial, and the page number. The abbreviations for the volume numbers are listed below.

Volume 1, 1937: *Slovak, Carpatho-Russian, Roumanian, Czech* is abbreviated as 1937–1.

Volume 2, 1937: *Italian, German* is abbreviated as 1937–2.

Volume 3, 1937: *Lithuanian, Jewish* is abbreviated as 1937–3

Volume 4, 1937: *Hungarian, Polish* is abbreviated as 1937–4.

Volume 5, 1937: *Slovenian* abbreviated as 1937–5.

Volume 1, 1938: *Slovak, Carpatho-Russian, Roumanian, Czech* is abbreviated as 1938–1.

Volume 2, 1938: *Italian, German* is abbreviated as 1937–2.

Volume 3, 1938: *Lithuanian, Jewish* is abbreviated as 1938–3.

Volume 4, 1938: *Hungarian, Polish* is abbreviated as 1938–4.

COCE   *Comments on Current Events.* Available in the Cleveland Public Library, 325 Superior Ave., NE, Cleveland, OH, and the Ohio State University Library, Columbus, OH. This collection contains articles and editorials from selected foreign language and black newspapers published in Cleveland. The articles and editorials are about a wide variety of events and developments. They were drawn from various newspapers between May 13, 1941, and July 31, 1942. This collection is a set of fifteen bound volumes, with each volume containing articles and editorials drawn from a period of several weeks. Each volume is identified by a specific number, and most of the volumes (thirteen of the fifteen) list the beginning and ending dates of the period that the articles and editorials are from. In citing from this collection, I give the name of the newspaper, date of the article or editorial (no titles are listed in the collection), the volume number, and the page number where the article or editorial can be found.

Introduction

1. Frank Julian Warne, *The Immigrant Invasion* (New York: Dodd, Mead, 1913).
2. Richard Abel, *Americanizing the Movies and "Movie-Mad" Audiences,* *1910–1914* (Berkeley: University of California Press, 2006); Lizabeth Cohen, *Making a New Deal: Industrial Workers in Chicago, 1919–1939* (New York: Cambridge University Press, 1990), 99–158; Lawrence A. Cremin, *Public Education* (New York: Basic Books, 1976; John Kasson, *Amusing the Million: Coney Island at the Turn of the Century* (New York: Hill and Wang, 1978), 39–40, 70, 108; Peter Levine, *Ellis Island to Ebbetts Field* (New York: Oxford University Press, 1992); Kathy Peiss, *Cheap Amusements: Working Women and Leisure in Turn-of-the-Century New York* (Philadelphia: Temple University Press, 1986), 31–33, 68–69, 150–153.
3. The principal is quoted in David B. Tyack, *The One Best System: A History of American Urban Education* (Cambridge: Harvard University Press, 1974), 232.
4. Carl F. Kaestle, Helen Damon-Moore, Lawrence C. Stedman, Katherine Tinsley, and William Vance Trollinger Jr., *Literacy in the United States* (New Haven: Yale University Press, 1991), 280–281.
5. See, for example, Lawrence A. Cremin, *The Transformation of the School: Progressivism in American Education, 1876–1957* (New York: Alfred A. Knopf, 1961), 66–75; Mark Krug, *The Melting of the Ethnics: Education of the Immigrants, 1880–1914* (Bloomington, IN: Phi Delta Kappa, 1976).
6. Joel Spring, *The American School: From the Puritans to No Child Left Behind* (New York: McGraw-Hill, 2008), 233, 214–215, 232–234. See also Clarence J. Karier, *Shaping the American Educational State, 1900 to the Present* (New York: Free Press, 1975), 225–274; Michael R. Olneck, "Americanization and the Education of Immigrants, 1900–1925: An Analysis of Symbolic Action," *American Journal of Education* 97:4 (August 1989), 402–405; Paul C. Violas, *The Training of the Urban Working Class* (Chicago: Rand McNally, 1978), 37–66.
7. Robert A. Carlson, *The Quest for Conformity: Americanization through Education* (London: Croom Helm, 1987), 12.
8. Walter Benn Michaels, *Our America: Nativism, Modernism, and Pluralism* (Durham: University of North Carolina Press, 1995), 67. See also James R. Barrett and David Roediger, "Inbetween Peoples: Race, Nationality, and the 'New Immigrant' Working Class," *Journal of Ethnic History* 16:3 (Spring 1997), 3–44; Arnold R. Hirsch, "E Pluribus Duo? Thoughts on 'Whiteness' and Chicago's 'New' Immigration as a Transient Third Tier," *Journal of American Ethnic History* 23:4 (Summer 2004), 7–44; Matthew Frye Jacobson, *Whiteness of a Different Color: European Immigrants and the Alchemy of Race* (Cambridge: Harvard University Press, 1998); David R. Roediger, *Working toward*

Whiteness: How America's Immigrants Became White (New York: Basic Books, 2005).

9. Nathan Glazer, "Is Assimilation Dead?" *Annals of the American Academy of Political and Social Science*, vol. 530 (November 1993), 123. For a superb overview of issues about assimilation and Americanization, see Michael Olneck, "Assimilation and American National Identity," in *Companion to Immigration*, ed. Reed Ueda (Malden, MA: Blackwell, 2006), 202–224. An excellent historiographic essay on assimilation is Russell A. Kazal, "Revising Assimilation: The Rise, Fall, and Reappraisal of a Concept in American Ethnic History," *American Historical Review* 100:2 (April 1995), 437–471.

10. Eugene E. Garcia, "Early Childhood Education Reinvention and Educational Policy: Addressing Linguistic and Cultural Diversity," *Early Childhood Development and Care* 123 (September 1996), 205, 203–205. For similar stances, see Joy Ann Williamson, Lori Rhodes, and Michael Dunson, "A Selected History of Social Justice in Education," *Review of Research in Education* 31 (March 2007), 198–201, 206, 211, 214; Bruce VanSledright, "Narratives of Nation-State, Historical Knowledge, and School History Education," in *Review of Research in Education* 38 (Washington, DC: American Educational Research Association, 2008), 109–146.

11. Arthur Evans Wood, quoted in William Carlson Smith, *Americans in the Making* (D. Appleton-Century, 1939), 115.

12. John J. Mahoney, "Americanization in the United States," *Biennial Survey of Education, 1920–21*, Bureau of Education Bulletin 1924, no. 13 (Washington, DC: U.S. Government Printing Office, 1924), 637.

13. Frank V. Thompson, *Schooling of the Immigrant* (New York: Harper and Brothers, 1920), 354–356, 367, 363–376; Michael Walzer, *What It Means to Be an American* (New York: Marsilio, 1996), 81–101.

14. See, for example, Gary Gerstle, *American Crucible: Race and Nation in the Twentieth Century* (Princeton: Princeton University Press, 2001); Michael Ignatieff, *Blood and Belonging: Journeys into the New Nationalism* (New York: Farrar, Straus and Giroux, 1992), 6; Noah Pickus, *True Faith and Allegiance: Immigration and Civic Nationalism* (Princeton: Princeton University Press, 2005); Rogers M. Smith, *Civic Ideals: Conflicting Visions of Citizenship in U.S. History* (New Haven: Yale University Press, 1997).

15. Ignatieff, *Blood and Belonging*, 6–8.

16. See, for example, Edward G. Hartmann's seminal study *The Movement to Americanize the Immigrant* (New York: Columbia University Press, 1948). See also Otis L. Graham Jr. and Elizabeth Koed, "Americanizing the Immigrant, Past and Future: History and Implications of a Social Movement," *Public Historian* 15:4 (Fall 1993), 24–49; John F. McClymer, "The Americanization Movement and the Education of the Foreign-Born Adult, 1914–25," in *American*

Education and the European Immigrant, 1840–1940, ed. Bernard J. Weiss (Urbana: University of Illinois Press, 1982); Olneck, "Americanization and the Education of Immigrants, 1900–1925"; Maxine S. Seller, "Success and Failure in Adult Education: The Immigrant Experience, 1914–1924," *Adult Education* 28:2 (1978). Exceptions to this pattern include Stephen F. Brumberg, *Going to School, Going to America: The Jewish Immigrant Public School Encounter in Turn-of-the Century New York City* (New York: Praeger, 1986); Ronald D. Cohen and Raymond A. Mohl, *The Paradox of Progressive Education: The Gary Plan and Urban Schooling* (Port Washington, NY: Kennikat Press, 1979), 84–109; Ronald D. Cohen, *Children of the Mill: Schooling and Society in Gary, IN, 1906–1960* (Bloomington: Indiana University Press, 1990), 31–36, 61–68, 88–89.

17. Susan B. Carter, Scott S. Gartner, Michael R. Haines, Alan L. Olmstead, Richard Sutch, and Gavin Wright, eds., *Historical Statistics of the United States,* vol. 1, pt. A, Population, "Aliens Naturalized by Provision," table Ad., 1030–1037 (New York: Cambridge University Press, 2006), 641–642. An additional reason for following Americanization efforts into the 1930s and 1940s is that several prominent "whiteness" scholars argue that during this period European immigrants made the transition from being racial outsiders or, as James Barrett and David Roediger argue, "inbetween" people (i.e., neither black nor Nordic) to taking their place as part of the white race. James Barrett and David Roediger, "Inbetween Peoples"; Guglielmo, *White on Arrival*; Hirsch, "E Pluribus Duo?"; Roediger, *Working toward Whiteness.*

18. Campbell Gibson and Emily Lennon, "Historical Census Statistics on the Foreign-Born Population of the United States: 1850 to 1990," Population Division Working Paper no. 29 (Washington, DC: U.S. Bureau of the Census1999), table 19.

19. U.S. Immigration Commission, *The Children of Immigrants in Schools,* vol. 1 (Washington, DC: U.S. Government Printing Office, 1911), 15.

20. For example, Carl F. Kaestle et al. use the work of a number of immigrant authors (e.g., Mary Antin) to examine how newcomers responded to their new homeland. Kaestle et al., *Literacy in the United States,* 234–244. Stephen Brumberg and Alan Wieder draw on interviews with elderly Jews who immigrated or whose parents immigrated. See Brumberg, *Going to School, Going to America;* and Alan Wieder, *Immigration, the Public School, and the 20th Century American Ethos: The Jewish Immigrant as a Case Study* (Lanham, MD: University Press of America, 1985). Thomas Guglielmo did extensive research in the Chicago newspaper *L'Italia* in his study. See Thomas A. Guglielmo, *White on Arrival* (New York: Oxford University Press, 2003).

21. The Chicago survey consists of complete translations of articles and editorials. The Cleveland digest contains summaries with some direct quotations. Overviews of the CFLPS and CFLND can be found in the Chicago Public

Library Omnibus Project, *The Chicago Foreign Language Press Survey: A General Description of Its Contents* (Chicago: Works Projects Administration, 1942), 1–5; "Introduction: History of the Survey," CFLPS; "Preface," CFLND 1937, vol. 1, i–ii; Oscar Ban, "Cleveland's Foreign Language Newspaper Digest," *Common Ground* 1:4 (Summer 1941), 120–124.

22. *Comment on Current Events* (Cleveland: Works Projects Administration, 1942). The newspapers serving the black community of Cleveland were not included in the 1937 and 1938 digests, but were included in the COCE.

23. Smith, *Americans in the Making*, 191.

24. Lawrence H. Fuchs, *The American Kaleidoscope: Race, Ethnicity, and the Civic Culture* (Middletown, CT: Wesleyan University Press, 1990), 5. See also John Higham, *Hanging Together: Unity and Diversity in American Culture* (New Haven: Yale University Press, 2001), 100; Kathleen Neils Conzen, David A. Gerber, Ewa Morawska, George E. Pozzetta, and Rudolph J. Vicoli, "The Invention of Ethnicity: A Perspective from the U.S.A.," *Journal of American Ethnic History* 12:1 (Fall 1992), 3–41; Werner Sollors, *Beyond Ethnicity: Consent and Descent in American Culture* (New York: Oxford University Press, 1986), 87–88.

25. James R. Barrett, "Americanization from the Bottom Up: Immigration and the Remaking of the Working Class in the United States, 1880–1930," *Journal of American History* 79:3 (December 1992), 997, 996–1020.

26. In her marvelous study of Slovaks in the interwar years, June Granatir Alexander describes a stance toward Americanization that is quite similar to what I call patriotic pluralism. Her in-depth analysis of Slovak ethnic and fraternal organizations nicely complements the broader educational perspective that my book takes on efforts by European immigrants to be proud of both their Americanism and their Old World heritage. June Granatir Alexander, *Ethnic Pride, American Patriotism: Slovaks and Other New Immigrants in the Interwar Era* (Philadelphia: Temple University Press, 2004). See also Richard Alba and Victor Nee, "Assimilation," in *The New Americans: A Guide to Immigration since 1965*, ed. Mary C. Waters, Reed Udea, and Helen B. Marrow (Cambridge: Harvard University Press, 2007), 131.

27. Zoe Burkholder, "'With Science as His Shield': Teaching Race and Culture in American Public Schools, 1900–1954" (Ph.D. diss., New York University, 2008); Dan Shiffman, *Rooting Multiculturalism: The Work of Louis Adamic* (Cranbury, NJ: Fairleigh Dickinson University Press, 2003); Diana Selig, *Americans All: The Cultural Gifts Movement* (Cambridge: Harvard University Press, 2008).

1 The Single Greatest Factor in the Americanization of Immigrants

1. Leonard Dinnerstein and David M. Reimers, *Ethnic Americans: A History of Immigration* (New York: Columbia University Press, 1999), 19; Howard C. Hill,

"The Americanization Movement," *American Journal of Sociology* 24:6 (May 1919), 609–611.

2. "Report of the Committee on State School Systems: Compulsory Education," in National Education Association, *Addresses and Proceedings, 1891* (New York: J. J. Little, 1891), 295.

3. William H. Maxwell, "Education of the Immigrant Child," in U.S. Bureau of Education, *Education of the Immigrant*, U.S. Bureau of Education Bulletin 1913, no. 51 (Washington, DC: U.S. Government Printing Office, 1913), 18.

4. "Education," *Immigrants in America Review* 1:2 (June 1915), 5.

5. Henry Cabot Lodge, *North American Review* 152 (January 1891), 32, 35.

6. George Creel, "Melting Pot or Dumping Ground?" *Collier's* 68:10 (September 3, 1921), 9.

7. Edward George Hartmann, *The Movement to Americanize the Immigrant* (New York: Columbia University Press, 1948), 18–24.

8. John Higham, *Strangers in the Land: Patterns of American Nativism, 1860–1925* (New York: Atheneum, 1975), 222–233, 264–299.

9. Gary Gerstle, *American Crucible: Race and Nation in the Twentieth Century* (Princeton: Princeton University Press, 2000).

10. For an example of this categorization scheme, see Philip Gleason, "American Identity and Americanization," in *Harvard Encyclopedia of American Ethnic Groups*, ed. Stephen Thernstrom (Cambridge: Harvard University Press, 1980), 46, 31–58. For a categorization scheme that also stresses the importance of education, see Joel M. Roitman, *The Immigrants, the Progressives, and the Schools: Americanization and the Impact of the New Immigration upon Public Education in the United States, 1890–1920* (Stark, KS: De Young Press, 1996), 19–21.

11. Such ideas were deeply embedded in the intellectual zeitgeist of this era, in which Jim Crow laws took a devastating toll on the education and lives of African Americans. James Anderson, *The Education of Blacks in the South, 1860–1935* (Chapel Hill: University of North Carolina Press, 1988).

12. This is the classic problem of using what Max Weber referred to as "ideal types" to aid in explaining and understanding historical and sociological phenomena. Gianfranco Poggi, *Weber: A Short Introduction* (Cambridge, UK: Polity Press, 2006), 24–27.

13. On Cubberley, see Eamonn Callan, *Creating Citizens: Political Education and Liberal Democracy* (Oxford, UK: Clarendon Press, 1997), 172–173; on Ford, see Neil Baldwin, *Henry Ford and the Jews: The Mass Production of Hate* (New York: Public Affairs, 2001); on Kallen, see David A. Hollinger, *Postethnic America* (New York: Basic Books, 2000), 116.

14. Campbell Gibson and Emily Lennon, "Historical Census Statistics on the Foreign-Born Population of the United States: 1850 to 1990," Population

Division Working Paper no. 29, table 19 (Washington DC: U.S. Bureau of the Census, 1999).

15. Thomas Muller, *Immigrants and the American City* (New York: New York University Press, 1993), 74–75; Justin B. Galford, "The Foreign Born and Urban Growth in the Great Lakes, 1850–1950: A Study of Chicago, Cleveland, Detroit, and Milwaukee" (Ph.D. diss., New York University, 1957), 64–66; Glenn A. Bishop and Raymond E. Craig, *Chicago's Accomplishments and Leaders* (Chicago: Bishop, 1932), 56, 60, 298–300, 492.

16. Sidney Glazer, *Detroit: A Study in Urban Development* (New York: Bookman, 1965), 79–96; Galford, "Foreign Born and Urban Growth in the Great Lakes, 1850–1950," 178–181.

17. David C. Hammack, Gudrun Birnbaum, Lazlo Katus, and Gabor Gyani, "Identity, Conflict, and Cooperation: Central Europeans in Cleveland, 1850–1930," in *Identity, Conflict, and Cooperation: Central Europeans in Cleveland, 1850–1930,* ed. David C. Hammack, Diane L. Grabowski, and John Grabowski (Cleveland: Western Reserve Historical Society, 2002), 27; Edward M. Miggins, "Businessmen, Pedagogues, and Progressive Reform: The Cleveland Foundation's 1915 School Survey" (Ph.D. diss., Case Western Reserve University, 1975), 12–13; Galford, "Foreign Born and Urban Growth in the Great Lakes, 1850–1950," 112–115.

18. In the previous decade, over 75 percent of the immigrants coming to the United States were from eastern and southern Europe. See Lawrence H. Fuchs, *The American Kaleidoscope: Race, Ethnicity, and the Civic Culture* (Middletown, CT: Wesleyan University Press, 1995), 56; Dinnerstein and Reimers, *Ethnic America,* 19; Raymond E. Cole, "The City's Responsibility to the Immigrant," *Immigrants in America Review* 1:2 (June 1915), 36–41.

19. Dinnerstein and Reimers, *Ethnic America,* 53–54; Higham, *Strangers in the Land,* 159; John Higham, *Send These to Me: Immigrants in Urban America* (Baltimore: Johns Hopkins University Press, 1984), 14.

20. Muller, *Immigrants and the American City,* 73. Thomas Archdeacon notes that despite the large numbers of immigrants in this era, the ratio of immigrants to the total American population was higher at certain times in the nineteenth century than in the early twentieth (e.g., the 2.8 million immigrants who arrived between 1850 and 1859 equaled 12.1 percent of the U.S. population, but the 8.2 million immigrants who came between 1900 and 1909 equaled only 10.1 percent). Archdeacon also found that a substantial number of the new immigrants, perhaps 30 percent, "remigrated" back to their home countries. Greeks, Italians, Magyars, and Poles were among the most frequent returnees. Thomas Archdeacon, *Becoming American: An Ethnic History* (New York: Free Press, 1983), 113, 115–116, 118–119, 139.

21. The twenty-two states were "Maine, New Hampshire, Vermont, Massachusetts, Rhode Island, Connecticut, Delaware, Florida, the two Dakotas, Kansas, Montana, Idaho, Wyoming, Colorado, New Mexico, Arizona, Utah, Nevada, California, Oregon, and Washington." Frank Julian Warne, *The Immigrant Invasion* (New York: Dodd, Mead, 1913), 21.

22. On ethnic concentration, see Olivier Zunz, *The Changing Face of Inequality: Urbanization, Industrial Development, and Immigrants in Detroit, 1880–1920* (Chicago: University of Chicago Press, 1982), 340–351.

23. On Italians in New York, see Carl H. Grabo, "Americanizing the Immigrants," *Dial* 66:791 (May 31, 1919), 539; and Robert E. Park and Herbert A. Miller, *Old World Traits Transplanted* (New York: Harper and Brothers, 1921), 259. On the centrality of Chicago to Polish America, see Edward R. Kantowicz, *Polish-American Politics in Chicago, 1888–1940* (Chicago: University of Chicago Press, 1975), 12–27; Helena Znaniecki Lopata, *Polish American: Status Competition in an Ethnic Community* (Englewood Cliffs, NJ: Prentice-Hall, 1976), 90; and Edmund G. Olszyk, *The Polish Press in America* (Milwaukee: Marquette University Press, 1940), 7. See also Galford, "Foreign Born and Urban Growth in the Great Lakes, 1850–1950," 82–83. On Lithuanians in Chicago, see "Chicago Is Capital of the Lithuanians," *Lietuva* (December 11, 1908), p. 1, CFLPS, Lithuanian, IIIA. On Hungarians in Cleveland, see Susan M. Papp, *Hungarian Americans and Their Communities of Cleveland* (Cleveland: Cleveland State University, 1981), 229.

24. John Dewey, "My Pedagogic Creed," in *Dewey on Education*, ed. Martin S. Dworkin (New York: Teachers College Press, 1959), 30.

25. Mary J. Herrick, *The Chicago Public Schools: A Social and Political History* (Beverly Hills: Sage, 1971), 403; Diane Ravitch, *The Great School Wars* (Baltimore: Johns Hopkins University Press, 2000), 405; Jeffrey Mirel, *The Rise and Fall of an Urban School System: Detroit, 1907–81* (Ann Arbor: University of Michigan Press, 1999), 425 (table 1).

26. U.S. Immigration Commission, *The Children of Immigrants in Schools*, vol. 1 (Washington, DC: U.S. Government Printing Office, 1911), 14.

27. Edward W. Stitt, "Recreation for the Immigrant," in U.S. Bureau of Education, *Education of the Immigrant*, 25.

28. Ronald D. Cohen, *Children of the Mill: Schooling and Society in Gary, IN, 1906–1960* (Bloomington: Indiana University Press, 1990); David John Hogan, *Class and Reform: School and Society in Chicago, 1880–1930* (Philadelphia: University of Pennsylvania Press, 1985), 194–227; Mirel, *Rise and Fall of an Urban School System*, 43–88; Paul Peterson, *The Politics of School Reform, 1870–1940* (Chicago: University of Chicago Press, 1985),

138–172; David Tyack, *The One Best System: A History of American Urban Education* (Cambridge: Harvard University Press, 1974), 126–255; Ravitch, *Great School Wars*, 189–232.

29. See, for example, Mirel, *Rise and Fall of an Urban School System*, 25–26, 1–42.

30. Peterson, *Politics of School Reform, 1870–1940*, 138–153; Judith Rosenberg Raftery, *Land of Fair Promise: Politics and Reform in Los Angeles Schools, 1885–1941* (Stanford, CA: Stanford University Press, 1992); Ravitch, *Great School Wars*, 134–158; Tyack, *One Best System*, 147–167.

31. Selma C. Berrol, *Julia Richman: A Notable Woman* (Philadelphia: Balch Institute Press, 1993), 53; Stephen Brumberg, *Going to America, Going to School* (New York: Praeger, 1986); Cohen, *Children of the Mill*, 1–107; Lawrence A. Cremin, *The Transformation of the School* (New York: Alfred A. Knopf, 1961), 72; Mirel, *Rise and Fall of an Urban School System*, 1–88; Peterson, *Politics of School Reform, 1870–1940*, 138–153; Raftery, *Land of Fair Promise*, 32–40; Ravitch, *Great School Wars*, 107–86; Tyack, *One Best System*, 126–255.

32. John H. Haaren, "Education of the Immigrant Child," in U.S. Bureau of Education, *Education of the Immigrant*, 20.

33. Helen L. Cohen, "Americanization by Classroom Practice," *Teachers College Record* 20:3 (May 1919), 238.

34. David M. Kennedy, *Over Here: The First World War and American Society* (New York: Oxford University Press, 2004), 46.

35. Kennedy, *Over Here*, 24–25, 63–69; Dinnerstein and Reimers, *Ethnic Americans*, 83–84; Hartmann, *Movement to Americanize the Immigrant*, 105–107.

36. Kennedy, *Over Here*, 24.

37. Peter Conolly-Smith, *Translating America: An Immigrant Press Visualizes American Popular Culture, 1895–1918* (Washington, DC: Smithsonian Books, 2004), 10–11; Higham, *Strangers in the Land*, 196; Russell A. Kazal, *Becoming Old Stock: The Paradox of German-American Identity* (Princeton: Princeton University Press, 2004), 2; Kennedy, *Over Here*, 67–68.

38. Lloyd Jorgenson, *The Founding of Public Education in Wisconsin* (Madison: State Historical Society of Wisconsin, 1958), 146–148; Carl F. Kaestle, *Pillars of the Republic* (New York: Hill and Wang, 1983), 164–166; Tyack, *One Best System*, 104–109.

39. Peterson, *Politics of School Reform*, 8–9, 57–58, 73–74.

40. Conolly-Smith, *Translating America*, 94–96; Nancy Gentile Ford, *Americans All! Foreign-Born Soldiers in World War I* (College Station: Texas A&M Press, 2001), 18–20; Higham, *Strangers in the Land*, 197; Kazal, *Becoming Old Stock*, 156–157; David Montgomery, "Nationalism, American Patriotism, and Class Consciousness among Immigrant Workers in the United States in the Epoch

of World War I," in *"Struggle a Hard Battle": Essays on Working-Class Immigrants*, ed. Dirk Hoerder (DeKalb: Northern Illinois University Press, 1986), 334–336.

41. Hartmann, *Movement to Americanize the Immigrant*, 106–107; Higham, *Strangers in the Land*, 197; Kazal, *Becoming Old Stock*, 160–170.

42. Woodrow Wilson, State of the Union address, December 7, 1915, *The Congressional Record: Proceedings and Debates of the First Session of the Sixty-fourth Congress*, vol. 53 (Washington, DC: U.S. Government Printing Office, 1916), 99.

43. Archdeacon, *Becoming American*, 167–168; James M. Bergquist, "The German-American Press," in *The Ethnic Press in the United States*, ed. Sally M. Miller (Greenwood, CT: Greenwood Press, 1987), 147–149; Edward Hale Bierstadt, *Aspects of Americanization* (Cincinnati: Stewart Kidd, 1922), 82–84; Timothy R. Cain, "Academic Freedom in an Age of Organization, 1913–1941" (Ph.D. diss., University of Michigan, 2005), 350–405; Conolly-Smith, *Translating America*, 252–254; Higham, *Strangers in the Land*, 196–198; Kazal, *Becoming Old Stock*, 171–194; Kennedy, *Over Here*, 67–68; Frederick C. Luebke, *Bonds of Loyalty: German-Americans and World War I* (DeKalb: Northern Illinois University Press, 1974); Miggins, "Businessmen, Pedagogues, and Progressive Reform," 270–271; Robert Park, *The Immigrant Press and Its Control* (New York: Harper and Brothers, 1922), 412–413; 434–447; Carl Brent Swisher, "Civil Liberties in War Time," *Political Science Quarterly* 55:3 (September 1940), 355.

44. See, for example, Public Schools of the City of Chicago, *Sixty-fourth Annual Report of the Board of Education* (Chicago: The Board, 1918), 11–12, 38–39, 150–151.

45. Gleason, "American Identity and Americanization," 39–41; King, *Making Americans*, 90–91.

46. Robert Livingston Schuyler, "The Movement for Americanization," *Columbia University Quarterly* 18 (March 1916), 181. See also Hartmann, *Movement to Americanize the Immigrant*, 105–163.

47. Hartmann, *Movement to Americanize the Immigrant*, 38–63, 112–113, 174–176; Hill, "The Americanization Movement," 612; Frances A. Kellor, "Americanization by Industry," *Immigrants in America Review* 2:1 (April 1916), 15–16; Frank V. Thompson, *Schooling of the Immigrant* (New York: Harper and Brothers, 1920), 26–74.

48. Hartmann, *Movement to Americanize the Immigrant*, 38–63, 105–126. See also Hill, "Americanization Movement," 616–619; Kellor, "National Americanization Day—July 4, 1915," *Immigrants in America Review* 1:3 (September, 1915), 18.

49. To see how one city celebrated this day, see "Hope to Instill Americanism in Latest Citizens," *Detroit News* (July 2, 1915), 16; "Wilson Endorses

Americanization Day Celebration," *Detroit News* (July 3, 1915), 16; Theodore Roosevelt, "Americanization Day," *Detroit News* (July 4, 1915), 4; "Flag Decked Churches Greet Nation's Holiday," *Detroit News* (July 3, 1915), 6.

50. Hartmann, *Movement to Americanize the Immigrant*, 124–133.

51. John F. McClymer, "The Americanization Movement and the Education of the Foreign-Born Adults, 1914–1925," in *American Education and the European Immigrant, 1840–1940*, ed. Bernard J. Weiss (Urbana: University of Illinois Press, 1982), 99–103. The American Red Cross, *The Work of the Foreign Language Information Service of the American Red Cross* (Washington, DC: The American Red Cross, 1920); Fred Clayton Butler, *State Americanization*, Bureau of Education Bulletin 1919, no. 77 (Washington, DC: U.S. Government Printing Office, 1920); Richard C. Campbell, "Americanization: The Public Schools as Participants in Federal Administration," in *Immigration and Americanization: Selected Readings*, ed. Philip Davis (New York: Ginn, 1920), 673–701; Frederic Ernest Farrington, "Public Facilities for the Alien," Bulletin 1916, no. 18 (Washington, DC: U.S. Government Printing Office 1916); Josephine Gratia, "Making Americans: How the Library Helps," in *Pamphlets on Americanization*, vol. 1 (Eugene: University of Oregon, 1920); Hartmann, *Movement to Americanize the Immigrant*, 24–37, 134–163; Kellor, "Americanization by Industry"; John J. Mahoney, "Americanization in the United States," Bulletin 1924, 1:20 in the *Biennial Survey of Education, 1920–22* (Washington, DC: U.S. Government Printing Office, 1924), 637–673; National Catholic War Council, *A Program for Citizenship*, Reconstruction Pamphlet no. 5 (Washington, DC: The Council, 1919).

52. Tyack, *One Best System*, 232.

53. See, for example, David A. Hollinger, *Postethnic America* (New York: Basic Books, 2000), 92–97; Milton M. Gordon, *Assimilation in American Life: The Role of Race, Religion, and National Origins* (New York: Oxford University Press, 1964), 85.

54. This definition of the assimilationist position is similar to what Milton Gordon refers to as "Anglo-conformity." Gordon, *Assimilation in American Life*, 85. See also Michael Olneck, "Assimilation and American National identity," in *Companion to Immigration*, ed. Reed Ueda (Malden, MA: Blackwell, 2006), 202–211.

55. Calvin Stowe, "On the Americanization of the Immigrant," in *Education in the United States: A Documentary History*, vol. 2, ed. Sol Cohen (New York: Random House, 1974), 993–994. See also Carl Kaestle, *Pillars of the Republic: Common Schools and American Society, 1780–1860* (New York: Hill and Wang, 1983), 99–100, 161–164.

56. As Robert Zeidel argues, Roosevelt had "inconsistent and at times contradictory views on immigration," at times endorsing immigration restriction and at others strongly supporting entry of "all but the most incorrigible foreigners," certain that those who arrived could be assimilated. Zeidel finds that over the years, that latter perspective became increasingly prominent in Roosevelt's words and actions. Robert F. Zeidel, *Immigrants, Progressives, and Exclusion Politics: The Dillingham Commission, 1900–1917* (DeKalb: Northern Illinois University Press, 2004), 22–25. For a detailed and nuanced account of Roosevelt's views on race and immigration, see also Gerstle, *American Crucible*, 14–80.

57. Theodore Roosevelt, "True Americanism," in *The History and the Government of the United States*, ed. Jacob Harris Patton and John Lord (New York,: University Society, 1903), 246.

58. Roosevelt, "True Americanism," 248.

59. Theodore Roosevelt, "Americanization Day," *Metropolitan Magazine* 42:3 (July 1915), 3. In another speech, given several months later in New York City, Roosevelt repeated his ideas about hyphenated Americans even more bluntly, declaring, "There is no room in this country for hyphenated Americans." Theodore Roosevelt, "Americanism," in Davis, *Immigration and Americanization*, 648. See also Kellor, "National Americanization Day—July 4th," 18–20.

60. Roosevelt, "Americanization Day," 3; See also Roosevelt, "True Americanism," 250.

61. Woodrow Wilson, *A History of the American People* (New York: Harper and Brothers, 1902), 212.

62. Woodrow Wilson, "Address of President Wilson, Delivered at Convention Hall, Philadelphia, May 10, 1915," *Immigrant in America Review* 1:3 (September 1915), 30. Many leading newspapers shared these views. For example, about a year after Wilson gave that speech, an editorial in the *Chicago Tribune* declared, "The United States cannot continue long to be composed of Poles, Swedes, Bohemians, Germans, Canadians, Italians, etc. It must come around to being composed of Americans." "Nationalism," *Chicago Tribune* (July 6, 1916), 6.

63. Ellwood Cubberley, *Changing Conceptions of Education* (Boston: Houghton Mifflin, 1909), 15–16. Cubberley used a slightly edited version of this statement in his hugely successful textbook on the history of American education, *Public Education in the United States* (Boston: Houghton Mifflin, 1919), 338. The quote still could be found in the 1947 edition of *Public Education in the United States* (Boston: Houghton Mifflin, 1947), 485–486.

64. On these efforts in Detroit, Gary, Los Angeles, and New York, see Mirel, *Rise and Fall of an Urban School System*, 1–88; Cohen, *Children of the Mill*, 1–107;

Ronald D. Cohen and Raymond A. Mohl, *The Paradox of Progressive Education: The Gary Plan and Urban Schooling* (Port Washington, NY: Kennikat Press, 1979), 84–101; Raftery, *Land of Fair Promise*; Ravitch, *Great School Wars*, 107–186. See also Mary E. Mumford, "The Public School and the Immigrant," *Child-Welfare Magazine* 4 (April 1910), 226–229; Cohen, "Americanization by Classroom Practice," 239–249.

65. Antin was, for example, a featured speaker at the National Conference on Immigration and Americanization held in Philadelphia in January 1916. See "The National Conference on Immigration and Americanization," *Immigrants in America Review* 2:1 (April 1916), 39, 43–44. On the role that literacy (gained both in school and through other institutions) played in Antin's metamorphosis (as well as the great changes literacy brought to several other immigrants, such as Emma Goldman and Bella Dodd), see Carl F. Kaestle, Helen Damon-Moore, Lawrence C. Stedman, Katherine Tinsley, and William Vance Trollinger Jr., *Literacy in the United States: Readers and Reading since 1880* (New Haven: Yale University Press, 1991), 237–238, 237–243.

66. Mary Antin, *The Promised Land* (Boston: Houghton Mifflin, 1912), xi, 209, 206–240. The same policy apparently was also enforced in the New York City public schools. See Leonard Covello, *The Heart Is the Teacher* (New York: McGraw-Hill, 1958), 26.

67. Antin, *Promised Land*, 225, 222.

68. Covello, *Heart Is the Teacher*, 43–44, 129.

69. Leonard Covello, *The Social Background of the Italo-American Child* (Leiden, The Netherlands: E. J. Brill, 1967), 411.

70. Horace M. Kallen, "Democracy versus the Melting Pot," *Nation* 100 (February 18–25, 1915), 190–194, 217–220; Horace Kallen, *Culture and Democracy in the United States* (New York: Boni and Liveright, 1924); Randolph Bourne, "Trans-National America," *Atlantic Monthly* 118 (July 1916), 86–97. For two very useful discussions of Kallen and Bourne, see Hollinger, *Postethnic America*, 92–97; and Gleason, "American Identity and Americanization," 43–45.

71. Gordon, *Assimilation in American Life*, 85.

72. Louis Brandeis, "True Americanism," in Davis, *Immigration and Americanization*, 644.

73. Kallen, *Culture and Democracy in the United States*, 80–81.

74. Ibid., 124–125.

75. Bourne, "Trans-National America," 88–90, 95–96. A thoughtful account of the differences between what Noah Pickus calls "Bourneian and Rooseveltian" civic nationalism can be found in Noah Pickus, *True Faith and Allegiance: Immigration and American Civic Nationalism* (Princeton: Princeton University Press, 2005), 147–152.

76. Gleason, "American Identity and Americanization," 45. See also Hollinger, *Postethnic America*, 93.

77. Horace Kallen, *Cultural Pluralism and the Democratic Idea: An Essay in Social Philosophy* (Philadelphia: University of Pennsylvania Press, 1956), 87–88.

78. Jane Addams, "The Public School and the Immigrant Child," in *National Education Association, Journal of Addresses and Proceedings, 1908* (Winona, MN: National Education Association, 1908), 99–100.

79. Ibid., 100. See also pro–cultural pluralism comments of Mary McDowell quoted in "Americanization of Immigrants," *Denni Hlasatel* (March 5, 1918), 3, CFLPS, Bohemian, IIIA. Rev. Enrico C. Sartorio makes the same argument about language and history instruction in public schools, in Enrico C. Sartorio, *The Social and Religious Life of Italians in America* (Boston: Christopher, 1918), 69–72. See also Peter Roberts, "Night Schools," in National Conference of Charities and Correction, *Proceedings of the National Conference of Charities and Correction, 1909* (Indianapolis: National Conference of Charities and Correction, 1909), 236, and *The Problem of Americanization* (New York: Macmillan, 1920), 29–32.

80. John Dewey, "Nationalizing Education," in *National Education Association, Addresses and Proceedings, 1916* (Ann Arbor, MI: National Education Association, 1916), 184–186.

81. John Dewey, "The Child and the Curriculum," in Dworkin, *Dewey on Education*, 97.

82. John Dewey, *Democracy and Education: An Introduction to the Philosophy of Education* (New York: Macmillan, 1964 [1916]), 4. For an astute discussion of these ideas, see Rivka Shpak Lissak, *Pluralism and Progressives: Hull House and the New Immigrants, 1890–1919* (Chicago: University of Chicago Press, 1989).

83. Dewey, "Child and the Curriculum," 97. In the early 1970s, there was some controversy about the degree to which Dewey really embraced cultural pluralism. In 1918, Dewey did a study on the Polish American community in which he criticized Poles for their resistance to Americanization and for the large role that the Catholic church played in Polish life. Philosopher Walter Feinberg viewed Dewey's stance on the Poles as hypocritical. Other scholars came to Dewey's defense, arguing convincingly that Dewey was much more culturally sensitive than Feinberg claimed. See Walter Feinberg, "Progressive Education and Social Planning," *Teachers College Record* 73 (May 1972), 491–495; Charles L. Zirby, "John Dewey and the Polish Question: A Response to the Revisionist Historian," *History of Education Quarterly* 15 (Spring 1975), 17–30; J. Christopher Eisele, "John Dewey and the Immigrants," *History of Education Quarterly* 15 (Spring 1975), 67–85.

84. Thompson, *Schooling of the Immigrant*, 11–15.

85. J. V. Breitwieser, "Adult Immigrant Education," *American Review* 3 (January 1925), 62; Fred Clayton Butler, *Community Americanization: A Handbook for Workers*, Bulletin 1919, no. 76 (Washington, DC: U.S. Government Printing Office, 1920), 13–14.

86. Ibid., 13–14. One year earlier, Franklin K. Lane, U.S. secretary of the interior, also endorsed the cultural-gifts perspective in a speech given in New York. Franklin K. Lane, *America, Americanism, Americanization* (Washington, DC: U.S. Government Printing Office, 1919), 4.

87. Gordon, *Assimilation in American Life*, 85.

88. Julius Drachsler, *Democracy and Assimilation: The Blending of Immigrant Heritages in America* (New York: Macmillan, 1920), 233. See also Hollinger, *Postethnic America*, 91–92.

89. Hollinger, *Postethnic America*, 92.

90. J. Hector St. John de Crèvecoeur, "Letters from an American Farmer," in *The American Reader*, ed. Diane Ravitch (New York: HarperCollins, 1991), 34.

91. Emerson is quoted in Hollinger, *Postethnic America*, 87–88. See also Gleason, "American Identity and Americanization," 38–39; and Eric P. Kaufmann, *The Rise and Fall of Anglo-America* (Cambridge: Harvard University Press, 2006), 43, 42–46.

92. Learned is quoted in "Words of Praise," *Abendpost* (April 12, 1908), 3, CFLPS, German, IIIF. For a similar statement, see J. Dyneley Prince, "Educating the Adult Immigrant," *Charity and the Commons* 17:20 (February 16, 1907), 890. Praise for Prince can be found in "Dr. John D. Prince," *Ukrainian Youth* (December 1935), CFLPS, Ukrainian, IA1b.

93. Israel Zangwill, *The Melting Pot* (North Stratford, NH: Ayer, 2004 [1909]), 34. In 1917, a judge presiding over a naturalization ceremony in Portland, Oregon, echoed Zangwill, telling the new citizens, "Here the best blood of the world is mingled; here the races are fused into a great mixt [sic] racial family, forming a composite citizenship, the greatest the world has known." John Kavanaugh, "Address to Applicants for Citizenship," in *Addresses and Proceedings of the Fifty-fifth Annual Meeting of the National Education Association, 1917* (Washington, DC: The Association, 1917), 97. For a superb analysis of Zangwill's play and its ramifications for ideas about American identity, see Werner Sollors, *Beyond Ethnicity: Consent and Descent in American Culture* (New York: Oxford University Press, 1986), 66–75, 92–101.

94. Zangwill, *Melting Pot*, 33.

95. Ibid., 184–185. It is important to note that contrary to many descriptions of Zangwill's play, this quote demonstrates that he was *not* imagining the amalgamation of only European groups in the making of a new American race (indeed, neither were Emerson and Learned). John J. Miller makes a similar

point, see John J. Miller, *The Unmaking of Americans* (New York: Free Press, 1998), 59–61.

96. Graham Taylor, "The Melting Pot and Social Agencies" (typescript, no date, probably 1922), in the Graham Taylor Papers, Box 29, Folder 1667, Newbury Library, Chicago, IL.

97. Drachsler, *Democracy and Assimilation*, 234; 235–236, 237.

98. Zadie Smith, *White Teeth* (New York: Vintage, 2001), 272.

99. Edward Hale Bierstadt, *Aspects of Americanization* (Cincinnati: Stewart Kidd, 1922), 14.

100. Tyler Anbinder, *Nativism and Slavery: The Northern Know Nothings and the Politics of the 1850s* (New York: Oxford University Press, 1992), 107; Archdeacon, *Becoming American*, 143–150; Gleason, "American Identity and Americaniza-tion," 34–38; Hartmann, *Movement to Americanize the Immigrant*, 13–21; Higham, *Strangers in the Land*, 3–11, 35–67; Noel Ignatiev, *How the Irish Became White* (New York: Routledge, 1995), 148–152; Mathew Frye Jacobson, *Whiteness of a Different Color* (Cambridge: Harvard University Press, 1998), 68–72.

101. Thomas F. Gosset, *Race: The History of an Idea in America* (Dallas; Southern Methodist University, 1963), 287; Jacobson, *Whiteness of a Different Color*; King, *Making Americans*.

102. Audrey Smedley calls these prejudices "folk classifications," which grow out of "ideologies, distinctions, and selective perceptions that constitute a society's popular imagery and interpretations of the world." Audrey Smedley, *Race in North America* (Boulder, CO: Westview Press, 1993), 27. See also Higham, *Strangers in the Land*, 12–18, 23–25; Ronald Takaki, *Strangers from a Different Shore: A History of Asian Americans* (Boston: Little, Brown, 1998), 102–103, and *A Different Mirror: A History of Multicultural America* (Boston: Little, Brown, 1993), 200, 204–209.

103. Smedley, *Race in North America*, 28.

104. Gosset, *Race*, 345; Archdeacon, *Becoming American*, 161–162.

105. The Immigrant Restriction League boasted a number of leading educators as members, including A. Lawrence Lowell, president of Harvard; Charles Thwing, president of Western Reserve; and David Starr Jordan, president of Stanford, as well as such well-known professors as John R. Commons and Edward A. Ross, of Wisconsin, and Robert DeCourcy Ward of Harvard. Barbara Miller Solomon, *Ancestors and Immigrants* (Cambridge: Harvard University Press, 1956), 122–151. See also Fuchs, *American Kaleidoscope*, 59–60; Hartmann, *Movement to Americanize the Immigrants*, 17–21; John Higham, *Strangers in the Land*, 264–330. Gosset, *Race: The History of an Idea in America*, 340; John Higham, *Send These to Me: Immigrants in Urban America* (Baltimore: Johns Hopkins University Press, 1984), 29–59.

106. The one exception to this trend was W. E. B. DuBois, who, for the most part, opposed restriction. See David J. Hellwig, "Black Leaders and United States Immigration Policy, 1917–1929," *Journal of Negro History* 66:2 (Summer 1981), 110–127.

107. For an excellent discussion of the prominent nineteenth-century American historians who contributed to ideas about the United States as a Nordic nation, see Edward Norman Saveth, "Race Nationalism in American Historiography: The Late Nineteenth Century," *Political Science Quarterly* 54:3 (September 1939), 421–441. See also Hartmann, *Movement to Americanize the Immigrant*, 13–21; Gleason, "American Identity and Americanization," 43–45; Higham, *Strangers in the Land*, 270–277; King, *Making Americans*, 52–54.

108. Francis A. Walker, "Restriction of Immigration" in Davis, *Immigration and Americanization*, 370. On Walker, see Gossett, *Race*, 302–303.

109. Alfred Schultz, *Race or Mongrel* (L. C. Page, 1906), 326, 246–247, 256–257, 272, 278, 324, 329. For a very similar analogy featuring draft horses and trotters, see Robert DeCourcy Ward, "Our New Immigration Policy," *Foreign Affairs* 3:1 (September 15, 1924), 102–103.

110. Schultz, *Race or Mongrel*, 261, 262–263, 266.

111. Madison Grant, *The Passing of the Great Race* (New York: Charles Scribner's Sons [1916], 1921), 216–220. John Higham called Grant "intellectually the most important nativist in recent American history." See Higham, *Strangers in the Land*, 155–157; Jacobson, *Whiteness of a Different Color*, 80–81; King, *Making Americans*, 218.

112. Grant, *Passing of the Great Race*, 20–21, 60–61. Grant likely took the Rome analogy from the notorious French racist Count Arthur de Gobineau. On Gobineau, see Gosset, *Race*, 342–344.

113. Grant, *Passing of the Great Race*, 90–91. For similar comments, see Henry Fairchild Osborn, *Scientific Papers of the Second International Congress of Eugenics*, vol. 1: *Eugenics in Race and State* (Baltimore: Williams and Wilkins, 1923), 2.

114. Solomon, *Ancestors and Immigrants*, 123.

115. The monthly series in the *Century Magazine* began in November 1913 (vol. 87, no. 1) and ended in October 1914 (vol. 88, no. 6). The book appeared soon after the series ended. Edward A. Ross, *The Old World in the New* (New York: Century, 1914).

116. Ross, *Old World in the New*, 95–167, 113–116.

117. Henry Pratt Fairchild, "Americanizing the Immigrant," *Yale Review* 5:4 (July 1916), 732, 731–740.

118. Henry Pratt Fairchild, *The Melting Pot Mistake* (Boston: Little, Brown, 1926), 167. It is worth noting that Fairchild's view on the failure of Americanization to

erase deep racial ties to the homeland or the ethnic group to some extent
echoed those of Horace Kallen. But Kallen obviously thought that maintaining
these deep ancestral ties was positive and a great benefit to the United States,
while Fairchild saw this phenomenon contributing to the deterioration of the
country. On Kallen's racialism, see Gleason, "American Identity and Americanization," 44–45.

119. Fairchild, *Melting Pot Mistake,* 197, 107–135, 156–171.

120. According to Desmond King, "[e]ven after the Second World War, Fairchild
harbored doubts about the suitability of some peoples to imbibe democratic
values and institutions." King, *Making Americans,* 193. See also Gosset, *Race,*
38–87.

121. Calvin Coolidge, "Whose Country Is This?" *Good Housekeeping* 72:2 (February 1921), 14, 106, 109.

122. Archdeacon, *Becoming American,* 168–170; Gerstle, *American Crucible,*
91–95, 97–103; Higham, *Strangers in the Land,* 222–232; Kennedy, *Over
Here,* 278–279; Aristide R. Zolberg, *A Nation by Design: Immigration Policy
in the Fashioning of America* (Cambridge: Harvard University Press, 2006,
248–250.

123. Kennedy, *Over Here,* 191–230, 287–292; King, *Making Americans,* 199–200.

124. Lothrop Stoddard, *The Rising Tide of Color against White Supremacy* (New
York: Charles Scribner's Sons, 1921), 263. Zolberg points out that Stoddard's
book and Madison Grant's *The Passing of the Great Race* were published by
Charles Scribner's Sons, perhaps the most prestigious publishing house in the
country at this time. Zolberg, *Nation by Design,* 249. In addition, a version of
Grant's and Stoddard's racial ideas appears in another famous Scribner
publication: F. Scott Fitzgerald, *The Great Gatsby* (New York: Charles
Scribner's Sons, 1925), 13–14.

125. Gerstle, *American Crucible,* 89; Kennedy, *Over Here,* 41, 59–61, 63, 65–66.

126. Creel, "Melting Pot or Dumping Ground?" 10. For more on these attitudes
about postwar immigrants, see Zolberg, *Nation by Design,* 246–247.

127. George Creel, "Close the Gates!" *Collier's* 69:18 (May 6, 1922), 9, 18.

128. John Carson, *The Measure of Merit: Talents, Intelligence, and Inequality in the
French and American Republics, 1750–1940* (Princeton: Princeton University
Press, 2007), 197–228; Stephen Jay Gould, *The Mismeasure of Man* (New York:
W. W. Norton, 1981), 194–195.

129. See, for example, the criticism by Gould in *Mismeasure of Man,* 196–217.

130. The degree of influence Grant had on Brigham can be seen in a footnote (on
182) in which Brigham urges his readers to read *The Passing of the Great Race* in
order "to appreciate the soundness of Mr. Grant's position and the compelling
force of his arguments." Carl C. Brigham, *A Study of American Intelligence*

(Princeton: Princeton University Press, 1923), 192. While Brigham later disavowed these findings, their influence persisted for decades. See Gould, *Mismeasure of Man*, 232–233.

131. Brigham, *Study of American Intelligence*, 155, 182–195.

132. King, *Making Americans*, 170. On the flawed logic of these interpretations of the army IQ tests, see John L. Rury, "Race, Region, and Education: An Analysis of Black and White Scores on the 1917 Army Alpha Intelligence Test," *Journal of Negro Education* 57:1 (Winter 1988), 51–65.

133. For example, Madison Grant cites data from the army exams in a 1924 article urging severe restriction of "inferior" immigrants. Madison Grant, "The Racial Transformation of America," *North American Review* 219 (March 1924), 351–352.

134. "Recommendations," in U.S. Immigration Commission, *Abstracts of Reports of the Immigration Commission*, vol. 1 (Washington, DC: U.S. Government Printing Office, 1911), 47–49. See also Zeidel, *Immigrants, Progressives, and Exclusion Politics*, 112–129.

135. U.S. Immigration Commission, "Federal Immigration Legislation," in Davis, *Immigration and Americanization*, 342–344, 358–359; Fuchs, *American Kaleidoscope*, 58–59; Anne Ruggles Gere, *Intimate Practices: Literacy and Cultural Work in U.S. Women's Clubs, 1880–1920* (Urbana: University of Illinois Press, 1997), 17–53; Higham, *Strangers in the Land*, 202–204, 308; King, *Making Americans*, 78–79; U.S. Immigration Commission, "Federal Immigration Legislation," in Davis, *Immigration and Americanization*, 342–344.

136. An early example of this idea of limiting "the number of each race arriving each year to a certain percentage of the average of that race arriving during a given period of years" appears in the recommendations of the 1911 report of U.S. Immigration. See U.S. Immigration Commission, *Abstracts of Reports of the Immigration Commission*, vol. 1, 47.

137. Higham, *Strangers in the Land*, 308–312.

138. Laughlin is quoted in King, *Making Americans*, 186, 166–175. See also Higham, *Strangers in the Land*, 307, 312–316; Jacobson, *Whiteness of a Different Color*, 21, 82–83; Ann Gibson Winfield, *Eugenics and Education in America* (New York: Peter Lang, 2007), 73–75, 78–80.

139. "Reed Offers New Immigration Plan," *Cleveland Plain Dealer* (December 12, 1922), 13.

140. Higham, *Strangers in the Land*, 312–320; King, *Making Americans*, 203–228.

141. "Back to 1890," *Saturday Evening Post* 195:21 (November 18, 1922), 24.

142. Quoted in Fuchs, *American Kaleidoscope*, 61.

143. David A. Reed, "America of the Melting Pot Comes to End," *New York Times* (April 27, 1924), 3.

144. In the House of Representatives, support for the bill was overwhelming. As Thomas Archdeacon notes, House members from the South and West voted "150 to 0" in favor of it; and midwestern House members, including many from districts with large numbers of people with German and Scandinavian backgrounds, voted "125 to 15" in favor. The only section of the country in which House members rejected the bill was the Northeast, and even that vote was close: 56 to 53. Archdeacon, *Becoming American*, 174, 171–172. See also Higham, *Strangers in the Land*, 321–324; King, *Making Americans*, 199–218; "Reed Offers New Immigration Plan," *Cleveland Plain Dealer*, 13.

145. Calvin Coolidge, "State of the Union Speech, 1923," in Fred L. Israel, ed., *The State of the Union Messages of the Presidents, 1790–1966*, vol. 3 (New York: Chelsea House, 1967), 2651.

146. "'Americanizing' the Alien," *Immigrants in America Review* 1:2 (June 1915), 3.

147. Ibid., 3.

2 Americanization and the Public Schools, 1890–1930

1. For example, the 1906 law that created the Division of Naturalization within the Bureau of Immigration (housed at the time in the Department of Commerce and Labor) specified that applicants for naturalization "must have the ability to speak English and . . . must show attachment to the principles of the Constitution." Burritt C. Harrington, "The Government and Adult Citizenship Education," *Religious Education* 39 (January 1944), 197; Ruth Z. Murphy, "Government Agencies Working with the Foreign Born," *Annals of the American Academy of Political and Social Science* 262 (March 1949), 138.

2. Frank Cody, "Americanization Courses in the Public Schools," *Chicago Schools Journal* 1:5 (January 1919), 5.

3. Albert Shiels, "Education for Citizenship," National Education Association, *Proceedings of the Sixtieth Annual Meeting of the National Education Association, 1922* (Washington, DC: National Education Association, 1922), 938. On Shiels, see Judith Rosenberg Raftery, *Land of Fair Promise: Politics and Reform in Los Angeles Schools, 1885–1941* (Stanford, CA: Stanford University Press, 1992), 47–48, 62–67, 87.

4. See, for example, Selma Berrol, "The Open City: Jews, Jobs, and Schools in New York City, 1880–1915," in *Educating an Urban People: The New York City Experience*, ed. Diane Ravitch and Ronald K. Goodenow (New York: Teachers College Press, 1981), 101–115; Lawrence A. Cremin, *The Transformation of the School: Progressivism in American Education, 1876–1957* (New York: Alfred A. Knopf, 1961), 66–75; Clarence J. Karier, *Shaping the American Educational*

State, 1900 to the Present (New York: Free Press, 1975), 225–274; Mark Krug, *The Melting of the Ethnics: Education of the Immigrants, 1880–1914* (Bloomington, IN: Phi Delta Kappa, 1976); Michael R. Olneck, "Americanization and the Education of Immigrants, 1900–1925: An Analysis of Symbolic Action," *American Journal of Education* (August 1989), 402–405; Paul C. Violas, *The Training of the Urban Working Class* (Chicago: Rand McNally, 1978), 37–66.

5. Thomas Balliet, "The Organization of a System of Evening Schools," National Education Association, *Addresses and Proceedings, 1904* (Winona, MN: National Education Association, 1904), 281.

6. Gary Gerstle, "Liberty, Coercion, and the Making of Americans," *Journal of American History* 84:2 (September 1997), 524–558. For an opposing view, see David Hollinger, "National Solidarity at the End of the Twentieth Century: Reflections on the United States and Liberal Nationalism," *Journal of American History* 84 (September 1997), 559–569.

7. On these developments nationally, see John Higham, "Cultural Responses to Immigration," in *Diversity and Its Discontents: Cultural Conflict and Common Ground in Contemporary American Society*, ed. Neil J. Smelser and Jeffrey C. Alexander (Princeton: Princeton University Press, 1999), 39–61; Eric P. Kaufmann, *The Rise and Fall of Anglo-America* (Cambridge: Harvard University Press, 2004); Diana Selig, *Americans All: The Cultural Gifts Movement* (Cambridge: Harvard University Press, 2008).

8. Ella Flagg Young, *Isolation in the Schools* (Chicago: University of Chicago Press, 1901), 92.

9. Lawrence A. Cremin, ed., *The Republic and the School: Horace Mann and the Education of Free Men* (New York: Teachers College Press, 1957), 58–59.

10. Anne-Lise Halvorsen, "The Origins and Rise of Social Studies Education at the Elementary Level: 1884 to 1941" (Ph.D. diss., University of Michigan, 2006), 15–88; Carl Kaestle, *Pillars of the Republic* (Hill and Wang, 1983), 71–72; David Miller, *On Nationality* (New York: Oxford University Press, 1995), 33–34, 141–143.

11. This massive enrollment growth was facilitated in part by new policies that downplayed the aggressively Protestant tenor of public school instruction in such cities as Chicago and Detroit. As early as 1874, facing political pressure from both the Irish and the Germans, the Chicago Board of Education "ordered Bible readings eliminated from the curriculum and from opening exercises of the public schools as well." Similarly, in 1898, after protests from "free-thinking" Germans and Jews, the Detroit Board of Education withdrew the book *Readings from the Bible*, which teachers had read from on a daily basis. On these developments in Chicago, see Chicago Board of Education, *Thirty-sixth Annual Report of the Public Schools of the City of Chicago,*

1889–90 (Chicago: The Board, 1890), 19–20; Mary Herrick, *The Chicago Schools: A Social and Political History* (Beverly Hills: Russell Sage, 1971), 61; "Religious Instruction in Public Schools Ordered Stopped," *Illinois Staats-Zeitung* (September 30, 1875), 1–3; "The Bible in the Schools," *Abendpost* (July 1, 1896), 1, CFLPS, German, IA1a; "Against the Bible in Schools," *Svornost* (May 8, 1896), 1–2, CFLPS, Bohemian, IA2a; "No Bible Reading in Schools," *Svenska Amerikanaren* (December 2, 1907), 1, CFLPS, Swedish, IA1a. On Detroit, see Norman Drachler, "The Influence of Sectarianism, Non-Sectarianism, and Secularism upon the Public Schools of Detroit and the University of Michigan" (Ph.D. diss., 1951), 120–138.

12. Jeffrey Mirel, "Urban Public Schools in the Twentieth Century: The View from Detroit," in *Brookings Papers on Educational Policy, 1999*, ed. Diane Ravitch (Washington, DC: Brookings Institution Press, 1999), 9–18.

13. Educators used the term "steamer classes" because many of the students seemed to have just stepped off the ship and into the classroom. See Selma Berrol, "Public Schools and Immigrants: The New York City Experience," in *American Education and the European Immigrant, 1840–1940*, ed. Bernard J. Weiss (Urbana: University of Illinois Press, 1982), 36; Boston Public Schools, *Annual Report of the Superintendent, 1914* (Boston: Boston Public Schools Printing Office, 1914), 36–38; Stephen F. Brumberg, *Going to America, Going to School* (New York: Praeger, 1986), 86–87, 93, 218; Cleveland Board of Education, *Annual Report of the Superintendent of Schools, 1912–13* (Cleveland: The Board, 1913), 25–26, 119; Detroit Board of Education, *The Sixty-eighth Annual Report of the Detroit Board of Education, 1910–11* (Detroit: The Board, 1911), 130; Detroit Board of Education, *The Eighty-first Annual Report of the Detroit Board of Education, 1923–24* (Detroit: The Board), 33; John H. Haaren, "Education of the Immigrant Child," in U.S. Bureau of Education, *Education of the Immigrant* (Washington, DC: U.S. Government Printing Office, 1913), 20–22; Cecil A. Kidd, "Education of the Immigrant Child," in U.S. Bureau of Education, *Education of the Immigrant*, 23, 22–23; Philadelphia Board of Education, *Annual Report of the Superintendent of Schools, 1915* (Philadelphia: Walther, 1916), 25–26. Gustave Straubenmuller, "Teaching Our Language to Non-English-Speaking Pupils," National Education Association, *Journal of Proceedings and Addresses, 1905* (Winona, MN: National Education Association), 414–415.

14. For examples, see Brumberg, *Going to America, Going to School*, 14–15; David R. Roediger, *Working toward Whiteness: How America's Immigrants Became White* (New York: Basic Books, 2005), 193–195; David B. Tyack, "Becoming an American: The Education of the Immigrants," in *Turning Points in American Education History*, ed. David B. Tyack (Waltham, MA: Blaisdell, 1967), 228–239.

15. Detroit Board of Education, *Sixty-second Annual Report, 1904–05* (Detroit: The Board, 1905), 75, 124–127, 142–143; Detroit Board of Education, *Sixty-third Annual Report, 1905–06* (Detroit: The Board, 1906), 75.

16. "Detroit Public Schools Course of Study in the Elementary Grades," in Detroit Board of Education, *The Sixty-seventh Annual Report of the Detroit Public Schools, 1909–10* (Detroit: The Board, 1910), 31. For similar trends in teaching history and civics in Massachusetts at this time, see Marvin Lazerson, *Origins of the Urban School: Public Education in Massachusetts, 1870–1915* (Cambridge: Harvard University Press, 1971), 232–240.

17. Detroit Public Schools, *Course of Study in History* (Detroit: Detroit Public Schools, 1917), 4–25. "Detroit Public Schools Course of Study in the Elementary Grades," in Detroit Board of Education, *Sixty-seventh Annual Report, 1909–10.* See also Mary E. Mumford, "The Public School and the Immigrant," *Child-Welfare Magazine* 4 (April 1910), 228.

18. Cleveland Board of Education, *Annual Report of the Superintendent, 1907–08* (Cleveland: The Board, 1908), 7, 10, 19.

19. Gertrude E. English, "Teaching English to Foreigners," *Educational Bi-Monthly* 2:1 (October 1907), 60. John Kinzie was one of the earliest white settlers in Chicago. Donald L. Miller, *City of the Century: The Epic of Chicago and the Making of America* (New York: Simon and Schuster, 1996), 52, 55.

20. "History: Outline for the Committee on Elementary Schools with Summary of Reports from Seventy-two Schools," in Chicago Board of Education, *Sixtieth Annual Report, 1913–14* (Chicago: The Board, 1914), 274, 278.

21. Ibid., 275.

22. Ibid., 276.

23. Ibid., 274, 279. On the expanding environment curriculum in social studies, see Halvorsen, "The Origins and Rise of Social Studies Education at the Elementary Level: 1884 to 1941," 293–362.

24. Harold Rugg and Ann Shumaker, *The Child-Centered School* (Yonkers-on-Hudson, NY: World Book, 1928), 5. See also Herbert Kliebard, *The Struggle for the American Curriculum* (New York: RoutledgeFalmer, 2004); Jeffrey Mirel, "Old Educational Ideas, New American Schools: Progressivism and the Rhetoric of Educational Revolution," *Paedagogica Historica* 39:4 (August 2003), 477–486; Diane Ravitch, *Left Back: A Century of Failed School Reform* (New York: Simon and Schuster, 2004).

25. Selma C. Berrol, *Julia Richman: A Notable Woman* (Philadelphia: Balch Institute Press, 1993), 53; Cremin, *Transformation of the School*, 72; Raftery, *Land of Fair Promise*, 32–40; David B. Tyack, *The One Best System: A History of American Urban Education* (Cambridge: Harvard University Press, 1974), 231–232.

26. Cremin, *Transformation of the School*, 69–71.

27. On the development of kindergartens in Massachusetts, see Lazerson, *Origins of the Urban School*, 36–73. For a comprehensive and insightful study of the history of the kindergarten, see Kristen Dombkowski Nawrotzki, "The Anglo-American Kindergarten Movements and Early Education in England and the USA, 1850–1965" (Ph.D. diss., University of Michigan, 2004).

28. Richard W. Gilder, "The Kindergarten: An Uplifting Social Influence in the Home and District," National Educational Association, *Journal of Proceedings and Addresses, 1903* (Winona, MN: The Association, 1903), 390. See also Ida Mighell, "Discussion," National Educational Association, *Journal of Proceedings and Addresses, 1905* (Winona, MN: The Association, 1905), 420. On Americanization and kindergartens, see Barbara Beatty, "'The Letter Killeth': Americanization and Multicultural Education in Kindergartens in the United States, 1856–1920," in Roberta Wollons, *Kindergartens and Culture* (New Haven: Yale University Press, 2000), 42–57; Lawrence Cremin, *American Education: The Metropolitan Experience, 1876–1980* (New York: Harper and Row, 1988), 310, 299–300; Lazerson, *Origins of the Urban School*, 36–73; Frank Manny, "The Process of Americanization in the Kindergarten and the School," *Kindergarten–Primary Magazine* 22 (June 1910), 300–301, 323–325.

29. Gilder, "Kindergarten," 393. See also Ronald D. Cohen, *Children of the Mill: Schooling and Society in Gary, IN, 1906–1960* (Bloomington: Indiana University Press, 1990), 11.

30. Maxine Seller, "The Education of Immigrant Children in Buffalo, New York, 1890–1916," *New York History* 57 (April 1976), 187, 190.

31. Like many educational innovations of the Progressive Era, kindergartens initially were philanthropic ventures, often linked to settlement houses rather than public schools. In 1892, the Chicago schools took charge of ten kindergartens originally created by the Froebel Society. Herrick, *Chicago Schools*, 72. In 1895, Detroit added kindergartens originally started by private organizations to the public school system. See Detroit Public Schools, *Education in Detroit* (Detroit: Detroit Public Schools, 1916), 52. Cleveland followed, adding several privately organized kindergartens to the system in 1897. "The Cleveland Day Nursery and Free Kindergarten Association, Inc.," in *The Encyclopedia of Cleveland History*, ed. David D. Van Tassel and John J. Grabowski (Bloomington: Indiana University Press, 1996), 233; Edward M. Miggins, "Businessmen, Pedagogues, and Progressive Reform: The Cleveland Foundation's 1915 School Survey" (Ph.D. diss., Case Western Reserve University, 1975), 17, 203; Cleveland Board of Education,

Annual Report of the Superintendent of Schools, 1907–08 (Cleveland: The Board, 1909), 122; Cleveland Board of Education, *Annual Report of the Superintendent of Schools, 1909–10* (Cleveland: The Board, 1910), 130.

32. U.S. Immigration Commission, *The Children of Immigrants in Schools*, vol. 2 (Washington, DC: U.S. Government Printing Office, 1911), 547.

33. David John Hogan, *Class and Reform: School and Society in Chicago, 1880–1930* (Philadelphia: University of Pennsylvania Press, 1985), 82. At least one commentator in the immigrant press was not put off by the Americanizing aspects of kindergartens in the Chicago Public Schools. Writing in 1922 in the *Jewish Daily Courier*, Joshua Seligman praised the kindergartens and declared, "Every Jewish child should and must attend one of those classes for at least one year." Joshua Seligman, "The Great and Free American Public School," *Jewish Daily Courier* (January 16, 1922), 5, CFLPS, Jewish, IA1a.

34. "The Cleveland Day Nursery and Free Kindergarten Association, Inc.," 233; Miggins, "Businessmen, Pedagogues, and Progressive Reform," 17, 203; Cleveland Board of Education, *Annual Report of the Superintendent of Schools, 1907–08*, 122; Cleveland Board of Education, *Annual Report of the Superintendent of Schools, 1909–10*, 130. Kindergartens in Buffalo, New York, also were quite popular among immigrant families. Seller, "Education of Immigrant Children in Buffalo, New York, 1890–1916", 191.

35. Detroit Board of Education, *Eighty-fifth Annual Report of the Detroit Public Schools, 1927–28* (Detroit: The Board, 1928), 42–43; Detroit Board of Education, *Sixty-eighth Annual Report of the Detroit Board of Education, 1910–11*, 91–95. See also George Strayer, ed., *Report of the Survey of the Schools of Chicago, Illinois*, vol. 2 (New York: Bureau of Publications, Teachers College, Columbia University, 1932), 18; and Joel M. Roitman, *The Immigrants, the Progressives, and the Schools: Americanization and the Impact of the New Immigration upon Public Education in the United States, 1890–1920* (Stark, KS: De Young Press, 1996), 111–112.

36. Cohen, *Children of the Mill*, 12; Cremin, *American Education*, 310. On the playground movement in Kansas City, Milwaukee, Rochester, and Toledo, see William J. Reese, *Power and the Promise of School Reform* (New York: Teachers College Press, 2002), 144–157.

37. David Blaustein, "The Schoolhouse Recreation Center as an Attempt to Aid Immigrants in Adjusting Themselves to American Conditions," *Playground* 6:9 (December 1912), 334–335. As director of the Educational Alliance, Blaustein played a key role in Americanizing Jewish immigrants prior to World War I. See Irving Howe, *World of Our Fathers* (New York: Harcourt Brace Jovanovich, 1976), 231. On playgrounds and immigrants, see also Edward W. Stitt, "Recreation for the Immigrant," in *Education of the*

Immigrant, U.S. Bureau of Education Bulletin 1913, no. 51 (Washington, DC: U.S. Government Printing Office, 1913); Roitman, *Immigrants, the Progressives, and the Schools*, 118–133.

38. On the development of playgrounds in Chicago, see Mary E. McDowell, "The Children of Our Cities," National Educational Association, *Journal of Proceedings and Addresses*, 1896 (Chicago, IL: University of Chicago Press, 1896), 493; and Gerald R. Gems, *The Windy City Wars: Labor, Leisure, and Sport in the Making of Chicago* (Lanham, MD: Scarecrow Press, 1997), 102–114. Gems provides an engaging account of how sports such as baseball contributed to the Americanization of immigrants in Chicago, but also how the immigrants adapted these sports to promote their particular group. For example, by 1915, both Czechs and Poles in Chicago had formed their own Catholic baseball leagues, which "allowed for the adaptation of Americanized interests without adoption of secular influences." Gems, *Windy City Wars*, 112. Slovaks also adopted "American sports" in ways that supported *ethnic* identity formation. See June Granatir Alexander, *Ethnic Pride, American Patriotism: Slovaks and Other New Immigrants in the Interwar Years* (Philadelphia: Temple University Press, 2004), 116–119, 146–152. For a wonderful example of such ethnically based Americanization in sports, see the article "Serbian Eagles Baseball Team—Champion," Scrap Book of Adam Popovich (1931), CFLPS, IIB3, which announced the upcoming championship game between the Serbian Eagles and the Rumanian [sic] Junior League team taking place at Goldberg Field.

39. David John Hogan, "Capitalism and Schooling: A History of the Political Economy of Education in Chicago, 1880–1930" (Ph.D. diss., University of Illinois, Urbana-Champaign, 1978), 69–71.

40. A. K. Rutkauskas, "What I Have Noticed," *Lietuva* (April 10, 1908), CFLPS, Lithuanian, IIIA.

41. Brumberg, *Going to America, Going to School*, 76–77.

42. "Fine Arts Education," in *The Eightieth Annual Report of the Detroit Public Schools, 1922–23* (Detroit: Detroit Board of Education, 1923), 37–38; Henry G. Geilen, "Primary Grades Art Education," *Chicago Schools Journal* 12:1 (September 1929), 17.

43. Detroit Board of Education, *The Seventy-third Annual Report of the Superintendent, 1915–16* (Detroit: The Board, 1916), 115–116. On music, see also Cleveland Board of Education, *Annual Report of the Superintendent, 1914–15* (Cleveland: The Board, 1915), 32–33; Francis G. Blair, "The American Melting Pot," *Proceedings of the Sixty-fifth Annual Meeting of the National Education Association, 1927* (Washington, DC: National Education Association, 1927), 40.

44. David L. Angus and Jeffrey E. Mirel, *The Failed Promise of the American High School, 1890–1994* (New York: Teachers College Press, 1999), 203.

45. On how different immigrant groups approached schooling, particularly high school, see John Bodnar, "Schooling and the Slavic Family," in Weiss, *American Education and the European Immigrant, 1840–1940*, 78–95; David K. Cohen, "Immigrants and the Schools," *Review of Educational Research* 40:1 (1970), 13–27; Leonard Dinnerstein, "Education and the Advancement of American Jews" in Weiss, *American Education and the European Immigrant, 1840–1940*, 55, 44–60; Paula S. Fass, "Immigration and Education in the United States," in *A Companion to American Immigration*, ed. Reed Ueda (Malden, MA: Blackwell, 2006), 499–500; Salvatore J. LaGumina, "American Education and the Italian Immigrant Response," in Weiss, *American Education and the European Immigrant, 1840–1940*, 61–77, 71; Joel Perlmann, *Ethnic Differences: Schooling and Social Structure among the Irish, Italians, Jews and Blacks in an American City* (New York: Cambridge University Press, 1988).

46. Angus and Mirel, *Failed Promise of the American High School, 1890–1994*, 204, 32–56.

47. Indeed, Frances Fitzgerald argues that in response to the great wave of immigration, American history textbooks specifically "began to emphasize the English ancestry of Americans." Frances Fitzgerald, *America Revised: History Schoolbooks in the Twentieth Century* (Boston: Little, Brown), 77, 77–79.

48. Charles A. Beard and Mary R. Beard, *History of the United States* (New York: Macmillan, 1921), 120. Cleveland Board of Education, *Report of the Superintendent of Schools: The Senior High Schools, 1928–29* (Cleveland: The Board, 1929), 142.

49. Beard and Beard, *History of the United States*, 411.

50. Ibid., 582–586. Perhaps the best-selling American history textbooks in the 1910s and 1920s, those written by David Saville Muzzey, were even more disparaging about "unassimilated and unassimilable" immigrants who had arrived in the United States in the previous few decades. See Stuart J. Foster, "The Struggle for American Identity: Treatment of Ethnic Groups in United States History Textbooks," *History of Education* 28:3 (1999), 260–261.

51. Jane Addams, "The Public School and the Immigrant Child," in National Education Association, *Journal of Addresses and Proceedings, 1908* (Winona, MN: The Association, 1908), 99–100. For more on Addams's views on this issue, see Rivka Shpak Lissak, *Pluralism and Progressives: Hull House and the New Immigrants, 1890–1919* (Chicago: University of Chicago Press, 1989), 54–55.

52. Grace Abbott, "The Education of Foreigners in American Citizenship," in National Municipal League, *Proceedings of the National Municipal League*, 1910, vol. 18 (Philadelphia: The League, 1910), 377–378. On Abbott and the Immigrants' Protective League, see Henry B. Leonard, "The Immigrants' Protective League of Chicago, 1908–1921," *Journal of the Illinois State Historical Society* 66:3 (Autumn 1973), 271–282.

53. Abbott, "Education of Foreigners in American Citizenship," 377–378.

54. Chicago Board of Education, *Sixty-fourth Annual Report of the Board of Education, 1917–1918* (Chicago: The Board, 1918), 5.

55. Ibid., 35–39; Detroit Board of Education, *Seventy-fifth Annual Report, 1917–18* (Detroit: The Board, 1918), 129–130; Department of Education, City of New York, *Nineteenth Annual Report of the Superintendent of Schools, 1916–17: Kindergartens, Music, Sewing, Cooking, Modern Languages in the Elementary Schools* (New York: Department of Education, 1917), 22–23, 37. On similar developments in Kansas City, Milwaukee, Rochester, and Toledo, see Reese, *Power and the Promise of Progressive Reform*, 213–222.

56. Peter A. Mortenson, "To the Business Men," in Board of Education of the City of Chicago and the Chicago Association of Commerce, *A Year of Americanization Work, July 1918–July 1919* (Chicago: The Board, 1919), 1.

57. These programs proved to be popular with Germans and non-Germans alike. In 1916, for example, a report on the program noted that only about a third of the students enrolled were of German ancestry. An excellent summary of the school board debates and decisions about teaching German in the Chicago Public Schools from 1865 to 1918 can be found in Ana Maria Espinosa, "The Role of Communities in Bilingual Education: A Case Study of German and Mexican-American Communities in Chicago, 1865–1985" (Ed.D. diss., Northern Illinois University, 1994), 51–132. See also Chicago Board of Education, *Sixty-first Annual Report of the Board of Education, 1914–1915*, (Chicago: The Board, 1915), 134. Heinz Kloss, "German-American Language Maintenance Efforts," in *Language Loyalty in the United States*, ed. Joshua A. Fishman (London: Mouton, 1966), 233–43; Rudolf A. Hofmeister, *The Germans of Chicago* (Champaign, IL: Stripes, 1976), 172–175; Steven L. Schlossman, "Is There an American Tradition of Bilingual Education? German in the Public Elementary Schools, 1840–1919," *American Journal of Education* 91:2 (February 1983), 150–165.

58. Kloss, "German-American Language Maintenance Efforts," 233–43; Hofmeister, *Germans of Chicago*, 172–75; Chicago Board of Education, *Sixty-first Annual Report of the Board of Education, 1914–1915*, 134.

59. Linda L. Sommerfeld, "An Historical Descriptive Study of the Circumstances That Led to the Elimination of German from the Cleveland

Schools, 1860–1918" (Ph.D. diss., Kent State University, 1986), 291. See also
Edward M. Miggins, "Americanization," in *The Encyclopedia of Cleveland
History*, ed. David D. Van Tassel and John J. Grabowski (Bloomington:
Indiana University Press, 1996), 34; Cleveland Board of Education, *Annual
Report of the Superintendent, 1914–15*, 28–32, 148; Cleveland Board of
Education, *Annual Report of the Superintendent, 1916–17* (Cleveland: The
Board, 1918), 48–50; Cleveland Board of Education, *Proceedings of the Board
of Education, January 2, 1917–December 21, 1917* 38 (Cleveland: The Board,
1918), 301–302; Cleveland Board of Education, *Proceedings of the Board of
Education, January 7, 1918–December 30, 1918* 39 (Cleveland: The Board,
1919), 215, 219.

60. The May 1914 Chicago school census found that of the approximately 2.44
million people living in Chicago, nearly 400,000 (over 16 percent) had been
born in Germany or had a German-born father. Espinosa, "Role of Communities in Bilingual Education," 118.

61. Quoted in Espinosa, "Role of Communities in Bilingual Education," 129.
Chicago Board of Education, *Sixty-fourth Annual Report of the Board of
Education, 1917–1918*, 11–12.

63. Chicago Board of Education, *The Sixty-fifth Annual Report of the Board of
Education, 1918–19* (Chicago: The Board, 1919), 26.

64. For a superb study of the controversy about German in the Cleveland schools,
see Sommerfeld, "An Historical Descriptive Study of the Circumstances That
Led to the Elimination of German from the Cleveland Schools, 1860–1918,"
61–280. See also Miggins, "Americanization," 34; Cleveland Board of Education, *Annual Report of the Superintendent, 1914–15*, 28–32, 148; Cleveland
Board of Education, *Annual Report of the Superintendent, 1916–17*, 48–50;
Cleveland Board of Education, *Proceedings of the Board of Education, January 2,
1917–December 21, 1917*, 301–302; Cleveland Board of Education, *Proceedings of
the Board of Education, January 7, 1918–December 30, 1918*, 215, 219. Detroit did
not have a similar program of German language instruction on the elementary
level. The major controversy in the Motor City about German issues involved
an effort to rename schools "having names of Germanic origin," replacing
them "with names that are in keeping with the spirit of American ideals." This
effort failed. Loren H. Houtman, "Response of Detroit Public Schools to
Immigrant Groups" (Ed.D. diss., Michigan State University, 1965), 100.
Nevertheless, the wartime hysteria over German instruction led to a massive
enrollment decline in German course-taking in Michigan. See Calvin O.
Davis, "The Probable Future of the Study of German in the Public Schools of
Michigan," *School and Society* 7:182 (June 22, 1918), 744–750.

65. Schlossman, "Is There an American Tradition of Bilingual Education?"
175–178; Jonathan Zimmerman, "Ethnics against Ethnicity: European

Immigrants and Foreign-Language Instruction, 1890–1940," *Journal of American History* 87:1 (March 2002), 1392–1393.

66. Hartmann, *The Movement to Americanize the Immigrant* (New York: Columbia University Press, 1948), 243–245. On the movement to eliminate German teaching in public schools in various states, see William G. Ross, *Forging New Freedoms: Nativism, Education, and the Constitution, 1917–1927* (Lincoln: University of Nebraska Press, 1994), 52–56.

67. Quoted in Mark G. Yudof, David L. Kirp, Tyll van Geel, and Betsy Levin, *Educational Policy and the Law* (Berkeley: McCutchan, 1982), 172.

68. Ross, *Forging New Freedoms*, 74–133.

69. Sara H. Fahey, "How the Public Schools Can Foster the American Ideal of Patriotism," 51.

70. Detroit Board of Education, *Seventy-fifth Annual Report, 1917–18*, 130. For a very similar statement, see Fahey, "How the Public Schools Can Foster the American Ideal of Patriotism," 51.

71. Charles Chadsey, "Emphasize Patriotism and Citizenship," *Detroit Educational Bulletin* 2:1 (September 1918), 1. See also I. M. Allen, "Pupil Responsibility as a Training in Democracy," *Chicago School Journal* 2:2 (October 1919), 2, 2–8.

72. Richard J. Ellis, *To the Flag: The Unlikely History of the Pledge of Allegiance* (Lawrence: University of Kansas Press, 2005), 30–31, 54–80.

73. Arthur W. Dunn, "The Civic Training of Young America," *Addresses and Proceedings of the Fifty-ninth Annual Meeting of the National Education Association, 1921* (Washington, DC: National Education Association, 1921), 765.

74. Ellis, *To the Flag*, 78.

75. "Some Suggestions for Teaching the Federal and State Constitutions," *Chicago Schools Journal* 4:2 (October 1921), 41; Chicago Board of Education, *Annual Report of the Superintendent, 1924–25* (Chicago: The Board, 1925), 19.

76. Elmer F. Pflieger, "Social Studies," in *Improving Learning in the Detroit Public Schools*, vol. 2, ed. Paul T. Rankin (Detroit: Detroit Board of Education, 1969), 488. The civics course was the *only* state-mandated high school graduation requirement in Michigan until 2006.

77. Lucie H. Schacht, "On the Teaching of History," *Chicago Schools Journal* 9:1 (September 1926), 12.

78. On May 1, 1919, for example, members of "patriotic" groups attacked a large prosocialist march in Cleveland, resulting in one death, numerous injuries, and mass arrests mainly of foreign-born marchers. On January 2, 1920, some 800 Detroiters were arrested in one of the "Palmer Raids" and were "held incommunicado" for several days in miserable conditions. Perhaps the most

serious impact the Red scare had on education took place in Boston and
Buffalo, where several teachers were fired because of their alleged left-wing
views. See C. E. Ruthenberg, "The Cleveland May Day Demonstration,"
Revolutionary Age 1:30 (May 10, 1919), 4; John Higham, *Strangers in the
Land: Patterns of American Nativism, 1860–1925* (New York: Atheneum,
1975), 231; David M. Kennedy, *Over Here: The First World War and American Society* (New York: Oxford University Press, 2004), 288–289; Robert
Iversen, *The Communists and the Schools* (New York: Harcourt, Brace,
1959), 12–13.

79. Arthur Dondineau, "Social Science and the Teaching of Citizenship," *Detroit
Journal of Education* 2:3 (February 1922), 25.

80. Detroit Board of Education, "Social Science," *Eighty-seventh Annual Report of
the Detroit Public Schools, 1929–30,* 131. An early discussion of the debate
between advocates of these two approaches can be found in Edgar Dawson,
"The Social Studies in Civic Education," in U.S. Bureau of Education, *Biennial
Survey of Education, 1921–1922,* vol. 1 (Washington, DC: Government Printing
Office, 1924), 403–418. See also Julie Reuben, "Beyond Politics: Community
Civics and the Redefinition of Citizenship in the Progressive Era," *History of
Education Quarterly* 37:4 (Winter 1997), 399–420.

81. On curriculum issues in this period, see Halvorsen, "The Origins and Rise of
Social Studies Education at the Elementary Level: 1884 to 1941," 145–225.

82. "Public School Civics," *Chicago Schools Journal* 2:9 (January 1920), 6; Frances
K. Hepner, "Civics for Vocational Students," *Chicago Schools Journal* 2:9
(January 1920), 6–9; E. Lori Brown, "Civic Foundations," *Chicago Schools
Journal* 2:9 (January 1920), 11–14; J. Leroy Stockton, "The Project, Work, and
Democracy," *Chicago Schools Journal* 5:5 (January 1923), 185–188; Peter A.
Mortenson, "Morals and Education," *Chicago Schools Journal* 5:6 (February
1923), 225–226; Peter J. Ritzma, "The Chicago Course of Study in Citizenship,"
Chicago Schools Journal 8:1 (September 1925), 5–9.

83. "Public School Civics," 6; Hepner, "Civics for Vocational Students," 6–9;
Brown, "Civic Foundations," 11–14; Stockton, "Project, Work, and Democ-
racy," 185–188; Mortenson, "Morals and Education," 225–226; Ritzma, "Chi-
cago Course of Study in Citizenship," 5–9; Mary A. Gilbert, "Laboratory
Civics," *Chicago Schools Journal* 2:9 (January 1920, 9–11; Committee on
Morals and Civics of the Chicago Principals Club, "Report on Morals and
Civics," *Chicago Schools Journal* 4:1 (September 1921), 19–22; Will D. Ander-
son, "Character Training" *Chicago Schools Journal* 12:1 (September 1929), 8.

84. Detroit Public Schools, Department of Social Science, *Course of Study in
Social Science: Grades One to Six* (Detroit,: Detroit Board of Education,
1923), 98.

85. Ibid., 15, 34, 53, 72, 98, 104.
86. See "Application of the Curriculum to the Development of Character and Citizenship," in Cleveland Board of Education, *Annual Report of the Superintendent of Schools, 1925–26* (Cleveland: The Board, 1926), 8, 19, 32, 34–35, 47.
87. Joseph Moreau, *Schoolbook Nation: Conflicts over American History Textbooks from the Civil War to the Present* (Ann Arbor: University of Michigan Press, 2003), 175–218; Jonathan Zimmerman, *Whose America? Culture War in the Public Schools* (Cambridge: Harvard University Press, 2002), 16–25. See also "Words of Praise," *Abendpost* (April 12, 1908), 3, CFLPS, German, IIIF; and J. Dyneley Prince, "Educating the Adult Immigrant," *Charity and the Commons* 17:20 (February 16, 1907), 890.
88. The quote on "the cult of Anglo-Saxonism" is from Moreau, *Schoolbook Nation*, 177, 185–186, 194–195.
89. Ibid., 186.
90. Nancy Gentile Ford, *Americans All! Foreign-Born Soldiers in World War I* (College Station: Texas A&M Press, 2001), 3, 69, 73, 77, 80, 85. A powerful expression of these sentiments can be found in a speech that Graham Taylor, a Congregational theologian and settlement-house leader, delivered sometime after World War I. Graham Taylor, "Patriotism of Foreign-Born Citizens" (typescript, n.d., but after 1918), in the GT Papers, Box 29, Folder-1699.
91. Moreau, *Schoolbook Nation*, 204, 206.
92. Ibid., 194–196.
93. McSweeney is quoted in Zimmerman, *Whose America?* 21.
94. Moreau, *Schoolbook Nation*, 194–196. The Knights of Columbus pamphlet is quoted in Zimmerman, *Whose America?* 20.
95. "The Foreign Languages," *Skandinaven* (August 25, 1920), 3, CFLPS, Norwegian, IIIA.
96. A. Duncan Yocum, "Report of the Committee on the Teaching of Democracy," in the *Proceedings of the Sixtieth Annual Meeting of the National Education Association*, 1922, 509.
97. Moreau, *Schoolbook Nation*, 194–201. See also Lissak, *Pluralism and Progressives*, 58.
98. Thompson is quoted in Zimmerman, *Whose America?* 21. As early as 1905, Poles had been urging that Polish history, as well as the role of Poles in American history, be taught in the Chicago Public Schools. "Urge to Study Poland," *Chicago Chronicle* (February 20, 1905), 1–2, CFLPS, Polish, IA1a.
99. Moreau, *Schoolbook Nation*, 201–207; Zimmerman, *Whose America?* 9, 22–25.
100. Moreau, *Schoolbook Nation*, 208.

101. Ibid., 214.

102. Selig, *Americans All*, 68–112.

103. Cody, "What One Representative City Is Doing in Teaching Americanism," 761. In the same talk, Cody strongly denounced programs that compelled workers to take Americanization courses or lose their jobs. Cody's 1916 anti-hyphen remark can be found in Detroit Board of Education, *Seventy-third Annual Report of the Superintendent, 1915–16*, 115.

104. Detroit Board of Education, *Eighty-sixth Annual Report of the Detroit Public Schools, 1928–29* (Detroit: The Board, 1929), 42.

105. U.S. Bureau of the Census, *Fifteenth Census of the United States: 1930, Population, V. 3, Part I* (Washington, DC: Government Printing Office, 1932), 1158.

106. Mortenson, "To the Business Men," 1. On the centrality of public schools in this process, see also Peter A. Speck, "The Meaning of Nationality and Americanization," *American Journal of Sociology* 32:2 (September 1926), 248.

107. Francis G. Blair, "The American Melting Pot," 34.

108. Detroit Board of Education, *The Sixty-first Annual Report of the Board of Education, 1903–04* (Detroit: The Board, 1904), 11.

109. Herrick, *Chicago Schools*, 44; Houtman, "Response of the Detroit Public Schools to Immigrant Groups," 32–47; "Evening Schools," in Detroit Board of Education, *The Sixty-eighth Annual Report of the Detroit Board of Education, 1910–11*, 130, 162–164.

110. As early as 1903, the Chicago night school supervisor accurately predicted, "The teaching of English to foreign-speaking people is, and probably will long continue to be, the most important part of the evening school work in Chicago." Public Schools of the City of Chicago, *Forty-ninth Annual Report of the Chicago Board of Education, 1902–03*, 65–66. In 1910–1911, some 18,300 students enrolled in courses in the Elementary Division of the Chicago evening school program. Of those, about 12,700, just under 70 percent, enrolled in classes of "English for Foreigners." Public Schools of the City of Chicago, *Fifty-seventh Annual Report of the Chicago Board of Education, 1910–11* (Chicago: The Board, 1911), 176.

111. Hartmann, *Movement to Americanize the Immigrant*, 24.

112. Josef John Barton, "Immigration and Social Mobility in an American City: Studies of Three Ethnic Communities in Cleveland" (Ph.D. diss., University of Michigan, Ann Arbor 1971), 115.

113. Detroit Board of Education, *The Sixty-first Annual Report of the Board of Education, 1903–04*, 93–95.

114. Public Schools of the City of Chicago, *Fortieth Annual Report of the Chicago Board of Education, 1893–94* (Chicago: The Board, 1894), 173–174.

115. Public Schools of the City of Chicago, *Fiftieth Annual Report of the Chicago Board of Education, 1903–04* (Chicago: The Board, 1905), 104; Public Schools of the City of Chicago, *Fifty-seventh Annual Report of the Chicago Board of Education, 1910–11*, 178–179.

116. Cleveland Board of Education, *Annual Report of the Superintendent of Schools, 1906–07* (Cleveland: The Board, 1907), 35.

117. Cleveland Board of Education, *Annual Report of the Superintendent of Schools, 1911–12* (Cleveland: The Board, 1912), 18.

118. "Evening Schools Make for Citizenship," in Cleveland Board of Education, *Annual Report of the Superintendent of Schools, 1913–14* (Cleveland: The Board, 1914), 24–25, 27. The rank order of students by nationality was: Hungarians, Russian Jews, Austrians, Poles, Czechs, and Italians. These six groups accounted for almost two-thirds of all the students enrolled in the Cleveland evening school program in 1913–1914.

119. "Evening School Classes Opportunity for Foreign Born," in Cleveland Board of Education, *Annual Report of the Superintendent of Schools, 1912–13* (Cleveland: The Board, 1913), 23.

120. Immigrants filed their "First Papers" (later known as the "Declaration of Intention to Seek American Citizenship") at least two years prior to filing their Second Papers. Applying for Second Papers took place before a judge, and the petitioners had to be accompanied by two U.S. citizens who testified about the applicants' good character and length of time in the country. The judges could be from county courts, superior courts, or federal courts. Raymond E. Cole, "The Naturalization of Foreigners," in *Immigration and Americanization*, ed. Philip Davis (New York: Ginn, 1920), 600–604; C. C. Barnes, "Naturalization," *Detroit Education Bulletin* 8:6 (February 1925), 19.

121. Cole, "Naturalization of Foreigners," 604–606.

122. On the political battles over the school board membership and structure, see Jeffrey Mirel, *The Rise and Fall of an Urban School System: Detroit, 1907–81* (Ann Arbor: University of Michigan Press, 1999), 1–42. On poor night-school enrollments, see Detroit Board of Education, *The Fifty-sixth Annual Report of the Board of Education, 1898–99* (Detroit: The Board, 1899), 79; Detroit Board of Education, *Sixty-seventh Annual Report of the Board of Education, 1909–10*, 133, 135.

123. Detroit Board of Education, *Sixty-ninth Annual Report of the Board of Education, 1911–12*, 148.

124. Detroit Board of Education, *Sixty-seventh Annual Report of the Board of Education, 1909–10*, 135; Detroit Board of Education, *The Seventy-second Annual Report of the Board of Education, 1914–15* (Detroit: The Board, 1915), 125–127.

125. Detroit Board of Education, *The Seventy-first Annual Report of the Board of Education, 1913–14* (Detroit: The Board, 1914), 143; Public Schools of the City of Chicago, *Forty-ninth Annual Report of the Chicago Board of Education, 1902–03* (Chicago: The Board, 1904), 67; Public Schools of the City of Chicago, *Fiftieth Annual Report of the Chicago Board of Education, 1903–04*, 103.

126. Frederic E. Farrington, *Public Facilities for Educating the Alien* (Washington, DC: U.S. Government Printing Office, 1916), 23–24. For an example of a school leader who supported employing teachers who spoke the immigrants' language, see Balliet, "Organization of a System of Evening Schools," 281.

127. Detroit Board of Education, *Seventy-second Annual Report of the Board of Education, 1914–15*, 123.

128. Herbert A. Miller, *The School and the Immigrant* (Cleveland: Survey Committee of the Cleveland Foundation, 1916), 90–95.

129. Public Schools of the City of Chicago, *Fifty-third Annual Report of the Chicago Board of Education, 1906–07* (Chicago: The Board, 1907), 144–145.

130. Public Schools of the City of Chicago, *Fifty-seventh Annual Report of the Chicago Board of Education, 1910–11*, 115.

131. Gregory Mason, "An Americanization Factory," *Outlook* 113 (February 23, 1916), 442. During this period, Rochester had nationally renowned evening school programs. See Reese, *Power and the Promise of School Reform*, 166–176; Edwin A. Rumball, "'To Express Our Gladness That We Are Americans,'" in *National Municipal Review, 1912* vol. 1, ed. Clinton Rogers Woodruff (Baltimore: Williams and Wilkins, 1912), 663–667.

132. Mason, "Americanization Factory," 443–445.

133. Harry A. Lipsky, "The Problem of Our People's Education," *Jewish Daily Courier* (August 1, 1916), 3, CFLPS, Jewish, IA3. See also "Men as Teachers in Evening Classes," *Jewish Daily Courier* (September 22, 1916), 2, CFLPS, Jewish, IK. Two years later, a leader of the Lithuanian community reiterated these complaints about the evening schools, stating, "We must devise better methods to interest immigrants in these schools." Another speaker also denounced efforts to force immigrants to learn English. "A Conference of Lithuanians and Americans" *Lietuva* (December 19, 1918), 3, CFLPS, Lithuanian, IIIA.

134. Chicago Board of Education, *Sixtieth Annual Report, 1913–14*, 398–399.

135. Department of Education, City of New York, *Nineteenth Annual Report of the Superintendent of Schools, 1916–17*, 43.

136. Miller, *School and the Immigrant*, 95.

137. Ibid., 99, 85–102. Miller's attack was a dramatic change from previous reports on Cleveland's evening school program. For more positive assessments, see Frances A. Kellor, "The Tie That Binds Immigration, Work and Citizenship,"

Survey 34 (March 21, 1914), 766–767; "Survey of Adult Immigrant Education," *Immigrants in America Review* 1:2 (June 1915), 52.

138. Miller, *School and the Immigrant*, 91, 94, 99–100.

139. "The City's Night Schools," *Detroit Free Press* (August 30, 1915), 4.

140. Ruth Robinson, "Report for the National Conference on Community Centers and Related Problems (Immigration)" (typescript, 1916), ACD Papers, Box 1, Folder 1, 4.

141. Frank V. Thompson, *Schooling of the Immigrant* (New York: Harper and Brothers, 1920), 68.

142. Massachusetts did require illiterate, non-English-speaking young people between sixteen and twenty-one years of age to attend English classes. See Boston Public Schools, *Annual Report of the Superintendent, 1920* (Boston: Boston Public Schools Printing Department, 1920), 45.

143. Howard C. Hill, "The Americanization Movement," *American Journal of Sociology* 24:6 (May 1919), 612.

144. National Americanization Committee and the Committee for Immigrants in America, *Americanizing a City: The Campaign for the Detroit Night Schools Conducted in Cooperation with the Detroit Board of Commerce and Board of Education, August–September, 1915* (New York: The Committees, 1915), 3.

145. Ibid., 4.

146. Thompson, *Schooling of the Immigrant*, 53–54; Hill, "Americanization Movement," 622; and Robert Livingston Schuyler, "The Movement for Americanization," *Columbia University Quarterly* 18:2 (March 1916), 188–189.

147. Mirel, *Rise and Fall of an Urban School System*, 18–19.

148. Detroit Board of Education, *Seventy-second Annual Report of the Board of Education, 1914–15*, 125; Campbell Gibson and Emily Lennon, "Historical Census Statistics on the Foreign-Born Population of the United States: 1850–1990," Population Division Working Paper no. 29 (Washington, DC: U.S. Bureau of the Census, 1999), table 19.

149. For a thoughtful overview of this campaign in Detroit, see Anne Brophy, "'The Committee . . . has stood out against coercion': The Reinvention of Detroit Americanization, 1915–1931," *Michigan Historical Review* 29:2 (Fall 2003), 1–39. Another excellent overview is Robyn Renee Greenlee, "Adult Education and the Americanization Committee of Detroit" (honors thesis, Emory University, 1999). See also Olivier Zunz, *The Changing Face of Inequality: Urbanization, Industrial Development, and Immigrants in Detroit, 1880–1920* (Chicago: University of Chicago Press, 1982), 311–318.

150. Byers Gitchall to Detroit Civic Leaders (typescript, n.d., but after May 1915), ACD Papers, Box 1, Folder 2, 1; Brophy, "'The Committee . . . has stood out against coercion,'" 7–8.

151. Raymond E. Cole, "The Immigrant in Detroit" (typescript, May 1915), in the ACD Papers, Box 1, Folder 2, 4.

152. Ibid., 23–27. A number of Cole's suggestions were based on his previous work in Cleveland. Raymond E. Cole, "The City's Responsibility to the Immigrant," *Immigrants in America Review* 1:2 (June 1915), 39–41. See also Jonathan Schwartz, "Henry Ford's Melting Pot," in *Ethnic Groups in the City*, ed. Otto Feinstein (Lexington, MA: Heath Lexington Books, 1971), 192.

153. Cole, "Immigrant in Detroit," 11–14; Zunz, *Changing Face of Inequality*, 311; Allan Nevins and Frank Ernest Hill, *Ford: Expansion and Challenge, 1915–1933* (New York: Charles Scribner's Sons, 1957), 1914.

154. On the YMCA's Americanization work, see Peter Roberts, "Night Schools," in National Conference of Charities and Correction, *Proceedings of the National Conference of Charities and Correction*, 1909 (Indianapolis: National Conference of Charities and Correction, 1909), 232.

155. Cole, "Immigrant in Detroit", 11, 17, 23. Cole also urged Detroit's civic leaders to create a central services and information clearinghouse to provide help to immigrants and their families. This suggestion was based on a program that originated in Cleveland. Cole, "Immigrant in Detroit," 23–26, "City's Responsibility to the Immigrant," 40–41. In 1918, Detroit created a Free Information Bureau that offered such services to the immigrants and their families until the early 1930s.

156. Byers Gitchall to Oscar Marx (July 15, 1915), ACD Papers, Box 1, Folder 2, 1; Byers Gitchall to Detroit Civic Leaders (typescript, n.d., but probably late July 1915), 1–3.

157. Esther Everett Lape, "The 'English First' Movement in Detroit," *Immigrants in America Review* 1:3 (September 1915). 46; National Americanization Committee and the Committee for Immigrants in America, *Americanizing a City*, 6–7, 19, 12–22.

158. "Minutes of the Committee on Education" (August 24, 1915), ACD Papers, Box 1, Folder 2; Lape, "The 'English First' Movement in Detroit," 47–49. For a sample of the English newspaper support, see "City's Night Schools,", 4; "Teaching English to Factory Employes [sic]," *Detroit News* (September 6, 1915), 4; "Night School Plan for Aliens Here to Aid Citizenship," *Detroit News Tribune* (September 5, 1915), 3.

159. Lape, "'English First' Movement in Detroit," 49.

160. Detroit Board of Education, *Seventy-third Annual Report of the Superintendent*, 1915–16, 108.

161. National Americanization Committee and the Committee for Immigrants in America, *Americanizing a City*, 12; Lape, "'English First' Movement in Detroit," 50.

162. Detroit Board of Education, *Seventy-third Annual Report of the Superinten-dent, 1915–16,* 113; "Record of Progress," *Immigrants in America Review* 2:1 (April 1916), 86; "Minutes of the Committee on Education, Detroit Board of Com-merce" (February 1, 1916), ACD Papers, Box 1, Folder 3, 1.

163. On YMCA Americanization work, see Thompson, *Schooling the Immigrant,* 57–59; "Evening Schools Make for Citizenship," 29; Hartmann, *Movement to Americanize the Immigrant,* 28; Peter Roberts, "The Y.M.C.A. among Immi-grants," *Survey* 33 (February 15, 1913), 697–700. See also C. Howard Hopkins, *History of the Y.M.C.A. in North America* (New York: Association Press, 1951), 477–478; Peter Roberts, "The Y.M.C.A. Teaching Foreign-Speaking Men," *Immigrants in America Review* 1:2 (June 1915), 18; Gerd Korman, "Americaniza-tion at the Factory Gate," *Industrial and Labor Relations Review* 18:3 (April 1965), 399–404.

164. Roberts, *Problem of Americanization,*; "Night Schools," "Y.M.C.A. among Immigrants," "Y M C A Teaching Foreign-Speaking Men."

165. Hartmann, *Movement to Americanize the Immigrant,* 28–29. The YMCA may have been the first organization to offer factory classes. See William M. Leiserson, *Adjusting Immigrant and Industry* (1924; repr. Montclair, NJ: Patterson Smith, 1971), 120.

166. Ford, *Americans All!* 108. On naturalizations in the military during this time see Susan B. Carter, Scott S. Gartner, Michael R. Haines, Alan L. Olmstead, Richard Sutch, and Gavin Wright, eds., *Historical Statistics of the United States,* vol. 1, pt. A, Population, "Aliens Naturalized by Provision, 1907–1997," table Ad., 1030–1037 (New York: Cambridge University Press, 2006), 641.

167. "Minutes of the Committee on Education, Detroit Board of Commerce" (February 1, 1916), 1; Peter Roberts, *Reader for Coming Americans* (New York: Young Men's Christian Association Press, 1910), 7, "Y.M.C.A. Teaching Foreign-Speaking Men," 20; "Minutes of the Committee on Education, Detroit Board of Commerce" (February 1, 1916), 1; Roberts, *Problem of Americanization,* 89–108.

168. Roberts, "Y.M.C.A. Teaching Foreign-Speaking Men," 20–21.

169. Roberts, *Reader for Coming Americans,* 7.

170. Detroit Board of Education, *Seventy-third Annual Report of the Superinten-dent, 1915–16,* 113–114. The "diploma" method, in which a certificate of course completion from a public school citizenship class sped up the naturalization process, was pioneered in Los Angeles. Americanizers in Detroit were aware of this process and probably used it as the model for their program. "Los Angeles Plan" (typescript, n.d., probably 1915), ACD Papers, Box 1, Folder 3.

171. Quoted in Schwartz, "Henry Ford's Melting Pot," 192. Nevins and Hill report that as late as 1919 Ford was still firing people who refused to take the English

course, but the number of people fired was small. In that year, thirty-eight people lost their jobs for refusing to take the English course. Nevins and Hill, *Ford: Expansion and Challenge, 1915–1933*, 340. See also National Americanization Committee and the Committee for Immigrants in America, *Americanizing a City*, 12.

172. National Americanization Committee and the Committee for Immigrants in America, *Americanizing a City*, 7–8, 10–11; Gregory Mason, "Americans First," *Outlook* 114 (September 27, 1916), 195; Frances Kellor, "Americanization by Industry," *Immigrants in America Review* 2:1 (April 1916), 24–25; Brophy, "'The Committee . . . has stood out against coercion,'" 14.

173. National Americanization Committee and the Committee for Immigrants in America, *Americanizing a City*, 11.

174. Mason, "Americans First," 196.

175. Brophy, "'The Committee . . . has stood out against coercion,'" 16.

176. Stephen Meyer III, *The Five Dollar Day: Labor Management and Social Control in the Ford Motor Company, 1908–1921* (Albany: State University of New York Press, 1981), 123–168.

177. Schwartz, "Henry Ford's Melting Pot," 192.

178. Mason, "Americans First," 200. Regarding his disdain for hyphenated citizenship, see Mason, "An Americanization Factory," 448. On how the Roberts system was used in the Ford schools, see Meyer, *Five Dollar Day*, 157–158, 162. In a supplementary pamphlet that contained one hundred important facts that Ford school students needed to know, only two of these facts, one about Columbus and another about Thaddeus Kosciusco [sic], had any relationship to someone with a background similar to that of any of the immigrants. See Ford Literary Club, *100 Facts* (Dearborn: Ford Motor Company, 1917), AJT Papers, Box 20, Ford English School Folder, 6.

179. Jeffrey Eugenides, *Middlesex* (New York: Farrar, Straus and Giroux, 2002), 104–105. Eugenides gives a terrific picture of the Ford graduation ceremony, but his timing of the event is off. The Greek immigrants who are central to his story came to the United States after the Turkish massacre of the Greek population of Smyrna in September 1922. By that time, Henry Ford had already closed down his Americanization schools and ended the pageants.

180. Mason, "Americans First," 199. The Ford school administrator is quoted in Meyer, *Five Dollar Day*, 160–161. See also Neil Baldwin, *Henry Ford and the Jews: The Mass Production of Hate* (New York: Public Affairs, 2001), 39–42; James R. Barrett, "Americanization from the Bottom Up: Immigration and the Remaking of the Working Class in the United States, 1880–1930," *Journal of American History* 79 (December 1992), 996; Schwartz, "Henry Ford's Melting Pot," 193.

181. Meyer, *Five Dollar Day*, 156.

182. Detroit Board of Education, *Seventy-third Annual Report of the Superinten-dent, 1915–16*, 115.

183. "Minutes of the Committee on Education, Detroit Board of Commerce" (December 16, 1915), in the ACD Papers, Box 1, Folder 2, 1–3.

184. "Minutes of the Americanization Committee" (August 21, 1916), in the ACD Papers, Box 1, Folder 2, 1. Leaders from various immigrant groups continued to meet with ACD leaders. See, for example, "Minutes of the Americanization Committee" (November 20, 1916), in the ACD Papers, Box 1, Folder 2, 1; "Minutes of the Americanization Committee" (August 13, 1917), in the ACD papers, Box 1, Folder 1916–17, 2.

185. "Information for the Committee on Education" (January 10, 1916), in the ACD Papers, Box 1, Correspondence, Minutes, Reports, 1916–17 Folder, 1–2.

186. For example, the 1925 annual report of the Americanization Committee of Detroit declared, "The Americanization Committee of Detroit wishes to take this opportunity of extending words of appreciation to the local foreign language press for the valuable support it has received during the past year." "Annual Report of the Americanization Committee of Detroit, 1925," in the ACD papers, Box 1, Folder 1922–25, 19. See also Mary O'Donnell Turner to Arthur J. Tuttle (May 27, 1929), in the ACD Papers, Box 1, Folder 1926–31, 1.

187. Ford, *Americans All!* 24.

188. "First National Conference on Americanization and Immigration" (typescript, n.d., but probably February 1916), ACD Papers, Box 1, Folder 1916–17, 1. See also "The National Conference on Immigration and Americanization," *Immigrants in America Review* 2:1 (April 1916), 38–47; Hartmann, *Movement to Americanize the Immigrant*, 134–135.

189. Hartmann, *Movement to Americanize the Immigrant*, 131.

190. Ibid., 149, 184.

191. Henry Hoyt, "Michigan's Sad Failure in Americanization Work," *Detroit Saturday Night* (December 15, 1917), 4. The failure Hoyt refers to was the inability of the Michigan legislature to pass a bill supporting Americanization efforts in the state.

192. "Minutes of the Committee on Education, Detroit Board of Commerce" (April 13, 1916), ACD Papers, Box 1, Folder 1916–17, 1. Prior to the visit, the Immigrants' Protective League of Chicago brought together the Association of Commerce, the City Club, the Union League Club, and various women's groups, to form the Joint Committee on the Education of the Foreigner, whose goal was improving the quality of Americanization education efforts in Chicago, with particular emphasis on bolstering the city's night schools. Hartmann, *Movement to Americanize the Immigrant*, 160. "City Observes Fourth, Sane but Patriotic," *Chicago Daily Tribune* (July 5, 1917), 5.

193. "Record of Progress," 84.
194. The Americanization Committee of the Pittsburgh Chamber of Commerce, *First Annual Report of the Americanization Bureau, 1921–22* (Pittsburgh: The Committee, 1922), i–ii.
195. Hoyt, "Michigan's Sad Failure in Americanization Work"; Raymond E. Cole, *A Hand Book of Industrial Americanization* (Cleveland: Mayor's War Advisory Committee, 1917), 4. See also Edward M. Miggins, "Becoming American: Americanization and the Reform of the Cleveland Public Schools," in *The Birth of Modern Cleveland, 1865–1930*, ed. Thomas F. Campbell and Edward M. Miggins (Cleveland: Western Reserve Historical Society, 1988), 361.
196. Boston Public Schools, *Annual Report of the Superintendent*, 1917 (Boston: Boston Public Schools Printing Department, 1918), 61; Cohen, *Children of the Mill*, 33, 66–67; Hartmann, *Movement to Americanize the Immigrant*, 150–163.
197. Thompson, *Schooling of the Immigrant*, 79.
198. Detroit Board of Education, *Seventy-fourth Annual Report of the Board of Education, 1916–17* (Detroit: The Board, 1917), 12–13. On the continuing publicity campaign in Detroit, see "Minutes of the Americanization Committee" (January 2, 1917), ACD papers, Box 1, 1916–17 Folder, 1–2.
199. Cleveland Public Schools, *The Eighty-second Annual Report of the Board of Education, 1917–18* (Cleveland: The Board, 1918), 115. The 1916–1917 total is the one listed in a table showing a decade of evening elementary school enrollments. However, the 1916–1917 annual report gives a higher figure: 5,309. I cannot explain the discrepancy but chose the smaller number because it was used for future discussions of developments in Cleveland. Cleveland Board of Education, *The Eighty-first Annual Report of the Superintendent of Schools, 1916–17* (Cleveland: The Board, 1917), 54,
200. Cleveland Board of Education, *Eighty-first Annual Report of the Superintendent of Schools, 1916–17*, 57.
201. These enrollment numbers are based on the annual table "Countries of Birth of Pupils in Evening Schools" that appeared in the statistical section on evening schools. This table lists high school and elementary school enrollments. I subtracted the students listed as born in the United States. Boston Public Schools, *Annual Statistics of the Boston Public Schools, 1913–14* (Boston: Boston Public Schools Printing Department, 1914), 47; Boston Public Schools, *Annual Statistics of the Boston Public Schools, 1916–17* (Boston: Boston Public Schools Printing Department, 1917), 49. Massachusetts had a law requiring immigrants who were illiterate minors (defined as young people between the ages of sixteen and twenty-one) to attend literacy classes. These students were not included in the numbers

cited above. However, in both cases, the trends were identical. In 1914–1915 there were over 5,000 minors in mandatory evening school classes. In November 1920, only 427 students enrolled in these classes. Boston Public Schools, *Annual Report of the Superintendent, 1920*, 45. On the passage of the compulsory education law for these students and the development of evening schools in Massachusetts generally, see Lazerson, *Origins of the Urban School*, 215, 213–233.

202. I computed these numbers from the table that listed distribution by nativity, age, and sex in the evening elementary schools, by subtracting U.S.-born students from the totals listed. Philadelphia Board of Education, *Annual Report of the Superintendent of Schools, 1914* (Philadelphia: Walther Printing, 1915), Table 24; Philadelphia Board of Education, *Annual Report of the Superintendent of Schools, 1917* (Philadelphia: Walther Printing, 1918), Table 29.

203. Department of Education, City of New York, *The Nineteenth Annual Report of the Superintendent of Schools, 1916–17: Evening Schools* (New York: The Board, 1917), 45, 24.

204. Detroit Board of Education, *The Seventy-fourth Annual Report of the Board of Education, 1916–17*, 12; Cleveland Board of Education, *Eighty-first Annual Report of the Superintendent of Schools, 1916–17*, 51, 57.

205. Brophy, "'The Committee . . . has stood out against coercion,'" 20.

206. Ford, *Americans All!* 3.

207. U.S. Bureau of the Census, *Historical Statistics of the United States, Colonial Times to 1970* (Washington, DC: Government Printing Office, 1975), 135.

208. U.S. Bureau of Education, *Americanization as a War Measure: Report of a Conference Called by the Secretary of the Interior, and Held in Washington, April 3, 1918* (Washington, DC: Government Printing Office, 1918), 27.

209. Boston Public Schools, *Annual Statistics of the Boston Public Schools, 1913–14)*, 47; Boston Public Schools, *Annual Statistics of the Boston Public Schools, 1917–18* (Boston: Boston Public Schools Printing Department, 1918), 54. Boston Public Schools, *Annual Report of the Superintendent, 1919* (Boston: Boston Public Schools Printing Department, 1919), 31.

210. Maxine S. Seller, "Success and Failure in Adult Education: The Immigrant Experience 1914–1924" *Adult Education* 28:2 (1978), 87.

211. Hartmann, *Movement to Americanize the Immigrant*, 174–176, 194–196. The bulletins included Fred Clayton Butler's *State Americanization: The Part of the State in the Education and Assimilation of the Immigrant* (Washington, DC; Government Printing Office, 1919) and *Community Americanization: A Handbook for Workers*, Bulletin 1919, no. 76 (Washington, DC: U.S. Government Printing Office, 1920).

212. Hartmann, *Movement to Americanize the Immigrant*, 183–184, 195. See also Kellor, "Americanization by Industry," 15–26.
213. "Minutes of the Americanization Committee" (August 13, 1917), 1–3; Americanization Committee of Detroit, "Annual Report of the Americanization Committee for the Year Ending March 31, 1919" (typescript, 1931), ACD Papers, Box 1, Folder 1918–21, 1–2.
214. Hill, "Americanization Movement," 623; J. S. Kershner, "Cleveland—Pioneer in Americanization," *I & N Reporter* 3 (April 1955), 60.
215. These numbers are based on data in George A. Green, "Americanization," in the Cleveland Foundation, *The Cleveland Yearbook*, 1921 (Cleveland: The Foundation, 1921), 195–196, 198. See also Hill, "The Americanization Movement," 622–623, 629–630; Miggins, "Becoming American, 361–362; Kershner, "Cleveland—Pioneer in Americanization," 60; Cole, *A Hand Book of Industrial Americanization*.
216. Board of Education of the City of Chicago and the Chicago Association of Commerce, *A Year of Americanization Work, July 1918–July 1919.*
217. Harry H. Merrick, "To the Members of the Chicago Association of Commerce," in the Board of Education of the City of Chicago and the Chicago Association of Commerce, *A Year of Americanization Work, July 1918–July 1919*, 1.
218. These data come from a table entitled "Nationalities of Pupils in Classes for Foreign-Born." However, neither the 1917–1918 nor the 1918–1919 totals in that table match the total number of students listed as being enrolled, provided in "Classes in English for the Foreign-Born." The 1917–1918 total for that table was 5,143, and the 1918–1919 total was 3,074. I cannot explain these discrepancies, but in both cases the total was substantially lower than the number enrolled listed for 1916–1917. Public Schools of the City of Chicago, *Sixty-fourth Annual Report of the Chicago Board of Education*, 1917–18, 217–218; Public Schools of the City of Chicago, *Sixty-fifth Annual Report of the Chicago Board of Education*, 1917–18, 146–147.
219. "Minutes of the Americanization Committee" (October 9, 1917), in the ACD papers, Box Three, 1. In a talk to the NEA in July 1922, Cody mentioned that Ford had indeed ended its Americanization school program. Frank Cody, "Remarks on Factory Classes," *Proceedings of the Sixtieth Annual Meeting of the National Education Association*, 1922, 968.
220. Nevins and Hill, *Ford: Expansion and Challenge, 1915–1933*, 340–341.
221. "Minutes of the Americanization Committee (October 29, 1917), in the ACD Papers, Box 1, Folder Three, 1–2,
222. Americanization Committee of Detroit, "Annual Report of the Americanization Committee for the Year Ending March 31, 1919," in the ACD Papers, Box 1, Folder 1918–21, 2. A considerable part of the decline in night school atten-

dance in the 1918–1919 school year in Detroit and the nation generally was the outbreak of the virulent and deadly Spanish flu. John M. Barry, *The Great Influenza: The Epic Story of the Greatest Plague in History* (New York: Penguin, 2004).

223. Philadelphia Board of Education, *Annual Report of the Superintendent of Schools, 1920* (Philadelphia: Walther Printing, 1921), 12–13; Philadelphia Board of Education, *Annual Report of the Superintendent of Schools, 1919* (Philadelphia: Walther Printing, 1920), Table 2. In his 1922 annual report, Peter Mortenson also blamed immigrants and their employers for the "decrease in the enthusiasm" for Americanization courses in previous years. He did note that in 1921–1922 enrollments were picking up. The Public Schools of the City of Chicago, *Sixty-sixth Annual Report of the Chicago Board of Education, 1921–22* (Chicago: The Board, 1922), 11.

224. Esther Everett Lape, "Americanization," *Columbia University Quarterly* 20:1 (January 1918), 59. See also Frances A. Kellor, "What Is Americanization?" *Yale Review* 8 (January 1919), 289; Seller, "Success and Failure in Adult Education," 87.

225. Kellor, "What Is Americanization?" 289.

226. Kenneth L. Roberts, "Guests from Italy," *Saturday Evening Post* 193:8 (August 21, 1920), 140. See also John J. Mahoney, "Americanization in the United States," in *Biennial Survey of Education, 1920–21*, U.S. Bureau of Education Bulletin 1924, no. 13 (Washington, DC: U.S. Government Printing Office, 1924), 639.

227. Cody, "What One Representative American City Is Doing in Teaching Americanism," 763.

228. Cody, "Remarks on Factory Classes," 968.

229. John McClymer's excellent analysis of the Americanization campaign argues that the campaign was more of a disappointment than a failure. He argues that between 1915 and 1925 "a minimum of 1,000,000 immigrants—and probably many more—enrolled in formal public school Americanization classes during the whole period," but due to the huge number of dropouts "the true minimum" reached by public school Americanization programs was "around 400,000." In other words, the campaign was neither a great success nor an utter disaster. John F. McClymer, "The Americanization Movement and the Education of the Foreign-Born Adult, 1914–25," in Weiss, *American Education and the European Immigrant, 1840–1940*, 103–105. For different views of the "failure" of these programs see Michael R. Olneck, "Americanization and the Education of Immigrants, 1900–1925," 398–423; Roediger, *Working toward Whiteness*, 143–145.

230. "Americanski," *Saturday Evening Post* 193 (May 14, 1921), 20. For similar statements, see Henry Pratt Fairchild, "Americanizing the Immigrant," *Yale*

Review 5:4 (July 1916), 731–740, and "Know Thy Pupil," *Journal of Educational Sociology* 1:9 (May 1928), 553–554.

231. Cleveland Board of Education, *The Eighty-fifth Annual Report of the Board of Education: The First of a Series of Surveys of Department of Instruction of the Cleveland Public Schools, 1920–21* (Cleveland: The Board, 1921), 28. See also "104 English Classes Open in 56 Different Centers," *Cleveland Americaniza-tion Bulletin* 1:1 (October 15, 1919), 1, and "A Brief Report of the Work of the Americanization Council," *Cleveland Americanization Bulletin* 1:4 (January 5, 1920), 1 in the WRHS.

232. Quoted in McClymer, "Americanization Movement and the Education of the Foreign-Born Adult, 1914–25," 98.

233. The Public Schools of the City of Chicago, *Sixty-sixth Annual Report of the Chicago Board of Education, 1921–22*, 105; Detroit Board of Education, *Seventy-ninth Annual Report of the Superintendent, 1921–22* (Detroit: The Board, 1922), 104; Houtman, "Response of the Detroit Public Schools to Immigrant Groups," 64; Detroit Board of Education, *Seventy-seventh Annual Report of the Superintendent, 1919–20* (Detroit: The Board, 1920), 42.

234. Boston Public Schools, *Annual Statistics of the Boston Public Schools, 1919–20* (Boston: Boston Public Schools Printing Department, 1920), 56; Boston Public Schools, *Annual Statistics of the Boston Public Schools, 1920–21* (Boston: Boston Public Schools Printing Department, 1921), 56.

235. John M. Blum, "Nativism, Anti-Radicalism, and the Foreign Scare, 1917–1920," *Midwest Journal* 3:1 (Winter 1950–1951), 51–53; Higham, *Strangers in the Land*, 231; Kennedy, *Over Here*, 288–289; Regin Schmidt, *Red Scare: The FBI and the Origins of Anticommunism in the United States, 1919–1943* (Copenhagen: Museum Tusculanum Press, 2000), 149, 293, 304.

236. Frank D. Loomis, *Americanization in Chicago* (Chicago: Chicago Community Trust, 1920), 15–18.

237. Higham, *Strangers in the Land*, 308–312.

238. Detroit Board of Education, *Seventy-second Annual Report of the Board of Education, 1914–15*, 127; Detroit Board of Education, *Seventy-third Annual Report of the Board of Education, 1915–16*, 120–121; Public Schools of the City of Chicago, *Sixty-fourth Annual Report of the Chicago Board of Education, 1917–18*, 218; Public Schools of the City of Chicago, *Sixty-fifth Annual Report of the Chicago Board of Education, 1918–19*, 147. The special educational problems of immigrant women were discussed as early as 1904, but school leaders did not focus on them until much later. See Balliet, "Organization of a System of Evening Schools," 284.

239. John Palmer Gavit, *Americans by Choice* (1922; repr. Montclair, NJ: Patterson Smith, 1971), 330–334.

240. "Annual Report of the Americanization Committee for the Year Ending March 31, 1920," in the ACD Papers, Box 1, Folder 1918–21, 8–9; "Americanization Committee—Report—April 1, 1921–March 31, 1922," in the ACD papers, Box 1, Folder 1922–25, 9–10; Frederick S. DeGalan, "Immigration v. Americanization," *Detroit Journal of Education* 2:1 (September 1921), 17–18.

241. "Americanization Announcements," *Detroit Education Bulletin* 3:5 (January 1920), 8. These efforts appear to have boosted enrollments of women to some degree. In 1916–1917, for example, women accounted for almost a third of the enrollments in English for Foreigners classes, up from merely 10 percent a decade earlier. Detroit Board of Education, *Eighty-fourth Annual Report of the Detroit Public Schools, 1926–27* (Detroit: The Board, 1927), 121.

242. Detroit Board of Education, *Seventy-ninth Annual Report of the Superintendent, 1921–22,* 104.

243. Loomis, *Americanization in Chicago,* 22; Catherine E. Wycoff, "The Shaping of an American Woman: The Chicago Settlement Houses and Immigrant Women, 1889–1928" (master's thesis, University of Illinois–Urbana-Champaign, 1995), 7; Cleveland Board of Education, *The Report of the Superintendent of Schools to the Board of Education of the City School District of the City of Cleveland, 1927–28* (Cleveland: The Board, 1928), 87. On Cincinnati, see Condon, "Education of the Immigrant," 559.

244. Prior to the passage of the Cable Act, the wives of U.S. citizens automatically became citizens when their husbands naturalized, as did minor children of the marriage. Schneider, "Naturalization and United States Citizenship in Two Periods of Mass Migration," 59–60. See also Marlene Gombach, "Slovenian Women in Cleveland Learning English" (paper presented at the History of Education Society Conference, Cleveland, 2007, in my possession), 15, 27; Aristide Zolberg, *A Nation by Design: Immigration Policy in the Fashioning of America* (Cambridge: Harvard University Press, 2006), 253–254; Butler, *Community Americanization,* 36–38.

245. The quote on Akron is in John J. Mahoney, "Americanization in the United States," *Biennial Survey of Education, 1920–1922* 1:13 (Washington, DC: Government Printing Office, 1924), 647. See also Chester A. Graham, "Akron Americanization Program at Work" (February 26, 1923), in the CAG Papers, Box 2, Folder–Americanization of Immigrants/Annual Reports #1,1.3. Los Angeles was particularly active in working with immigrant women. See the Los Angeles City School District, *Elementary Adult Education 1916–1919,* School Publication no. 27 (Los Angeles: The District, 1919), 38–77. On the Home Teacher Act in California, which was mainly devoted to educating immigrant women, see Raftery, *Land of Fair Promise,* 72–86.

246. Owen B. Hoban, "Americanization—Wise and Unwise," in *Proceedings of the Sixtieth Annual Meeting of the National Education Association*, 1922, 912.

247. Detroit Board of Education, *Seventy-ninth Annual Report of the Superintendent*, 1921–22, 104; Detroit Board of Education, *Eighty-third Annual Report of the Detroit Public Schools*, 1925–26 (Detroit, MI: The Board, 1926), 125.

248. On this, see Brophy, " 'The Committee . . . has stood out against coercion,' " 33.

249. In 1918, about 42 percent of all naturalizations were due to military service. This percentage leaped to about 59 percent the following year, fell off to 29 percent in 1920, and then dropped to just under 10 percent in 1921. In her comprehensive discussion of naturalizations in this era, Dorothee Schneider argues that, the "only naturalization program that could be called a success was military naturalization." See Dorothee Schneider, "Naturalization and United States Citizenship in Two Periods of Mass Migration: 1894–1930, 1965–2000," *Journal of American Ethnic History* 21:1 (Fall 2001), 61, 55–63. Carter et al., *Historical Statistics of the United States*, vol. 1, pt. A, Population, "Aliens Naturalized by Provision 1907–1997," table Ad., 1030–1037, 641.

250. Thompson, *Schooling of the Immigrant*, 13–14. Thompson argued that the European imperial efforts to force Germanization or Hungarianization were not models the United States should emulate (7–8). Detroit superintendent Frank Cody also noted that Americanization courses should be voluntary. Cody, "Remarks on Factory Classes," 968.

251. Julius Drachsler, *Democracy and Assimilation: The Blending of Immigrant Heritages in America* (New York: Macmillan, 1920), 195–196. On the immigrants' comparison of Americanization to Russification and other forms of European cultural hegemony, see Seller, "Success and Failure in Adult Education," 88; and "A Conference of Lithuanians and Americans."

252. Albert Shiels, "Education for Citizenship," in *Proceedings of the Sixtieth Annual Meeting of the National Education Association*, 1922, 939–940. John J. Mahoney also saw such coercion as a failure of Americans to live up to their democratic creed. Mahoney, "Americanization in the United States," 638. See also Lape, "Americanization," 59, 80. For a similar assessment, see Kellor, "What Is Americanization?" 289–290.

253. Frederic Woellner, "The Teaching of History as a Factor in Americanization," *Ohio Teacher* 41:7 (March 1920), 310. For similar sentiments, see Butler, *Community Americanization*, 13–14. See also Butler, *State Americanization*, 8.

254. For more than a decade, Roberts had been arguing that Americanization educators needed to know and respect the immigrants' culture in order to be effective in the classroom. See, for example, Roberts, "Night Schools," 236; "Minutes of the Committee on Education, Detroit Board of Commerce" (February 1, 1916), 1; Roberts, *Problem of Americanization*, 29–32.

255. Peter Roberts, "The Viewpoint of the Y.M.C.A. in Americanization," in *Proceedings of the First General State Conference of All Agencies Interested in Americanization* (December 1920), 51–52, in the WRHS. Roberts's sentiments apparently were shared by other leaders in the YMCA. Raymond A. Mohl and Neil Betten point out that in the 1920s and 1930s, the YMCA created a number of international institutes to aid immigrants in numerous cites across the country. While these institutes carried out many traditional Americanization activities, they also were centers for "helping various ethnic groups to maintain cultural identity and a positive self-image." Raymond A. Mohl and Neil Betten, "Ethnic Adjustment in the Industrial City: The International Institute of Gary, 1919–1940," *International Migration Review* 6:4 (Winter 1972), 362, 361–376. On the "cultural gifts" these immigrants brought to the United States, see Hoban, "Americanization—Wise and Unwise," 912, 912–914; and the poem by Robert Haven Schauffler, "Scum o' the Earth," in *The Little Book of Modern Verse*, ed. Jessie Belle Rittenhouse (Boston: Houghton Mifflin, 1913), 105–108.

256. Garry C. Myers, "The Human Wish in Americanization," *Ohio Teacher* 41:2 (October 1921), 65.

257. J. V. Breitwieser, "Adult Immigrant Education," *American Review* 3 (January 1925), 61. Robert Park and Herbert Miller make a similar argument. Park and Miller, *Old World Traits Transplanted* (Harper and Brothers, 1921), 273, 280.

258. Philip Davis, "How to Americanize the Immigrant: Definition of Americanization," in Davis, *Immigration and Americanization*, 668.

259. David Tyack, *Seeking Common Ground: Public Schools in a Diverse Society* (Cambridge: Harvard University Press, 2003), 79–80. See also Eric Kaufmann, *The Rise and Fall of Anglo-America* (Cambridge: Harvard University Press, 2004), 157–174; Moreau, *Schoolbook Nation*, 201–207; Zimmerman, *Whose America?* 9, 22–25.

260. Selig, *Americans All*, 6.

261. Brophy, "'The Committee . . . has stood out against coercion,'" 28, 31, 36, 21–39.

262. Ibid., 20–21.

263. On this process, see Higham, "Cultural Responses to Immigration," 52–53.

3 Americanization and the Foreign Language Press, 1890–1930

1. John Bodnar, *The Transplanted: A History of Immigrants in Urban America* (Bloomington: Indiana University Press, 1985), 184–205; Otis L. Graham Jr. and Elizabeth Koed, "Americanizing the Immigrants, Past and Future: History and Implication of a Social Movement," *Public Historian* 15:4 (Fall 1993), 37.

2. Maxine S. Seller, "Success and Failure in Adult Education: The Immigrant Experience 1914–1924," *Adult Education* 28:2 (1978), 88, 94.

3. For similar statements, see Lubomyr R. Wynar and Anna T. Wynar, *Encyclopedic Directory of Ethnic Newspapers and Periodicals in the United States* (Littleton, CO: Libraries Unlimited, 1976), 18; Hanno Hardt, "The Foreign-Language Press in American Press History," *Journal of Communication* 39:2 (Spring 1989), 122–125; Sally M. Miller, ed., *The Ethnic Press in the United States* (Greenwood, CT: Greenwood Press, 1987), xv–xvi; William Carlson Smith, *Americans in the Making: The Natural History of the Assimilation of Immigrants* (New York: D. Appleton-Century, 1939), 191.

4. Joshua Fishman et al, *Language Loyalty in the United States* (London: Mouton, 1966), 52, 53, 56, 57, 58, 63, 64.

5. Robert Park, *The Immigrant Press and Its Control* (New York: Harper and Brothers, 1922), 6–7; Seller, "Success and Failure in Adult Education," 94.

6. Park, *The Immigrant Press and Its Control*, 79–87; Carl F. Kaestle, Helen Damon-Moore, Lawrence C. Stedman, Katherine Tinsley, and William Vance Trollinger Jr., *Literacy in the United States: Readers and Reading since 1880* (New Haven: Yale University Press, 1991), 281; Horace M. Kallen, *Culture and Democracy in the United States* (New York: Boni and Liveright, 1924), 162–163. Perhaps the best-known example of a foreign language newspaper providing advice about life in the United States was the "Bintel Brief" section of the *Jewish Daily Forward.* See Isaac Metzker, *A Bintel Brief* (New York: Ballantine Books, 1971).

7. Edward Hale Bierstadt, *Aspects of Americanization* (Cincinnati: Stewart Kidd, 1922), 85.

8. Harry Lipsky, "Cooperation of Foreign-Language Press," in *Immigration and Americanization,* ed. Philip Davis (New York: Ginn, 1920), 721. For other examples, see Park, *The Immigrant Press and Its Control*, 87; Marshall Beuick, "The Declining Immigrant Press," *Social Forces* 6:2 (December 1927), 257–259; Bierstadt, *Aspects of Americanization*, 72; Lawrence A. Cremin, *American Education: the Metropolitan Experience, 1876–1980* (New York: Harper and Row, 1988), 144; Hyman Horowitz, "The Jew and the Jewish Press in America," CFLND, 1937–3, 129; Charles Jaret, "The Greek, Italian, and Jewish American Press: A Comparative Analysis," *Journal of Ethnic Studies* 7:2 (Summer 1979), 47; Kaestle et al., *Literacy in the United States*, 281; George E. Pozzetta, "The Italian Immigrant Press of New York City: The Early Years, 1880–1915," *Journal of Ethnic Studies* 1:3 (Fall 1973), 32; Jerzy Zubzycki, "The Role of the Foreign Language Press in Migrant Integration," *Population Studies* 12:1 (July 1958), 79. A very useful examination of the role of the Yiddish press of New York City in Americanization can be found in Mordecai Soltes, *The Yiddish Press: An*

Americanizing Agency (1925; repr. New York: Arno Press and the New York Times, 1969).

9. Fred Clayton Butler, *State Americanization*, Department of the Interior Bulletin 1919, no. 77 (Washington, DC: Government Printing Office, 1920), 10; Bureau of Foreign Language Information Service, *The Work of the Foreign Language Information Service of the American Red Cross* (Washington, DC: American Red Cross, 1920), 7–8; Edward G. Hartmann, *The Movement to Americanize the Immigrant* (New York: Columbia University Press, 1948), 222–223; Frances A. Kellor, "Straight America," *Immigrants in America Review* 2:2 (July 1916), 15; National Americanization Committee and the Committee for Immigrants in America, *Americanizing a City: The Campaign for the Detroit Night Schools Conducted in Cooperation with the Detroit Board of Commerce and Board of Education, August–September, 1915* (New York: The Committees, 1915), 19. Some people, however, vehemently denounced the foreign language press, seeing it as an agent of division and disloyalty. See, for example, U.S. Department of the Interior, Bureau of Education, *Americanization as a War Measure*, Bulletin 1918, no. 18 (Washington, DC: Government Printing Office, 1918), 24–25; Henry Pratt Fairchild, *The Melting Pot Mistake* (Boston: Little, Brown, 1926), 231–232; Desmond King, *Making Americans: Immigration, Race, and the Origins of Diverse Democracy* (Cambridge: Harvard University Press, 2000), 110–113.

10. Mary O'Donnell Turner to Arthur J. Tuttle (May 27, 1929), AJT Papers, Box 1, Folder 1926–31.

11. Board of Education of the City of Chicago and the Chicago Association of Commerce, *A Year of Americanization Work, July 1918–July 1919* (Chicago: The Board, 1919), 20.

12. Frank D. Loomis, *Americanization in Chicago* (Chicago: Chicago Community Trust, 1920), 26.

13. Peter Lambros, *Scrapbook* (February 22, 1922), 1, CFLPS, Greeks, IJ. Under Lambros's more than four decades of leadership, the *Greek Star*, or *Star*, became "the leading Greek-language newspaper" in Chicago. Andrew T. Kopan, "The Greek Press," in Miller, *Ethnic Press in the United States*, 166.

14. Julianna Puskas, "The Magyars in Cleveland, 1880–1930," in *Identity, Conflict, and Cooperation: Central Europeans in Cleveland, 1850–1930*, ed. David C. Hammack, Diane L. Grabowski, and John J. Grabowski (Cleveland: Western Reserve Historical Society, 2002), 170; Adam Walaszek, "Polish Americans," in Hammack, Grabowski, and Grabowski, *Identity, Conflict, and Cooperation*, 224, 230. See also "Cleveland Americanization Council" *Cleveland Americanization Bulletin* 1:1 (October 15, 1919), 1, in the WRHS. On other cities, see the Americanization Committee of the Pittsburgh Chamber of Commerce, *First*

Annual Report of the Americanization Bureau, 1921–22 (Pittsburgh: The Committee, 1922), 8; "Annual Report of the Americanization Department of the Akron [Ohio] Public Schools, September 1, 1923 to August 31, 1924" (typescript), 16, CAG, Box 2, Folder: Americanization of Immigrants, Annual Reports, 1. During World War I, the federal government also enlisted foreign language newspapers in Americanization efforts, as did the Carnegie Corporation. See David Kennedy, *Over Here* (New York: Oxford University Press, 2004), 41, 59–66; Daniel Erwin Weinberg, "The Foreign Language Information Service and the Foreign Born, 1918–1939: A Case Study of Cultural Assimilation Viewed as a Problem in Social Technology" (Ph.D. diss., University of Minnesota, 1973).

15. Two notable exceptions are Jonathan Zimmerman, "Ethnics against Ethnicity: European Immigrants and Foreign-Language Instruction, 1890–1940," *Journal of American History* 87:1 (March 2002), 1383–1404; and John F. McClymer, "The Americanization Movement and the Education of the Foreign-Born Adults, 1914–1925," in *American Education and the European Immigrant, 1840–1940,* ed. Bernard J. Weiss (Urbana: University of Illinois Press, 1982), 110–111. In his classic study of Americanization, Edward Hartmann quotes a number of foreign language press editorials. See Hartmann, *Movement to Americanize the Immigrant,* 256–258. Given that these editorials appeared in 1919–1920, the period of intensely aggressive Americanization efforts, some of the editorials are quite critical of Americanization programs, while others sought to redefine it in ways similar to that of the Chicago papers.

16. Ronald D. Cohen and Raymond A. Mohl make a similar argument in their book *The Paradox of Progressive Education: The Gary Plan and Urban Schooling* (Port Washington, NY: Kennikat Press, 1979), 108.

17. Horace Kallen, *Culture and Democracy in the United States* (New York: Boni and Liveright, 1924), 200–201; Michael Walzer, *What It Means to Be an American* (New York: Marsilio, 1996), 37.

18. For examples of stances similar to patriotic pluralism, see June Granatir Alexander, *Ethnic Pride, American Patriotism: Slovaks and Other New Immigrants in the Interwar Years* (Philadelphia: Temple University Press, 2004); James R. Barrett, "Americanization from the Bottom Up: Immigration and the Remaking of the Working Class in the United States, 1890–1930," *Journal of American History* 79 (December 1992), 996–1020: Gary Gerstle, *Working-Class Americanism: The Politics of Labor in a Textile City, 1914–1960* (Princeton: Princeton University Press, 2002), 153–195; Thomas Gobel, "Becoming Americans: Ethnic Workers and the Rise of the CIO," *Labor History* 29 (Spring 1988), 173–198.

19. "The Public Schools Are the Bulwark of the Nation," *Star* (October 21, 1904), 1, CFLPS, Greek, IA1a. On the support for public education among immigrant

leaders, also based on newspapers in the CFLPS, see Kathryn M. Neckerman, *Schools Betrayed: Roots of Failure in Inner-City Education* (Chicago: University of Chicago Press, 2007), 65–66.

20. "Attention! To What Kind of Schools Should We Send Our Polish Children[?]" *Dziennik Ludowy* (September 4, 1907), 1, CFLPS, Polish, IA2a. On *Dziennik Ludowy*, see Edward R. Kantowicz, *Polish-American Politics in Chicago* (Chicago: University of Chicago Press, 1975), 29. For a very similar statement, see "In Regard to Parochial Schools," *Tribuna Italiana* (September 9, 1906), 1, CFLPS, Italian, IA1a.

21. "Prof. Ross's Attack on Foreign-Born Citizens," *L'Italia* (February 1, 1914), 4, CFLPS, Italian, IIIG. For other examples of strong support for public schools, see also "How to Obtain Education," *Lietuva* 16:50 (December 13, 1907), 1, CFLPS, Lithuanian, IA1a; "Leave Your Children in School," *Denni Hlasatel* (September 11, 1915), 1, 7, CFLPS, Bohemian IA1a; "Child Labor" *Radnicka Straza* (May 10, 1916), 3, 4, CFLPS, Croatian, IH; "Graduation Day Has Become a Jewish Holiday," *Jewish Daily Forward* (June 15, 1924), 1, CFLPS, Jewish, IA1a; "Against the Menace of Closing the Public Schools," *Vita Nuova* (June 1929), 1–2, CFLPS, Serbian, IA1a. See also Alexandra Kuropas, "*Svoboda* and the Education of Rusyn-Ukrainians in America, 1893–1914: A Study of an Ethnic Newspaper" (master's thesis, Northern Illinois University, 1995), 129.

22. Joshua Seligman, "The Great and Free American Public School," *Jewish Daily Courier* (January 16, 1922), 1, CFLPS, Jewish, IA1a. The second article appeared on January 20, 1922, CFLPS, Jewish, IA1a. See also Soltes, *Yiddish Press*, 151–153. Czechs in Cleveland were largely positive in their assessment of the city's public schools as well. See Jeanne Kota Rossi, "Children of Czech Immigrants: Education and Acculturation in Cleveland, Ohio, 1920–1940" (Ph.D. diss., Cleveland State University, 2006), 111, 115–116, 136, 163–172.

23. On this issue, see Alexander, *Ethnic Pride, American Patriotism*, 60; John J. Kulczycki, *School Strikes in Prussian Poland: The Struggle over Bilingual Education* (Boulder, CO: East European Monographs, 1981); Robin Okey, *The Hapsburg Monarchy from Enlightenment to Eclipse* (New York: Palgrave Macmillan, 2002), 284–292.

24. The journalist is quoted in Zimmerman, "Ethnics against Ethnicity," 1383.

25. Richard Alba and Victor Nee, *Remaking the American Mainstream: Assimilation and Contemporary Immigration* (Cambridge: Harvard University Press, 2003), 72.

26. Zimmerman, "Ethnics against Ethnicity," 1386.

27. "The Polish Language in America," *Narod Polski* (July 5, 1911), 1, CFLPS, Polish, IA2b. On *Narod Polski*, see Jan Kowalik, *The Polish Press in America* (San Francisco: R & E Research Associates, 1978), 19.

28. "Our Schools and the Lithuanian Language," *Lietuva* (September 19, 1913), 2–3, CFLPS, Lithuanian, IA3. *Lietuva* was "the most distinguished [Lithuanian] newspaper during the first twenty years of the twentieth century." See Edgar Anderson and M. G. Slavenas, "The Latvian and Lithuanian Press," in Miller, *Ethnic Press in the United States*, 240.

29. "American Educational Facilities for the Foreign Born," *Saloniki* (June 25, 1921), 1, CFLPS, Greek, IA3. See also "What Can I Do," *Saloniki* (January 28, 1922), CFLPS, Greek, IC. For other examples of this stance, see "All Italian Children Must Learn English Language," *L'Italia* (March 23, 1889), CFLPS, Italian, IA1a; "Americanization," *Magyar Tribune* (November 22, 1918), 1, CFLPS, Hungarian IIIA. Hungarians in Cleveland responded in similar ways. See also Juliana Puskas, "The Magyars in Cleveland, 1880–1930," in Hammack, Grabowski, and Grabowski, *Identity, Conflict, and Cooperation*, 173. Slovaks also saw learning English as "indispensable" but they were equally committed to teaching their native language to their children. See Alexander, *Ethnic Pride, American Patriotism*, 61–63, 140.

30. "Evening Schools," *Dziennik Zwiazkowy* (October 8, 1910), 1, CFLPS, Polish, IA1a. On the wide range of Polish newspapers in Chicago and the rest of the United States, see Kantowicz, *Polish-American Politics in Chicago*, 30–37; A. J. Kuzniewski, "The Polish-American Press," in Miller, *Ethnic Press in the United States*, 278–282; Edmund G. Olszyk, *The Polish Press in America* (Milwaukee: Marquette University Press, 1940), 84. On the PNA, see Donald E. Pienkos, *P. N. A. Centennial History* (New York: Columbia University Press, 1984).

31. "Learn the English Language," *Ujednujeno Srbstvo* (October 31, 1922), 2, CFLPS, Serbian, IA3.

32. For other examples, see "About Evening Schools," *Lietuva* 3:43 (October 26, 1895), CFLPS, Lithuanian, IA3; "Evening School for Adults Opens," *Svenska Tribunen-Nyheter* (October 23, 1906), 1, CFLPS, Swedish IA3; "More Greeks Enrolled at Scammon School," *Greek Star* (November 30, 1906), 1, CFLPS, Greek, IA3; "New Evening School for Study of English Language Established," *Naujienos* (January 2, 1915), 1, CFLPS, Lithuanian, IA3; "Americanization," *Polonia* 13:19 (May 6, 1920), 1, CFLPS, Polish, IC; "Free English Schools," *Otthon* ((September 14, 1924), 1, CFLPS, Hungarian, IA3; "Learn English," *Russkoye Obozrenie* (August 1928), 1–3, CFLPS, Russian IA3. On adult education programs in Chicago for Polish immigrants, see Frederick J. Augustyn Jr., "Polish-American Positions towards Adult Literacy and Acculturation in Chicago, 1890–1930: Professional and Popular Perspectives" (paper presented at the History of Education Society Annual Meeting, 2003, Evanston, IL), 33. On Slovak leaders urging people to master English, see Alexander, *Ethnic Pride, American Patriotism*, 59–61.

33. "Polish Language in America," 1. See also Thomas I. Monzell, "The Catholic Church and the Americanization of the Polish Immigrant," *Polish American Studies* 26:1 (January–June 1969), 13.

34. Zimmerman, "Ethnics against Ethnicity," 1392.

35. An excellent overview of the battle between German Americans and Slavic groups in Chicago is Melvin G. Holli, "Teuton vs. Slav: The Great War Sinks Chicago's German *Kultur*," *Ethnicity* 8:4 (December 1981), 406–451.

36. "German in the Public Schools," *Svornost* (July 31, 1890), 3, CFLPS, Bohemian, IA1b. The piece in *Svornost* was responding to "On a Slippery Road: Bohemians Oppose German Instruction in the Public Schools," *Illinois Staats-Zeitung* (July 26, 1890), 1–7, CFLPS, German, IA1b. One Jewish leader also opposed dual-language instruction in the elementary grades. See "Concerning Foreign-Language Teaching," *Reform Advocate* (May 22, 1891), 1–2, CFLPS, Jewish, IA1b.

37. "Against German in the Public Schools," *Svornost* (July 25, 1890), 1–3, CFLPS, Bohemian, IA1b; Zimmerman, "Ethnics against Ethnicity," 1387–1388.

38. "Numbers Are Proof," *Abendpost* (January 16, 1896), CFLPS, German, IA1b; "Value of the German Language Teaching," *Abendpost* (December 28, 1897), CFLPS, German, IA1b.

39. Zimmerman, "Ethnics against Ethnicity," 1388; "For the Italian Language," *L'Italia* (June 30, 1900) 1, CFLPS, Italian, IIIH.

40. See, for example, "The Polish Language in the Schools," *Dziennik Zwiazkowy* (November 26, 1910), CFLPS, Polish, IA1b. Zimmerman, "Ethnics against Ethnicity," 1388–1392.

41. Bohumil Kral, "The Bohemian Language in Public Schools," *Denni Hlasatel* (June 27, 1915), 2, CFLPS, Bohemian, IA1b.

42. "Immigrants and Politicians," *Denni Hlasatel* (October 28, 1915), 1–2, CFLPS, Bohemian, IIIG. See also "Immigration in the Limelight," *Denni Hlasatel* (September 14, 1915), 1–8, CFLPS, Bohemian, IIIG.

43. "Away with the Kaiser's Spelling Book," *Dziennik Zwiazkowy* (April 25, 1917), 1–2, CFLPS, Polish, IA1a; "The Kaiser Wins," *Denni Hlasatel* (August 8, 1917), 1–2, CFLPS, Bohemian, IC; "Chicago Finally Destroys Dangerous Propaganda," *Denni Hlasatel* (August 14, 1917), 1–2, CFLPS, Bohemian, IC; Holli, "Teuton vs. Slav," 433–437; Zimmerman, "Ethnics against Ethnicity," 1393.

44. "Honor to Whom Honor Is Due," *Denni Hlasatel* (July 14, 1917), 1, CFLPS, Bohemian, IC; "Some Disgusting Thoughts," *Denni Hlasatel* (July 21, 1917), 1–2, CFLPS, Bohemian, IC; "What to Do with the Mayor," *Denni Hlasatel* (September 6, 1917), 1, CFLPS, Bohemian, IC; "Polish and Other Slavic Delegates Attend School Board Meeting," *Dziennik Zwiazkowy* (March 28,

1918), 1–2, CFLPS, Polish, IA1a; "Kosciusko or Bismarck?" *Dziennik Zwiaz-kowy* (April 26, 1918), 1–5, CFLPS, Polish, IC; Holli, "Teuton vs. Slav," 438–439.

45. Chicago Board of Education, *Proceedings of the Chicago Board of Education, 1917–18* (Chicago: The Board, 1918), 343–344. On Czarnecki, see "Gratitude," *Denni Hlasatel* (May 26, 1917), 1, CFLPS, Bohemian, IC; and Holli, "Teuton vs. Slav," 434–435, 439.

46. See Linda L. Sommerfeld, "An Historical Descriptive Study of the Circumstances That Led to the Elimination of German from the Cleveland Schools, 1860–1918" (Ph.D. diss., Kent State University, 1986), 137–138.

47. On Young's support of these efforts, see Rivka Shpak Lissak, *Pluralism and Progressives: Hull House and the New Immigrants, 1890–1919* (Chicago: University of Chicago Press, 1989), 56–58.

48. "Demand That Lithuanian Be Taught at the Armour School," *Lietuva* (February 10, 1911), 1, CFLPS, Lithuanian, IA1b; "Let's Teach Norwegian," *Scandia* (May 27, 1911), 1, CFLPS, Norwegian, IA1b; "The Swedish Language in the High Schools," *Svenska Kuriren* (June 3, 1911), 1, CFLPS, Swedish, IA1a; "Polish Language in Chicago High Schools," *Dziennik Zwiazkowy* (September 20, 1911), 1–5, CFLPS, Polish, IA1a; "The Struggle for the Bohemian Language," *Denni Hlasatel* (March 11, 1912), 1, CFLPS, Bohemian, IA1a; "Yiddish and Hebrew in the Public Schools," *Jewish Daily Courier* (May 2, 1912), 1, CFLPS, Jewish, IA1b; "Danish Taught in American High Schools," *Revyen* (February 1, 1913), 1, CFLPS, Danish, IA1b.

49. "Count Frantisek Luetzow among the Czechs," *Denni Hlasatel* (February 24, 1912), 5, CFLPS, Bohemian, IIIH.

50. See, for example, "First Jewish School Teacher of Hebrew Hired," *Jewish Daily Courier* (July 30, 1917), 1, CFLPS, Jewish, IA1b; "Czech Language in High Schools," *Denni Hlasatel* (June 14, 1917), 1, CFLPS, Bohemian, IA1b; A Mario Pei, "Italian Language in the High Schools," *Mens Italica* (October 1928), 1, CFLPS, Italian, IA1b; "High Schools Give Instruction in Greek," *Saloniki-Greek Press* (January 30, 1936), 1–2, CFLPS, Greek, IA1b.

51. "Czech Pupils' Club at Harrison High," *Denni Hlasatel* (March 2, 1917), CFLPS, Bohemian, IIIE; H. A. Lipsky, "Marshall High School and Hebrew," *Jewish Daily Courier* (May 12, 1922), 2–3, CFLPS, Jewish, IA1b.

52. David L. Angus and Jeffrey Mirel, *The Failed Promise of the American High School, 1890–1995* (New York: Teachers College Press, 1999), 203.

53. Not all factions in ethnic communities welcomed these courses. In the fall of 1911, for example, the religiously oriented Polish paper *Dziennik Chicagoski* denounced the introduction of Polish in Schurz High School, because the course might encourage students to leave parochial schools for public schools. The more secular paper *Dziennik Zwiazkowy* blasted this response, noting that

this course would aid thousands of Polish students in public schools in their efforts to retain their Polish heritage. "The Polish Language in the Public High Schools," *Dziennik Zwiazkowy* (November 4, 1911), 1–3, CFLPS, Polish, IA1b. On similar controversies in other immigrant groups, see Zimmerman, "Ethnics against Ethnicity," 1400.

54. "Beginning of the School Year," *Dziennik Zwiazkowy* (September 5, 1914), 2–3, 5, CFLPS, Polish, IA1b.

55. Zimmerman, "Ethnics against Ethnicity," 1383–1384, 1390, 1394–1395, 1399–1401. On the problem of getting immigrant children into these courses, see "Not Enough Pride," *Denni Hlasatel* (September 11, 1913), CFLPS, Bohemian, IA1b; "More Interest in Czech Classes Urged," *Denni Hlasatel* (February 5, 1917), CFLPS, Bohemian, IA1b.

56. Zimmerman, "Ethnics against Ethnicity," 1395–1400.

57. For example, in his 1916 study of the education of immigrants in Cleveland, Herbert A. Miller found that Poles, Slovaks, and Slovenians had more children in dual-language parochial schools than in public schools. Nevertheless, approximately 47 percent of children from Polish families, 40 percent from Slovak families, and 40 percent from Slovenian families attended public elementary schools. Herbert A. Miller, *The School and the Immigrant* (Cleveland: Survey Committee of the Cleveland Foundation, 1916), 25, 33. On the large percentage of Catholic students attending the Chicago Public Schools in this era, see Mary Herrick, *The Chicago Schools: A Social and Political History* (Beverly Hills: Russell Sage, 1971), 403. On Catholic schools in Chicago, see Christian Dallavis, "Extending Theories of Culturally Responsive Pedagogy: An Ethnographic Examination of Catholic Schooling in an Immigrant Community in Chicago" (Ph.D. diss., University of Michigan, 2008), 70–91; Ann Marie Ryan, "Negotiating Assimilation: Chicago Catholic High Schools' Pursuit of Accreditation in the Early Twentieth Century," *History of Education Quarterly* 46:3 (Fall 2006), 354, 363; James W. Sanders, *The Education of an Urban Minority: Catholics in Chicago, 1833–1965* (New York: Oxford University Press, 1977), 4.

58. "Education," *Dziennik Chicagoski* (June 2, 1891), 8, CFLPS, Polish, IA2a.

59. James T. Fisher, *Communion of Immigrants: A History of Catholics in America* (New York: Oxford University Press, 2002), 77–83; "Polish Language in Churches," *Zagoda* (December 20, 1900), 1–5, CFLPS, Polish, IIIA.

60. On Ireland, see Timothy Walch, *Parish School: American Catholic Parochial Education from Colonial Times to the Present* (New York: Crossroad, 1996), 81, 71–83.

61. According to one historian, in the early 1920s "[p]arochial schools in Chicago enrolled 70% of Polish children, in Detroit 65%, in Milwaukee 60%, in

Philadelphia 40%." Jozef Miaso, *The History of the Education of Polish Immigrants in the United States* (Warsaw: Polish Scientific, 1977), 230. See also David John Hogan, *Class and Reform: School and Society in Chicago, 1880–1930* (Philadelphia: University of Pennsylvania Press, 1985), 127; Zimmerman, "Ethnics against Ethnicity," 1400.

62. Walch, *Parish School*, 77–80; "Editorial," *Katalikas* (January 12, 1899), CFLPS, Lithuanian, IB3b; "Roman Catholic Day School Opened," *Otthon* (September 21, 1930), 1, CFLPS, Hungarian, IA2a; "Send Your Children to Catholic Schools," *Amerikanski Slovenec* (August 25, 1925), 1–2, CFLPS, Slovene, IA2a; "Catholic School," *Osadne Hlasy* (September 1928), 1, CFLPS, Slovak, IA2a.

63. The Lutheran church supported a number of dual-language German and Slovak parochial schools. Miller, *School and the Immigrant*, 31–33. On Czech dual-language parochial schools in Cleveland, see Rossi, "Children of Czech Immigrants," 92, 105–106, 173–176.

64. JoEllen McNergney Vinyard, *For Faith and Fortune: The Education of Catholic Immigrants in Detroit* (Urbana: University of Illinois Press, 1998), 177, 172–180.

65. "Is a Higher School of Learning Really Necessary for Lithuanians?" *Lietuva* (October 27, 1905), 2, CFLPS, Lithuanian, IA1b.

66. "Polish Language in Chicago High Schools," *Dziennik Zwiazkowy* (September 20, 1911), 2, CFLPS, Polish, IA1b. In addition, as Walch points out, conditions in some schools were deplorable. Walch, *Parish School*, 80. One Polish woman said she spent only two hours per day studying English at her parochial school, in essence learning English "like a foreign language." Augustyn, "Polish-American Positions towards Adult Literacy and Acculturation in Chicago, 1890–1930," 13. See also King, *Making Americans*, 320, fn. 22; and Vinyard, *For Faith and Fortune*, 178,

67. Edward A. Ross, "American and Immigrant Blood: A Study of the Social Effects of Immigration," *Century Magazine* 87:2 (December 1913), 232.

68. William G. Ross, *Forging New Freedoms: Nativism, Education, and the Constitution, 1917–1927* (Lincoln: University of Nebraska Press, 1994), 50–52, 94l; Walch, *Parish School*, 80–82.

69. "Americanization," *Narod Polski* (February 5, 1919), 1, CFLPS, Polish, IIIA. Se also William J. Galush, "What Should Janek Learn? Staffing and Curriculum in Polish-American Parochial Schools, 1870–1940," *History of Education Quarterly* 40:4 (Winter 2000), 395–417.

70. Edward D. Kantowicz, "Cardinal Mundelein of Chicago and the Shaping of Twentieth-Century American Catholicism," *Journal of American History* 68:1 (June 1981), 53–55, 63–65; Sanders, *Education of an Urban Minority*, 115–120; Vinyard, *For Faith and Fortune*, 93–95.

71. Sanders, *Education of an Urban Minority*, 147–149; Charles Shanabruch, *Chicago's Catholics: Evolution of an American Identity* (Notre Dame, IN: University of Notre Dame Press, 1981), 187–189.

72. See, for example, "The Polish Language in Parochial Schools," *Dziennik Zwiazkowy* (November 21, 1911), 1–2, CFLPS, Polish, IA2b; Ryan, "Negotiating Assimilation," 368–369. See also Daniel S. Buczek, "The Polish-American Parish as an Americanizing Factor," in *Studies in Ethnicity: The East European Experience in America*, ed. Charles A. War, Philip Shashko, and Donald E. Pienkos (New York: East European Monographs, 1980), 153–165; John J. Bukowczyk, *And My Children Did Not Know Me: A History of Polish-Americans* (Bloomington: Indiana University Press, 1987), 69–70; Miaso, *History of the Education of Polish Immigrants in the United States*, 229; Leslie W. Tentler, *Seasons of Grace: A History of the Catholic Archdiocese of Detroit* (Detroit: Wayne State University Press, 1990), 247–249; Vinyard, *For Faith and Fortune*, 186–187.

73. Tentler, *Seasons of Grace*, 248–249. On other factors that contributed to the decline of these schools, see Sanders, *Education of an Urban Minority*, 105–114.

74. Quoted in Miaso, *History of the Education of Polish Immigrants in the United States*, 229–230. On similar concerns in Detroit, see Tentler, *Seasons of Grace*, 242, 249. See also Bukowczyk, *And My Children Did Not Know Me*, 72–73.

75. "Let's Treasure Our National Wealth," *Dziennik Zjednoczenia* (June 12, 1923), 2, CFLPS, Polish, IC. See also "Is It True That We Are Denationalizing Ourselves[?]" *Dziennik Zjednoczenia* (October 6, 1927), 1, CFLPS, Polish, IIIA. Lizabeth Cohen found substantial resilience in dual-language parochial schools in the 1920s. Lizabeth Cohen, *Making a New Deal: Industrial Workers in Chicago, 1919–1939* (New York: Cambridge University Press, 1990), 84–86.

76. Walch, *Parish School*, 81–82; Dorota Praszalowic, "The Cultural Changes of Polish-American Parochial Schools in Milwaukee, 1866–1988," *Journal of Ethnic Studies* 13:4 (Summer 1994), 35; Galush, "What Should Janek Learn?" 414–416; Joseph S. Roucek, "The Yugoslav Immigrants in America," *American Journal of Sociology* 40:5 (March 1935), 606. Holli notes that in this period many German language parochial schools "dropped German language instruction." Holli, "Teuton vs. Slav," 446.

77. "Hebrew Schools," *Chicago Tribune* (December 8, 1879),1–2, CFLPS, Jewish, IA2a.

78. "Remember the Youth," *Jewish Daily Courier* (February 2, 1923), 1–3, CFLPS, Jewish, IIIA; Soltes, *Yiddish Press*, 152–153; Nathan Glazer, *American Judaism* (Chicago: University of Chicago Press, 1957), 85–87, 111. More recent immigrant

groups also rely on weekend or after-school schools, and summer camp programs, to help maintain their ethnic and/or religious heritage. See Zinta Sanders, "Latvian Education in the United States: Antecedents and Development of Supplementary Schools," *Journal of Ethnic Studies* 7:1 (Spring 1979), 31–42; Neela Banerjee, "Camp Joins Summer Fun with Teaching the Hindu Faith," *New York Times* (July 21, 2007), A8.

79. "The Greek Language and the Duty of the Community," *Star* (August 11, 1905), 2, CFLPS, Greek, IA2b. See also "Send Your Children to Greek Schools," *Saloniki-Greek Press* (September 19, 1935), CFLPS, Greek, IA2b.

80. As the editor of *Denni Hlasatel* put it, "Let us . . . send our children not only to public schools but also to our own Bohemian schools." "On the Threshold of the School Year," *Denni Hlasatel* (September 4, 1915), 6, CFLPS, Bohemian, IA1a; Kral, "Bohemian Language in Public Schools," 5. As early as 1880, Czechs in Cleveland organized a Czech Sunday school that taught "Czech language, geography, history, literature, and folklore." Winston Chrislock, "Cleveland Czechs," in Hammack, Grabowski, and Grabowski, *Identity, Conflict, and Cooperation*, 95.

81. "For Czech Parents to Consider," *Denni Hlasatel* (September 14, 1917), 1–2, CFLPS, Bohemian, IA1b. On after-school and weekend Czech schools in Cleveland, see Rossi, "Children of Czech Immigrants," 83, 109–110, 137–138.

82. "The Fire beneath the Melting Pot," *Jewish Daily Courier* (June 5, 1918), 2, CFLPS, Jewish, IG.

83. See, for example, "School for Children," *Novi Svijet* (March 19, 1925), 1, CFLPS, Croatian, IA1a; Roucek, "Yugoslav Immigrants in America," 606; "Schools for the Children," *Rassviet* (August 12, 1926), 1–2, CFLPS, Russian, IA2a; Kuropas, "*Svoboda* and the Education of Rusyn-Ukrainians in America, 1893–1914," 127–46. The Hungarian community also offered summer programs. "Hungarian Summer Schools," *Otthon* (July 6, 1920), 1, CFLPS, Hungarian, IA2a; "Hungarian Summer School," *Magyar Tribune* (July 1, 1927), CFLPS, Hungarian, IA2a.

84. Kuropas, "*Svoboda* and the Education of Rusyn-Ukrainians in America, 1893–1914," 128–129.

85. "The Children of the Russian Colony," *Ruskii Viestnik* (April 12, 1924), 1–2, CFLPS, Russian, IA1a.

86. Among the numerous examples of this stance are "Patriotism the Duty of the Greek in America," *Star* (June 15, 1906), 3, CFLPS, Greek, IIIG; "A Closer Relationship with Americans," *Lietuva* (February 24, 1911), 1–2, CFLPS, Lithuanian, IIIA; "Our Duty to This Country," *Saloniki* (December 22, 1917), 1–2, CFLPS, Greek IG; "Why the Hungarian Worker Is Well Liked in America," *Magyar Tribune* (January 4, 1918), 2, CFLPS, Hungarian, IG; "An Important Decision," *Onze Toekomst* (June 20, 1923), 3, CFLPS, Dutch, IA1b;

"The Foreign Languages," *Skandinaven* (August 25, 1920), 3, CFLPS, Norwegian, IIIA; "The Campaign of Incitement," *Magyar Tribune* (March 27, 1931), 3, CFLPS, Hungarian, IC; "We Must Know Our Language," *Januimas* (February 15, 1937), 2, CFLPS, Lithuanian, IIIA.

87. Michael Olneck, "What Have Immigrants Wanted from American Schools? What Do They Want Now? Historical and Contemporary Perspectives on Immigrants, Language, and American Schooling," *American Journal of Education* 115:3 (May 2009), 398, 379–389. Jonathan Zimmerman goes further, arguing that in these struggles over language, immigrants discovered that they "could preserve distinctive identities without maintaining distinctive language, contrary to the claims of ethnic leaders in the past as well as ethnic theorists in the present." Zimmerman, "Ethnics against Ethnicity," 1403.

88. On this process, see Jonathan Zimmerman, *Whose America? Culture Wars in the Public Schools* (Cambridge: Harvard University Press, 2002).

89. "The Whole World Glorified Columbus," *Vita Nuova* (October 1930) [monthly], 1, CFLPS, Italian, IIIB3a. Columbus was not the only Italian explorer touted by the community. See also "Carnovale in the Vindication of Henry Tonti," *Vita Nuova* (January 1926), 1–2, CFLPS, Italian, IIIF.

90. "Jonathan D. Sarna, "Columbus and the Jews," *Commentary* 94:4 (November 1992), 38.

91. "Yugoslavs in the United States," *National Print and Publication Company* (December 9, 1934), 1, CFLPS, Croatian, IIIF.

92. "Leif Erickson," *Skandinaven* (October 4, 1891), 1–2, CFLPS, Norwegian, IJ; "An Appeal," *Skandinaven* (June 29, 1919), 4, CFLPS, Norwegian, IJ; "Poles in the United States," *Chicago Society News* (July 1926), 1, CFLPS, Polish, IIIF; William Seabrook, "Americans All," *American Magazine* (August 1937), 1.

93. "The First Swedes in America," *Svenska Kuriren* (July 10, 1913), 1–9, CFLPS, Swedish, IIIG; "Jews in Celebration of Reaching America," *Record-Herald* (November 25, 1905), CFLPS, Jewish, IC; "Heroes of American Democracy," *Abendpost* (October 20, 1918), 1–3, CFLPS, German, IIIF; Frank Spiecker, "Thoughts on the Pastorius Celebration," *Abendpost* (October 6, 1933), 1–2, CFLPS, German, IIIF; "Lithuanians Were among the Early Settlers of the New World," *Sandara* (October 10, 1930), 1, 5, CFLPS, Lithuanian, IIIF. One of the most clever attempts to read a group back into early American history appeared in a Croatian publication which maintained that the word "Croatoan," the mysterious clue carved on a tree in the "lost colony" on Roanoke Island, referred to a Croatian ship that had visited the colony and perhaps saved the colonists "from the destruction that was taking place" there. Untitled piece, First All-Slavic Singing Festival announcement in English (December 9, 1934), 1, CFLPS, Croatian, IJ.

94. "Thanksgiving Day," *Dziennik Zwiazkowy* (November 1911), 11, CFLPS, Polish, IIIB3. See also "The First Thanksgiving," *Polonia* (November 24, 1921), CFLPS, Polish IJ; "Lithuanians Were among the Early Settlers of the New World," 1. For a brief discussion of every American holiday, see Leonard Deutelbaum, "Decoration Day," *Reform Advocate* (May 30, 1931), CFLPS, Jewish, IJ.

95. "George Washington," *Dziennik Chicagoski* (February 21, 1891), 1, CFLPS, Polish IJ. See also "George Washington's Birthday Party," *Svenska Tribunen* (February 25, 1880), CFLPS, Swedish, IIIB3a; "Washington and Lincoln," *Svenska Tribunen* (February 27, 1901), CFLPS, Swedish IJ; "Lithuanians Will Participate in the Washington Anniversary Celebration," *Lietuva* (February 17, 1911), CFLPS, Lithuanian IIIA; "An Evening for New Citizens," *Denni Hlasatel* (February 10, 1916), CFLPS, Bohemian, IIIB2; Washington's Birthday," *Polonia* 12:8 (February 21, 1918), 1, CFLPS, Polish IIIB3a; Peter Lambros, "Immigrant Reveres Washington's Name," *Scrapbook* (February 22, 1922), CFLPS, Greek, IJ; "The George Washington Bicentennial," *Bulletin, Italian Chamber of Commerce in Chicago* (June 1930), CFLPS, Italian, IIIB3a; "George Washington," *Weekly Zagoda* (February 26, 1931), CFLPS, Polish, IJ.

96. Peter Lambros, "Adopted Father of the Immigrant," *Scrapbook* (February 22, 1922), 1, CFLPS, Greek, IJ. See also "George Washington," *Saloniki* (February 20, 1926), 1, CFLPS, Greek, IJ.

97. "Celebration of the Two-Hundredth Anniversary of the Birth of George Washington," *Osadne Hlasy* (June 10, 1932), 1–2, CFLPS, Slovak, IIIB3a. See also "Immigration on the Wane," *Abendpost* (October 17, 1925), CFLPS, German, IIIG.

98. "George Washington's Birthday," *Dziennik Zwiazkowy* (February 22, 1917), 1, CFLPS, Polish, IIIB3a.

99. "Independence Day," *Dziennik Zwiazkowy* (July 3, 1911), 1, CFLPS, Polish, IIIB3a.

100. The local PNA constitution is quoted in Peter A. Ostafin, "The Polish Peasant in Transition: A Study of the Group Interaction as a Function of Symbiosis and Common Definitions" (Ph.D. diss., University of Michigan, 1948).

101. "A Repetition of the Declaration of Independence," *Lietuva* (July 5, 1918), 1–2, CFLPS, Lithuanian, IIIB3a. See also "Magnificent Day of Loyalty," *Narod Polski* (July 10, 1918), CFLPS, Polish, IIIB3a; "The Celebration of the Fourth of July by the Greeks of Chicago," *Loxias* (July 11, 1918), CFLPS, Greek, IIIB3a; "Celebration of the Fourth of July in Our Community," *Saloniki* (July 6, 1918), CFLPS, Greek, IIIB3a.

102. "George Washington's Birthday," *Dziennik Chicagoski* (February 22, 1906), 1, CFLPS, Polish, IIIB3a. See also "Attention," *Dziennik Chicagoski* (January 23,

1907), 1–2, CFLPS, Polish, IIIH; "Honoring the American Flag," *Dziennik Zwiazkowy* (June 15, 1908), 2, CFLPS, Polish, IIIB3a.

103. "Independence Day," 4. See also "Poles in the United States," 1; "Thaddeus Kosciuszko," *Chicago Society News* 4:6 (February 26, 1926), 1–3, CFLPS, Polish, IIIF. For a marvelous contemporary view of Kosciusko, see Bill Moyers's Sol Feinstone Lecture on The Meaning of Freedom, delivered at the United States Military Academy on November 15, 2006, http://www.tompaine.com/print/message_to_west_point.php.

104. "Lithuanians Were among the Early Settlers of the New World," 3; "Poles Plan to Erect Statue of Lithuanian in Washington," *Lietuva* (April 2, 1909), 1–2, CFLPS, Lithuanian, IC.

105. "In the German Club," *Illinois Staats Zeitung* (March 11, 1917), 1–2, CFLPS, German, IIIF. See also "Von Steuben's Birthday," *Abendpost* (September 1923), CFLPS, German, IIIB3a.

106. See, for example, "A Distinguished Page in German American History: General Niklas Hershheimer," *Abendpost* (August 14, 1927), CFLPS, German, IIID; "German Influence upon the American Constitution," CFLPS, German, IIIF.

107. "Greeks Taken as an Example," *Star* (July 1, 1904), 4, CFLPS, Greek, IIIH; "Greeks Must Be Naturalized," *Loxias* (March 17, 1909), CFLPS, Greek, IIIA.

108. "The Fourth of July Should Also Be a Greek Holiday," *Saloniki* (July 5, 1919), 1, CFLPS, Greek, IIIB3a.

109. Peter Lambros, "The March of Progress of the Greeks in Chicago," *Aster* (November 11, 1927), 1, CFLPS, Greek, IIIA. See also "Greeks Taken as an Example," 4. In 1899, a Norwegian newspaper offered a similar perspective, namely, that "Scandinavia is the cradle of what is known as Anglo-Saxon liberty and institutions." "History in the Schools," *Skandinaven* (December 31, 1899), 3, CFLPS, Norwegian, IA1a. Slovaks took a similar approach describing themselves as having "done their goodly share of building America." Alexander, *Ethnic Pride, American Patriotism*, 162.

110. "American and Polish Ideals," *Dziennik Zwiazkowy* (March 20, 1919), 1–3, CFLPS, Polish, IJ.

111. "The Racial Conflict," *Jewish Daily Courier* (July 30, 1919), 3, CFLPS, Jewish, IC. Several years earlier, the paper ran an article praising celebrations of the fiftieth anniversary of the signing of the Emancipation Proclamation. "The Liberation of Negroes," *Jewish Daily Courier* (January 6, 1913), CFLPS, Jewish, IIIB3a.

112. "Lincoln Enjoyed Wide Popularity among Immigrants," *Rassviet* (February 13, 1936), 2, CFLPS, Russian, IJ.

113. Gary Gerstle notes that reverence for Lincoln continued well into the 1940s, among mainly French Canadian union members. Gerstle, *Working-Class Americanism*, 290.

114. "The Heart of the Germans," *Illinois Staats Zeitung* (April 18, 1890), 2, CFLPS, German, IIIB3a. Another German paper suggested that Lincoln was actually German. "Was Lincoln of German Descent?" *Abendpost* (February 26, 1901), CFLPS, IJ. See also "Fifty Years Later," *Svenska Tribunen-Nyheter* (April 27, 1915), CFLPS, Swedish, IJ.

115. "Abraham Lincoln," *Skandinaven* (February 11, 1909), CFLPS, Norwegian, IJ. See also "Naturalized Citizens and Lincoln," *Skandinaven* (February 13, 1896), 1–2, CFLPS, Norwegian, IJ; "Abraham Lincoln," *Zagoda* (February 18, 1897), CFLPS, Polish, IIIB3a.

116. "The Hundred-Per-Cent Patriots Should Be Reminded," *Polonia* (March 27, 1924), CFLPS, Polish, IC. See also "Abraham Lincoln," *Polonia* (June 30, 1921), CFLPS, Polish, IJ.

117. "The Battle of Raclawice," *Dziennik Chicagoski* (April 4, 1894), CFLPS, Polish, III3a; "Kosciusko–Lincoln" *Dziennik Zwiazkowy* (February 12, 1915), CFLPS, Polish, IJ; "Commemoration of the Birthdays of Lincoln and Kosciusko," *Dziennik Zwiazkowy* (February 10, 1917), CFLPS, Polish, IIIB3a; "If Kosciusko Had Been Lincoln," *Dziennik Zwiazkowy* (February 12, 1918), CFLPS, Polish, IJ; "Lincoln–Kosciusko Birthday Observed," *Dziennik Zwiazkowy* (February 14, 1918), CFLPS, Polish, IIIB3a.

118. Stanislaus Orpiszowski, "Kosciusko and Lincoln," *Dziennik Zwiazkowy* (October 15, 1917), 2, CFLPS, Polish, IJ.

119; "Pericles and Lincoln Alike in Democracy," *Chicago Herald and Examiner* (February 10, 1924), 7, CFLPS, Greek, IJ. Lambros was not the first person to make that comparison. See Garry Wills, *Lincoln at Gettysburg: The Words That Remade America* (New York: Simon and Schuster, 1992), 41–62.

120. "Abraham Lincoln," February 12, 1918, CFLPS, Jewish, IJ.

121. "The Seventy-Fifth Anniversary of the Liberation of the Peasants," *Rassviet* (March 7, 1936), 1–2, CFLPS, Russian, IIIB3a.

122. "The Germans of 1848," *Abendpost* (April 16, 1924), CFLPS, German, IJ. As many as 200,000 Germans served in the Union army during the Civil War. See Ella Lonn, *Foreigners in the Union Army and Navy* (Baton Rouge: Louisiana State University Press, 1951), 577–579. See also William L. Burton, *Melting Pot Solders: The Union's Ethnic Regiments* (Ames: Iowa State University Press, 1988), 72–111.

123. "German Defenders of the Union," *Illinois Staats Zeitung* (August 29, 1900), 2, CFLPS, German, IIID. See also "Roaring Applause! Major General Osterhaus the Object of Great Honors. A Pride of the Germans," *Abendpost* (June 23, 1904), CFLPS, German, IIID.

124. "May Ceremonials on Bohemian Cemetery," *Svornost* (June 1, 1891), CFLPS, Bohemian, IIIB3a. See also "Decoration Day," *Denni Hlasatel* (May 31, 1906), CFLPS, Bohemian, IIIB3a.

125. "Decoration Day Celebration," *Denni Hlasatel* (May 31, 1913), 1–2, CFLPS, Bohemian, III3Ba.

126. "General Edward Salomon in Chicago," *Illinois Staats Zeitung* (October 5, 1887), CFLPS, German, IIID; [No title] *Chicago Chronicle* (March 30, 1923), CFLPS, Jewish, IIID.

127. "Decoration Day," *Dziennik Zwiazkowy* (May 29, 1911), 2, CFLPS, Polish, IJ. About 4,000 Poles served in the Union army. See also "The Swedish Immigration to America," *Svenska Tribunen* (February 27, 1895), 2–3, CFLPS, Swedish, IIIA; "An Appeal," *Svenska Kuriren* (April 25, 1918), 2–3, CFLPS, Swedish, IIID. Some 3,000 Swedes served in the Union army. On these groups, see Lonn, *Foreigners in the Union Army and Navy*, 579–581, 625–626; Burton, *Melting Pot Soldiers*, 168.

128. Nancy Gentile Ford, *Americans All! Foreign-Born Soldiers in World War I* (College Station: Texas A&M Pres, 2001), 3, 27–44. See also "Poles, Bohemians and Chicago Recruiting," *Chicago Evening Post* (May 9, 1917), 5.

129. George Creel, "Our 'Aliens'—Were They Loyal or Disloyal?" *Everybody's Magazine* (March 1919), 38.

130. "A Day of Touching Memories," *Denni Hlasatel* (May 31, 1922), 7–8, CFLPS, IIIB3a. See also "Chicago Poles Honor War Dead," *Dziennik Zjednoczenia* (June 1, 1927), CFLPS, Polish, IIIB3a.

131. "Americanization," *Chicago Tribune* (November 16, 1922), 8.

132. On the adoption of the American "we," see the speech by a German Lutheran leader who began by declaring, "When our forefathers fought for liberty. . . ." "Reverend Herzberger Takes Up Battle against Nativists and Protests against Persecution of Catholics," *Illinois Staats Zeitung* (November 16, 1892), 3, CFLPS, German, IIIA. See also "Decoration Day," *Dziennik Zwiazkowy*; and Lipsky, "The Problem with Our People's Education," 2

133. Zimmerman, *Whose America?* 214.

134. See, for example, Lothrop *Stoddard, Re-Forging America: The Story of Our Nationhood* (New York: Charles Scribner's Sons, 1927); Aristide Zolberg, *A Nation by Design: Immigration Policy and the Fashioning of America* (Cambridge: Harvard University Press, 2006), 248–251.

135. Henry Louis Gates, "Native Sons of Liberty," *New York Times* (August 6, 2006), sect. 4, 12.

136. On the changing requirements for naturalization and the requirement for an oath of allegiance, see John Palmer Gavit, *Americans by Choice* (1922; repr. Montclair, NJ: Patterson Smith, 1971, 74–75, 86, 69–88. See also Richard A. Easterlin, David Ward, William S. Bernard, and Reed Ueda, *Immigration* (Cambridge: Belknap Press, 1982), 117.

137. See, for example, Joel Perlmann, *Ethnic Differences: Schooling and Social Structure among the Irish, Italians, Jews, and Blacks in an American City, 1880–1935* (New York: Cambridge University Press, 1988).

138. On the support that New York's Yiddish newspapers gave to naturalization efforts and their call for Jewish citizens to become involved in local, state, and national politics, see Soltes, *Yiddish Press*, 127–133.

139. Norman Davies, *Heart of Europe: The Past in Poland's Present* (New York: Oxford University Press, 2001), 229–235; Misha Glenny, *The Balkans: Nationalism, War, and the Great Powers, 1804–1999* (New York: Penguin Books, 1999), 1–306; Kulczycki, *School Strikes in Prussian Poland*, 12–47; Paul Robert Magocsi, *A History of Ukraine* (Toronto: University of Toronto Press, 1996), 351–457; Okey, *The Hapsburg Monarchy from Enlightenment to Eclipse*, 292–335; Andrew Wilson, *The Ukrainians: Unexpected Nation* (New Haven: Yale University Press, 2000), 73–118.

140. However, as Thomas Archdeacon notes, substantial numbers of new-stock immigrants did not stay in the United States permanently, and thus did not seek citizenship. He argues that perhaps 30 percent of these immigrants "re-migrated" to their home countries. He estimates that prior to 1924, 54 percent of Greeks, 46 percent of Italians, 47 percent of Magyars, 37 percent of Slovaks, and 33 percent of Poles returned to their home countries. Thomas Archdeacon, *Becoming American: An Ethnic History* (New York: Free Press, 1983), 115–116, 118–119, 139.

141. Timothy Smith, "Immigrant Social Aspirations and American Education, 1880–1930," *American Quarterly* 21: 3(Autumn 1969), 542.

142. "America and Poland," *Dziennik Chicagoski* (February 14, 1891), 1, CFLPS, Polish, IC. See also "The Polish Language in America," *Narod Polski*.

143. "Patriotism the Duty of the Greek in America," *Star*. See also "Greek Schools," *Saloniki* (March 18, 1916), 1, CFLPS, Greek, IA2a. For other similar statements, see "How to Obtain Education," *Lietuva* (December 13, 1907), 2, CFLPS, Lithuanian, IA1a. See also "Editorial," *Katalikas*; "From the Foreign Newspapers," *Lietuva* (February 8, 1901), CFLPS, Lithuanian, IC.

144. Leopold Deutelbaum, "The American Flag," *Reform Advocate* (June 13, 1931), 3, CFLPS, Jewish ,IC. See also "Letter to Jewish Children," *Jewish Daily Courier* (September 3, 1916), 2, CFLPS, Jewish, IA1a.

145. Ronald Sanders, "The *Jewish Daily Forward*," *Midstream* 8:4 (December 1962), 79. See also Soltes, *Yiddish Press*, 178–180.

146. Not all foreign language newspapers were as supportive of such accommodations to American life as those in Chicago. George E. Pozzetta argues that prior to 1915, the Italian foreign language press in New York City paid little attention to "the American scene" and in many cases had "a strong anti-American bias." Pozzetta, "The Italian Immigrant Press of New York City," 37, 39. Park and Miller reported on similar sentiments. Robert E. Park and Herbert A. Miller, *Old World Traits Transplanted* (Harper and Brothers,

1921), 291. However, other scholars, such as Charles Jaret, have questioned the degree to which the New York papers were representative of Italians in the United States, noting that Italian papers in Chicago, particularly *L'Italia*, which had a very large readership, "stressed the importance of adjusting to American conditions by acquiring citizenship, attending school, voting responsibly, resisting padroni domination, and adopting habits acceptable to urban Americans." Jaret argues that the difference between the New York and other Italian papers might have been due to the ease of departure from New York, which made Italians in that city more transient than those in cities like Chicago. Jaret, "Greek, Italian, and Jewish American Press," 51–53.

147. Rev. Jan Rynda, "Duties of the American Czechs to Their New Homeland," *Denni Hlasatel* (May 18, 1917), 1–2, CFLPS, Bohemian, IC. See also "More about Hyphens," *Denni Hlasatel* (October 13, 1915), 2, CFLPS, Bohemian, IIIA.

148. Mr. Alfange, "The Greeks of America," *Saloniki* (May 19, 1928), 9–10, CFLPS, Greek, IIIB2.

149. On this phenomenon, see Lawrence Fuchs, *The American Kaleidoscope: Race, Ethnicity, and the Civic Culture* (Middletown, CT: Wesleyan University Press, 1990), 23; Barrett, "Americanization from the Bottom Up," 1009.

150. A 1915 editorial in *Denni Hlasatel* declared, "The much abused hyphen is not a sign of cleavage, but a sign of unity." "More about Hyphens," *Denni Hlasatel* (October 13, 1915), 1, CFLPS, Bohemian, IIIA.

151. "Citizenship," *Narod Polski* (September 8, 1909), 3, CFLPS, Polish, IIIA.

152. "Meaning of American Citizenship," *Dziennik Zwiazkowy* (November 17, 1911), 3–4, CFLPS, Polish, IIIG.

153. "The Italian Electoral Force in Chicago," *L'Italia* (August 17, 1889), 1, CFLPS, Italian, IIIA. At the time, *L'Italia* "was the largest circulating Italian newspaper in the U.S." Jaret, "Greek, Italian, and Jewish American Press," 52.

154. "Compulsory Citizenship," *L'Italia* (April 5, 1914), 1, CFLPS, Italian, IIIA.

155. "News from the Political Front," *Dziennik Zwiazkowy* (August 28, 1918), 1, CFLPS, Polish, IF1. On other groups, see "A Jew for Jews," *Jewish Daily Courier* (April 1, 1910), CFLPS, Jewish, IF1; "[Vote for a Bohemian]," *Denni Hlasatel* (April 2, 1914), 1–2, CFLPS, Bohemian, IF1; "Swedish-American Candidate for State Senator," *Svenska Tribunen-Nyheter* (March 1, 1922), CFLPS, Swedish, IF1; "Ignatio Izsak Candidate for County Commissioner," *Magyar Tribune* (April 4, 1930), CFLPS, Hungarian, IF1; "For the Italian Candidates," *Vita Nuova* (October 1930); Pail Koken, "The Power of United Vote," *Hellenic Center News* (October 1, 1932), CFLPS, Greek, IF1.

156. See, for example, "Citizenship," *L'Italia* (March 7, 1891), 1, CFLPS, Italian, IIIA; "Get Your Citizenship Papers," *Skandinaven* (December 1, 1893),

CFLPS, Norwegian, IIIA: "Get Your Citizenship Papers before Sept. 27," *Dziennik Chicagoski* (September 14, 1906), 1, CFLPS, Polish, IIIA; "Strive for Citizenship," *Dziennik Chicagoski* (February 22, 1907), 1, CFLPS, Polish, IIIA; "The Greek and American Citizenship," *Star* (August 30, 1907), CFLPS, Greek, IIIA; "Greeks Must Be Naturalized," *Loxias* (March 17, 1909), CFLPS, Greek, IIIA; "Offers Aid in Naturalization Proceedings," *Denni Hlasatel* (January 4, 1914), CFLPS, Bohemian, IIIG; Anthony Czarnecki, "Polish Cause in Danger," *Dziennik Zwiazkowy* (October 10, 1914), CFLPS, Polish, IFA.

157. On the problems facing immigrant women and naturalization, see Gavit, *Americans by Choice*, 296–334.

158. The German newspaper *Abendpost* and the Greek paper *Saloniki* were notable exceptions to this trend. See "Let Us Hope for the Best," *Abendpost* (April 5, 1919), CFLPS, German IK; "Are Men and Women of Equal Ability[?]" *Saloniki* (March 1, 1919), CFLPS, Greek, IK.

159. "To the Italian Women," *La Parola Socialisti* (February 18, 1914), CFLPS, Italian, IK; "The First Duty of Women Voters," *Jewish Daily Courier* (March 18, 1914), CFLPS, Jewish, IK; "Vote Socialistic," *Revyen* (April 4, 1914), CFLPS, Danish, IK; "Parade of Women Voters" *Denni Hlasatel* (May 1, 1914), CFLPS, Bohemian, IK; "The Struggle for Equal Rights" *Narod Polski* (October 16, 1918), CFLPS, Polish, IK.

160. "Need Chicago Fear Women's Political Might?" *Jewish Daily Courier* (March 18, 1914), 1, CFLPS, Jewish, IK. See also "The Duty of the Women," *Jewish Daily Courier* (February 2, 1914), CFLPS, Jewish, IK.

161. "The Struggle for Equal Rights," *Narod Polski* (October 16, 1918), CFLPS, Polish, IK: "Congress Acts on the Woman Suffrage Question," *Naujienos* (January 14, 1915), CFLPS, Lithuanian, IK; "Why Women Must Have the Right to Vote," *Radnicka Straza* (April 19, 1916), 1, CFLPS, Croatian, IK; "Women's Vote," *Radnicka Straza* (October 31, 1917), CFLPS, Croatian, IK.

162. "Women's Suffrage," *Narod Polski* (August 25, 1920), 3–4, CFLPS, Polish, IK. See also "Women's Affairs," *Ranna Zorya* (July 1919), CFLPS, Ukrainian, IK; "Much-Needed Reform," *Svenska Tribunen-Nyheter* (November 24, 1920), CFLPS, Swedish, IB3a; "The Position of Women in the World," *Magyar Tribune* (August 13, 1926), CFLPS, Hungarian, IK.

163. "To All Bohemians and Slovaks," *Denni Hlasatel* (July 16, 1915), 1, CFLPS, Bohemian, IIIH. See also "An Evening for New Citizens," *Denni Hlasatel* (February 10, 1916), CFLPS, Bohemian, IIIB2. Two years earlier, *Denni Hlasatel* reported that Austria had passed a law making it "a crime to evade military service by emigrating to the United States." "The Attack of Foes of Immigration Repulsed," *Denni Hlasatel* (January 22, 1913), 2, CFLPS,

Bohemian, IIIG. America's entry into the war also spurred immigrants from the enemy nations—Austria, Germany, and Hungary—to seek citizenship to protect themselves from the allegations of dual loyalty. See "Masses Acquire Citizenship," *Magyar Tribune* (March 30, 1917), CFLPS, Hungarian, IIIA. The acquisition of American citizenship had one enormous potential benefit during the war. Former subjects from one of the Central Powers who joined the U.S. military and were captured faced the prospect of summary execution for treason if they did not have U.S. citizenship. Gavit, *Americans by Choice*, 257.

164. Ford, *Americans All!* 108–111. See also Gavit, *Americans by Choice*, 255–295.

165. Quoted in Gavit, *Americans by Choice*, 294. Gavit was quite critical of the quality of Americanization education that the soldiers and sailors received in the military, but he provided scant data to support that conclusion.

166. Susan B. Carter, Scott S. Gartner, Michael R. Haines, Alan L. Olmstead, Richard Sutch, and Gavin Wright, eds., *Historical Statistics of the United States*, vol. 1, pt. A, Population (New York: Cambridge University Press, 2006), 642, 643. On the "Act of May 9, 1918," see Henry B. Hazard, "The Trend toward Administrative Naturalization," *American Political Science Review* 21:2 (May 1927), 346.

167. Carter et al., *Historical Statistics of the United States*, 641.

168. Reed Ueda, *Postwar Immigrant America: A Social History* (Boston: Bedford Books, 1994), 128.

169. "Polish Youth," *Dziennik Zjednoczenia* (July 29, 1929), 2, CFLPS, Polish, IC. See also "Americanization of Poles by Poles," *Dziennik Zjednoczenia* (May 13, 1922) 4, CFLPS, Polish, IIIA.

170. National Catholic War Council, *A Program for Citizenship* (Washington, DC: The Council, 1919), 6, 7–12, in the Committee on History and Education for Citizenship in the Schools, Correspondence 1919 Folder, Box 766, American Historical Association Papers, Library of Congress, Washington, DC. I am indebted to Anne-Lise Halvorsen for getting me a copy of this pamphlet.

171. See, for example, "Americanization and Citizenship," *Saloniki* (September 1, 1923), CFLPS, Greek, IJ; "Citizenship School," *Bulletin of the Italo-American National Union* (August 1927), 1, CFLPS, Italian, IIIA; [No title], *Jewish Daily Forward* (July 6, 1922), CFLPS, Jewish, IIIA; "A Naturalization Bureau," *Jewish Daily Forward* (October 2, 1920), CFLPS, Jewish, IIIA; "Civics and Citizenship," [Chicago Hebrew Institute] *Observer* (1929), CFLPS, Jewish IIIA; "Poles Organize Naturalization League. They Will Conduct Schools in All Parts of the City," *Dziennik Zjednoczenia* (May 8, 1922), 1–4, CFLPS, Polish, IIIA; "New Citizenship Course," *Dziennik*

Zjednoczenia (January 5, 1922), CFLPS, Polish, IIIA; "American Citizenship Course," *Dziennik Zjednoczenia* (March 7, 1922), CFLPS, Polish, IIIA; "School of Citizenship of Poles," *Dziennik Zjednoczenia* (March 11, 1922), CFLPS, Polish, IIIA; "We Should Become Citizens. Political Clubs at the Parishes," *Dziennik Zjednoczenia* (May 19,1922), CFLPS, Polish, IIIA; "Special Correspondence Course on Citizenship," *Dziennik Zjednoczenia* (September 9, 1922), CFLPS, Polish, IIIA; "The Duties of the American Citizen," *Polonia* (March 8, 1923), CFLPS, Polish, IIIA; "Naturalization of Foreigners," *Rassviet* (March 10, 1927), CFLPS, Russian, IIIA; "Citizenship School in South Chicago," *Amerikanski Slovenec* (October 18, 1928), CFLPS, Slovenian, IIIA. For similar efforts in a very different locale, see John Bieter and Mark Bieter, *An Enduring Legacy: The Story of Basques in Idaho* (Reno: University of Nevada Press, 2000), 74.

172. "Naturalization Schools in Chicago," *Dziennik Zjednoczenia* (February 11, 1928), 1, CFLPS, Polish, IIIA. See also S. L. Kolanowski, "34,983 Poles Received Their Citizenship Papers; Italians Rank Highest," *Dziennik Chicagoski* (January 12, 1928), CFLPS, Polish, IIIG.

173. Andrew J. Vlachos, "The Federal Constitution of the United States of America," *Greek Star* (February 21, 1908), 1–22, Greek, CFLPS, IJ.

174. "Important Announcement," *Denni Hlasatel* (February 19, 1913), CFLPS, Bohemian, IIIG; "The Constitution of the United States Is a Protection against Injustice," *Jugoslavia* (December 10, 1921), CFLPS, Croatian, IJ; "Register Next Tuesday: Jews Must Not Neglect the Gift Given Them by the Constitution of the United States," *Jewish Daily Courier* (October 15, 1916), CFLPS, Jewish, IIIA; "A Repetition of the Declaration of Independence," *Lietuva* (July 5, 1918), 2, CFLPS, Lithuanian, IIIB3a; "What Does the Constitution of the United States Give Us?" *Dziennik Chicagoski* (December 15, 1921), CFLPS, Polish, IJ; "The Constitution of the United States Assures Us Justice Always," *Saloniki* (February 4, 1922), CFLPS, Greek, IC; "The Duties of American Citizenship," *Polonia* (March 8, 1923), CFLPS, Polish, IIIA; "The ABC of American Politics," *Magyar Tribune* (April 13, 1928), CFLPS, Hungarian, IC. Editorials in Jewish newspapers from this era focused on "American government, economics, society, particularly free elections, democratic ideals, and high government officials, in spite of the fact that some of these papers were at the same time quite critical of the capitalist basis of the economy." See Jaret, "Greek, Italian, and Jewish American Press," 48.

175. Reed Ueda, "Naturalization and Citizenship," in Easterlin, Ward, Bernard, and Ueda, *Immigration*, 150.

176. Woodrow Wilson, "Address of President Wilson, Delivered at Convention Hall, Philadelphia, May 10, 1915," *Immigrants in America Review* 1:3 (September 1915), 30.

177. Sollors argues that this metaphor has been "pervasive" in America since colonial times. Warner Sollors, *Beyond Ethnicity: Consent and Descent in American Culture* (New York: Oxford University Press, 1986), 152–155. For a contemporary example, see Ha Jin's novel on Chinese immigrants, *A Free Life* (New York: Pantheon Books, 2007), 489–490.

178. "Public Education," *Magyar Tribune* (August 21, 1925), 2–3, CFLPS, Hungarian, IA1a.

179. "One Who Understands," *Revyen* (June 10, 1916), Danish, IC. See also "Polish Patriotism in America," *Dziennik Chicago* (February 13, 1891), CFLPS, Polish, IIIA; A. G. Witting, "A Speech Addressed to Swedish Americans," *Svenska Tribunen-Nyheter* (April 25, 1923), 6, CFLPS, Swedish, III. Jacob Riis also used this metaphor. See Sollors, *Beyond Ethnicity*, 153.

180. Fred Clayton Butler, *Community Americanization*, Department of the Interior Bulletin 1919, no. 76 (Washington, DC: Government Printing Office, 1920), 15.

181. *Ameriska Domovina* (October 23, 1937), CFLND 1937:5, Abstract 20535, 433.

182. "The Question of American Citizenship," *Greek Star* (December 13, 1907), CFLPS, Greek, IIIG.

183. "The Vote Is Our Weapon," *Narod Polski* (September 2, 1914), 2, CFLPS, Polish, IF1.

184. Victor Greene, "'Becoming American': The Role of Ethnic Leaders—Swedes, Poles, Italians, and Jews," in *The Ethnic Frontier: Essays in the History of Group Survival in Chicago and the Midwest*, ed. Melvin G. Holli and Peter d'A. Jones (Grand Rapids, MI: Erdmans, 1977), 143–175.

185. On the rise of "new immigrants'" political power in Chicago, see John M. Allswang, *A House for All Peoples: Ethnic Politics in Chicago, 1890–1936* (Lexington: University of Kentucky Press, 1971); John D. Buenker, "Dynamics of Chicago Ethnic Politics, 1890–1930," *Journal of the Illinois State Historical Society* 67:2 (April 1974), 175–199.

186. John Bodnar, *Remaking America: Public Memory, Commemoration, and Patriotism in the Twentieth Century* (Princeton: Princeton University Press, 1992), 96, 98, 96–104. On the music program, see the MHF Papers, City of Cleveland, "Free Open Air Concerts, 1929," Container 1, Folder 1.

187. Paul G. Perrault, "The Campaigns to Abolish Parochial Education in Michigan, 1920 and 1924" (seminar paper, University of Michigan, in my possession); Neil Baldwin, *Henry Ford and the Jews: The Mass Production of Hate* (New York: Public Affairs, 2001), 94.

188. Archdeacon, *Becoming American: An Ethnic History*, 173–201.

189. Robert Dahl, *Who Governs?* (New Haven: Yale University Press, 1961), 59; Michael Parenti, "Ethnic Politics and the Persistence of Ethnic Identification," *American Political Science Review* 61:3 (September 1967), 725–726.

190. John Higham, "Cultural Responses to Immigration," in *Diversity and Its Discontents: Cultural Conflict and Common Ground in Contemporary American Society,* ed. Neil J. Smelser and Jeffrey C. Alexander (Princeton: Princeton University Press, 1999), 52.

191. "Proposals Restricting Immigration to America," *Dziennik Chicagoski* (December 19, 1892), 3–4, CFLPS, Polish, IIIG.

192. "What Awaits Us?" *Svornost* (March 10, 1892), 1, CFLPS, Bohemian, IIIA.

193. "Italians! Stop! Now Is the Time! *Tribuna Italiana* (June 9, 1906), CFLPS, Italian, IIIC; "What America Owes to the Immigrants," *Dziennik Zwiazkowy* (December 30, 1910), CFLPS, Polish, IIIG; "The Immigration Question," *Dziennik Zwiazkowy* (December 18, 1911), 1, CFLPS, Polish IIIG; "A Big Protest Meeting," *Denni Hlasatel* (May 15, 1912), CFLPS, Bohemian, IIIG; "Exclusion of Illiterates," *Parola del Socialisti* (January 18, 1913), CFLPS, Italian, IIIG; "A Mass Meeting without Masses," *Jewish Daily Courier* (March 4, 1914), CFLPS, Jewish, IC; "Protest against the Immigration Bill," *Dziennik Zwiazkowy* (January 11, 1915), CFLPS, Polish, IIIG.

194. "Prof. Ross's Attack on Foreign-Born Citizens," *L'Italia* (February 1, 1914), 2, CFLPS, Italian, IIIG. See also "Discussion of Immigration," *L'Italia* (March 1, 1914), CFLPS, Italian, IIIG; "E. A. Ross," *Denni Hlasatel* (April 14, 1914), 2, CFLPS, Bohemian, IIIB2.

195. "National Festivals Succeed," *Denni Hlasatel* (May 31, 1915), 22, CFLPS, Bohemian, IIIB3a.

196. "Nationalism," *Chicago Tribune* (July 6, 1916), 6. For a response to this editorial, see "Nationalism," *Narod Polski* (July 12, 1916), CFLPS, Polish, IIIA.

197. For additional expressions of loyalty to the United States and devotion to the immigrants' homelands, see "More about Hyphens"; "The New Americanism," *Svenska Kuriren* (June 22, 1916), Swedish, IG; "Our Duty To This Country"; "The Fire beneath The Melting Pot."

198. On enlistments and support of the war, see "For the Liberation of Slovakia," *Denni Hlasatel* (April 29, 1917), CFLPS, Bohemian, IG; "Join the American Army," *Denni Hlasatel* (December 12, 1917), CFLPS, Bohemian, IIID; "The Jew Is No Slacker," *Sunday Jewish Courier* (June 9, 1918), CFLPS, Jewish, IG; "The American Jews in the Great World War," *Jewish Daily Courier* (May 19, 1919), CFLPS, Jewish, IG; "A Gigantic Lithuanian Demonstration," *Lietuva* (July 12, 1918), CFLPS, Lithuanian, IIIB3a; "25,000 Poles Honor Polish Army," *Dziennik Zwiazkowy* (October 15, 1917), CFLPS, Polish, IG; "Minutes of the Ukrainian Women's Alliance of America," *Ranna Zorya* (June 1919), CFLPS, Ukrainian, IIIB1. On the purchase of war bonds, see "Poles in First Place: Results of Third Liberty Bond Sale among Foreign National Groups," *Dziennik Zwiazkowy* (May 8, 1918), CFLPS, Polish, IG; "Russians and the Third Liberty Loan," *Russkoye Zhan* (May 11, 1918), CFLPS, Russian, IG;

"News of Liberty Loans," *Loxias* (May 16, 1918), CFLPS, Greek, IG; "The Foreign Born and the Third Liberty Loan," *Svenska Kuriren* (September 19, 1918), CFLPS, Swedish, IG; "Liberty Bonds and Slovenes in Chicago," *Proletarec* (September 24, 1918), CFLPS, Slovenian, IG.

199. "Nicoli La Franco Arouses Great Enthusiasm among Italian Soldiers of Camp Grant," *L'Italia* (August 4, 1918), CFLPS, Italian, IIID; "Russians and the Third Liberty Loan," *Russkaya Zhizn* (May 11, 1918), CFLPS, Russian, IG; "Russian in America," *Novaya Russkaya Zhizn* (September 1918), CFLPS, Russian, IG; "Thousands of Chicago Greeks Celebrate War Entry at Mass Meeting," *Daily Journal* (June 23, 1918), CFLPS, Greek, IG; "Greeks Beg for Release from Turkish Rule," *Chicago Tribune* (December 16, 1918), CFLPS, Greek, IIIB1.

200. "Timely Topics," *Dziennik Zwiazkowy* (May 10, 1917), 2, CFLPS, Polish, IIID.

201. "The Immigrant Problem," *Denni Hlasatel* (October 23, 1917), 2, CFLPS, Bohemian, IIIG. See also "Finally!" *Lietuva* (May 10, 1918), CFLPS, Lithuanian, IG.

202. Quoted in Park and Miller, *Old World Traits Transplanted*, 273–274.

203. "Poles, Bohemians and Chicago Recruiting," *Chicago Evening Post* (May 9, 1917), 10.

204. "Fire beneath the Melting Pot." For similar sentiments, see "Americanization Temptations," *Dziennik Zwiazkowy* (August 7, 1918), 5–6, CFLPS, Polish, IIIA.

205. "Americanization Temptations," 3.

206. See, for example, "European Hordes Keen to Enter U.S.," *Cleveland Plain Dealer* (December 6, 1922), 12.

207. George Creel, "Melting Pot or Dumping Ground?" *Collier's* 68:10 (September 3, 1921), 9.

208. "Struggle of Congressman Adolph J. Sabath Useless: House of Representatives Expected to Pass Law Forbidding Immigration," *Denni Hlasatel* (December 10, 1920), 1–2, CFLPS, Bohemian, IIIG.

209. "Preserving the American Race," *New York Times* (May 2, 1924), 14.

210. "Protest against the Restrictive Laws of Immigration," *Bulletin of the Italian Chamber of Commerce of Chicago* (March 1920), 2–3, CFLPS, Italian, IIIB1.

211. Higham, *Strangers in the Land*, 411; "The Regulation of Immigration," *Svenska Tribunen-Nyheter* (November 22, 1922), CFLPS, Swedish, IIIG.

212. "Let's Have the Congress Conference," *Chicago Chronicle* (December 28, 1923), 1, CFLPS, Jewish, IC. See also "The Misapprehension of *The Chicago Tribune*," *Jewish Daily Courier* (May 17, 1923), CFLPS, Jewish, IIIA; L. Carnovale, "The Non-Americanization of Immigrants," *La Fiamma* (November 1, 1923), CFLPS, Italian, IIIG; "Resolution," *Saloniki* (February 9, 1924), CFLPS, Greek, IIIG; "Chicago Organization Urges Senators and Congressmen to Vote against 1890 Basis of Entry," *Chicago Daily Journal* (February 18, 1924), CFLPS, Greek, IIIG.

213. "To the U.S. Senate Immigration Committee," *Italian Chamber of Commerce* 2 (April 1924), CFLPS, Italian, IIIB1.

214. Such immigrant groups as Germans and Scandinavians that the legislation favored generally supported the act. See, for example, "The Regulation of Immigration"; "The Immigration Law of 1924," *Abendpost* (May 30, 1926), CFLPS, German, IIIG. However, in 1929, when Congress sought to further reduce immigration and cut down on the number of people coming to the United States from all parts of Europe (including northwest Europe), these newspapers responded with outrage. "Oppose the National Origins Provisions," *Svenska Tribunen-Nyheter* (April 10, 1929), CFLPS, Swedish, IIIG; "Mass Protest against the National Origins Clause," *Abendpost* (March 30, 1929), CFLPS, German, IC.

215. "Persecution of Immigrants Unanimously Condemned by Council Committee and Representatives of All Nationalities in Chicago," *Jewish Daily Courier* (March 5, 1924), 2, CFLPS, Jewish IIIB1; "Chicago's Delegation to Protest against Immigration Bill en Route to Washington," *Jewish Daily Courier* (March 7, 1924), CFLPS, Jewish, IIIB1. See also "Protest," *Bulletin of the Italo-American National Union* (March 1924), CFLPS, Italian, IIIG; "Foreigners," *Radnik* (June 26, 1924), CFLPS, Croatian, IIIA.

216. Robert H. Clancy, "Speech, April 8, 1924," *Congressional Record: Proceedings and Debates of the First Session of the Sixty-eighth Congress*, vol. 65:6 (Washington DC: Government Printing Office, 1924), 5929.

217. See for example, "American of Foreign Origin," *Abendpost* (January 2, 1919), 2–3, CFLPS, German, IC; "The Value of Citizenship," *Minute Man* (March 1922), 1–2, CFLPS, Greek IJ; "Religion and American Politics," *Jewish Daily Forward* (April 13, 1924), 5–6, CFLPS, Jewish, IF4.

218. Anonymous, "A Real National Danger," *Chicago Society News* (April 1924), 1, 4 5, CFLPS, Polish, IIIG. See also "Polish American Veterans: The Proof of Loyalty," *Dziennik Zjednoczenia* (September 3, 1927), 1–2, CFLPS, Polish.

219. King, *Making Americans*, 117. "Our New 'Nordic' Immigration Policy," *Literary Digest* 81:6 (May 10, 1924), 12–13. On Sabath, see "A Man Who Served Well His People," *Jewish Daily Courier* (March 26, 1924), CFLPS, Jewish, IF5.

220. "Enemies of Immigration Planning to Adopt New Cruelties in the Next Congress," *Jewish Daily Forward* (August 2, 1926), 2, CFLPS, Jewish, IIIB1.

221. See, for example, "Italophobia," *Bulletin of the Italian-American National Union* (April 1925), CFLPS, Italian, IC; "Aliens Are in Great Danger," *Vilnis* (March 9, 1926), CFLPS, Lithuanian, IIIA; "Polish American Veterans the Proof of Loyalty," *Dziennik Zjednoczenia* (September 3, 1927), CFLPS, Polish, IIID; "The Problem among the Nationalities in the United States," *Dziennik*

Chicagoski (January 7, 1928), CFLPS, Polish IIIA; "America and Her People in the Eyes of the European: Contradiction of Ideals," *Dziennik Chicagoski* (January 11, 1928), 8, CFLPS, Polish, IIIG.

222. See, for example, "What Do Ukrainians Want?" *Dziennik Zwiazkowy* (August 3, 1918), CFLPS, Polish, IIID; "Anti-Polish Propaganda by the Jews," *Polonia* (December 12, 1918), CFLPS, Polish, IC; "Jews Are Inventing Pogroms, Say Chicago Polish Anti-Semites," *Jewish Daily Courier* (May 23, 1919), CFLPS, Jewish, IC; "Here Is No Poland, You Polacks, but the United States of America," *Ukrainia* (October 18, 1919), CFLPS, Ukrainian, IC; "Lithuanians Demand Recognition: Desire No Ties with Poland," *Jewish Daily Forward* (June 9, 1919), CFLPS, Jewish, IC; "Loathsome Jewish Attacks on Poland," *Narod Polski* (August 18, 1920), CFLPS, Polish, IC; "Chicago Lithuanians Slander Poland," *Narod Polski* (June 8, 1921), CFLPS, Polish, IC.

223. Gary Gerstle, *American Crucible: Race and Nation in the Twentieth Century* (Princeton: Princeton University Press, 2001), 120–121.

224. See, for example, the message of support Sabath sent to the National Negro Congress's tenth-anniversary celebration in 1946. He wrote, "The acid test of any democratic government is that, under majority rule, the rights of all minorities are protected. As long as one-tenth of the population of the United States is arbitrarily deprived of equal rights in earning a living, in getting an education, in living decently, merely because of the color of their skin, we have failed in our struggle toward democratic living. . . . I have fought for 40 years against every discrimination based on race, religion, or national derivation, and I shall continue that fight as long as there is breath in my body." Adolph J. Sabath to Dr. Max Yergen [president of the National Negro Congress], May 23, 1946, in the Adolph J. Sabath Papers, American Jewish Archives, Box 1, Folder 19. See also Joseph Pierro, "'Everything in My Power': Harry S. Truman and the Fight against Racial Discrimination" (master's thesis, Virginia Polytechnic Institute and State University, 2004), 15–16; Alexander von Hoffman, "A Study in Contradictions: The Origins and Legacy of the Housing Act of 1949," *Housing Policy Debate* 11:2 (2000) 309; Burton A. Boxerman, "Adolph Joachim Sabath in Congress: The Roosevelt and Truman Years," *Journal of the Illinois State Historical Society* 66:4 (Winter 1973), 441.

225. "Jews and Negroes" *Svenska Nyheter* (June 30, 1903), CFLPS, Swedish, IIIH; "Americanization and the Lynch Law" *Star* (August 4, 1904), 11, CFLPS, Greek, IIIA.

226. "Jews and Negroes a Comparison," *Jewish Daily Courier* (August 5, 1912), CFLPS, Jewish, IC. The murder of Leo Frank in 1915 provided Jews with

another reason to abhor lynching. "The Murder of Leo M. Frank," *Jewish Daily Courier* (August 18, 1915), CFLPS, Jewish, IC. See also "Miss Jane Addams and the Frank Case," *Jewish Daily Courier* (March 29, 1914), CFLPS, Jewish, 1914.

227. In the early twentieth century, Italians had been lynched in the South, thus giving Italian immigrants a powerful reason to identify with blacks on this issue. Thomas A. Guglielmo, *White on Arrival: Italians, Race, Color, and Power in Chicago, 1890–1945* (New York: Oxford University Press, 2003), 36. A study of articles about lynching in several Slovak newspapers offers a different perspective. Robert M. Zecker, "'Negrov Lyncovanie' and the Unbearable Whiteness of Slovaks: The Immigrant Press Covers Race," *American Studies* 43:2 (Summer 2002), 52, 50–54.

228. "1776–1924," *Radnik* (July 5, 1924), 2, CFLPS, Croatian, IJ.

229. "Norwegian Independence Day," *Scandia* (May 15, 1930), 3, CFLPS, Norwegian, IIIB3a.

230. "Due to Prejudice," *Jewish Daily Courier* (April 22, 1914), 3–4, CFLPS, Jewish, IC. The Polish newspaper *Narod Polski* also compared blacks and Jews, but in racist and anti-Semitic terms, arguing that race riots in the United States and pogroms in Europe were due to evils perpetrated by these two groups. "Pogroms of Negroes," *Narod Polski* (August 6, 1919), CFLPS, Polish, IC.

231. "The War of Colors," *Jewish Daily Courier* (May 31, 1917), CFLPS, Jewish, IC; Elliot M. Rudwick, *Race Riot at East St. Louis, July 2, 1917* (Carbondale: Southern Illinois University Press, 1964), 27–57.

232. "The Racial Conflict," *Jewish Daily Courier* (July 30, 1919), 5, CFLPS, Jewish, IC.

233. Guglielmo, *White on Arrival*, 40.

234. "Admissions about the Klan," *Magyar Tribune* (August 29, 1924), 3–4, CFLPS, Hungarian, IF1. See also "Meditations of the Day," *Sunday Jewish Courier* (April 22, 1923), CFLPS, Jewish, IC; "The Ku-Klux Klan and the Democratic Convention," *Jewish Daily Forward* (June 16, 1924), CFLPS, Jewish, IE; "From Eve of the Sabbath to the Eve of the Sabbath," *Jewish Daily Courier* (April 27, 1923), CFLPS, Jewish, IC; "Religion and American Politics," *Jewish Daily Forward* (April 13, 1924), 5–6, CFLPS, Jewish, IF4; "The Horizon Is Clearing," *Magyar Tribune* (October 16, 1925), CFLPS, Hungarian, IE.

235. "A Students' Strike," *Rassviet* (September 30, 1927), 2–3, CFLPS, Russian, IC.

236. Abraham Lincoln, "Speech at Chicago, Illinois, July 10, 1858," in *The Collected Works of Abraham Lincoln*, vol. 2 (New Brunswick: Rutgers University Press, 1953), 499–500. John J. Miller makes a similar point about this speech. John J. Miller, *The Unmaking of Americans: How Multiculturalism Has Undermined America's Assimilation Ethic* (New York: Free Press, 1998), 28–29.

237. John U. Ogbu, "Understanding Cultural Diversity and Learning," *Educational Researcher* 21:8 (November 1992), 7.

238. Eric Foner, *The Story of American Freedom* (New York: W. W. Norton, 1998), 246.

239. M. E. [Marcus Eli] Ravage, *An American in the Making* (1917; repr. New York: Dover, 1971), xi.

240. Langston Hughes, "Let America Be America Again," in *A Patriot's Handbook*, ed. Caroline Kennedy (New York: Hyperion, 2003), 54–56.

241. Gerstle, *American Crucible*, 46–47.

242. The quote is from New York City public school superintendent William Ettinger in "Americanization—What Do We Mean by It?" [New York] *Evening Post* (August 9, 1918), 7.

243. John Higham, *Hanging Together: Unity and Diversity in American Culture* (New Haven: Yale University Press, 2001), 116.

244. Pei, "Italian Language in the High Schools," 4. For a similar statement, see Myron B. Kuropas, *The Ukrainian Americans: Roots and Aspirations, 1884–1954* (Toronto: University of Toronto Press, 1991), 79. As June Granatir Alexander finds, Slovak ethnic and fraternal organizations also promoted a "both/and" stance in regard to their Americanism and pride in their Old World heritage. See Alexander, *Ethnic Pride, American Patriotism*.

245. For a fascinating essay on taking a "both/and" stance in current debates about immigration, see Robert D. Putnam, "E Pluribus Unum: Diversity and Community in the Twenty-first Century, The 2006 Johan Skytte Lecture," *Scandinavian Political Studies* 30:2 (2007), 137–174.

246. Kaufmann, *Rise and Fall of Anglo-America*, 2, 110, 85–110. See also Higham, "Cultural Responses to Immigration," 52.

247. Diana Selig, *Americans All: The Cultural Gifts Movement* (Cambridge: Harvard University Press, 220), 3–6.

4 "They have never been—they are not now—half-hearted Americans"

1. Gerhart H. Saenger, "Assimilation and the Minority Problem," *Journal of Educational Sociology* 14:3 (November 1940), 131–132; Gerhart Saenger, *Today's Refugees, Tomorrow's Citizens: A Story of Americanization* (New York: Harper and Brothers, 1941), ix–x.

2. See, for example, John F. McClymer, "The Americanization Movement and the Education of the Foreign-Born Adult, 1914–25," in *American Education and the European Immigrant, 1840–1940*, ed. Bernard J. Weiss (Urbana: University of Illinois Press, 1982); Michael R. Olneck, "Americanization and the Education of Immigrants, 1900–1925: An Analysis of Symbolic Action," *American Journal of Education* 97 (August 1989); Maxine S. Seller, "Success

and Failure in Adult Education: The Immigrant Experience, 1914–1924," *Adult Education* 28:2 (1978).

3. Mildred J. Wiese, *Helping the Foreign-Born Achieve Citizenship: A Teachers' Guide*, U.S. Office of Education, Education and National Defense Series, Pamphlet no. 21 (Washington, DC: United States Government Printing Office, 1942), 2, 6.

4. M. E. [Marcus Eli] Ravage, *An American in the Making* (1917; repr. New York: Dover, 1971), xi.

5. Mark Mazower, *Dark Continent: Europe's Twentieth Century* (New York: Vintage Books, 1998), 42, 51–55.

6. Ibid., 5.

7. Richard Weiss, "Ethnicity and Reform: Minorities and the Ambience of the Depression Years," *Journal of American History* 66:3 (December 1979), 566–585.

8. Louis Adamic, "Aliens and Alien-Baiters," *Harper's Magazine* 173 (November 1936), 561–574. Adamic accurately noted that in the early 1930s more people left the United States than immigrated to it. See Susan B. Carter, Scott S. Gartner, Michael R. Haines, Alan L. Olmstead, Richard Sutch, and Gavin Wright, eds., *Historical Statistics of the United States*, vol. 1 pt. A, Population, "Immigrants, Emigrants, and Net Migration," table Ad., 1–2 (New York: Cambridge University Press, 2006), 1–541.

9. Adamic, "Aliens and Alien-Baiters," 562–563.

10. The Educational Policies Commission and the American Association of School Administrators, *Education and the Defense of American Democracy* (Washington, DC: National Education Association and the American Association of School Administrators, August 1940), 2.

11. Stanley High, "Star Spangled Fascists," *Saturday Evening Post* 211 (May 27, 1939), 5–7, 70–73; Neil Baldwin, *Henry Ford and the Jews: The Mass Production of Hate* (New York: Public Affairs Press, 2001), 278–279.

12. Adolf Hitler, *Mein Kampf* (1925, 1926; repr. Boston: Houghton Mifflin, 1971), vol. 2, chap. 3, 439–440. See also Gerhard L. Weinberg, "Hitler's Image of the United States," *American Historical Review* 69:4 (July 1964), 1009; Edwin Black, *War against the Weak: Eugenics and America's Campaign to Create a Master Race* (New York: Four Walls Eight Windows, 2003), 7–8, 261–318.

13. Black, *War against the Weak*, 311–313, 317–318.

14. Lothrop Stoddard, *Re-Forging America: The Story of Our Nationhood* (New York: Charles Scribner's Sons, 1927).

15. High, "Star Spangled Fascists."

16. Hoover is quoted in Lawrence H. Fuchs, *The American Kaleidoscope: Race, Ethnicity, and the Civic Culture* (Middletown, CT: Wesleyan University Press), 66.

17. For example, a May 1938 Roper/*Fortune* survey asked if the U.S. should welcome political refugees from Germany and Austria. Over two-thirds of the respondents said "no." Conducted by Roper Organization during May 1938 and based on personal interviews with a national adult sample of 5,151 [USROPER.38–01.Q07]. Data provided by the Roper Center for Public Opinion Research, University of Connecticut.

18. Salvatore J. LaGumina, "The New Deal, the Immigrants and Congressman Vito Marcantonio," *International Migration Review* 4:2 (Spring 1970), 58. See also Robert A. Divine, *American Immigration Policy, 1924–1952* (New Haven: Yale University Press, 1957), 77–109.

19. John Diggins, *Mussolini and Fascism: The View from America* (Princeton: Princeton University Press, 1972), 27, 26–28.

20. Isaac F. Marcosson, "The Alien in America," *Saturday Evening Post* 207:40 (April 6, 1935), 86, 22–23, 110, 112–113. See also Aristide R. Zolberg, *A Nation by Design: Immigration Policy in the Fashioning of America* (New York: Russell Sage Foundation, 2006), 254–258.

21. Marcosson, "Alien in America," 23.

22. Martin Dies, "The Immigration Crisis," *Saturday Evening Post* 207:42 (April 20, 1935), 27–28.

23. "The Alien Problem Is the Severest," *National Republic* (June 1935), 10. See also the editorial "Alien Quarrels in America", *Saturday Evening Post* 208 (November 23, 1935), 22.

24. Raymond G. Carroll, "Alien Workers in America," *Saturday Evening Post* 208:30 (January 25, 1936), 85.

25. Lester V. Chandler, *American's Greatest Depression, 1929–1941* (New York: Harper and Row, 1970), 37.

26. The editor of *Liberty Magazine* and the statement from the American Legion are both from Mary Ann Thatcher, *Immigrants and the 1930s: Ethnicity and Alienage in Depression and On-Coming War* (New York: Garland Press, 1990), 169. See also Raymond G. Carroll, "The Alien on Relief," *Saturday Evening Post* 208:28 (January 11, 1936), 16–17, 100–103.

27. Thatcher, *Immigrants and the 1930s*, 153–201.

28. On anti-Semitism in this period, see Leonard Dinnerstein, *Anti-Semitism in America* (New York: Oxford University Press, 1994), 105–149. On anti-Catholic attitudes, see David M. Kennedy, *Freedom from Fear: The American People in Depression and War, 1929–1945* (New York: Oxford University Press, 2005), 228. See also John Tracy Ellis, *American Catholicism* (Chicago: University of Chicago Press, 1969), 150–151; John T. McGreevy, "Thinking on One's Own: Catholicism in the American Intellectual Imagination, 1928–1960," *Journal of American History*, 84:1 (June 1997), 106–111.

29. Harry H. Laughlin, *Immigration and Conquest* (New York: Special Committee on Immigration and Naturalization of the Chamber of Commerce of the State of New York, 1939), 19, 37, 90.

30. The demands of the New York Chamber of Commerce were successfully resisted. See Zoe Burkholder, "'With Science as His Shield': Teaching Race and Culture in American Public Schools, 1900–1954" (Ph.D. diss., New York University, 2008), 57, 57–70. On Chamber of Commerce demands for slashing public school budgets in this era, see David Tyack, Elisabeth Hansot, and Robert Lowe, *Public Schools in Hard Times* (Harvard University Press, 1984), 58, 75.

31. Westbrook Pegler, "America for Americans," *Washington Post* (July 3, 1941), 9. He reiterated this position three weeks later. Westbrook Pegler, "Citizenship Restricted to Natives" *Washington Post* (July 26, 1941), 7. The same year that he wrote these columns, Pegler became the first syndicated columnist to win a Pulitzer Prize. On Pegler's career, see Oliver Pilat, *Pegler, Angry Man of the Press* (Boston: Beacon Press, 1963).

32. *Alien Registration Act of 1940*, Public Law 670, 76th Cong., 3rd sess., C.H. 439 (June 28, 1940), 671, 673–74.

33. In 1942, the U.S. Office of Education reported that over 4.7 million aliens had registered. Two years later, Burritt C. Harrington claimed the figure was over 4.9 million. See Wiese, *Helping the Foreign-Born Achieve Citizenship*, 4, 6. Burritt C. Harrington, "The Government and Adult Citizenship Education," *Religious Education* 39 (January 1944), 198.

34. Gary Gerstle, *American Crucible: Race and Nation in the Twentieth Century* (Princeton: Princeton University Press, 2001), 187–237. The internment of "enemy aliens" was not unprecedented. During World War I, the U.S. government arrested some 6,300 enemy aliens (mostly Germans) and interned 2,300 of them. Carl Brent Swisher, "Civil Liberties in War Time," *Political Science Quarterly* 55:3 (September 1940), 355.

35. Diana Selig, *Americans All: The Cultural Gifts Movement* (Cambridge: Harvard University Press, 2008).

36. On this trend, see Weiss, "Ethnicity and Reform: Minorities and the Ambience of the Depression Years," 566–585.

37. I. F. Stone, "America for Americans," *Washington Post* (July 29, 1941), 9. See also the anti-Pegler comments by Read Lewis, executive director of the Council for American Unity, in the Cleveland Czech newspaper *Svet-American* (August 8, 1941), COCE, vol. 4 (July 20–August 19, 1941), 19–20. Lewis's attack on Pegler was reprinted in *Hlas* (August 7, 1941); *Szabadsag* (August 1, 1941); *L'Araldo* (August 8, 1941), and the *Yidishe Welt* (July 24, 1941); all of which are listed in COCE, vol. 4 (July 20–August 19, 1941), 20. Note that the name of the Jewish newspaper the *Yidishe Welt* only contains one "d"

which is how the paper is identified in both the CFLND and COCE. I have
kept this unconventional spelling throughout this chapter.

38. Franklin D. Roosevelt, "Address on the Occasion of the Fiftieth Anniversary of
the Statue of Liberty," Franklin D. Roosevelt, *The Public Papers and Addresses
of Franklin D. Roosevelt*, vol. 5, 1936 (New York: Random House, 1938), 542–543.

39. Franklin D. Roosevelt, "Address at Roosevelt Park, New York City," in Roosevelt, *Public Papers and Addresses of Franklin D. Roosevelt*, , 544–545.

40. Ibid., 544.

41. For a less sanguine view of the New Deal efforts regarding immigrants, see
LaGumina, "The New Deal, the Immigrants and Congressman Vito Marcantonio," 67, 70–74

42. Tyack, Hansot, and Lowe, *Public Schools in Hard Times.*

43. "An Appraisal of the Effects of the Depression on the Public Schools,"
Elementary School Journal 36:4 (December 1935), 248; Marian Schibsby,
"Educational Opportunities for Applicants for American Citizenship,"
*Proceedings of the Seventy-second Annual Meeting of the National Educa-
tion Association*, 1934 (Washington, DC: National Education Association,
1934), 281.

44. Tyack, Hansot, and Lowe, *Public Schools in Hard Times*, 92–138.

45. Harry Zeitlin, "Federal Relations in American Education, 1933–43: A Study of
New Deal Efforts and Innovations" (Ph.D. diss., Columbia University, 1958),
136.

46. Jerome Davis, "Adult Education in the United States," *Journal of Educational
Sociology* 14:3 (November 1940), 166. Adjusted for inflation, $20 million in 1940
was equal to about $267 million in 2004 dollars. Bureau of Labor Statistics,
Cost of Living Adjustments, Inflation Calculator, http://www.bls.gov/ppi/home
.htm.

47. Cleveland Board of Education, *Annual Report of the Superintendent of
Schools, 1941–42* (Cleveland: The Board, 1942), 45.

48. Henry B. Hazard, "Trends and Accomplishments in the Field of Immigration
and Naturalization," in *Proceedings of the Seventy-second Annual Meeting of
the National Education Association*, 1934, 276–280; Schibsby, "Educational
Opportunities for Applicants for American Citizenship," 280–282.

49. Daniel W. MacCormack, "The Furtherance of Unity among the People of
Widely Variant Racial Origins," *Proceedings of the Seventy-fourth Annual
Meeting of the National Education Association*, 1936 (Washington, DC: The
Association, 1936), 166.

50. In 1913, Congress moved the Division of Naturalization and Bureau of
Immigration into the newly created Department of Labor. In 1933, an
Executive Order merged the two agencies into the Immigration and Natural-
ization Service. Seven years later, the INS was moved to the Department of

Justice. Harrington, "The Government and Adult Citizenship Education," 197; Ruth Z. Murphy, "Government Agencies Working with the Foreign Born," *Annals of the American Academy of Political and Social Science* 262 (March 1949), 138.

51. Franklin L. Burdette, "Education for Citizenship," *Public Opinion Quarterly* 6:2 (Summer 1942), 276, 278; Murphy, "Government Agencies Working with the Foreign Born," 138; Glenn Kendall, "Educational Activities of the United States Immigration and Naturalization Service," *Journal of Educational Sociology* 17:1 (September 1943), 41.

52. Mark Starr, "Why Union Education? Aims, History, and Philosophy of the Educational Work of the International Ladies' Garment Workers' Union," *Proceedings of the American Philosophical Society* 92:3 (July 19, 1948), 197, 198, 202; Mildred Allen Beik, *The Miners of Windber: The Struggles of New Immigrants for Unionization, 1890s–1930s* (University Park: Pennsylvania State University Press, 1996), 338–339. The United Mine Workers strongly supported Americanization education as early as 1916. See also Joel M. Roitman, *The Immigrants, the Progressives, and the Schools: Americanization and the Impact of the New Immigration upon Public Education in the United States, 1890–1920* (Stark, KS: De Young Press, 1996), 49–50.

53. *Nationality Act of 1940*, Public Law 853, 76th Cong., 3rd sess., CH. 876, (October 14, 1940), 1140, 1151. See also Charles Cheney Hyde, "The Nationality Act of 1940," *American Journal of International Law* 35:2 (April 1941), 316–317; Harrington, "Government and Adult Citizenship Education," 197. On the educational implications of the Nationality Act, see Murphy, "Government Agencies Working with the Foreign Born," 137.

54. On the continuing controversies about the nature and content of the citizenship test, see Jack Schneider, "Gatekeepers: A History of Naturalization and the U.S. Citizenship Test" (seminar paper, Stanford University, 2007, in my possession).

55. Mark Van Pelt "'A Vigorous and Violent Program of Education': The National Citizenship Education Program" (seminar paper, University of Wisconsin, 2006, in my possession), 10.

56. Kendall, "Educational Activities of the United States Immigration and Naturalization Service," 40–41.

57. Van Pelt, "'A Vigorous and Violent Program of Education,'" 3.

58. Murphy, "Government Agencies Working with the Foreign Born," 134–135.

59. Van Pelt, "'A Vigorous and Violent Program of Education,'" 13–14; Kendall, "Educational Activities of the United States Immigration and Naturalization Service," 37–41; Bureau of Labor Statistics, Cost of Living Adjustments, Inflation Calculator, http://www.bls.gov/ppi/home.htm.

60. William B. Russell, "The National Citizenship Education Program," *School Life* 27:1 (October 1941), 21. In a number of ways, the actions of the NCEP paralleled or continued efforts taken by the Foreign Language Information Service (FLIS), which ended its operation in 1939. Daniel Erwin Weinstein, "The Foreign Language Information Service and the Foreign Born, 1918–1939: A Case Study of Cultural Assimilation Viewed as a Problem in Social Technology" (Ph.D. diss., University of Minnesota, 1973), 73–73, 86, 93–94, 149–158.

61. Burdette, "Education for Citizenship," 274–275.

62. Van Pelt, "'A Vigorous and Violent Program of Education,'" 19–20.

63. Ibid., 31–32.

64. Works Projects Administration, National Citizenship Education Project (Illinois), *Citizenship Education*, Bulletin no. 5 (Champaign: Division of University Extension, University of Illinois, November 1941). See also Frederick M. Lash, "Methods in the Teaching of Americanization Classes," in *Proceedings of the Seventy-fourth Annual Meeting of the National Education Association, 1936*, 164–165.

65. Works Projects Administration, National Citizenship Education Project (Illinois), *Citizenship Education*, 1, 8, 10, 16, 20, 36, 40, 48, 50, 52.

66. Selig, *Americans All*, 17.

67. See, for example, Harriette F. Ryan, "How Has Our Concept of Americanization Changed?" *Interpreter Releases* 14 (August 10, 1937), 280–282; Weinberg, "Foreign Language Information Service and the Foreign Born, 1918–1939," 180–247.

68. "Self-Made Citizens," *New York Times* (June 2, 1939), 22. On this newspaper's support of the National Origins Act, see "Preserving the American Race," *New York Times* (May 2, 1924), 14.

69. Carl A. Marsden, "A WPA Program of Adult Education, Schuylkill County, Pennsylvania," *Journal of Educational Sociology* 10:9 (May 1937), 558–559.

70. On the CFLND, see Oscar Ban, "Cleveland's Foreign Language Newspaper Digest," *Common Ground* 1:4 (Summer 1941); "Preface," CFLND, 1937–1, i–iii; and Theodore Andrica, "WPA Digests Reveal Story of the Foreign–Born," *Cleveland Press* (February 4, 1941), 12. On immigrants in the American Folk Life interviews, see Dorothee Schneider, "Polish Peasants into Americans: U.S. Citizenship and Americanization among Polish Immigrants in the Inter-War Era," *Polish Sociological Review* 2 (2007), 161, 159–171. On the Federal Writers' Project initiative, see Jerre Mangione, *The Dream and the Deal: The Federal Writers' Project, 1935–1943* (Boston: Little Brown, 1972), 277–285. On Cleveland's Cultural Gardens, see John Bodnar, *Remaking America: Public Memory, Commemoration, and Patriotism in the Twentieth Century* (Princeton: Princeton University Press, 1992), 96–104.

71. Nicholas V. Montalto, *A History of the Intercultural Education Movement, 1924–1941* (New York: Garland Press, 1982), 149–156.

72. Wiese, *Helping the Foreign-Born Achieve Citizenship*, 1. This belief that the "anti-German mania of World War I [should] not to be repeated" was a guiding principle of the NCEP, as well. See Van Pelt, "'A Vigorous and Violent Program of Education,'" 14–15.

73. Weiss, "Ethnicity and Reform," 566.

74. Educational Policies Commission, *The Education of Free Men in American Democracy* (Washington, DC: National Education Association 1941), 29–30, 33, 37, 54.

75. Victor Morey, "Present Objectives of Citizenship Education," *Monthly Review* 3:6 (December 1945), 234–235.

76. Ibid., 235.

77. Chicago Board of Education, *Annual Report of the Superintendent of Schools*, 1937–38 (Chicago: The Board, 1938), 296–301. Chicago had been offering a modest adult *day school* program from as early as 1907, but it was not until 1929 when the Dante School opened that the school system created a permanent elementary program to serve adult students (mainly immigrants) during the day. In February 1940, the system established a high school program in the Dante School. Chicago Board of Education, *Annual Report of the Superintendent of Schools*, 1940–41 (Chicago, IL: The Board, 1941), 330–334.

78. Chicago Board of Education, *Annual Report of the Superintendent of Schools*, 1937–38, 437.

79. Chicago Board of Education, *Annual Report of the Superintendent of Schools*, 1938–39 (Chicago: The Board, 1939), 339.

80. Chicago Board of Education, *Annual Report of the Superintendent of Schools*, 1939–40 (Chicago: The Board, 1940), 198.

81. Chicago Board of Education, *Annual Report of the Superintendent of Schools*, 1939–40, 199. For similar comments, see Chicago Board of Education, *Annual Report of the Superintendent of Schools*, 1937–38, 437; Chicago Board of Education, *Annual Report of the Superintendent of Schools*, 1938–39, 242. On the differences between immigrants in the 1930s and previous newcomers, see Saenger, *Today's Refugees, Tomorrow's Citizens*.

82. Chicago Board of Education, *Annual Report of the Superintendent of Schools*, 1939–40, 199.

83. Chicago Board of Education, *Annual Report of the Superintendent of Schools*, 1940–41 (Chicago: The Board, 1941), 334–335.

84. Ibid., 334.

85. Chicago Board of Education, *The Chicago Public Schools in Wartime* (Published as the Annual Report of the Superintendent of Schools for the School Years 1941–42, 1942–43), 28, 31.

86. See, for example, *Szabadsag* (January 2, 1937), CFLND 1937–4, Abstract 10070, 117; *Wiadomosci Codzienne* (January 2, 1937), CFLND 1937–4, 496; *Ameriska Domovina* (January 4, 1937), CFLND 1937–5, Abstract 19530, 284; *Waechter und Anzeiger* (April 1, 1937), CFLND 1937–2, Abstract 4345, 287; *Hlas* (April 8, 1937), CFLND 1937–1, Abstract 144, 27; *Yidishe Welt* (April 29, 1937), CFLND 1937–3, Abstract 7683, 313–314; *America* (August 17, 1937), CFLND 1937–1, Abstract 1022, 179–180; *Enakopravnost* (October 4, 1937), CFLND 1937–5, Abstract 20489, 426; ; *Yidishe Welt* (January 28, 1938), CFLND 1938–3, Abstract 7700, 336; *Waechter und Anzeiger* (February 8, 1938), CFLND 1938–2, Abstract 4048, 217; *La Voce del Popolo Italiano* (February 13, 1938), CFLND 1938–2, Abstract 2671, 27; *Rodina* (April 14, 1938), CFLND 1938–1, Abstract 381, 72; *Szabadsag* (April 16, 1938), CFLND 1938–4, Abstract 10236, 122; *Dirva* (June 3, 1938), CFLND 1938–3, Abstract 5333, 80; *Wiadomosci Codzienne* (July 4, 1938), CFLND 1938–4, Abstract 12855, 477.
87. *Wiadomosci Codzienne* (March 22, 1938), CFLND 1938–4, Abstract 13240, 531.
88. *American* (February 4, 1938), CFLND, 1938–1, Abstract 2164, 362–363.
89. Cleveland Board of Education, *Annual Report of the Superintendent of Schools, 1941–42*, 45.
90. On Reynolds, see Rob Christensen, *The Paradox of Tar Heel Politics* (Chapel Hill: University of North Carolina Press, 2008), 101–106. *Szabadsag* (September 17, 1941), COCE, vol. 5 (August 20–September 19, 1941), 32.
91. *Waechter und Anzeiger* (June 24, 1942), COCE, vol. 15 (June 20–July 31, 1942), 25.
92. *Yidishe Welt* (September 8, 1941), COCE, vol. 5 (August 20–September 19, 1941), 35.
93. Van Pelt, "'A Vigorous and Violent Program of Education,'" 68–69.
94. Harrington, "Government and Adult Citizenship Education," 195–196, 199–204; Kendall, "Educational Activities of the United States Immigration and Naturalization Service," 36–41; Peter Rachleff, "Class, Ethnicity, and the New Deal: The Croatian Fraternal Union of the 1930s," in *The Ethnic Enigma: The Salience of Ethnicity for European-Origin Groups*, ed. Peter Kivisto (Philadelphia: Balch Institute Press, 1989), 90.
95. Murphy, "Government Agencies Working with the Foreign Born," 134–135, 137–138.
96. Detroit Board of Education, *Learning to Live: The Superintendent's Annual Report for the 105th Year of the Detroit Public Schools* (Detroit: The Board, 1947), 22–23; Chicago Board of Education, *Our Chicago Public Schools: Annual Report of the General Superintendent of Schools, 1950–51* (Chicago: The Board, 1951), 22. See also Cleveland Board of Education, *Report of the Superintendent of Schools, 1943–44* (Cleveland: The Board, 1944), 80–81;

Ralph E. Crow, "Adult Education in the Cleveland Public Schools," *Report to the Superintendent* (Cleveland: Cleveland Board of Education, 1948), 2–3; Detroit Board of Education, *Your School Report: The Superintendent's Annual Report for the Detroit Public Schools, 1950* (Detroit: The Board, 1950), 11; Detroit Board of Education, *Citizens All: The Superintendent's Annual Report for the Detroit Public Schools, 1951* (Detroit: The Board, 1951), 23.

97. Murphy, "Government Agencies Working with the Foreign Born," 138. The quote is from Wiese, *Helping the Foreign-Born Achieve Citizenship*, 20. See also Kendall, "Educational Activities of the United States Immigration and Naturalization Service," 41.

98. Dorothee Schneider, "Naturalization and United States Citizenship in Two Periods of Mass Migration: 1894–1930, 1965–2000," *Journal of American Ethnic History* 21:1 (Fall 2001), 63–64; Wiese, *Helping the Foreign-Born Achieve Citizenship*, 2, 6.

99. Franklin D. Roosevelt, "Speech to the Daughters of the American Revolution" (April 21, 1938), in Roosevelt, *The Public Papers and Addresses of Franklin D. Roosevelt, 1938* (New York; Macmillan, 1941), 259.

100. Franklin D. Roosevelt, "Radio Address to the New York *Herald Tribune* Forum" (October 24, 1940), in Roosevelt, *Public Papers and Addresses of Franklin D. Roosevelt, 1941*, 496–497.

101. Byron Darnton, "Vast Throng Jams Mall to Cheer American Day Fete: City's Greatest Patriotic Rally Draws Estimated 750,000 to Reaffirm Loyalty to U.S.," *New York Times* (May 19, 1941), 1, 3.

102. Harold Ickes, "Interior Secretary Harold Ickes Lashes Isolationists and Defeatists?" ["I Am an American Day" speech in New York City, May 18, 1941], in *Lend Me Your Ears: Great Speeches in History*, ed. William Safire (New York: W. W. Norton, 1992), 59.

103. Murphy, "Government Agencies Working with the Foreign Born," 134.

104. Unlike during the World War I years, in the 1940s only a small number of new naturalizations (about 125,000) were due to military service. Carter et al., *Historical Statistics of the United States*, vol. 1, pt. A, Population, "Aliens Naturalized by Provision," table Ad., 1030–1037, 641–642. See also Murphy, "Government Agencies Working with the Foreign Born," 132.

105. Richard Polenberg, *One Nation Divisible: Class, Race, and Ethnicity in the United States since 1938* (New York: Penguin Books, 1980), 36. On the number of papers in Cleveland, see "Preface," CFLND, 1937–1, i–iii.

106. The CFLPS essentially ended its work in 1936, although there are occasional entries from 1937. The CFLND project translated articles and editorials for all of 1937 and 1938. The COCE project excerpted articles and editorials from foreign language and black newspapers in Cleveland from May 1941 to July 1942.

107. Articles on the growing power of groups like the Ku Klux Klan can be found in *Szabadsag* (October 7, 1937), CFLND 1937:1, Abstract 10736, 221; *Yidishe Welt* (March 19, 1937), CFLND 1937–3, Abstract 8018, 373; *Yidishe Welt* (July 30, 1937), CFLND 1937–3, Abstract 8189, 408; *America* (March 29, 1938), CFLND 1938–1, Abstract 1042, 174.

108. "A Narrow-Minded Editorial Writer" *Svenska-Tribunen-Nyheter* (February 18, 1933), 2–3, CFLPS, Swedish, IIIG. For similar editorial attacks on the *Saturday Evening Post*, see "Immigration Crisis," *Abendpost* (April 19, 1935), CFLPS, German, IIIG; and "Advance of Nativism," *Abendpost* (June 25, 1935), CFLPS, German, IIIG.

109. *Szabadsag* (September 23, 1938), CFLND 1938–4, Abstract 10698, 195.

110. *Wiadomosci Codzienne* (November 1, 1938), CFLND, 1938:4, Abstract 13862, 620. The *Wiadomosci Codzienne* was the first Polish daily newspaper in Cleveland. It had a reputation for being a "free-thinking" but not anticlerical paper that had some leftist leanings. See John J. Grabowski, Judith Zielinski-Zak, Alice Boberg, and Ralph Wroblewski, *Polish Americans and Their Communities of Cleveland* (Cleveland: Cleveland Ethnic Heritage Series, 197), 204. For additional examples of opposition to Dies and other anti-immigrant politicians, see *Szabadsag* (October 18, 1938), CFLND 1938–4, Abstract 10728, 200; *Szabadsag* (November 1, 1938), CFLND 1938–4, Abstract 10750, 204; *Waechter und Anzeiger* (October 29, 1938), CFLND 1938–2, Abstract 4389, 283. *Wiadomosci Codzienne* (August 15, 1938) CFLND, 1938–4, Abstract 13657, 593; *La Voce del Popolo Italiano* (October 28, 1938), CFLND 1938–2, Abstract 2854, 60; *Yidishe Welt* (November 25, 1938), CFLND 1938–3, Abstract 8323, 466.

111. "Hundred-Per-Cent Americans and the Foreigners," *Otthon* (June 28, 1935), 1, CFLPS, Hungarian, IIIA. See also *Wiadomosci Codzienne* (September 11, 1937), CFLND, 1937–4, Abstract 14643, 667.

112. *Enakopravnost* (May 8, 1937), CFLND, 1937–5, Abstract 21063, 516–517.

113. For other examples of such sentiments, see Franco D'Amico, "Nordic Myths," *Bulletin of the Sons of Italy of Illinois* 8:11 (1936), CFLPS, Italian, IIIA. In the Cleveland papers, see *Hlas* (September 7, 1937), CFLND 1937–1, Abstract 157, 29; *Rodina* (September 9, 1937), CFLND 1937–1, Abstract 327, 66; *Ameriska Domovina* (July 3, 1937), CFLND 1937–5, Abstract 21187, 535; *Svet-American* (September 20, 1937), CFLND 1937–1, Abstract 1993, 345.

114. "Lithuanians Were among the Early Settlers of the New World," *Sandara* (October 10, 1930), 1, 5, CFLPS, Lithuanian, IIIF. See also "Norwegian Independence Day," *Scandia* (May 15, 1930), 2, CFLPS, Norwegian, IIIB3a.

115. *Rodina* (November 11, 1937), CFLND 1937-1, Abstract 331, 67. See also *Rodina* (September 9, 1937), CFLND 1937–1, Abstract 327, 66–67; *Rodina* (September 24, 1937), CFLND, 1937–1, Abstract 328, 67.

116. *America* (January 12, 1937), CFLND 1937–1, Abstract 829, 139. For other expressions of this idea, see *Waechter und Anzeiger* (January 13, 1937), CFLND 1937–2, Abstract 4290, 278; *Waechter und Anzeiger* (April 17, 1938), CFLND 1938–2, Abstract 4133, 235.

117. On Germans in American history, see "Americans of German Origin," *Abendpost* (March 9, 1930), CFLPS, German, IC; "The German Element in the 100 Year History of Chicago," *Abendpost* (May 28, 1933), CFLPS, German, IIIF; "The Parent Country of the United States," *Sonntagpost* (July 1, 1934), 4–5, CFLPS, German, IJ; *Waechter und Anzeiger* (July 5, 1937), CFLND 1937-2, Abstract 4490, 312; *Waechter und Anzeiger* (August 8, 1937), CFLND 1937–2, Abstract 4528, 320; *Waechter und Anzeiger* (June 20, 1938), CFLND 1938–2, Abstract 3877, 189–190; *Waechter und Anzeiger* (May 30, 1938), CFLND 1938–2, Abstract 4186, 247–248; *Waechter und Anzeiger* (September 12, 1938), CFLND 1938–2, Abstract 4323, 271. On Greeks, see "Enlightening the Americans about Grecian Contributions," *Greek Press* (January 29, 1931), CFLPS, Greek, IIIF; "We Have Two Countries," *Saloniki-Greek Press* (October 11, 1934), CFLPS, Greek, IIIG. On Hungarians, see "The Campaign of Incitement," *Magyar Tribune* (March 27, 1931), CFLPS, Hungarian, IC; *Szabadsag* (March 12, 1938), CFLND 1938–4, Abstract 10428, 150; *Szabadsag* (July 13, 1938), CFLND, 1938–4, Abstract 10601, 178. On Italians, see *La Voce del Popolo Italiano* (July 31, 1938), CFLND 1938:2, Abstract 2690, 30. On Poles, see, for example, *Wiadomosci Codzienne* (January 13, 1937), CFLND 1937–4, Abstract 13911, 556; *Wiadomosci Codzienne* (July 4, 1938), CFLND, 1938–4, Abstract 13531, 575. On Romanians, see *America* (February 18, 1937), CFLND 1937:1, Abstract 856, 145. On Slovenians and other Yugoslavs, see *Enakopravnost* (September 11, 1937), Abstract 21286, 551; *Enakopravnost* (October 2, 1937), CFLND 1937–5, Abstract 21311, 555.

118. *Wiadomosci Codzienne* (May 28, 1938), CFLND, 1938–4, Abstract 13407, 557.

119. Richard Brenne, "German American Achievements," CFLND 1937–2, 104. According to Carl Wittke, *Waechter und Anzeiger* was the second-oldest German language newspaper in the United States and was, by the late 1930s, one of only twelve German language dailies left in the country. Carl Wittke, *The German-Language Press in America* (Lexington: University of Kentucky Press, 1957), 287.

120. See John Pankuch, "Slovaks in Cleveland," CFLND 1937–1, 1; Ivan A. Ladizinsky, "Historical Sketch of the Carpatho-Russian People," CFLND 1937–1, 44; J. N. Barbu, "Roumanians [sic] in America," CFLND 1937–1, 73; F. J. Kutak, "The Czech People," CFLND 1937–1, 242; Hyman Horowitz, "The

Jew and the Jewish Press in America," CFLND 1937–3, 129; Zoltan Gumbos, "Hungarians in America," CFLND 1937–4, 4; Z. B. Dybowski, "Historical Sketch of the Polish People," CFLND 1937–4, 320; James Debevec, "The Nation of Slovenes," CFLND 1937–5, 2.

121. Hannah Arendt, *The Origins of Totalitarianism* (1948; repr. New York: Harvest Book/Harcourt,1994).

122. Moshe R. Gottleib, *American Anti-Nazi Resistance, 1933–1941* (New York: Ktav, 1982).

123. *Yidishe Welt* (April 1, 1937), CFLND 1937–3, Abstract 8978, 542.

124. The Cleveland Jewish community was home to two of the most nationally prominent anti-Nazi leaders—Rabbi Barnett Brickner and Rabbi Abba Hillel Silver. See Gottleib, *American Anti-Nazi Resistance, 1933–1941*, 91–92, 99–100, 160–161, 271. Cleveland was the first city in the United States to boycott German goods following the Nazi takeover in 1933. *Yidishe Welt* (January 24, 1937), CFLND 1937–3, Abstract 7609, 301.

125. Lucy S. Dawidowicz, *The War against the Jews, 1933–1945* (New York: Holt, Rinehart, and Winston, 1973), 63, 67, 63–69.

126. On Jews' loss of civil rights in Hungary, including the right to naturalize, see Dawidowicz, *The War against the Jews, 1933–1945*, 380–381; *Yidishe Welt* (May 24, 1938), CFLND 1938–3, Abstract 8632, 537. On the loss of civil rights for Polish Jews and loss of citizenship for some of them, see Dawidowicz, *War against the Jews, 1933–1945*, 396; *Yidishe Welt* (September 13, 1937), CFLND 1937–3, Abstract 8705, 497; *Yidishe Welt* (April 4, 1938), CFLND 1938–3, Abstract 7964, 389–390. On Jews' loss of civil rights and citizenship in Romania, see Misha Glenny, *The Balkans: Nationalism, War, and the Great Powers, 1804–1999* (New York: Penguin Books, 1999), 449; see also *Yidishe Welt* (August 23, 1937), CFLND 1937–3, Abstract 8652, 487; *Yidishe Welt* (January 7, 1938), CFLND 1938–3, Abstract 8380, 477–78. For denunciations of the idea of racial purity generally, see *Yidishe Welt* (January 30, 1938), CFLND 1938–3, Abstract 9077, 632.

127. Dawidowicz, *War against the Jews, 1933–1945*, 88–106; Gregory Paul Wegner, *Anti-Semitism and Schooling under the Third Reich* (New York: Routledge-Falmer, 2002), 196–197; *Yidishe Welt* (October 12, 1937), CFLND 1937–3, Abstract 7832, 340; *Yidishe Welt* (February 3, 1937), CFLND 1937–3, Abstract 8365, 434: *Yidishe Welt* (January 27, 1938), CFLND 1938–3, Abstract 8420, 489.

128. *Yidishe Welt* (October 14, 1938), CFLND 1938–3, Abstract 7792, 352.

129. Hyman Horowitz, "The Jew and the Jewish Press in America," CFLND 1937–3, 129. See also *Yidishe Welt* (November 12, 1937), CFLND 1937–3, Abstract 7871, 346.

130. Mazower, *Dark Continent*, 50–51, 53–60.
131. *Dirva* (February 5, 1937), CFLND 1937–3, Abstract 5735, 98. On the mistreatment of Lithuanians, see *Dirva* (July 1, 1938), CFLND 1938–3, Abstract 5515, 113. On *Dirva*, see John F. Cadzow, *Lithuanian Americans and Their Communities of Cleveland* (Cleveland: Cleveland Ethnic Heritage Studies, 1978), 133.
132. *Ameriska Domovina* (March 3, 1937), CFLND 1937–5, Abstract 21628, 607.
133. *Enakopravnost* (April 6, 1937), CFLND 1937–5, Abstract 21471, 581.
134. Vatro J. Grill, "American Slovenes," CFLND 1937–5, 2.
135. *Rodina* (March 11, 1937), CFLND 1937–1, Abstract 340, 69.
136. *Szabadsag* (May 16, 1937), CFLND 1937–4, Abstract 10961, 261. See also *Szabadsag* (March 30, 1937), CFLND 1937–4, Abstract 10946, 258; *Szabadsag* (April 12, 1937), CFLND 1937–3, Abstract 10950, 259; *Szabadsag* (February 3, 1938), CFLND 1938–4, Abstract 10364, 142.
137. *Svet-American* (January 21, 1937), CFLND 1937–1, Abstract 2017, 349.
138. *Szabadsag* (May 17, 1938), CFLND 1938–4, Abstract 10527, 166. See also *Szabadsag* (April 19, 1937), CFLND 1937–4, Abstract 10452, 174–75.
139. In the section "Nationality Organizations," Consiliu National Roman American (Romanian National Council) speech by Mr. Barber (May 10, 1938), CFLND 1938–1, Abstract 576, 109.
140. Saul Friedlander, *Nazi Germany and the Jews: The Years of Persecution, 1933–1939* (New York: Harper Perennial, 1997), 214–215; C. E. Black and E. C. Helmreich, *A History of Twentieth Century Europe* (New York: Alfred A. Knopf, 1972), 355–357, 359–361, 545–546; Glenny, *The Balkans*, 447–460; Dennis Deletant, *Hitler's Forgotten Ally: Ion Antonescu and His Regime, Romania, 1940–1944* (New York: Palgrave Macmillan, 2006).
141. On denunciations of Nazism and fascism generally and concern about the dictatorships in Hungary and Romania specifically, see *Szabadsag* (May 6, 1937), CFLND 1937–4, Abstract 10488, 180; *Szabadsag* (January 14, 1938), CFLND 1938–4, Abstract 10329, 136; *America* (March 2, 1937), CFLND 1937–1, Abstract 868, 148; *America* (April 20, 1937), CFLND 1937–1, Abstract 924, 160; *America* (May 14, 1938), CFLND 1938–1, Abstract 580, 109. On their opposition to anti-Semitism, see *Szabadsag* (July 9, 1937), CFLND 1937–1, Abstract 11190, 297; *Szabadsag* (May 10, 1938), CFLND 1938–4, Abstract 10912, 233; *America* (February 27, 1937), CFLND 1937–1, Abstract 864, 147; *America* (February 5, 1938), CFLND 1938–1, Abstract 1342, 237. On support for antitotalitarian protests, see *Szabadsag* (January 19, 1938), CFLND 1937–4, Abstract 10336, 137; *America* (September 18, 1937), CFLND 1937–1, Abstract 790, 132.
142. *America* (March 19, 1938), CFLND 1938–1, Abstract 1036, 172.

143. *Szabadsag* (September 17, 1938), CFLND 1937–4, Abstract 11310, 303. For similar predictions, see *Szabadsag* (December 31, 1938), CFLND 1938–4, Abstract 10822, 218; *Svet-American* (October 23, 1937), CFLND 1937–1, Abstract 2235, 379.

144. The weekly Romanian paper *Foaia Poporului (People's News)* probably should be in this category also. It supported the dictatorial regime in Romania and was fiercely anti-Semitic. On these stands, see *Foaia Poporului* (May 15, 1938), CFLND 1938–1, Abstract 899, 143; *Foaia Poporului* (June 19, 1938), CFLND 1938–1, Abstract 909, 144; *Foaia Poporului* (July 10, 1938), CFLND 1938–1, Abstract 918, 147; *Foaia Poporului* (January 23, 1938), CFLND 1938–1, Abstract 986, 16. However, the CFLND abstracted the paper only in 1938, and it was rarely cited in the COCE. Thus, it is difficult to know whether it changed its views prior to the U.S. entry into World War II.

145. Wittke, *German-Language Press in America*, 272.

146. Ronald H. Bayor, "Historical Encounters: Intergroup Relations in a 'Nation of Nations,'" *Annals of the American Academy of Political and Social Science* 530 (November 1993), 22.

147. On the rebirth of the German economy, see, for example, *Waechter und Anzeiger* (May 30, 1938), CFLND 1938–2, Abstract 4530, 311. On uniting all Germans in one state, see *Waechter und Anzeiger* (April 1, 1938), CFLND 1938–2, Abstract 4115, 232. On U.S. support for Britain in World War I, see *Waechter und Anzeiger* (April 6, 1937), CFLND 1937–2, Abstract 4351, 288.

148. On the German American Bund, see *Waechter und Anzeiger* (January 8, 1937), CFLND 1937–2, Abstract 2872, 131; *Waechter und Anzeiger* (January 22, 1937), CFLND 1937–2, Abstract 2874, 131; *Waechter und Anzeiger* (November 15, 1937), CFLND 1937–2, Abstract 4257, 272–273. On the activities of the German consul, see *Waechter und Anzeiger* (February 11, 1937), CFLND 1937–2, Abstract 3500, 185.

149. *Waechter und Anzeiger* (January 26, 1937), CFLND 1937–2, 1937), Abstract 3996, 231. See also *Waechter und Anzeiger* (February 20, 1937), CFLND 1937–2, 1937), Abstract 4017, 234.

150. *Yidishe Welt* (April 29, 1937), CFLND 1937–3, Abstract 7683, 313; *Yidishe Welt* (August 20, 1937), CFLND 1937–3, Abstract 8644, 486. On anti-Jewish actions in education, see Wegner, *Anti-Semitism and Schooling under the Third Reich*, 18–19, 67–179. On Nazi education generally, see Erika Mann, *School for Barbarians: Education under the Nazis* (New York: Modern Age Books, 1938). For other criticisms of the student exchange, see *Yidishe Welt* (April 27, 1937), CFLND 1937–3, Abstract 7678, 312–313; *Yidishe Welt* (May 2, 1937), CFLND 1937–3, Abstract 7690, 314; *Yidishe Welt* (September 3, 1937), CFLND 1937–3, Abstract 7807, 336; *Yidishe Welt* (September 5, 1937), CFLND 1937–3, Abstract 7810, 337.

151. Silver is quoted in *Yidishe Welt* (May 4, 1937), CFLND 1937–3, Abstract 7695, 316.

152. *Waechter und Anzeiger* (May 3, 1937), CFLND 1937–2, Abstract 4079, 243; *Waechter und Anzeiger* (June 2, 1937), CFLND 1937–2, Abstract 4120, 250; *Waechter und Anzeiger* (June 2, 1937), CFLND 1937–2, Abstract 4121, 250; *Waechter und Anzeiger* (June 8, 1937), CFLND 1937–2, Abstract 4125, 261; *Waechter und Anzeiger* (September 28, 1937), CFLND 1937–2, Abstract 4219, 267. On the angry Jewish response, see *Yidishe Welt* (April 30, 1937), CFLND 1937–3, Abstract 7688, 314; *Yidishe Welt* (May 4, 1937), CFLND 1937–3, Abstract 7696, 316; *Yidishe Welt* (May 3, 1937), CFLND 1937–3, Abstract 7692, 315; *Yidishe Welt* (May 4, 1937), CFLND 1937–3, Abstract 7694, 318.

153. *Waechter und Anzeiger* (June 21, 1938), CFLND 1938–2, Abstract 42206, 254.

154. *Yidishe Welt* (April 26, 1938), CFLND 1938–3, Abstract 7733, 342. In fact, in December 1941, an article in *Waechter und Anzeiger* proudly declared that relations between the German paper and *Yidishe Welt* were so good that the Jewish paper actually "printed our paper [*Waechter und Anzeiger*] recently while we were in the process of moving to other quarters." *Waechter und Anzeiger* (December 12, 1941), COCE, vol. 8 (November 20, 1941–December 19, 1941), 27.

155. *Waechter und Anzeiger* (April 5, 1937), CFLND 1937–2, Abstract 4349, 288.

156. *Waechter und Anzeiger* (April 27, 1938), CFLND 1938–2, Abstract 4146, 238. As a Bund publication explained in October 1936, "By obtaining your [U.S.] citizenship you have not lost your German character. You remain what you were, Germans in America . . . we do not become Americans by taking out our second papers." Quoted in Timothy J. Holian, *The German-Americans and World War II: An Ethnic Experience* (New York: Peter Lang, 1996), 29–30. For a later editorial criticizing this position, see *Waechter und Anzeiger* (June 24, 1938), CFLND 1938–2, Abstract 4224, 255.

157. *Yidishe Welt* (April 28, 1938), CFLND 1938–2, Abstract 7735, 342. Two days earlier, the *Yidishe Welt* ran an editorial praising the *Waechter und Anzeiger's* denunciation of Nazi violence against Jews in Austria. *Waechter und Anzeiger* (April 23, 1938), CFLND 1938–2, Abstract 4519, 309; *Yidishe Welt* (April 26, 1938), CFLND 1938–2, Abstract 7733, 342. About two weeks after the German newspaper ran its anti-Bund editorial, it received a letter from the League for Human Rights, an anti-Nazi organization in Cleveland, congratulating "the *Waechter und Anzeiger* on its stand against Nazi propaganda." *Waechter und Anzeiger* (May 8, 1938), CFLND 1938–2, Abstract 4164, 242.

158. *Szabadsag* (April 29, 1938), CFLND 1937–4, Abstract 10242, 123.

159. Dawidowicz, *War against the Jews*, 101–104.

160. "The German Name Disgraced," *Waechter und Anzeiger* (November 17, 1938), 2. This editorial was not included in the CFLND. I am indebted to Ana Margarida Abrantes from Case Western Reserve University for locating this editorial for me, and to Sara Jackson of the German Language and Literature Department at the University of Michigan for translating it. Two days after this editorial appeared, the Romanian newspaper *America* applauded the stand taken by *Waechter und Anzeiger*. *America* (November 19, 1938), CFLND 1938–1, Abstract 953, 153. The *Waechter und Anzeiger* renewed its condemnation of Nazi Germany the following week. See *Waechter und Anzeiger* (November 26, 1938), CFLND 1938–2, Abstract 4609, 323.

161. *Waechter und Anzeiger* (December 12, 1941), COCE, vol. 8 (November 20, 1941–December 19, 1941), 27.

162. Holian, *German-Americans in World War II*, 58. See also Wittke, *German-Language Press in America*, 284–285, and Yaroslav J. Chyz, "The War and the Foreign-Language Press," *Common Ground* 3:3 (Spring 1943), 7. For a contrary view on the German American press, see David G. Singer, "The Prelude to Nazism: The German-American Press and the Jews, 1919–1933," *American Jewish Historical Quarterly* 66:3 (March 1977), 419–420.

163. Black and Helmreich, *A History of Twentieth Century Europe*, 390; Edward R. Kantowicz, *Polish-American Politics in Chicago* (Chicago: University of Chicago Press, 1975), 3, 110–119; Helena Znaniecki Lopata, *Polish Americans: Status Competition in an Ethnic Community* (Englewood Cliffs, NJ: Prentice-Hall, 1976), 23; Mazower, *Dark Continent*, 53. On the increasingly onerous laws against Jews in Poland, see Dawidowicz, *War against the Jews*, 396. In the 1920s, Polish newspapers in Chicago also vehemently attacked any group that questioned undemocratic and racist developments in the new Polish state. They directed particular outrage at American Jewish protests about mistreatment of their coreligionists in Poland. See, for example, "Anti-Polish Propaganda by the Jews," *Polonia* (December 12, 1918), CFLPS, Polish, IC; "Jews Are Inventing Pogroms, Say Chicago Polish Anti-Semites," *Jewish Daily Courier* (May 23, 1919), CFLPS, Jewish, IC; "Loathsome Jewish Attacks on Poland," *Narod Polski* (August 18, 1920), CFLPS, Polish, IC.

164. On praise of American democratic values, see *Wiadomosci Codzienne* (October 13, 1937), CFLND 1937–4, Abstract 14725, 681. On urging Poles to learn about the U.S. Constitution, see *Wiadomosci Codzienne* (September 11, 1937), CFLND 1937–4, Abstract 14643, 667; *Wiadomosci Codzienne* (September 18, 1937), CFLND 1937–4, Abstract 14662, 671. For responses to criticism of Poland in English language newspapers, see, for example, *Wiadomosci Codzienne* (September 4, 1937), CFLND 1937–4, Abstract 13758,

532; *Wiadomosci Codzienne* (December 14, 1937), CFLND 1937–4, Abstract 14915, 709.

165. On Polish anti-Semitism during these years, see Friedlander, *Nazi Germany and the Jews,* 215–219.

166. *Wiadomosci Codzienne* (January 19, 1937), CFLND 1937–4, Abstract 15003, 724.

167. *Wiadomosci Codzienne* (March 10, 1937), CFLND 1937–4, Abstract 15135, 743.

168. *Wiadomosci Codzienne* (May 25, 1937), CFLND 1937–4, Abstract 15306, 771; *Wiadomosci Codzienne* (May 25, 1937), CFLND 1937–4, Abstract 15308, 771. On Polish efforts to actually expel large numbers of Jews to Madagascar, see Friedlander, *Nazi Germany and the Jews,* 219.

169. *Wiadomosci Codzienne* (July 18, 1937), CFLND 1937–4, Abstract 15413, 788.

170. On Lithuanians, see *Wiadomosci Codzienne* (February 27, 1937), CFLND 1937–4, Abstract 14046, 577; *Wiadomosci Codzienne* (March 17, 1938), CFLND 1938–4, Abstract 14163, 665. On Ukrainians, see *Wiadomosci Codzienne* (November 11, 1938), CFLND 1938–4, Abstract 14716, 745.

171. On opposition to lynching, see *Wiadomosci Codzienne* (April 17, 1937), CFLND 1937–4, Abstract 14193, 600 and *Wiadomosci Codzienne* (January 18, 1938), CFLND 1938–4, Abstract 13067, 507. On support for the Scottsboro Boys see *Wiadomosci Codzienne* (July 29, 1937), CFLND 1937–4, Abstract 14526, 649. On denunciations of Bilbo, see *Wiadomosci Codzienne* (June 8, 1938), CFLND 1938–4, Abstract 13437, 561 and *Wiadomosci Codzienne* (June 13, 1938), CFLND 1938–4, Abstract 13455, 564.

172. For example, *Enakopravnost, Szabadsag,* the *Waechter und Anzeiger,* and the *Yidishe Welt* strongly condemned lynching and supported federal legislation to end the practice. See *Enakopravnost* (April 16, 1937), CFLND 1937–5, Abstract 20993, 506; *Enakopravnost* (August 21, 1937), CFLND 1937–5, Abstract 21253, 546; *Szabadsag* (February 8, 1938), CFLND 1938–4, Abstract 10371, 143; *Waechter und Anzeiger* (April 17, 1937), CFLND 1937–2, Abstract 4375, 293; *Yidishe Welt* (April 27, 1937), CFLND 1937–3, Abstract 8060, 381; *Yidishe Welt* (November 29, 1937), CFLND 1937–3, Abstract 8301, 381; *Yidishe Welt* (January 16, 1938), CFLND 1938–3, Abstract 7858, 365. On the Scottsboro boys, see *Szabadsag* (November 10, 1937), CFLND 1937–4, Abstract 10795, 232. On support for black voting rights, see *Yidishe Welt* (November 2, 1938), CFLND 1938–3, Abstract 8279, 459.

173. *Wiadomosci Codzienne* (June 16, 1938), CFLND 1938–4, Abstract 13470, 566.

174. Friedlander, *Nazi Germany and the Jews,* 266–267.

175. *Wiadomosci Codzienne* (October 31, 1941), COCE, vol. 7 (October 20–November 19, 1941), 8–9; *Wiadomosci Codzienne* (October 28, 1941), COCE, vol. 7 (October 20–November 19, 1941), 33.

176. Stefano Luconi, "The Italian-Language Press, Italian American Voters, and Political Intermediation in Pennsylvania in the Interwar Years," *International Migration Review* 33:4 (Winter 1999), 1037, 1031–61; John Patrick Diggins, *Mussolini and Fascism: The View from America* (Princeton: Princeton University Press, 1972), 107, 81–86; 106–110. On the pro-Fascist leanings of the editor of *La Voce del Popolo Italiano*, see Gene Veronesi, *Italian Americans and Their Communities of Cleveland* (Cleveland: Cleveland Ethnic Heritage Series, 1977), 252–261.

177. *La Voce del Popolo Italiano* (July 14, 1937), CFLND 1937–2, Abstract 2523, 53–54. On Leonard J. Melaragno, see Veronesi, *Italian Americans and Their Communities of Cleveland*, 260.

178. On citizenship classes, see *La Voce del Popolo Italiano* (February 13, 1938), CFLND 1938–2, Abstract 2671, 27. On patriotic holidays and support for democratic values, see *La Voce del Popolo Italiano* (June 4, 1937), CFLND 1937–2, Abstract 2513, 51; *La Voce del Popolo Italiano* (July 4, 1937), CFLND 1937–2, Abstract 2517, 52; *La Voce del Popolo Italiano* (May 29, 1938), CFLND 1938–2, Abstract 2764, 43.

179. On support for Mussolini and Fascism, see, for example, *La Voce del Popolo Italiano* (April 25, 1937), CFLND 1937–2, Abstract 2429, 35; *Voce del Popolo Italiano* (October 28, 1937), CFLND 1937–2, Abstract 2694, 89. For attacks on the English language press, see *Voce del Popolo Italiano* (April 18, 1937), CFLND 1937–2, Abstract 2427, 34; *Voce del Popolo Italiano* (September 28, 1938), CFLND 1938–2, Abstract 2969, 81.

180. On Rapone and Olindo Melaragno, the longtime editor of *La Voce*, who, at the behest of Mussolini, received a Chevalier of the Crown from King Victor Emanuel III, see Veronesi, *Italian Americans and Their Communities of Cleveland*, 252, 261. On support for the invasion of Ethiopia, see *La Voce del Popolo Italiano* (January 8, 1937), CFLND 1937–2, Abstract 2591, 66–67; *La Voce del Popolo Italiano* (January 30, 1938), CFLND 1938–2, Abstract 2731, 38. Thomas Guglielmo found similar pro-war sentiments among Italian Americans in Chicago. Guglielmo, *White on Arrival*, 115–125. On the Munich agreement and Sudeten Germans, see *La Voce del Popolo Italiano* (September 15, 1938), CFLND 1938–2, Abstract 2964, 80. On the adoption of racial laws in Italy, see Diggins, *Mussolini and Fascism*, 318–320, 342–343; *La Voce del Popolo Italiano* (February 25, 1938), CFLND 1938–2, Abstract 2903, 70. On Jewish opposition to these laws, see *Yidishe Welt* (September 12, 1938), CFLND 1938–3, Abstract 8220, 448; *Yidishe Welt* (September 14, 1938), CFLND 1938–3, Abstract 8222, 449.

181. Diggins, *Mussolini and Fascism*, 26–29, 58–72, 81–86; Guglielmo, *White on Arrival*, 114–115; Luconi, "Italian-Language Press, Italian American Voters, and Political Intermediation in Pennsylvania in the Interwar Years," 1037–39. On why many Italians fell under the spell of Il Duce, see Michael de Capite, "War Comes to Little Italy," *Common Ground* 2:3 (Spring 1942), 50–52; and Max Ascoli, "On the Italian Americans," *Common Ground* 3:1 (Autumn 1942), 45–49.

182. While there is some debate about exactly when this change occurred, there is no doubt that by mid-December 1941, the majority of Italian Americans were backing away from their past support for Mussolini and the Fascist regime in Italy. See Veronesi, *Italian Americans and Their Communities in Cleveland*, 262–263, and Diggins, *Mussolini and Fascism*, 349–352.

183. Both the Sons of Italy leader and the editor *of L'Araldo* are quoted in Veronesi, *Italian Americans and Their Communities in Cleveland*, 262.

184. DeMaiorbus is quoted in Veronesi, *Italian Americans and Their Communities in Cleveland*, 262–263. DeMaiorbus was the first Italian American elected to the Cleveland city council. See Charles D. Ferroni, *The Italians of Cleveland: A Study in Assimilation* (New York: Arno Press, 1980), 128.

185. For example, see *Svet-American* (May 28, 1941), COCE, vol. 1 (May 12–June 14, 1941), 18; *Szabadsag* (May 24, 1941), COCE, vol. 1 (May 12–June 14, 1941), 18; *Wiadomosci Codzienne* (May 29, 1941), COCE, vol. 1 (May 12–June 14, 1941), 19; *America* (May 29, 1941), 19–20; *Ameriska Domovina* (May 31, 1941), COCE, vol. 1 (May 12–June 14, 1941), 20; *Enakopravnost* (May 28, 1941), COCE, vol. 1 (May 12–June 14, 1941), 20–21; *Hlas* (May 20, 1941), COCE, vol. 1 (May 12–June 14, 1941), 20. While *Hlas* was quite clear about its opposition to the pro-Nazi regime in Slovakia, June Granatir Alexander notes that there was considerable division among Slovak Americans about supporting the regime. Nevertheless, following Slovakia's declaration of war against the United States in December 1941, the Slovak American community united in fierce opposition to the Axis powers, including Slovakia. June Granatir Alexander, *Ethnic Pride, American Patriotism: Slovaks and Other New Immigrants in the Interwar Years* (Philadelphia: Temple University Press, 2004), 192–219. Similarly, until the attack on Pearl Harbor, the German and Italian papers still argued that the United States should not enter the war to rescue Britain. See, for example, *Waechter und Anzeiger* (July 11, 1941), COCE, vol. 3 (June 20–July 19, 1941), 9; *L'Araldo* (July 18, 1941), COCE, vol. 3 (June 20–July 19, 1941), 10.

186. *Svet-American* (May 28, 1941), COCE, vol. 1 (May 12–June 14, 1941), 18.

187. *Hlas* (October 30, 1941), COCE, vol. 4 (October 20–November 19, 1941), 13.

188. On the isolationists generally, see Robert A. Divine, *The Reluctant Belligerent: American Entry into World War II* (New York: John Wiley & Sons, 1979), 7–24, 103–104.

189. *Wiadomosci Codzienne* (June 18, 1941), COCE, vol. 2 (June 6–June 25, 1941), 13. See also *America* (July 19, 1941), COCE, vol. 3 (June 20–July 19, 1941), 7; *America* (July 8, 1941), COCE, vol. 3 (June 20–July 19, 1941), 21; *Svet-American* (August 20, 1941), COCE, vol. 5 (August 20–September 19, 1941), 5; *Yidishe Welt* (September 7, 1941), COCE, vol. 5 (August 20–September 19, 1941), 8. On Coughlin, see *Wiadomosci Codzienne* (September 19, 1941), COCE, vol. 5 (August 20–September 19, 1941), 10–11; *Svet-American* (December 1, 1941), COCE, vol. 8 (November 20–December 19, 1941), 40; *Bratstvo* (April 2, 1942), COCE, vol. 12 (March 20–April 19, 1942), 35; *Wiadomosci Codzienne* (April 4, 1942), COCE, vol. 12 (March 20–April 19, 1942), 56.

190. Westbrook Pegler and Senator Robert Rice Reynolds were nativists *and* isolationists. See Pilat, *Pegler, Angry Man of the Press*, 182–185; Christensen, *Paradox of Tar Heel Politics*, 101–106.

191. *Hlas* (September 18, 1941), COCE, vol. 5 (August 20–September 19, 1941), 41. On Lindbergh's speech and the reaction to it, see Dinnerstein, *Anti-Semitism in America*, 129–130. On opposition to Lindbergh and America First, the main isolationist organization in the country, see *Yidishe Welt* (September 26, 1941), COCE, vol. 6 (September 20–October 19, 1941), 24; *Szabadsag* (October 15, 1941), COCE, vol. 6 (September 20–October 19, 1941), 26; *Yidishe Welt* (September 26, 1941), COCE, vol. 6 (September 20–October 19, 1941), 24.

192. *Szabadsag* (September 19, 1941), COCE, vol. 5 (August 20–September 19, 1941), 39.

193. *Enakopravnost* (September 13, 1941), COCE, vol. 5 (August 20–September 19, 1941), 37. For other examples of this argument, see *Bratstvo* (April 2, 1942), COCE, vol. 12 (March 20–April 19, 1942), 34; *Svet-American* (May 30, 1942), COCE, vol. 14 (May 20–June 19, 1942), 1.

194. *Wiadomosci Codzienne* (February 23, 1942), COCE, vol. 11 (February 20–March 19, 1942), 42.

195. *Szabadsag* (July 19, 1941), COCE, vol. 3 (June 20–July 29, 1941), 14. On these issues, see Anthony S. Chen, "'The Hitlerian Rule of Quotas': Racial Conservatism and Fair Employment Legislation in New York State, 1941–45," *Journal of American History* 92:4 (March 2006), 1242–1243.

196. *Waechter und Anzeiger* (October 8, 1941), COCE, vol. 6 (September 20–October 19, 1941), 17–18. See also *Yidishe Welt* (January 11, 1942), COCE, vol. 9 (December 20, 1941–January 19, 1942), 19.

197. Louis Adamic, "No 'Hyphens' This Time," *New York Times Sunday Magazine* (November 1, 1942), 18–19. On Poles in the war, Joseph A. Wytrwal,

Poles in American History and Tradition (Detroit: Endurance Press, 1969), 390–391. Franklin Roosevelt described the U.S. military in very similar terms; see Michael Olneck, "Assimilation and American National Identity" in *Companion to Immigration*, ed. Reed Ueda (Malden: Blackwell, 2006), 207.

198. Deborah Dash Moore, *GI Jews: How World War II Changed a Generation* (Cambridge: Belknap Press of Harvard University Press, 2004), 257.

199. Wytrwal, *Poles in American History and Tradition*, 414, 440–441; "Poles Form National Unit," *Detroit Free Press* (May 30, 1944), 3. See also Paul M. Deac, "3,000 Delegates Open Polish-American Congress," *Detroit Free Press* (May 29, 1944), 11.

200. Alexander, *Ethnic Pride, American Patriotism*, 219. See also Andrew M. Greeley, "American Sociology and the Study of Ethnic Immigrant Groups," *International Migration Digest* 1:2 (Autumn 1964), 109.

201. Jeanine Basinger, *The World War II Combat Film* (Middletown, CT: Wesleyan University Press, 2003), 47–57. That these films were produced by an industry dominated by immigrants is not surprising. See Neal Gabler, *An Empire of Their Own: How the Jews Invented Hollywood* (New York: Anchor Books, 1989), 347–350.

202. Richard Rorty, *Achieving Our Country* (Cambridge: Harvard University Press, 1998), 100.

203. John Hersey, *A Bell for Adano* (New York: Alfred A. Knopf, 1944).

204. Louis Adamic, "Thirty Million New Americans," *Harper's Magazine* 169:11 (November 1934), 684. On Adamic's newspaper career and his critique of traditional Americanization programs, see Dan Shiffman, *Rooting Multiculturalism: The Works of Louis Adamic* (Cranbury, NJ: Fairleigh Dickinson University Press, 2003).

205. For a similar view of second-generation Americans, see Read Lewis, "Immigrants and Their Children," in *Social Work Year Book, 1935* (New York: Russell Sage Foundation, 1935), 202.

206. Adamic, "Thirty Million New Americans," 687, 692.

207. Ibid., 692–694. Five years after his "second generation" article appeared, Adamic wrote a pamphlet titled, "Let's Become Americanized—All of Us!" that promoted this new vision of Americanization and echoed many of the themes of patriotic pluralism articulated by the foreign language press. Shiffman, *Rooting Multiculturalism*, 19.

208. James Marshall, "How the Schools Can Help Solve the Second Generation Problem," *Interpreter Releases* (May 13, 1935), 195, 196.

209. "Problems of the American Schools," *Rassviet* (June 15, 1935), CFLPS, Russian, IIIA, 1–2.

210. Montalto, *History of the Intercultural Education Movement, 1924–1941*, 111; Rachel Davis DuBois with Corann Okorodudu, *All This and Something More: Pioneering Intercultural Education* (Bryn Mawr, PA: Dorrance, 1984), 66; American Historical Association, Report of the Commission on the Social Studies, *Conclusions and Recommendations of the Commission* (New York: Charles Scribner's Sons, 1934), 24, 38.

211. American Youth Commission, *Youth and the Future* (Washington, DC: American Council on Education, 1942), 211; National Council for the Social Studies, *The Social Studies Look beyond the War* (Washington, DC: The Council, 1944), 19–20, WVT Papers, Box 39, no folder.

212. Selig, *Americans All*, 84–85.

213. Marion Edman, *Unity through Understanding: Study Guide and Discussion Manual for Use with* Americans All (Washington, DC: Department of Supervisors and Directors of Instruction, National Education Association, 1942), 3–6.

214. Burkholder, "'With Science as His Shield'"; Selig, *Americans All*; Shiffman, *Rooting Multiculturalism*.

215. Charles I. Glicksberg, "Intercultural Education: Utopia or Reality," *Common Ground* 6:4 (Summer 1946), 61.

216. Chicago took some steps toward intercultural education about the time that the movement was starting to fade. See Kathryn M. Neckerman, *Schools Betrayed: Roots of Failure in Inner-City Education* (Chicago: University of Chicago Press, 2007), 98–105. See also Don C. Rogers, "Human Relations," *Chicago Schools Journals* 29:1–4 (September–December 1947), 12–15; S. C. Watkins, "Cultural Contributions of the Negro," *Chicago Schools Journal* 30:5–6 (January–February 1949), 137–140; Henrietta Haffemann, "Vitalizing Intercultural Relations," *Chicago Schools Journal* 28:5–10 (January–June 1947), 54–61; Paul R. Pierce, "Developing Intergroup Education," *Chicago Schools Journal* 30:2 (October 1948), 36.

217. See also Adamic, "No 'Hyphens' This Time," 19; Eric P. Kaufmann, *The Rise and Fall of Anglo-America* (Cambridge: Harvard University Press, 2004), 110, 108–110.

218. Louis Adamic's *A Nation of Nations* highlights the contributions of thirteen immigrant and minority groups (ranging from African Americans to Yugoslavs). Louis Adamic, *A Nation of Nations* (New York: Harper and Brothers, 1944).

219. Burkholder, "'With Science as His Shield,'" 41–90; Kaufmann, *The Rise and Fall of Anglo-America*, 108–110; Selig, *Americans All*, 10–39.

220. John Carson, *The Measure of Merit* (Princeton: Princeton University Press, 2008), 260–261. See also Stephen J. Gould, *The Mismeasure of Man* (New York: W. W. Norton, 1981), 232–233.

221. Montalto, *History of the Intercultural Education Movement, 1924–1941*, 77–108. On her friendship with Adamic, see DuBois with Okorodudu, *All This and Something More*, 68, 62–98. On her friendship with Covello, see Michael C. Johanek and John L. Puckett, *Leonard Covello and the Making of Benjamin Franklin High School: Education as If Citizenship Mattered* (Philadelphia: Temple University Press, 2007), 165. See also Montalto, *History of the Intercultural Education Movement, 1924–1941*, 103, 111–112, 118–121; Selig, *Americans All*, 9–11, 68–112, 272.

222. DuBois is quoted in Selig, *Americans All*, 85.

223. Rachel Davis DuBois, *National Unity through Intercultural Education*, U.S. Office of Education, Education and Defense series, Pamphlet no. 10 (Washington, DC: Government Printing Office, 1942), 5.

224. Selig, *Americans All*, 79.

225. On DuBois's and the Bureau's involvement with the New York City Public Schools, see Johanek and Puckett, *Leonard Covello and the Making of Benjamin Franklin High School*, 167–169; Montalto, *A History of the Intercultural Education Movement, 1924–1941*, 109–111; Nicholas V. Montalto "Multicultural Education in the New York City Public Schools, 1919–1941," in *Educating an Urban People: The New York City Experience*, ed. Diane Ravitch and Ronald Goodenow (New York: Teachers College Press, 1981), 71–72; Lauri Johnson, "'We Declare That Teachers Need More Intercultural Education, Not Less': The Politics of Intercultural Education in the New York City Schools, 1944–1950," (paper presented at the History of Education Society Annual Meeting, October 2001), 3.

226. The resolution is quoted in Montalto, "Multicultural Education in the New York City Public Schools, 1919–1941," 72.

227. Hilda Taba and William Van Til, eds., *Democratic Human Relations: Promising Practices in Intergroup and Intercultural Education in the Social Studies*. Sixteenth Yearbook of the National Council of Social Studies (Washington, DC: National Council of Social Studies, 1945). On Taba, see Jane Bernard-Powers, "Composing Her Life: Hilda Taba and Social Studies History," in Margaret Smith Crocco and O. L. Davis Jr., eds., *"Bending the Future to Their Will": Civic Women, Social Education, and Democracy* (Lanham, MD: Rowman and Littlefield, 1999), 185–206.

228. Bernard-Powers, "Composing Her Life: Hilda Taba and Social Studies History": American Council on Education, *Bulletin of Cooperating Schools* 3 (November 25, 1945), RFB Papers, Box 2, Wisconsin Workshop Folder.

229. The survey is summarized and quoted in Leo Shapiro, "Intergroup Education," *Common Ground* 7:1 (Autumn 1946), 102.

230. James Waterman Wise, *The Springfield Plan* (New York: Viking Press, 1945); G. H. Reavis, "The Cincinnati Program," *Intercultural Education News* 6:3

(April 1945), 1–2, RFB Papers, Box 4, Intergroup Relations Folder; Harold J. Harrison, "A Study of the Work of the Coordinating Committee on Democratic Human Relations in the Detroit Public Schools from September 1943 to June 1952" (Detroit: Ed.D. diss., Wayne [State] University, 1953), 14; Yoon K. Pak, " 'If there is a better intercultural plan in any school system in America, I do not know where it is': The San Diego City Schools' Intercultural Education Program, 1946–49," *Urban Education* 37:5 (November 2002), 588–609; Lillian A. Lamoreaux, "Santa Barbara Intercultural Educational Program," *Proceedings of the Eightieth Annual Meeting of the National Education Association, 1942* (Washington, DC: National Education Association, 1942), 316–318.

231. "The Cleveland Council for American Unity," *Common Ground* 1:1 (Autumn 1940), 79.

232. See, for example, Selig, *Americans All*, 90.

233. David L. Angus and Jeffrey E. Mirel, *The Failed Promise of the American High School, 1890–1995* (New York: Teachers College Press, 1999), 57–101, 203.

234. Cleveland Board of Education, *Report of the Superintendent of Schools, 1939–1940* (Cleveland: The Board, 1940), 291.

235. An indication of the increasing number of high school students from immigrant backgrounds in Cleveland in the 1930s can be found in the CFLND. The Hungarian, Italian, Polish, Romanian, and Slovenian newspapers regularly ran articles praising recent high school graduates in 1937 and 1938. Virtually all of these articles applauded students graduating from *public* high schools. See, for example, *Szabadsag* (January 19, 1938), CFLND 1938–4, Abstract 10180, 116; *La Voce del Popolo Italiano* (January 22, 1937), CFLND 1937–2, Abstract 2408, 31; *Wiadomosci Codzienne* (June 18, 1937), CFLND 1937–4, Abstract 13683, 522; *Enakopravnost* (May 29, 1937), CFLND 1937–5, Abstract 20145, 376.

236. Carter et al., *Historical Statistics of the United States*, vol. 1, pt. A, Population, "Immigrants, Emigrants, and Net Migration," Table Ad., 1–2, 1–541; Cleveland Board of Education, *Annual Report of the Superintendent of Schools, 1941–42* (Cleveland: The Board, 1942), 206.

237. United States Department of Commerce, *Sixteenth Census of the United States: 1940, Population*, vol. 2, pt. 5, *New York-Oregon* (Washington, DC: U.S. Government Printing Office, 1943), 710, table D-36; United States Department of Commerce, *Seventeenth Census of the United States: 1950, Population*, vol. 2, pt. 35, *Ohio* (Washington, DC: U.S. Government Printing Office, 1952), 91, table 34.

238. [Allen Y. King], "Do the Social Studies Give Emphasis to Intercultural Education?" in Cleveland Board of Education, *Report of the Superintendent of*

Schools, 1943–44 (Cleveland: The Board, 1945), 102–108. King is not listed in the superintendent's report, but he clearly was the author. See Allen Y. King, "Intercultural Education in the Cleveland Social Studies Program," *Social Education* 11:2 (February 1947), 61–64.

239. [King], "Do the Social Studies Give Emphasis to Intercultural Education?" 103.

240. Ibid., 104.

241. Ibid., 105.

242. Ibid.; Selig, *Americans All*, 206–234. For two fascinating accounts of how these ideas were put into practice in one Cleveland high school, see Edith F. Erickson, "Intergroup Education at Collinwood," *Clearing House* 22:1 (September 1947), 3–8; Mabel S. Finley, "The Book Approach: An Experiment in Intergroup Education," *English Journal* 38:7 (September 1949), 384–388. On similar efforts in other cities, see Burkholder, "'With Science as His Shield,'" 277–301.

243. Erickson, "Intergroup Education at Collinwood," 3–4; American Council on Education, *Bulletin of Cooperating Schools* 3 (November 25, 1945); American Council on Education, *Reading Ladders for Human Relations* (Washington, DC: The Council, 1949), ii. The major cities with intercultural programs were New York, Chicago, Detroit, Los Angeles, Cleveland, St. Louis, and Pittsburgh.

244. In Detroit, high school enrollments jumped from over 25,000 in 1929–1930 to almost 49,000 in 1939–1940. These enrollments dropped sharply during World War II, but after the war they climbed back to late 1930s levels. Jeffrey Mirel, *The Rise and Fall of an Urban School System: Detroit, 1907–81* (Ann Arbor: University of Michigan Press, 1999), 131–134, 459–460. In terms of immigration, in 1938–1939, Detroit offered eleven classes "for the adjustment of foreign children into regular grades." Between 800 and 1,000 pupils registered for these classes. Detroit Board of Education, *Superintendent's Annual Report, Detroit Public Schools, 1938–39* (Detroit: The Board, 1939), 93. On the postwar increase of foreign-born children, see Detroit Public Schools, "Annual Report, Foreign Children's Classes, 1946–47" (typescript, June 1947), 134, in the Detroit Public Schools, *Department of Special Education Annual Report, 1946–47* (Detroit: Detroit Public Schools, 1947).

245. United States Department of Commerce, *Sixteenth Census of the United States: 1940, Population V. II, Part 3: Kansas-Michigan* (Washington, DC: U.S. Government Printing Office, 1943), 892, table A-36; United States Department of Commerce, *Seventeenth Census of the United States: 1950, Population*, vol. 2, pt. 22, *Michigan* (Washington, DC: U.S. Government Printing Office, 1952), 78, table 34.

246. Mirel, *Rise and Fall of an Urban School System*, 3, 152–56; Dominic Capeci, *Race Relations in Wartime Detroit* (Philadelphia: Temple University Press, 1984); Thomas Sugrue, *Origins of Urban Crisis* (Princeton: Princeton University Press, 1996), 29, 72–75.

247. The CIUS was created by the Union for Democratic Action (UDA), which was chaired by the Detroit theologian Reinhold Niebuhr. The UDA merged with Americans for Democratic Action in 1946. For a discussion of the formation of the CIUS and a partial list of its member organizations, see Harrison, "Study of the Work of the Coordinating Committee on Democratic Human Relations," 67, 259.

248. The committee was originally called the Administrative Committee on Intercultural and Interracial Education. Over the next decade, the name of the committee changed to the Administrative Committee on Intercultural Education, and eventually to the Coordinating Committee on Democratic Human Relations. Harrison, "Study of the Work of the Coordinating Committee on Democratic Human Relations," 15, 35–37. The mission statement of the committee is quoted in Harrison on page 38.

249. Harrison, "Study of the Work of the Coordinating Committee on Democratic Human Relations," 71–77.

250. The January 1945 resolution was a direct response to a request made by the CIUS to the board in June 1944 asking for three things—a policy statement on intercultural education, in-service teacher training in this area, and the integration of intercultural material throughout the curriculum. The board agreed to all three requests. See *Detroit Board of Education Proceedings, 1943–44* (Detroit: The Board, 1944), 605; and Harrison, "Study of the Work of the Coordinating Committee on Democratic Human Relations," 69. The Detroit policy statement received national attention. See Leo Shapiro, *Intergroup Education* (Chicago: Anti-Defamation League, 1945), 7, RFB Papers, Box 1, 1945–46 Folder.

251. Detroit Public Schools, *Building One Nation Indivisible* (Detroit: Detroit Public Schools, Division of Instruction, 1944), 5. A copy of this book is available at the Michigan Historical Collection, Bentley Historical Library, University of Michigan, Ann Arbor.

252. Ibid., 37–43.

253. Stanley E. Dimond, "Detroit Uses School Committees," *Intercultural Education News* 6:2 (January 1945), 1–2, RFB Papers, Box 4, Intergroup Relations Folder. Between 1945 and 1952, about 84 percent of the senior high schools and 87 percent of the junior high schools (intermediate schools) had such committees. Harrison, "Study of the Work of the Coordinating Committee on Democratic Human Relations," 45–48.

254. Research conducted at Detroit's Wayne [State] University on intercultural teacher training programs at the college and university level is reviewed in Lloyd Allen Cook, *Intergroup Relations in Teacher Education* (Washington, DC: American Council for Education, 1951); Cherry A. McGee Banks, "The Intergroup Education Movement," in *Multicultural Education, Transformative Knowledge, and Action,* ed. James Banks (New York: Teachers College Press, 1996), 260–261.

255. Harrison, "Study of the Work of the Coordinating Committee on Democratic Human Relations," 76–87, 122–141.

256. Administrative Committee on Intercultural Education, *Promising Practices in Intergroup Education* (Detroit: Detroit Board of Education, 1946. Marion Edmon and Laurentine B. Collins, *Promising Practices in Intergroup Education* (New York: Bureau for Intercultural Education, 1947). On this development, see Harrison, "Study of the Work of the Coordinating Committee on Democratic Human Relations," 143–144, 152–155.

257. Administrative Committee on Intercultural Education, *Promising Practices in Intergroup Education* (Detroit: Detroit Board of Education), 7.

258. Ibid., 17, 19.

259. Ibid., 15–16.

260. Rankin is quoted in Harrison, "Study of the Work of the Coordinating Committee on Democratic Human Relations," 64.

261. Administrative Committee on Intercultural Education, *Promising Practices in Intergroup Education,* 15–16.

262. "NAACP Aide Praises School Race Conditions," *Detroit Free Press* (April 9, 1944), 5.

263. See, for example, Horace F. Bradfield to Gloster Current (April 18, 1944), National Association for the Advancement of Colored People Papers, Part 17: National Staff Files, 1940–1955; Mirel, *Rise and Fall of an Urban School System,* 190–196; Harrison, "Study of the Work of the Coordinating Committee on Democratic Human Relations," 142–159.

264. Burkholder, "'With Science as His Shield,'" 477–484.

265. Allen Y. King, "The Social Studies and Current Affairs in the Cleveland Public Schools" (Cleveland: Cleveland Board of Education, 1949), Cleveland Public Library, Cleveland Board of Education Superintendents Reports.

266. Harrison, "Study of the Work of the Coordinating Committee on Democratic Human Relations," 63.

267. Emilie Stern, Elizabeth Nolan, and Harold Bailey, "Some Experiences in Democratic Living," *Intercultural Education News* 8:3 (Spring 1947), 1–2, RFB Papers, Box 37, Intergroup Relations Folder.

268. On this trend in Detroit, see Anne-Lise Halvorsen and Jeffrey Mirel, "Educating Citizens: Social Problems Meet Progressive Education in Detroit, 1930–

52," in *Clio at the Table: Using History to Inform and Improve Educational Policy*, ed. Robert Rothman and Kenneth Wong (New York: Peter Lang, 2009), 9–36.

269. Banks, "Intergroup Education Movement," 269–270; Burkholder, "'With Science as His Shield,'" 485–506; Johnson, "'We Declare That Teachers Need More Intercultural Education, Not Less,'" 10–14; Gerstle, *American Crucible: Race and Nation in the Twentieth Century*, 258–259; Selig, *Americans All*, 16–17.

270. On this process, see Diane Ravitch, *Left Back: A Century of Failed School Reform* (New York: Simon and Schuster, 2004); Halvorsen and Mirel, "Educating Citizens."

271. Detroit Board of Education, *A Progress Report of the Detroit Public Schools since 1940 Published as the Superintendent's Annual Report, 1955* (Detroit: The Board, 1955), 20; Detroit Board of Education, *Learning to Live: The Superintendent's Annual Report for the 105th Year of the Detroit Public Schools* (Detroit: The Board, 1947), 12; Detroit Board of Education, *Learning for Living: Superintendent's Annual Report, 1952* (Detroit: The Board 1952), 4. Many organizations at this time shifted terminology from intercultural relations to human relations. Burkholder, "'With Science as His Shield,'" 480–481.

272. Mirel, *Rise and Fall of an Urban School System*, 306–308, 375.

273. Harrison, "Study of the Work of the Coordinating Committee on Democratic Human Relations," 70, 103, 169.

274. Mirel, *Rise and Fall of an Urban School System*, 306–308, 375.

275. Joseph Moreau, *Schoolbook Nation: Conflicts over American History Textbooks from the Civil War to the Present* (Ann Arbor: University of Michigan Press, 2003), 264–283. See also Jonathan Zimmerman, *Whose America?* (Cambridge: Harvard University Press, 2002), 112–113, 127.

276. Cleveland Board of Education, *Annual Report of the Superintendent of Schools, 1941–42*, 137, 139–140. Another example of a high school student who recently immigrated to the United States, in this case from Germany, espousing devotion to America and pride in her European cultural background can be found in Detroit Public Schools, *Building One Nation Indivisible*, 39. See also Paula Fass, *Outside In: Minorities and the Transformation of American Education* (New York: Oxford University Press, 1989), 73.

277. The dinner took place on January 13, 1942. Adamic believed that the president had invited him to help drive home the point to Churchill that America was *not* an Anglo-Saxon country, but a polyglot nation with diverse ethnic interest groups. This diversity made gaining U.S. support for Great Britain more complicated than Churchill imagined. Louis Adamic, *Dinner at the White House* (New York: Harper and Brothers, 1946), 65–69.

278. Philip Gleason, "Americans All: World War II and the Shaping of American Identity," *Review of Politics* 43:4 (October 1981), 518.

279. See, for example, James R. Barrett and David Roediger, "Inbetween Peoples: Race, Nationality, and the 'New Immigrant' Working Class," *Journal of Ethnic History* 16:3 (Spring 1997), 3–44; Guglielmo, *White on Arrival: Italians, Race, Color, and Power in Chicago, 1890–1945*; Arnold R. Hirsch, "E Pluribus Duo? Thoughts on 'Whiteness' and Chicago's 'New" Immigration as a Transient Third Tier," *Journal of American Ethnic History* 23:4 (Summer 2004), 7–44.

280. Gunnar Myrdal, *An American Dilemma; The Negro Problem and Modern America*, vol. 1 (New York: Harper and Brothers, 1944), 603.

281. See, for example, Sugrue, *The Origins of the Urban Crisis: Race and Inequality in Postwar Detroit*, 77–81.

282. Walter Benn Michaels, *Our America: Nativism, Modernism, and Pluralism* (Durham: University of North Carolina Press, 1995), 67. Roediger makes a similar point, stating, "Malcolm X therefore had a good deal of the story right when he argued that in the process of Americanizing, European immigrants acquired a sense of whiteness and of white supremacy." David R. Roediger, *Towards the Abolition of Whiteness: Essays on Race, Politics, and Working Class History* (New York: Verso, 1994), 187.

283. David R. Roediger, *Working toward Whiteness: How America's Immigrants Became White* (New York: Basic Books, 2005), 8.

284. Roediger briefly discusses K–12 education in *Working toward Whiteness*, 193–195.

285. See, for example, James D. Anderson, *The Education of Blacks in the South, 1860–1935* (Chapel Hill: University of North Carolina, 1988); Mirel, *Rise and Fall of an Urban School System*, 186–96; Moreau, *Schoolbook Nation*, 52–91, 163–175; Zimmerman, *Whose America?* 32–55.

286. David Miller, *On Nationality* (New York: Oxford University Press, 1995), 40, 17–47.

287. Eric Arnesen, "Whiteness and Historians' Imagination," *International Working-Class History* 60 (Fall 2001), 15.

288. Myrdal, *American Dilemma*, V. 2, 1011.

289. Ibid., 1011–12, 1011–1015. On the importance of Myrdal's views on the American Creed, see Olneck, "Assimilation and American National identity," 207–208.

Conclusion

1. Gregory Rodriguez, "Identify Yourself," *New York Times* (September 23, 2001), sec. 4, 1,4.

2. James A. Banks, "Diversity, Transformative Citizenship Education, and School Reform," in *Just Schools: Pursuing Equality in Societies of Difference*, ed.

Martha Minow, Richard A. Shweder, and Hazel Rose Marcus (New York: Russell Sage Foundation, 2008), 230.

3. Patrick J. Buchanan, *State of Emergency: The Third World Invasion and Conquest of America* (New York: St. Martin's Press, 2006), 248–251. See also Ryan Lizza, "Return of the Nativist," *New Yorker* (December 17, 2007).

Table 1 Chicago Foreign Language Press Circulation, 1900–1930

Publication	Circulation Period	1900[a]	1910[b]	1920[c]	1930[d]
Abendpost (German)	Evenings (except Sun)	37,335	47,667	47,449	45,925
Denni Hlasatel (Czech)	Daily	6,090	34,000	35,000	47,321
Dziennik Chicagoski (Polish)	Evenings (except Sun)	8,235	7,000	26,534	29,789
Dziennik Zjednoczenia (Polish)	Evenings (except Sun)	–	–	–	18,630
Dziennik Zwiazkowy Zgoda (Polish)	Evenings (except Sun)	–	30,000	41,728	32,435
Aster (Greek Star)	Thursdays	1,900 (Wed)	–	138,000	136,319
Illinois Staats-Zeitung (German)	Friday	–	10,000	–	–
	Mornings (except Sun)	–	49,325	–	–
	Wednesdays	–	32,926	–	–
	Sundays	34,000	72,521	–	–
Italia (Italian)	Saturdays	22,000	30,000	–	–
	Sundays	–	–	38,426	–
	Tri-weekly (Wed, Thurs, Sun)	–	–	35,674	37,115
Jewish Daily Courier (Yiddish)	Mornings/Evenings (except Sat)	6,500 (e)	11,000	42,040	48,041
	Sundays	8,000	(m)	(m)	(m)
Jewish Daily Forward (Yiddish)	Mornings	–	–	31,353	38,898
	Saturdays	–	–	32,510	39,525
	Sundays	–	–	31,906	41,063
Lietuva (Lithuanian)	Friday	4,366	7,500	–	–
Loxias (Greek)	Mornings (except Sun)	–	–	9,000	–
	Wednesdays	–	–	–	–
Narod Polski (Polish)	Wednesdays	–	–	80,000	105,600

Table 1 (continued)

	Circulation Period	1900[a]	1910[b]	1920[c]	1930[d]
Naujienos (Lithuanian)	Mornings/Evenings (except Sun)	–	–	19,100 (e)	37,504 (m)
Radnik (Yugoslavian)	Mornings (except Sun)	17,401	17,500	20,000	16,226
Reform Advocate (Jewish/ published in English)					–
Russian Daily News (Russian)	Mornings (except Sun)	–	–	–	20,000
Saloniki (Greek)	Saturdays	–	–	–	15,250
Skandinaven (Norwegian/ Danish)	Evenings (except Sun)	17,526	22,500	18,701	11,175
	Wed & Fri	–	50,000	29,438	21,705
	Wed & Sat	44,468	–	–	–
	Sundays	17,278	–	–	11,175
Svenska Amerikanaren (Swedish)	Tuesdays	38,500	–	–	–
	Thursdays	–	33,305	59,747	68,970
Svenska Kuriren (Swedish)	Tuesdays	36,450	–	–	–
	Thursdays	–	–	46,157	–
	Saturdays	–	32,500	–	–
Svenska Tribunen-Nyheter (Swedish)	Tuesdays	23,500	54,097	59,776	58,922
Svornost (Czech)	Mornings/Evenings	23,750 (m)	24,983 (m)	25,634 (e)	49,813 (e)
	Sunday		32,200	30,504	50,782
Tribuna Italiana Transatlantica (Italian)	Saturdays	–	22,500	25,000	25,000

a. N. W. Ayer & Sons American Newspaper Annual and Directory (Philadelphia: N. W. Ayer & Sons, 1901).
b. N. W. Ayer & Sons American Newspaper Annual and Directory (Philadelphia: N. W. Ayer & Sons, 1911).
c. N. W. Ayer & Sons American Newspaper Annual and Directory (Philadelphia: N. W. Ayer & Sons, 1921).
d. N. W. Ayer & Sons American Newspaper Annual and Directory (Philadelphia: N. W. Ayer & Sons, 1931).

Table 2   Cleveland Foreign Language Press Circulation, 1930–1940

	Circulation Period	1930[1]	1940[2]
America (Romanian)	Evenings (except Sun)	18,900	—
	Tri-Weekly (Tues, Thurs, Sat)	—	10,500
Ameriska Domovina (Slovenian)	Mornings	—	—
	Mornings (except Sun)	—	6,800
Brotherhood (Carpatho-Russian)	Monthly	—	7,000
Dirva (Lithuanian)	Fridays	12,330	9,700
Enakopravnost (Slovenian)	Evenings (except Sun)	7,350	5,620
La Voce del Popolo Italiano (Italian)	Mornings (except Mon)	25,312	—
	Mornings (except Mon, Tues, Sat)	—	18,543
L'Araldo (Italian)	Fridays	—	11,990
Svet-American (Czech)	Mornings (except Sun)	13,275	26,200
Szabadsag (Hungarian)	Evenings/Sun morning	43,491	—
	Evenings	—	40,085
Waechter und Anzeiger (German)	Evenings (except Sun)	17,924	—
	Sunday morning	11,630	—
	Evenings	—	15,895
Wiadomosci Codzienne (Polish)	Evenings (except Sun)	21,416	29,485
Yidishe Welt (Jewish)	Mornings (except Sat)	20,944	14,948

1. N. W. Ayer & Son's Directory of Newspapers and Periodicals (Philadelphia: N. W. Ayer & Son, 1931).
2. N. W. Ayer & Son's Directory of Newspapers and Periodicals (Philadelphia: N. W. Ayer & Son, 1941).

ACKNOWLEDGMENTS

This book, like many of the immigrants it discusses, has its roots in eastern Europe. In 1995, I began an exciting collaboration with a group of educators who were working on issues of civic education in eastern Europe and the former Soviet Union. Over the years, I spent countless hours with them in venues ranging from the shore of the Black Sea to the Transcarpathian Mountains, discussing the role of education in changing former totalitarian states into functioning democracies. These conversations invariably led me to one of the main questions of this book: what role can education play in transforming people with little or no experience in democracy into knowledgeable and committed democratic citizens? It is a great pleasure to thank the people who started me on this journey: Alden Craddock, Joe Davis, David Dorn, Steve Fleishman, Alexandra Kuropas, Myron Kuropas, Bill McCready, Rimma Perelmuter, and Ruud Veldhuis. I particularly want to thank my dear friends Alexander Gungov and Maria Dimitrova at Sophia University, Sofia, Bulgaria, and Natalia Lominska and Alexi Izmentinov at the National University of Ostroh Academy, Ostroh, Ukraine, whose graciousness and generosity during my visits to their countries have been a continuing inspiration. I treasure their friendship.

Writing this book would not have been possible without the help and support of many individuals and institutions. I am deeply grateful to the Earhart Foundation for a Faculty Fellowship to begin my research. A Small Grant from the Spencer Foundation funded most of my research on Chicago. A Smith Richardson Foundation Research Grant provided me with time and graduate student support that allowed me to begin writing the book much sooner than I thought possible. I would especially like to thank Mark Steinmeyer, senior program officer at Smith Richardson, for his continuing interest and enthusiasm for the book. For their support and encouragement of this project I also would like to thank Karen Wixson and Deborah Ball, who successively served as the dean of the School of Education at the University of Michigan while I was writing the book.

As all historians know, it is impossible to do what we do without the support of knowledgeable and committed archivists. I have been very lucky in having been aided by a number of wonderfully helpful archivists from around the country. At the University of Michigan, I particularly want to thank Francis Blouin, Nancy Bartlett, and Karen Jania at the Bentley Historical Collection, who, as always, made long hours of research at the Bentley a pleasure; Marija Freeland, the Education Librarian at the Harlan Hatcher Library was unfailingly supportive in helping me and my graduate student assistants track down virtually everything we sought. I would also like to thank Daniel Golodner and the staff at the Archives of Labor and Urban Affairs, Walter P. Reuther Library, Wayne State University, Detroit; Ann Sindelar and the staff of the Western Reserve Historical Society in Cleveland; Mark Moore and the staff of the Social Sciences Department, and the staff of the General Reference Department, of the Cleveland Public Library; the staff of the Newberry Library in Chicago; the staff of the Microfilm Reading Room and the Municipal Reference Room of the Harold Washington Library in Chicago; the staff of the Richard J. Daley Library at the University of Illinois–Chicago; the staff of the Chicago Historical Library; and Carol Leadenham and the staff of the Hoover Institution Archives at Stanford University.

Over the many years that I have been working on this project, a number of friends and colleagues routinely have offered support ranging from comments on chapter drafts, to suggestions of books and articles that I ought to read, to new ways to think about this topic. I am deeply grateful to David K. Cohen, Robb Cooper, Mary Ann Dzuback, Michael J. Feuer, David Kamens, Michael D. Kennedy, Deborah Dash Moore, Juliette Moutinou, Beth Schulman, Guy Senese, Addison Stone, Neta Sher-Hadar, David Tyack, Alan Wieder, and James P. Young for their wise and encouraging counsel.

I especially want to thank Catherine E. Wycoff and Wayne Urban, whose impact on this project was enormous. In a chance conversation at a History of Education Society conference, Cate told me about the Chicago Foreign Language Press Survey and convinced me of the survey's importance for this book. In a similar conversation at a Southern History of Education Society conference, Wayne told me about an equally exciting collection of translated foreign language newspapers in Cleveland. These conversations and the collections they sent me to utterly changed the nature, scope, and argument of this book. I cannot thank Cate and Wayne enough.

While at Michigan I have had the privilege of working with some of the best graduate students in the country. Drew Ciancia, Anthony Francis, Deborah Michaels, Gwynne Morrissey, Paul Perrault, Seneca Rosenberg, and Nathaniel Schwartz, most of whom served at one time or another as my graduate research assistants, were indispensable partners on this project. Several of them (Deborah, Gwynne, Seneca, and Nate) read the entire manuscript and offered meticulous and invaluable criticism. In addition, a number of close friends took time away from their already overloaded schedules to read and offer detailed criticism of every chapter in this book. Robert Bain, Gary Fenstermacher, Anne-Lise Halvorsen, and Maris Vinovskis provided me with astute, honest, and at times painful criticism that improved this book in every possible way. They also boosted my often-deflated spirits when the writing got difficult. I am deeply grateful for their generosity, friendship, and good humor. I would also like to thank the two manuscript reviewers for Harvard

University Press, William Reese and Jonathan Zimmerman, whose suggestions for improving the manuscript were superb. My editor, Elizabeth Knoll, has been an enthusiastic supporter of this book ever since I described it to her many years ago over drinks at a bar in the Drake Hotel. It has been a pleasure working with her. I would also like to thank Meredith Phillips of Westchester Book Group for her careful overseeing of the production process. All of these people saved me from many blunders and errors; those that remain are my responsibility alone.

This book is dedicated to my wife, Barbara. No one has been more crucial to the writing and completion of this book than she. She has read and edited every chapter in it, some of them several times. Her remarkable skills as a rhetorician helped sharpen my arguments and polish my prose. She has shown more forbearance than humanly possible in listening to me run on endlessly about this project. That she has done all this while advancing her own academic career is a tribute to her strength, will, and amazing talent. Thank you, my love, for everything.

Grateful acknowledgment is given for permission to reprint portions of my previously published material.

Educational Review for material from "Civic Education and Changing Definitions of American Identity, 1900–1950," in vol. 54:2 (2002), 143–152.

INDEX